Luke:
Illuminating the Sage of Galilee

Luke:
Illuminating the Sage of Galilee

Kenneth L. Hanson

AN IMPRINT OF THE
GLOBAL CENTER FOR RELIGIOUS RESEARCH
1312 17TH STREET • SUITE 549
DENVER, COLORADO 80202

INFO@GCRR.ORG • GCRR.ORG

GCRR Press
An imprint of the Global Center for Religious Research
1312 17th Street Suite 549
Denver, CO 80202
www.gcrr.org

DOI: 10.33929/GCRRPress.2022.05

Typesetter: Christian Farren
Series Editor: Darren M. Slade
Consulting Editors: Kimberly Dell, Alexandra Hademenos
Front Cover Images: Kenneth L. Hanson
Cover Design: Abdullah Al Mahmud
                    fiverr.com/mahmuddidar

Library of Congress Cataloging-in-Publication Data

Luke : illuminating the sage of Galilee / Kenneth L. Hanson
p.   cm. – (The Hebraic gospels series)
Includes bibliographic references and index.
ISBN (Print): 978-1-959281-00-9
ISBN (eBook): 978-1-959281-01-6
1. Bible. N.T. Luke—Commentaries.   2. Bible. N.T. Gospels—Criticism interpretation, etc.   3. Bible. N.T.—Hermeneutics.   I. Title.   II. Series.

BS2595.3.H36   2022

ॐ

To Nikol—
freshly minted American citizen

Advanced Endorsements

Acknowledgments

I wish to acknowledge Prof. Zev Garber, whose boundless encouragement has sustained me in my efforts.

A Selection of Publications by Kenneth L. Hanson

The Annotated Passover Haggadah (co-editor and contributor with Zev Garber) (Denver: GCRR Press, 2021)

Whose Holy Land? Archaeology Meets Geopolitics in Today's Middle East (Nashville: New English Review Press, 2020)

Judaism and Jesus (with Zev Garber) (Newcastle Upon Tyne: Cambridge Scholars Publishing, 2020)

The Eagle and the Bible (Nashville: New English Review Press, 2013)

Blood Kin of Jesus (San Francisco: Council Oak Books, October, 2009)

Secrets from the Lost Bible (San Francisco: Council Oak Books, 2004)

Contents

Introduction: The Synoptic Gospels and a Hypothetical *Grundschrift*   1

Introduction to Luke   12

Commentary

Act I   Luke's Prelude   15

Act II   The Baptist, the Genealogy, the Temptation and Galilee   34

Act III   The Judean Sojourn   49

Act IV   The Return to Galilee   93

Act V   Up to Jerusalem   142

Act VI   Temple to Tomb   170

Act VII Resurrection and Post-Resurrection   213

Afterword   235

Bibliography   237

Index   243

Hypothetical Evolution of the Synoptic Gospels

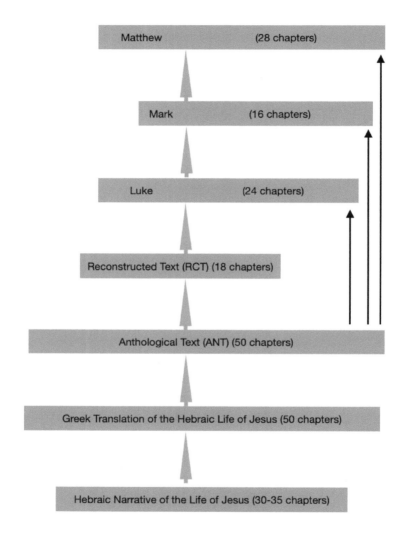

Introduction:
The Synoptic Gospels
and a Hypothetical *Grundschrift*

S everal decades ago, a collaborative group of Jewish and Christian scholars based in Israel advanced what was then, and still is, considered a radical theory regarding the birth, growth, and development of the Synoptic Gospels. What began as a joint effort between two Jerusalem-based scholars, American Robert L. Lindsey (a Southern Baptist minister) and Professor David Flusser (director of the Department of Comparative Religion at the Hebrew University of Jerusalem), blossomed into a fledgling "movement" and spawned what came to be known as the Jerusalem School of Synoptic Research.

Lindsey had originally noticed that the Gospel of Luke, though said to lack Aramaisms, can be translated into a Hebrew text much more easily than Mark, which is almost universally assumed to have been the first of the four Gospels. For example, Mark frequently interjects the Greek expression καὶ εὐθὺς ("and immediately"). He does this a total of forty-one times; yet, the phrase has no Hebrew equivalent. Luke, by contrast, employs this expression only once, and not in a story unit shared with Mark. Lindsey's question was that if Luke were copying Mark, who supposedly wrote first, why did he not reproduce Mark's wording: καὶ εὐθὺς? He concluded that Luke did not copy Mark's text because he did not see it.[1] Matthew, in a number of instances, reproduces καὶ εὐθὺς, but only in passages which parallel Mark. A

---

[1] See Robert Lindsey, *Jesus Rabbi and Lord* (Oak Creek, WI: Cornerstone, 1990), 20.

test of other expressions and phrases yielded similar results. Moreover, Lindsey discovered that in places where Matthew most closely follows Mark, his text does not translate well into Hebrew. However, when Matthew follows Luke as opposed to Mark, it is relatively easy to render a Hebrew version of the narrative. Lindsey was forced to conclude that Luke indeed wrote first. When he met David Flusser, who had independently become convinced of the strong editorial redaction in Mark's Gospel, a healthy working relationship began.

They suggested that beneath the Greek texts of Matthew, Mark, and Luke lay a long-vanished Semitic, indeed a Hebrew subtext, or "undertext" (*grundschrift*), the haunting tones of which may be imperfectly glimpsed through the occasionally awkward syntax of the traditional Gospel narratives. As a literary product the Gospels betray their origins, not as a collection of oral compositions, slapped together by Greek-speaking redactors decades after the life and death of their principal subject, but as a multi-layered translation project, dissecting, rearranging, reassembling, and parroting what theoretically began as a single Hebraic document—a hypothetical life of Jesus of Nazareth.[2]

The evidence for such an Ur-text is hiding in plain sight, in the multiple Hebraisms (Greek words and phrases which almost certainly represent translations of Hebrew idioms) scattered across the Synoptic narratives. Syntactical evidence in the form of sentence structure that appears to mimic biblical Hebrew is equally abundant. Indeed, the Greek of the Synoptic Gospels is said to resemble what might be called "translation Greek," similar to the ancient Greek rendering of the Hebrew Scriptures, known as the Septuagint. Language of composition being the fundamental element of any literary work, the implications of this avant-garde theory are astounding. They suggest that the Christian Gospels are inherently the product of "homegrown" Jewish thought during the

---

[2] See Pinchas Lapide, "The Missing Hebrew Gospel," *Christian News From Israel*, XXIV (1974): 167–70.

days of the Second Temple. Moreover, they present us with the serious prospect that the language in which the words of the historical Jesus were recorded, and by extension the "mother tongue" in which he taught, was not, as long supposed, Aramaic, but Hebrew. Hardly a dead or dormant language, this was the Hebrew of the Dead Sea Scrolls, and subsequently the Mishnah. In a real sense, the Jesus of history becomes Jesus the Jewish Sage.

　　Some have argued that Aramaic source material of some kind lay behind the Synoptic Gospels, while others have argued just as convincingly that the Aramaic theory is without merit. The case presented here is that looking to proposed Aramaic sources behind the Synoptics is, in fact, seriously flawed. There are certainly several Aramaisms peppering the Gospel narratives, including ταλιθά, κοῦμι ("*talita cumi*," Mark 5:41), ἐφφαθά ("*ephphata*," Mark 7:34), ῥαββουνί ("*rabboni*," Mark 10:51) and most notably Ἐλωΐ Ἐλωΐ, λιμᾶ σαβαχθανί; ("*Eloí, Eloí, lima savachthaní?*" Mark 15:34). It is significant, however, that most Hebrew literature from the Second Temple and Tanniatic periods, including the Mishnah, the Dead Sea Scrolls, and the Bar Kokhba letters, also contain Aramaisms that had filtered into common use. It is equally notable that multiple Hebrew words are also represented in the Greek Gospels. These include:

λίβανον (לְבוֹנָה) ("frankincense," Matt 2:11),

Ῥακά (רקא) "empty," Matt 5:22),

ζιζάνια (זונים) "tares," Matt 13:25),

Ῥαββί (רַב) "Rabbi," Matt 23:7–8),

κύμινον (כמון) "cummin," Matt 23:23),

Βοανεργές (בואנגרס) Boanerges, Mark 3:17),

κορβᾶν (קרבן) "sacrifice," Mark 7:11),

μύρου (מוֹר) "myrrh," Luke 7:37),

σατανᾶν (שָׂטָן) "Satan," Luke 10:18),

Βεελζεβοὺλ (בעל זבוב) "Beelzebub," Luke 11:15),

βάτους (בט) "bath" as a measure, Luke 16:6),

κόρους (כור) "kor" as a measure, Luke 16:7),

μαμωνᾶ (מָמוֹן "mammon," Luke 16:9),

συκομορέαν (שִׁקְמָה "sycamore," Luke 19:4),

Οὐαὶ (אוֹי "Woe!") and

ἀμήν (אָמֵן *amen*), appearing hundreds of times in Gospels.[3]

In the early twentieth century, the renowned Jewish scholar, M. H. Segal wrote:

...what was the language of ordinary life of educated native Jews in Jerusalem and Judea from 40 B.C. to 150 A.D.? The evidence presented by Mishnaic Hebrew and its literature leaves no doubt that that language was Mishnaic Hebrew. Of course those educated Judeans also understood Aramaic, and used it even in writing, but only occasionally...[4]

As recently observed by Michael Wise in his study of language patterns in Roman Judea, "Most scholars today would agree that Judeans in the first century C.E. and the first third of the second century were a trilingual society, using Hebrew, Aramaic, and Greek."[5] He also notes that prior to the discoveries of the manuscripts of the Judean Desert (between 1945 and 1965) it was commonly assumed that the dominant language for daily life in Judea was Aramaic. However, "It was the discoveries associated with the later period—the contracts and documents of the Bar Kokhba period—that provided the more direct argument for Hebrew as a vernacular; and it was the letters that advance this view."[6]

In the final analysis, those who insist that the Greek of the Synoptics does not rely on Hebrew source material of any kind are

---

[3] See David Bivin and Roy Blizzard, *Understanding the Difficult Words of Jesus* (Arcadia, CA: Makor Foundation, 1983), 32–34.

[4] M. H. Segal, *A Grammar of Mishnaic Hebrew* (Oxford: Clarendon Press, 1927), 13.

[5] Michael Wise, *Language and Literacy in Roman Judaea: A Study of the Bar Kokhba Documents* (New Haven and London: Yale University Press, 2015), 7.

[6] Ibid., 12.

forced to conclude that in the many instances in which the Greek seems to betray a Hebraic flavor ("and it came to pass" being an example) the writers were deliberately attempting to mimic biblical Hebrew (something not done with such regularity in John's Gospel or other Greek compositions of the New Testament). The other logical option is they were, in fact, relying on authentically Hebraic source texts, subsequently translated to Greek. Indeed, those who cannot hear the rich resonance of Hebrew coursing through the printed words of the Greek text are arguably not sufficiently trained in Hebrew to appreciate the phenomenon.

The burden of this research is to "read through" the Greek of the Synoptic Gospels to the vestigial remnants of this underlying Hebraic source. It is a monumental undertaking of scholarly sleuthing, which seeks to reconstruct this most elusive of all Ur-texts, vaguely akin to a Dead Sea Scroll, some thirty to thirty-five Hebrew chapters in length and likely reduced to writing within just a few years of the events it describes. According to the Jerusalem School, this text, which was subsequently lost, was translated to Greek, for consumption in the Hellenistic communities to the west, where the apostle Paul was busily casting his own theological net over this uniquely Jewish messianic sect. For the sake of scholarship, it may be referred to as a "Proto-Narrative" (PN). The obvious question is how this single *grundschrift* became three separate Synoptic accounts.

On a literary level, it is a Darwinian endeavor, positing The Origin of Gospel Species. It amounts to what might be called "evolutionary textology." The operating theory advanced by the Jerusalem School is that PN was taken in hand by a Greek-speaking redactor and cleverly subdivided into three separate topical sections. It likely consisted of a narrative of the life of Jesus (including the multiple miracle stories linked to him, his death and resurrection), a "sayings" section (recording the words and teachings/*ipsissima verba* of Jesus), and a compilation of Jesus' parables. It may be referred to as the "Anthological Text" (ANT), approximately fifty Greek chapters in length. It is the "sayings" section of the ANT that presents an intriguing alternative to what is normally supposed to be an entirely separate collection of the words of Jesus, referred to as the "Q" source.

To be sure, the application of Occam's razor is most helpful in deciphering this textual puzzle: "Entities [in this case texts] should not be multiplied without necessity." Nonetheless, any understanding of the "Synoptic problem" requires at least some such multiplication. It is theorized that at some point the Anthological Text (ANT) was taken in hand by another redactor, who, according to the theory of the Jerusalem School, attempted to reconstruct a fresh narrative of Jesus according to the supposed original order, weaving together stories, parables, and sayings as they might have originally appeared. The result was a hypothetical "Short Gospel" or "Reconstructed Text" (RCT, approximately eighteen chapters in length), by its description less developed and more concise than its predecessor. It might well be titled "Condensed Gospel," which, along with PN, became the source material for the three Synoptics to follow. In essence, it is a radical variation of the "two source" hypothesis, and it does much to reconcile many of the conundrums involved in Synoptic research.[7]

It is at this point that the Jerusalem School offers the sweeping suggestion that Luke was composed first, relying on both the ANT and the RCT. The fatal flaw in the conventional reasoning, it is argued, is that the length of a book as a whole is the most compelling evidence for its primacy. Following a curiously Darwinian logic, it is assumed that all texts evolve from primitive to complex states and that the "evolutionary development" of the Synoptic Gospels must therefore have begun with Mark. It is a serious mistake, however, to consider overall length as the "holy grail" of textual primacy. It is much more appropriate to consider the inner workings of the texts, their "genetic code," as it were. On that level, the conventional wisdom is upended, as we lay specific

---

[7] See Robert Lindsey, "A Modified Two-Document Theory of the Synoptic Dependence and Interdependence," *Novum Testamentum* 6 (1963): 239–63.

passages side by side to observe over and over again that Mark appears to be expanding on Luke as if to explain to a Greek-speaking audience what Lucan idioms actually signify.

A case in point, among myriad examples, is when Jesus is reported by Luke (18:29–30) as saying:

There is no one who has left house, or parents, or brothers, or wife, or children, for the sake of the kingdom of God, who shall not receive manifold more in this present time, and in the world to come eternal life.

Mark (10:29–30) appears to explain what Luke means by the word "house" (in Hebrew בית). His account reads:

There is no one who has left house, or brothers, or sisters, or father, or mother, or wife, or children, or lands, for my sake, and the Gospel's, but he shall receive a hundredfold now in this time, houses, and brothers, and sisters, and mothers, and children, and land, with persecutions; and in the world to come eternal life.

The word "parents" in Luke has been elaborated in Mark as "father or mother." Mark also adds "sisters" and "lands," as well as a reference to the "Gospel" and the words "with persecutions." The promise of future land is inconsistent with the Jesus of Luke, who is not in the habit of promising physical rewards for dedication to his movement. Indeed, while Mark on the whole is considerably shorter than Luke, the Markan redactor is in the habit of supplementing the Lucan account on a verse-by-verse basis. As another example, the pericope regarding the healing of a demon-possessed boy contains 124 words as recorded in Luke (9:37–43) and 270 words in Mark (9:14–29).

To employ Hebraic terminology, Mark might well be called a kind of "targumist," who went well beyond the task of translating one language to another, clarifying the presumed intent of idioms, phrases, and sundry expressions, as conveyed from text to text. A separate case, involving a theological interpretation, is the statement in the mouth of the Roman centurion at the crucifixion of Jesus. Luke records him as saying, "Surely, this was a righteous man." Mark, however, has him say, "Surely, this was the son of God." It is much easier to recognize Luke as reproducing an earlier and more "authentic" text, which was later embellished by Mark so as to extol Jesus to a level of near divinity. It was later writers who had every reason to elevate Jesus, in line with an evolving theology. Mark, it is argued, relied on the ANT and Luke, but did not know the RCT directly. Instead, he essentially "lifted" the RCT out of Luke, adapting it as he saw fit.

Finally, we have Matthew's Gospel, which also relies on two sources: the ANT and Mark, without knowing Luke. Matthew ordered his story units (pericopes) after Mark while taking other material (such as minor corrections of Mark's wording) from the ANT. For the discriminating mind, Matthew presents a whole gamut of challenges in its own right. It is in Matthew's narrative that we find, at the trial of Jesus before Pilate, a boisterous Jewish mob demanding his crucifixion with the libelous chant, "His blood be upon us and on our children." It is a charge absent in Luke and Mark. Given the use of such language across the centuries for the accusation that the Jewish people are history's quintessential "Christ killers," it is by no means difficult to understand why Matthew, and by extension all the Gospels, would be viewed by Jews as beyond the pale of serious consideration, even on a purely literary level. However, if we can wrestle with Matthew as part of the larger Synoptic Problem, we might catch a glimpse of a tertiary writer, theorized to have been part of an Aramaic-speaking, Judeo-Christian group, with an exclusivist mindset that conceived of itself as the "new Israel," the "true Israel." Such a mentality would go a long way toward explaining the writer's occasionally vicious rhetoric directed against what became traditional Judaism.

On a textual level, though Matthew did not know Luke, the common source material is responsible for many passages and pericopes common to both (the so-called "double tradition"), with minor variations. In other instances, the same or similar pericope is repeated across all three Synoptics: the "triple tradition." It is precisely in these cases where Matthew appears conflicted between Mark and the ANT. Often he seems to "pick up" Mark's elaborations to suit his own exegetical and theological purposes. Robert Lindsey, in seeking a new approach to the Synoptic Problem, examined a phenomenon he called the "Marcan cross-factor." He noted that in the triple tradition Matthew and Luke evince high agreement in pericope order and low verbal agreement in the narrative. In the double tradition, however, Matthew and Luke evince low agreement in pericope order and high agreement in verbal identity. This is quite consistent with the theory of Lucan priority.

Another contention of Lindsey and the Jerusalem School is that Jesus may well have spent a good deal of his time ("ministry") to the south of his native Galilee, in Judea. Certain aspects of his teaching seem particularly suited to an environment that included Jerusalem and points south, rather than the Galilean environment with which he is almost exclusively associated, save for the last week of his life. It is clear from the Gospels themselves that Jesus' family was wealthy enough to afford trips to Jerusalem, as recorded in the narratives surrounding his childhood. Later we are told (Luke 5:17) that he encountered "Pharisees and teachers of the Law ... who had come out of every town of Galilee, and Judea, and Jerusalem." It should hardly be surprising if Jesus had in fact returned to Judea regularly during his adult life, and it would indeed be unusual if he had not ventured into this region to his immediate south.

An important value of this admittedly avant-garde approach to the Synoptic problem is that it mitigates what often appears as a troublesome, anti-Jewish tone in many New Testament passages, even as it forces us to consider, not Mark, but Luke as the earliest Synoptic record. The potential of such an understanding is of huge consequence in the realm of interfaith relations. For Christians, there is considerable value in reading through the Greek Gospels to uncover, at least potentially, the *ipsissima verba* of Jesus himself, unadorned by layers of subsequent theological overlay. For Jews the prospect of vivisecting the Gospels to encounter, not the progenitor of another faith, but an ancient Israelite sage, perhaps an ancient Hasid, or perhaps harboring serious sympathies for the Zealot freedom fighters of his day, opens a door to appreciating the great Nazarene in a manner not thought possible since the inception of Christianity, nearly two millennia ago. It is in that spirit and with that aspiration that the following annotated version of the Synoptic Gospels is presented. It is sincerely hoped that it will add to the discussion of the Jewish Jesus, in all his color and first-century flavor.

A Note to the Reader

This volume is designed for those who are familiar to some extent with New Testament scholarship. However, it "bridges the gap" between material considered "accessible" and high scholarship. A knowledge of Hebrew and Greek is certainly helpful, though not required, as important terms and quotations appear in English as well as in the original languages.

One important textual note is that Lindsey himself wrote relatively little in his lifetime, and perhaps his most important work, *Jesus, Rabbi and Lord*, was written not in an academic style, but in his role as a Baptist minister. Nevertheless, its contents represent the sum of his decades long partnership with David Flusser. Many of his insights, virtually unattested in New Testament scholarship, deserve serious scholarly treatment and consideration. His suggested pericope order carries profound implications for synoptic research, and the text presented here represents a serious attempt to re-order the complete Gospel of Luke in accordance with Lindsey and Flusser's proposed schema, albeit purely hypothetical.

It is not the purpose of this modest volume to make a conclusive or exhaustive argument for Lucan priority. I have therefore made only a brief summary of the evidence for the theory while pointing to others who have defended it in greater detail. The Jerusalem School of Synoptic Research, along with its publications and related website (jerusalemperspective.com/696/) continue to advance important scholarly arguments with respect to the primacy of Luke. The Jerusalem School is currently compiling an exhaustive online resource, attempting to reconstruct this Proto-Narrative, admittedly from an evangelical Christian perspective. As of this writing, it remains only partially complete. Rather than restating these arguments or belaboring their fine points, the value of the current work is to get a glimpse of what the Gospel may have resembled, hypothetically, if the primacy of Luke were accepted. It may provide a sense of what the narrative of the life of Jesus may have resembled in its earliest compilation. The work presented here is intended to provide a much-needed overview, from a non-sectarian vantage point, of the entirety of this research. As with any academic debate, the important thing is not to arrive at conclusive proof, which every serious scholar knows is unattainable, but to glean insights that greatly enhance the understanding of all.

Moreover, whatever the validity of the theory, the abundant parallels to the Lucan narrative in multiple ancient sources, from the Dead Sea Scrolls to rabbinic literature (cited in the original Hebrew and/or Aramaic wherever possible), should serve as an important reference for those seeking a better understanding of the Jewish Jesus movement and its earliest historical milieu, prior to the imposition of multiple layers of subsequent religious and theological dogma. In the final analysis, the approach presented here is by no means the "last word" on contemporary Jesus research, but admittedly a work in progress, as enlightened scholarship grapples with the Sage of Galilee. It is therefore with a considerable dose of humility that Hebraic Luke is set forth as follows. Let the learning begin…

Introduction to Luke

The author of Luke begins by acknowledging that other accounts of the life of Jesus have preceded him. The operating theory espoused here is that two of the prior sources available to him were: a hypothetical "Anthological Text" (ANT) and a "Reconstructed Text" (RCT), which we may also refer to as a "Short Gospel." Following the introductory narratives of the first two chapters, it is argued that Chapter 3 through the middle of Chapter 9, as well as Chapters 19 to 24, are taken from RCT. The Reconstructed Text is known only to Luke. (Purple-colored font is used to highlight RCT.) The Anthological Text (ANT) is reproduced by Luke from the middle of Chapter 9 through Chapter 18. One textual conundrum potentially resolved by this theory is the fact that many of the Lucan sayings of Jesus are repeated later in the Gospel, as "doublets." The "two-source hypothesis" presented here explains this phenomenon. Additionally, the theory that Jesus embarked on a Judean sojourn is emphasized. The relevant passages appear in a separate section. Other passages have been rearranged from their order in the traditional Lucan text. This corresponds with the theorized notion that in the earliest "Proto-Narrative," a typical Gospel story unit (pericope) would have been built of an incident and a teaching, followed by two parables. Consequently, the flow of original chapters and verses is often interrupted, and explanatory notes have been placed in the text to indicate the transposition of certain sections. The text has therefore been rearranged according to hypothetical "Acts" and "Scenes." These include:

1. Luke's "Prelude"
2. The Baptist, the Genealogy, the Temptation and Galilee
3. The Judean Sojourn
4. The Return to Galilee
5. Up to Jerusalem
6. Temple to Tomb
7. Post-Resurrection

Some of the sayings and teachings of Jesus are also theorized to belong to a final, "post-resurrection" section of the Luke-Acts, originally appearing after Luke 24:50 or Acts 1:3. Such sayings have been transposed to the end. Occasional imports from the Gospels of Matthew and John are in red font. It should be noted that the first two chapters of Luke (excluding Luke's dedication to Theophilus in the first four verses) also betray a Hebraic syntax, likely stemming from an earlier Hebrew "nativity" source.

It is worth noting that beginning with the first two chapters of Luke, there has been much source-critical discussion of "aberrations" in the Greek. M. Wilcox noted the influence of "Aramaic and/or Hebrew traditional material" on New Testament Greek. He argued that there is something more going on than mere imitation of the Greek of the Septuagint. It is arguably the case, however, that a Hebrew *Vorlage* explains such aberrations better than a supposed Aramaic source or sources.[1]

In any case, such an unknown Hebrew source is distinct from either the ANT or the RCT. This section is color-coded in brown. Throughout the text, the words and phrases in bold font are notable for their Hebraic significance, and the extensive footnotes at the bottom of each page explain their meaning and importance.

---

[1] See Max Wilcox, "Semitisms in the New Testament," *ANRW* II.25.1 (1984): 978-1029. See also Albert L. A. Hogeterp and Adelbert Denaux, *Semitisms in Luke's Greek: A Descriptive Analysis of Lexical and Syntactical Domains of Semitic Language Influence in Luke's Gospel* (Tübingen: Mohr Siebeck, 2018), 29.

A brief outline of Luke's sources is as follows:

Chapters 1–3: Unknown "Nativity" source
Chapters 3–9: RCT (Reconstructed Text)—known only to Luke
Chapters 9–18: ANT (Anthological Text)
Chapters 19–24: RCT (Reconstructed Text)—known only to Luke

A note on the text: I have chosen the King James version of the Gospels since it slavishly preserves, often in an awkward fashion, much of the original syntax of the Greek, which itself awkwardly renders a hypothetical Hebrew Ur-text. I have, however, made extensive edits to the KJV, consulting the original Greek text, in order to conform it to modern idiomatic English.

Luke's Prelude

B eginning with the story of the birth of John the Baptist, we find a thoroughly Hebraic cadence, with the word "and" being employed multiple times to preserve the flow of the narrative. This mirrors the "vav consecutive" verb form, which, while stylistically common in Hebrew, sounds monotonously repetitive when reproduced in Greek (and English translation).[1]

While it has been pointed out that there is in general a lack of Aramaisms in Luke, the case can be made (notwithstanding a cadre of scholarly detractors) that there are abundant Hebraisms.[2] Reading "beneath" the Greek, we may imagine a Hebrew subtext, in which the word "and" is a perfectly common literary device, the "*vav* consecutive." Other Hebraisms begin to appear, such as the statement, "And it came to pass." While the first two chapters of Luke (seen by some as second century additions) are not theorized to derive from either RCT or ANT, the author/redactor likely relied on Hebraic source material of some kind. Luke's account of the virgin birth is often considered part of a hypothetical oral tradition, known as "L," but it can easily be argued that the Greek of these passages suggests a written Hebrew *grundschrift*. Such an argument is considered avant-garde in the context of the majority of contemporary scholarship, but it is entirely reasonable, given the universal recognition of the text's Semitic characteristics and overall "flair."

---

[1] The same phenomenon is frequently found in the Apocrypha and Pseudepigrapha. See R. H. Charles, *The Apocrypha and Pseudepigrapha of the Old Testament*, I (London: Oxford University Press, 1913), 641.

[2] See R. Steven Notley, "Non-Septuagintal Hebraisms in the Third Gospel: An Inconvenient Truth," in *The Language Environment of First Century Judaea*, eds. Randall Buth and R. Steven Notley (Leiden: Brill, 2014), 320–46.

Dedication to Theophilus

Writing to Theophilus ("friend of God"), likely a non-Jew, Luke's author/redactor declares his objective as setting forth a narrative "in order." This is consistent with the "two-source hypothesis." Although the consensus of critical scholarship places the Gospel's composition later in the first century, it is theorized that Luke's first recension may date to as early as 58–60 CE.[3]

Luke 1:1 Inasmuch as **many have attempted to set forth in order a narrative**[4] of the things that have been accomplished among us, **2** Even as they delivered them to us, who from the beginning were eyewitnesses, and servants of the word; **3** It seemed good to me also, having been acquainted with all things from the very first, to write to you in order, most excellent Theophilus, **4** so that you might know the certainty of the things in which you have been instructed.

Scene 1:
John the Baptist's Birth Announced

The focus of Chapter 1 is on the priestly service in the temple. The narrative betrays Hebraic syntactical features, with abundant references to the Hebrew Scriptures, rabbinic literature, and the Dead Sea Scrolls. As in the Hebrew Bible, there is an emphasis on the motif of a child born to a barren woman. Interestingly, the term "Holy Spirit," long considered uniquely Christian in usage, also finds a parallel in the Dead Sea Scrolls, indicating its adoption at

---

[3] See Robert Lindsey, *A Hebrew Translation of the Gospel of Mark*, (Jerusalem: Dugith Publishers, 1973), 44–45; Bivin and Blizzard, 93–98; Dan Barag and David Flusser, "The Ossuary of Yehohanah Granddaughter of the High Priest Theophilus," *Israel Exploration Journal* 36, no. 1–2 (1986): 39–44.

[4] The "many" who have attempted to produce an orderly narrative might have included the editors/redactors of both ANT (the hypothetical "anthological text") and RCT (the "short Gospel,") representing an attempt to restore the Greek text to its proper chronological sequence.

least by sectarian movements of the Second Jewish Commonwealth.

Luke 1:5 There was in the days of Herod, the king of Judea, a certain priest named Zechariah, of the **order of Abijah: and his wife was among the daughters of Aaron,**[5] and her name was Elizabeth. **6** And they were both **righteous before God,**[6] walking in all the commandments and ordinances of the Lord blameless. **7 And they had no child,**[7] because Elizabeth was barren, and they both were now well **advanced in years.**[8] **8 And it came to pass,**[9] that while he executed the priest's office before God in the order of his division, **9** According to the custom of the priest's office, the lot fell to him to burn incense when he went into the temple of the Lord. **10** And the whole multitude of the people were **praying**[10] outside at the time of incense. **11** And there appeared to him an angel of the Lord **standing on the right side of the altar of**

---

[5] See 1 Chr 24:1. The list of priestly divisions is dated to the fifth century, BCE, but no mention is made of the fixed order of service. This is a post-Biblical tradition. Priests lived in other settlements, aside from Jerusalem (*m. Ta'an.* 4:2), leaving their homes and traveling to Jerusalem for a week at a time: "When the time arrived [for the members of a certain] priestly watch to ascend, the priests and Levites of that watch would ascend to Jerusalem" (הִגִּיעַ זְמַן הַמִּשְׁמָר לַעֲלוֹת, כֹּהֲנִים וּלְוִיִם עוֹלִים לִירוּשָׁלָיִם). Abijah was the eighth division, serving in *Iyar* (Apr.–May) and again in *Marcheshvan* (Oct.–Nov.). The Abijah division was named after one of the priests returning with Zerubbabel (Neh 12:4). The phrase "among the daughters of Aaron" was an idiom of the period, meaning that she was a daughter of a priest.

[6] "Righteous" suggests that their childlessness was not the result of wickedness or unworthiness. "Before God" (ἐναντίον τοῦ Θεοῦ) translates the Hebrew לִפְנֵי אלהים, meaning "in the opinion of God."

[7] As in Gen 16:1, which relates that Sarah was barren. Note: *Pesiq. Rab.* 32: "R' Levi said anywhere that it says she does not have [a child], she has" (רבי לוי בכ"מ שהוא אומר אין לה יש).

[8] Sixty years was considered the beginning of agedness; note *m. Avot* 5:21: "At sixty old age" (בֶּן שִׁשִּׁים לַזִּקְנָה). See Luke 18:16.

[9] The Greek ἐγένετο δὲ translates the Hebrew וַיְהִי, which is used idiomatically throughout the Hebrew Bible, beginning with Gen 1:5: "And there was evening and there was morning, one day" (וַיְהִי-עֶרֶב וַיְהִי-בֹקֶר יוֹם אֶחָד).

[10] It is charged that people did not pray at the time of sacrifice or incense, and that Luke (the L source) is unfamiliar with the temple practices.

incense.[11] **12** And when Zechariah saw him, he was troubled, and fear fell upon him. **13** But the angel said to him: Do not fear, Zechariah; for your prayer has been heard; and your wife Elizabeth will bear you a son, **and you will call his name**[12] John. **14** And you will have joy and gladness; and many will rejoice at his birth. **15** For he will be great in the sight of the Lord, **and will drink neither wine nor strong drink;**[13] and he will be filled with the **Holy Spirit,**[14] even from his mother's womb. **16** And he will turn many of the children of Israel to the Lord their God. **17** And he will go before him in the spirit and power of Elijah, **to turn the hearts of the fathers to the children,**[15] and the disobedient to the

---

[11] See Num 28:3–4. The *Tamid*, the daily offering, was determined by casting lots. The culmination was the burning of incense (*m. Tam.* 3:1; 5:2). The most striking example of a vision at the time of incense was at the time of Simon the Just (c. 200 BCE). Note *b. Yom.* 39b: "On every Yom Kippur [upon entering the Holy of Holies], I was met by an old man who was dressed in white, and his head was wrapped up in white, and he would enter with me, and he would leave with me. But today, I was met by an old man who was dressed in black, and wrapped up in black, and he entered with me, but he did not leave with me. After the festival of *Sukkot*, he was ill for seven days and died" (בְּכָל יוֹם הַכִּפּוּרִים הָיָה מְזֻדַּמֵּן לִי זָקֵן אֶחָד לָבוּשׁ לְבָנִים וְעָטוּף לְבָנִים, נִכְנָס עִמִּי וְיָצָא עִמִּי, וְהַיּוֹם נִזְדַּמֵּן לִי זָקֵן אֶחָד לָבוּשׁ שְׁחוֹרִים וְעָטוּף שְׁחוֹרִים, נִכְנַס עִמִּי וְלֹא יָצָא עִמִּי. אַחַר הָרֶגֶל חָלָה שִׁבְעָה יָמִים וָמֵת). There are other instances of visions at the time of incense, e.g. John Hyrcanus—that his sons had defeated Antiochus (Josephus, *Ant.* 13:282); and again, that Caligula was dead (*Tos. Sot.* 13:6). Therefore, a vision at this time was not unheard of. However, visions always came to a high priest, never to an ordinary priest. The right side could indicate favorable circumstances. Note *b. Yom.* 33b: "And when he enters the Sanctuary it is the **altar** that he encounters first" (וְכִי עָיֵיל לְהֵיכָל פָּגַע בְּמִזְבֵּחַ בְּרֵישָׁא); *Targ. Cant.* 4:16: "... and on the **altar** the priests offered the sacrifice and on it sent up the spice incense" (וְעַל **מַדְבְּחָא** הֲווֹ כָּהֲנַיָּא מַסְקִין קְטוֹרֶת בּוּסְמִין). On the *Tamid*, see Exod 29:38–43.

[12] The Greek καὶ καλέσεις τὸ ὄνομα αὐτοῦ translates the perfectly idiomatic Hebrew וקראת את שמו, as in Gen 17:15: "And God said unto Abraham: 'As for Sarai your wife, you shall not **call her name** Sarai, but Sarah shall be her name'" (וַיֹּאמֶר אֱלֹהִים אֶל-אַבְרָהָם שָׂרַי אִשְׁתְּךָ לֹא-**תִקְרָא אֶת-שְׁמָהּ** שָׂרָי: כִּי שָׂרָה שְׁמָהּ).

[13] That is, a Nazirite vow, thus unshorn; see Num 6:5.

[14] The Greek Πνεύματος Ἁγίου/"Holy Spirit" translates the Hebrew רוח קודש. The Hebrew Bible refers to God's "holy spirit" only three times, in Isa 63:10–11, and Ps 51:13. Note Jubilees 1:33: "and I shall create in them a *holy spirit*, and I shall cleanse them so that they shall not turn away from Me from that day unto eternity" (ובראתי להם רוח **קדוש** וטיהרתים למען לא יסורו עוד ממני מיום ההוא עד עולם). The Dead Sea Scrolls mention a "holy spirit" at least four times, and on several more instances refer to an angel or spirit of truth. Note 1QS4:21: "... cleansing from every wicked deed by a *holy spirit*" (ולטהרו ברוח **קודש** מכול עלילות רשעה). The term falls out of use in the rabbinic period, though the concept is carried on in the idea of the *shekhinah*, referring to the divine presence, or "dwelling."

[15] See Mal 3:24: "And he shall turn the heart of the fathers to the children, and the heart of the children to their fathers" (וְהֵשִׁיב לֵב אָבוֹת עַל בָּנִים, וְלֵב בָּנִים עַל אֲבוֹתָם).

wisdom of the righteous; **to make ready a people prepared**[16] for the Lord. **18** And Zechariah said to the angel: How will I know this? For I am an old man, and my wife is well advanced in years. **19** And the angel answering said to him: I am Gabriel, who stands in the presence of God; and am sent to speak to you, and to show you these **glad tidings.**[17] **20 And, behold,**[18] you will become mute, and unable to speak, until the day that these things take place, because you did not believe my words, which will be fulfilled in their season. **21** And the people waited for Zechariah, **and marveled that he remained so long in the temple.**[19] **22** And when he came out, **he could not speak to them;**[20] and they perceived that he had seen a vision in the temple: for he gestured to them, and remained speechless. **23 And it came to pass,**[21] that, as soon as the days of his service were accomplished, he departed to his own house. **24** And after those days his wife Elizabeth conceived, and secluded herself for five months, saying: **25** Thus has the Lord dealt with me in the days in which he looked on me, to take away my reproach among men.

---

[16] Note Ben Sira 48:10: "… you who are *ready* at the appointed time."

[17] The Greek εὐαγγελίσασθαι translates the Hebrew לְבַשֵּׂר. Note Isa 61:1: "The spirit of the Lord GOD is upon me; because the LORD has anointed me *to bring good tidings* to the humble …" (רוּחַ אֲדֹנָי יְהוִה עָלָי יַעַן מָשַׁח יְהוָה אֹתִי לְבַשֵּׂר עֲנָוִים).

[18] The Greek καὶ ἰδού translates the Hebrew וְהִנֵּה. In the Septuagint ἰδού is the most common translation of the Hebrew demonstrative particle הִנֵּה. Either the Greek is deliberately mimicing the LXX or there is an underlying Hebraic source on which the Gospel writer is relying. M. Wilcox ("Semitisms in the New Testament") argued that such features are not simply the imitation of Septuagint Greek.

[19] People were always concerned when a priest entered the temple, lest something go amiss. Note *m. Yom.* 5:1 (regarding the high priest on the Day of Atonement): "And he would not extend his prayer there so as not to alarm the Jewish people [who would otherwise conclude that something happened and that he died in the Holy of Holies]" (וְלֹא הָיָה מַאֲרִיךְ בִּתְפִלָּתוֹ, שֶׁלֹּא לְהַבְעִית אֶת יִשְׂרָאֵל). It is charged, however, that several priests regularly entered the temple to offer incense, and that Luke is unfamiliar with these practices.

[20] He was *expected* to offer the priestly benediction (Num 6:24–26): "The Lord bless you and keep you …" (… יְבָרֶכְךָ יְהוָה וְיִשְׁמְרֶךָ).

[21] The Greek καὶ ἐγένετο translates the Hebrew וַיְהִי. Note the repetition throughout the narrative of the word "and" (καί), preserved in the King James version, and consistent with the concept of an underlying Hebrew text, where "and" (ו) is a common literary feature.

Scene 2:
Jesus' Birth Announced

The announcement of Jesus' birth is profoundly Hebraic in style and flavor. It bears syntactical features (including poetic parallelism and the equivalent of the "vav consecutive") that are rooted in the Hebrew language.

Luke 1:26 And in the sixth month the angel Gabriel was sent from God to a city of **Galilee,**[22] called **Nazareth,**[23] **27** To a **virgin**[24] espoused to a man whose name was Joseph, of the house of David; and the virgin's name was Mary. **28** And the angel came to her, and said: Greetings, you who are highly favored, **the Lord is with you: blessed are you among women. 29 And when she saw him, she was troubled**[25] at his saying, and pondered what kind of salutation this might be. **30** And the angel said to her: Do not fear, Mary: for you have found favor with God. **31 And, behold,**[26] you will conceive in your womb, and bring forth a son, **and you will call his name**[27] Jesus. **32** He will be great, and will be called the

---

[22] Galilean Jews regarded themselves as very devout and more pious than their compatriots in Jerusalem and Judea. In the Tannaitic age many most famous rabbis were from Galilee. See Richard A. Gabriel, *Gods of Our Fathers: The Memory of Egypt in Judaism and Christianity* (Westport, CT: Greenwood Press, 2002), 145.

[23] Nazareth is mentioned *only* in the New Testament, and not in Jewish sources until the seventh century. While it was an obscure town, this could also indicate a systematic expunging of the name by later rabbis in response to a *large* messianic movement among the Jews.

[24] The Hebrew of Isa 7:14 reads: "Therefore the Lord Himself shall give you a sign: behold, *the young woman* shall conceive ..." (לָכֵן יִתֵּן אֲדֹנָי הוּא לָכֶם אוֹת: הִנֵּה הָעַלְמָה הָרָה). However, the Septuagint translates הָעַלְמָה as παρθένος ("virgin") because it is hardly a "sign" for a young woman to bear a child.

[25] In the Biblical period, the Divine Name was used in greetings, but substitutes were used in the Second Temple period, such as המקום/*ha-Makom* ("the Place") and הגבורה/*ha-G'vurah* ("the Power"). That "the Lord" is invoked here is what "troubles" Mary. Later, the Jews returned to using the Divine Name in greetings, to distinguish themselves from the *Minim,* i.e. Nazarenes. Note *m. Ber.* 9:5: "The Sages also instituted that one should greet another in the name of God" (וְהִתְקִינוּ, שֶׁיְּהֵא אָדָם שׁוֹאֵל אֶת שְׁלוֹם חֲבֵרוֹ בַּשֵּׁם).

[26] The Greek καὶ ἰδού translates the Hebrew וְהִנֵּה. See Luke 1:20 n.

[27] The Greek καὶ καλέσεις τὸ ὄνομα αὐτοῦ translates the perfectly idiomatic Hebrew ותקרא את שמו; see Luke 1:13.

Son of the Most High:[28] And the Lord God will give to him the throne of his father David: **33** And he will reign over the house of Jacob forever; and there will be no end of his kingdom. **34** Then Mary said to the angel: How will this be, since I have not known a man? **35** And the angel answered and said to her: The **Holy Spirit**[29] will come upon you/and the **power of the Most High will overshadow you;**[30] therefore also the holy one born to you will be called the **Son of God.**[31] **36 And, behold,**[32] your **relative Elizabeth**[33] has also conceived a son in her old age; and this is the sixth month with her, who was called barren. **37** For with God nothing will be impossible. **38** And Mary said: **Behold**[34] the handmaid of the Lord; may it be to me according to your word. And the angel departed from her.

Scene 3:
Mary Visits Elizabeth

The text goes on to recount Mary's song of praise, where we find allusion not only to biblical literature but to the Dead Sea Scrolls. The "Magnificat" (Luke 1:47–55) likely originated as a

---

[28] See Wisdom of Solomon 2:18; 2:13–16. The righteous will be called "God's son." Note the Dead Sea "Son of God" text (4Q246 f1i:9–f1ii:1), regarding some unidentified person: "[… his son] will be called The Great, and be designated by his name. He will be called the ***Son of God***, they will call him the ***son of the Most High***" (יתקרא ובשמה יתכנה. **ברה די אל** יתאמר **ובר עליון** יקרונה).

[29] See Luke 1:15. Note Dead Sea Scrolls 1QS4:21: "… cleansing from every wicked deed by a ***holy spirit***" (ולטהרו **ברוח קודש** מכול עלילות רשעה).

[30] See Ruth 3:9: "Spread therefore your wing over your handmaiden…" (וּפָרַשְׂתָּ כְנָפֶךָ עַל-אֲמָתְךָ). Ruth, like Sarah and Rebecca, is said to have had *no womb; see Ruth R.* 4:13. Note the Hebraic parallelism: "The Holy Spirit will come upon you/the power of the Most High will overshadow you."

[31] See Luke 1:32; Note the Dead Sea "Son of God" text.

[32] The Greek καὶ ἰδού translates the Hebrew וְהִנֵּה. See Luke 1:20 n.

[33] According to Luke both Elizabeth and Zechariah her husband were of priestly descent, confirming the connection between Mary's Davidic roots and the tribe of Levi. Mary was therefore likely of mixed lineage. See James Tabor, *The Jesus Dynasty: The Hidden History of Jesus, His Royal Family, and the Birth of Christianity* (New York: Simon & Schuster, 2006), 56.

[34] The Greek ἰδού translates the Hebrew הִנֵּה. See Luke 1:20 n.

Maccabean hymn, during the reign of the Hasmonean king, Simon (142–135 BCE).[35]

Luke 1:39 And Mary arose in those days, and went into the hill country with haste, into a city[36] **of Judea;**[37] **40** And entered into the house of Zechariah,[38] and greeted Elizabeth. **41 And it came to pass,**[39] that, when Elizabeth heard the salutation of Mary, the baby leaped in her womb; and Elizabeth was filled with the **Holy Spirit:**[40] **42** And she cried out with a loud voice, and said: Blessed are you among women, and **blessed is the fruit of your womb.**[41] **43** And how is it to me, that the mother of my Lord should come to me? **44** For, **Behold,**[42] as soon as the **voice**[43] of your greeting came to my ears, the baby leaped in my womb for joy. **45** And blessed is she who believed; for there will be a fulfillment of those things that were spoken to her from the Lord. **46** And Mary said: **My soul magnifies the Lord,**[44] **47** And my spirit has rejoiced in God my Savior. **48** For he has regarded the **low estate**[45] of his handmaiden;

---

[35] See Randall Buth, "Hebrew Poetic Tenses and the Magnificat," *Journal for the Study of the New Testament,* 21 (1984): 67–83; Paul Haupt, "Magnificat and Benedictus," *American Journal of Philology* 40 1 (1919): 64–75; David Flusser, *Judaism and the Origins of Christianity* (Jerusalem: Magnes Press, 1988), 289.

[36] The Greek πόλιν translates the Hebrew word מדינה ("city"/"town"), which additionally came to mean: country, land or region.

[37] Unlike the stories of Isaac, Samson, and *Samuel* (after whom the nativity story is modeled), there is no mention that Mary *conceived*. This could be an error in transmission of the Semitic original, the Hebrew ותהר ("and she conceived") being mistaken for ותמהר ("and she hurried"). Hypothetical Hebrew Reconstruction: בימים ההם ותהר (ותמהר) מרים ותלך ההרה למדינת יהודה ("In those days Mary *conceived* and went to the hill country in the region of Judea").

[38] Followers of John the Baptist may have claimed that *he* was born in Bethlehem, linking him with David. The followers of Jesus may have felt compelled to do the same.

[39] The Greek καὶ ἐγένετο translates the Hebrew וַיְהִי; see Luke 1:23.

[40] See Luke 1:15. Note Dead Sea Scrolls 1QS4:21: "… cleansing from every wicked deed by a *holy spirit*" (ולטהרו ברוח קודש מכול עלילות רשעה).

[41] Note *PRK* (supplement 6): "Blessed is the house in which the Messiah was created. Blessed is the womb whence he came."

[42] The Greek ἰδού translates the Hebrew הִנֵּה. See Luke 1:20 n.

[43] A messianic proclamation; the Greek φωνὴ translates the Hebrew קול, as in בת קול ("daughter of the voice"). See Luke 9:35.

[44] Note 1 Sam 2:1: "My heart exults in the LORD …" (עָלַץ לִבִּי בַּיהוָה). Mary's words are patterned on Hannah's.

[45] The Greek ταπείνωσιν translates the Hebrew עָנְיִ.

for, **behold,**[46] from henceforth **all generations shall call me blessed.**[47] **49** For the Mighty One has done to me great things; and holy is his name. **50** And his mercy is on those who fear him from **generation to generation.**[48] **51 He has shown strength with his arm;**[49] he has scattered **the proud**[50] in the imagination of their hearts. **52 He has brought down the mighty from their thrones, and exalted the humble.**[51] **53** He has filled the hungry with good things; and the rich he has sent empty away. **54** He has helped his servant Israel, in remembrance of his mercy. **55** As he spoke to our fathers, to Abraham, and to his seed forever. **56** And Mary dwelt with her about three months, and returned to her own house.

Scene 4:
The Birth and Circumcision
of John the Baptist

The details regarding John the Baptist align well with Jewish tradition, which required circumcision on the eighth day, along with the naming of the child.

Luke 1:57 Now Elizabeth's full time came that she should give birth; and she brought forth a son. **58** And her neighbors and her relatives heard how the Lord had shown great mercy upon her; and

---

[46] The Greek ἰδού translates the Hebrew הִנֵּה. See Luke 1:20 n.

[47] Note *Pesiq. Rab.* 37: "Blessed is the generation whose eyes behold him" (אשרי **הדור** שעיניו רואות אותו). Regarding previous generations, note Luke 10:23–24: "Blessed are the eyes which see the things that you see … Many prophets and kings have desired to see the things which you see, and have not seen them; and to hear the things which you hear, and have not heard them." See also Matt 13:6.

[48] The Greek γενεὰς καὶ γενεὰς translates a common Hebrew idiom: מִדּוֹר לְדוֹר.

[49] This references the victories of the Maccabees.

[50] "The proud" were the Greeks/Seleucids.

[51] The "mighty" who were brought down were the Seleucid kings (Antiochus V Eupator and Demetrius I Soter). See note on Luke 2:38; Dead Sea Scrolls, 1QM 14:4–7, 11: "Blessed be the God of Israel" (ברוך אל ישראל). "He has called those who stumble unto wondrous accomplishments" (ויקרא כושלים לגבורות פלא). "He gives those whose knees shake strength to stand" (ונותן לנמוגי ברכים חזוק מעמד). "… by those whose way is perfect shall all wicked nations come to an end (ובתמימי דרך יתמו כול גויי רשעה). "Those who are great in height You will cut down to humble them" (ורמי קומה תגדע להשפילם).

they rejoiced with her. **59 And it came to pass,**[52] **that on the eighth day they came to circumcise the child; and they called him Zechariah, after the name of his father.**[53] **60** And his mother answered and said: No; but he shall be called John. **61** And they said to her: **There is no one among your relatives who is called by this name.**[54] **62** And they made signs to his father, how he would have him called. **63** And he asked for a writing tablet, and wrote, saying: His name is John. And they all marveled. **64** And his mouth was opened immediately, and his tongue loosed, and he spoke, and praised God. **65** And fear came on all who dwelt round around them: and all these sayings were talked about throughout all the hill country of Judea. **66** And all who heard them laid them up in their hearts, saying, What manner of child will this be? And the **hand of the Lord**[55] was with him.

Scene 5:
Zechariah's Prophecy

The prophecy of Zechariah (the "Benedictus") is also Hebraic in syntax, containing linguistic nuances that can only be appreciated in Hebrew. It is thought by some to have been composed during the Babylonian captivity, being one of the earliest Hebrew psalms.[56] Of particular note are the expressions "son of the Most High" (v. 32) and "son of God" (v. 35), which, far from being exclusively Christian formulations, have been found among the fragments of the Dead Sea Scrolls. We also see the concept of "salvation" for an exclusive group among the Israelites, elsewhere referenced as

---

[52] The Greek καὶ ἐγένετο translates the Hebrew וַיְהִי; see Luke 1:23.

[53] Note *PRE* (ch. 48): Moses was named יקותיאל (Yekutiel) on eighth day (from יקח + אל: suggesting "obedience to God"). Note also *Eccles. Rab.* 7:3: "A man is given three names: the one given by his father and mother, the one giving him by other people (his nickname), and the one which has been predestined for him" (שְׁלֹשָׁה שֵׁמוֹת נִקְרָא לָאָדָם: הֶדָּה, אֶחָד שֶׁקְּרָאוּ לוֹ אָבִיו וְאִמּוֹ, וְאֶחָד שֶׁקְּרָאוּ לוֹ אֲחֵרִים, וְאֶחָד שֶׁקְּרוּי לוֹ בְּסֵפֶר תּוֹלְדוֹת בְּרִיָּתוֹ).

[54] Note the Jewish practice of naming a child in honor of a family member, either deceased or living.

[55] Note Dead Sea Scrolls 1QM 1:14 "In the seventh lot the great **hand of God** shall overcome …" (ובגורל השביעי **יד אל** הגדולה מכנעת …).

[56] See Flusser, *Judaism*, 134–35.

the "elect." How many of such ideas were shared by Jesus and his followers is up for debate.

Luke 1:67 And his father Zechariah was filled with the **Holy Spirit,**[57] and prophesied, saying: **68 Blessed is the Lord God of Israel;** for he has **visited**[58] and **redeemed his people,**[59] **69** And **has raised up a horn of salvation**[60] for us in the house of his servant David; **70 As he spoke by the mouth of his holy prophets,**[61] of old: **71** That we should be saved from our enemies, and from the hand of all who hate us; **72** To fulfill mercy toward our fathers, and to remember his holy covenant; **73** The oath which he swore to **our father Abraham,**[62] **74** That he would grant to us, deliverance from the hand of our enemies, being saved to serve him without fear, **75** In holiness and righteousness before him, all the days of our life. **76** And you, child, shall be called **the prophet of the Most High:**[63] for you shall go before the face of the Lord to prepare his ways; **77** To give knowledge of salvation to his people by the forgiveness of their sins, **78** Through the tender mercy of

---

[57] See Luke 1:15. Note Dead Sea Scrolls 1QS4:21: "… cleansing from every wicked deed by a *holy spirit*" (ולטהרו **ברוח קודש** מכול עלילות רשעה).

[58] See Luke 19:44.

[59] See Luke 1:52; note Dead Sea Scrolls 1QM 14:4–15: "*Blessed is the God of Israel*, who guards lovingkindness for His covenant and the appointed times of *salvation* (*yeshuah*) for the *people He redeems*. He has called those who stumble unto wondrous accomplishments …" (… ויקרא .ותו**ד** **ישועה לעם פדותו** **ברוך אל ישראל** השומר חסד לבריתו ותעודות כושלים לגבורות פלא).

[60] The Greek Ἰησοῦν ("Jesus") transliterates the Hebrew ישועה ("Salvation"). Note the fifteenth benediction of the *Amidah* prayer: "Blessed are you, O Lord, who causes the *horn of salvation* (*yeshuah*) to flourish" (בָּרוּךְ אַתָּה יְיָ מַצְמִיחַ קֶרֶן יְשׁוּעָה).

[61] Not found in the Masoretic Text, but similar language appears in the Dead Sea Scrolls 1QS 1:3: "He commanded through the hand of Moses and the hand of all His servants the prophets" (צוה ביד מושה וביד כול עבדיו הנביאים).

[62] The "plebeian" class had derived the principle of the "merit of the fathers" (זכות אבות), which implied the pre-determination of one's fate. Shemaiah claimed that the Red Sea opened in reward for the faith of Abraham. Avtalion (the "patrician") said that it was due to the faith/merit of the Israelites themselves; see *Mekh.* 2:3, Luke 3:8. See Dead Sea Scrolls 1QM 14:8: "But we are the remnant of Your people. Blessed is Your name, O God of lovingkindness, the One who kept the *covenant for our forefathers*" (ואנו שארית **ברית לאבותינו** עמכה. ברוך שמכה אל החסדים השומר). See also Luke 11:72–73.

[63] Note *Test. Levi* 8:15; possibly a messianic title: "And his presence is beloved, *as a prophet of the Most High*, of the seed of Abraham our father" (וחזותו יאהבו **כנביא אל** מזרע אברהם אבינו **עליון**).

our God; whereby the **dayspring from on high**[64] has visited us, **79** To give light to those who sit in darkness and in the shadow of death, to guide our feet into **the way of peace.**[65] **80** And the child continued to grow strong in spirit, and was in the deserts until the day of his appearance to Israel.

Scene 6:
The Birth of Jesus

Luke's special "nativity" narrative continues (and concludes) in Chapter 2. Jesus is linked in this account with the city of Bethlehem (whether or not he was actually born there). The link with David is obviously messianic, but does this suggest (in addition to a messianic identification) militancy and insurrection against Roman domination?

Luke 2:1 And it came to pass[66] in those days, that there went out a decree from Caesar Augustus to register all the world. **2 This first registration took place when Quirinius**[67] was governor of Syria. **3** And all went to be registered, each one to his own city. **4** Joseph also went up from Galilee, out of the city of **Nazareth,**[68] into Judea, to the city of David, which is called **Bethlehem;**[69]

---

[64] Note Mal 3:20: "But to you that fear My name shall the *sun of righteousness* arise with healing in its wings" (וְזָרְחָה לָכֶם יִרְאֵי שְׁמִי שֶׁמֶשׁ **צְדָקָה** וּמַרְפֵּא בִּכְנָפֶיהָ).

[65] *PRK* 18:6 interprets Ps 72:7 messianically: "In his days let the righteous flourish, and abundance of *peace*" (יִפְרַח בְּיָמָיו צַדִּיק וְרֹב **שָׁלוֹם**).

[66] The Greek ἐγένετο δὲ translates the Hebrew וַיְהִי.

[67] Quirinius did not become governor until 6 CE. The census he conducted in Syria has been confirmed by an inscription purchased in Beirut in 1674, but it dates too late to match the account in Luke. It has been argued that Quirinius had been governor on a previous occasion (3 BCE–2 BCE), at which time an earlier census may have been conducted. Luke may have alluded to this when he mentions "this first registration." While theoretically possible, such a solution would require post-dating Herod's death to 1 BCE, as opposed to the accepted date, 4 BCE.

[68] See Luke 1:26; Nazareth is mentioned *only* in the New Testament …

[69] Note Mic 5:1: "But you, **Bethlehem** Ephrathah, too little to be among the thousands of Judah, out of you shall one come forth to Me one who is to be ruler in Israel; whose goings forth are from of old, from ancient days" (וְאַתָּה **בֵּית-לֶחֶם** אֶפְרָתָה צָעִיר לִהְיוֹת בְּאַלְפֵי יְהוּדָה מִמְּךָ לִי יֵצֵא לִהְיוֹת מוֹשֵׁל בְּיִשְׂרָאֵל; וּמוֹצָאֹתָיו מִקֶּדֶם, מִימֵי עוֹלָם). Some speculate that Jesus was born in Nazareth and that the Bethlehem story is intended as a messianic link. There is also archaeological evidence of another town in Galilee called Bethlehem.

because he was of the house and lineage of David; **5** To be registered with Mary who was betrothed to him, being with child. **6 And it came to pass**[70] that, while they were there, the days were fulfilled that she should deliver. **7** And she brought forth her firstborn son, and wrapped him in swaddling clothes, and laid him in a **manger;**[71] **because there was no room for them in the inn.**[72]

Scene 7:

The Shepherds

The reference to "peace" in this passage refers to the Messiah, who is sent to the "saved" people of God. The implication is that messianic peace is for an exclusive group of Israelites: the "elect."

Luke 2:8 And there were in the same region shepherds lodging in the fields, keeping watch over their flock by night. **9** And an angel of the Lord stood by them, and the glory of the Lord shone around them; and they were greatly afraid. **10** And the angel said to them: Do not fear; for, **behold,**[73] I bring you **good news**[74] of great joy,

---

[70] The Greek ἐγένετο δὲ translates the Hebrew וַיְהִי.

[71] The Hebrew term for a feeding trough ("manger") occurs only three times in the Hebrew Bible, most notably Isa 1:3: "The ox knows its owner and the donkey its master's **feeding trough**; *But* Israel does not know, My people do not consider" (יָדַע שׁוֹר קֹנֵהוּ, וַחֲמוֹר **אֵבוּס** בְּעָלָיו; יִשְׂרָאֵל לֹא יָדַע, עַמִּי לֹא הִתְבּוֹנָן). This detail in Luke is possibly a prophetic rebuke, though others suggest it associates Jesus with a feeding trough, prefiguring the Last Supper.

[72] The lack of room at the inn was possibly an excuse. There may indeed have been room, given that a man was allowed to share a room with more than one woman as long as one was his wife. Moreover, people slept in their clothes, only removing the outer garment. The real reason may have involved Mary's pregnancy since people would be inconvenienced if she had to leave the room. Nor would there be privacy for giving birth. Note *m. Kid.* 4:12: "A man may not be secluded with two women lest he sin with them, but one woman may be secluded with two men. Rabbi Shimon says: Even one man may be secluded with two women when his wife is with him" (לֹא יִתְיַחֵד אָדָם עִם שְׁתֵּי נָשִׁים, אֲבָל אִשָּׁה אַחַת מִתְיַחֶדֶת עִם שְׁנֵי אֲנָשִׁים. רַבִּי שִׁמְעוֹן אוֹמֵר, אַף אִישׁ אֶחָד מִתְיַחֵד עִם שְׁתֵּי נָשִׁים בִּזְמַן שֶׁאִשְׁתּוֹ עִמּוֹ).

[73] The Greek ἰδού translates the Hebrew הִנֵּה. See Luke 1:20 n.

[74] Note Dead Sea Scrolls 1QHa 23:15: "to raise up according to Your truth the **herald of good news**" (להרים כאמתכה **מבשר**).

which shall be for **all people.**[75] **11** For to you has been born today in the city of David a Savior, who is the Messiah, the Lord. **12** And this shall be a sign to you; You shall find the babe wrapped in **swaddling clothes,**[76] lying in a **manger.**[77] **13** And suddenly there was with the angel a multitude of the heavenly host praising God, and saying: **14** Glory to God in the highest, and **on earth peace among men of goodwill.**[78] **15 And it came to pass**[79] as the angels were going away from them into heaven, the shepherds said one to another: Let us now go indeed to Bethlehem, and see this thing which has come to pass, which the Lord has made known to us. **16** And they came with haste, and found Mary, and Joseph, and the baby lying in a **manger.**[80] **17** And when they had seen it, they proclaimed abroad the saying that was told them concerning this child. **18** And all those who heard it marveled at the things that were told to them by the shepherds. **19** But Mary treasured all these things, and pondered them in her heart. **20** And the shepherds returned, glorifying and praising God for all the things that they had heard and seen, as it was told to them.

------

[75] Reflecting the universalism of the Hebrew prophets, as in Isa 2:2: "And it shall come to pass in the end of days, that the mountain of the LORD'S house shall be established as the top of the mountains, and shall be exalted above the hills; and *all nations* shall flow unto it." (וְהָיָה בְּאַחֲרִית הַיָּמִים נָכוֹן יִהְיֶה הַר בֵּית-יְהוָה בְּרֹאשׁ הֶהָרִים וְנִשָּׂא מִגְּבָעוֹת; וְנָהֲרוּ אֵלָיו **כָּל-הַגּוֹיִם**).

[76] Note Wis. Sol. 7:4: "I was nursed with care *in swaddling cloths*" (אֻמָּנְתִּי **בַּסְּדִינִים** בִּדְאָגָה רַבָּה).

[77] See v. 7.

[78] "Of goodwill" (εὐδοκίας) is preferred, being the most difficult reading. The verse should read, "on earth peace for men of [God's] favor." Hypothetical Hebrew reconstruction: ובארץ שלום בבני רצונו. Note Dead Sea Scrolls 1QHa 12:33–34: "... to perfect a way for humankind so that they may know all His works by His mighty power and the abundance of His mercies upon all the *sons of His will*" (להתם דרך לבני אדם למען **בני רצונו** ידעו כול מעשיו בכוח גבורתו ורוב רחמיו על כול). The Coptic translation of Luke 2:14 contains "his." See Luke 19:38; Isa 6:3; Ezek 3:12; Deut 33:23.

[79] The Greek καὶ ἐγένετο translates the Hebrew וַיְהִי; see Luke 1:23.

[80] See v. 7.

Scene 8:
Circumcision and Presentation of Jesus

The Hebrew name for Jesus, Yeshua (ישועה), derives from the root yashah (ישע), meaning "salvation" and indicating that God "saves"/"delivers"/"redeems." The idea is not eschatological but suggests present tense deliverance from malady or calamity.

Luke 2:21 And when eight days were accomplished for the circumcising of the child, **his name was called Jesus,**[81] who was so named by the angel before he was conceived in the womb. **22** And when the days of their **[her] purification**[82] according to the law of Moses were fulfilled, they **brought him to Jerusalem.**[83] to present him to the Lord; **23 As it is written**[84] in the law of the Lord: Every male who opens the womb shall be called holy to the Lord; **24** And to offer a sacrifice according to what is said in the law of the Lord, **A pair of turtledoves, or two young pigeons.**[85]

Scene 9:
Simeon's Prophecy

The suggestion that ancient, militant hymns lie beneath the text is underscored by the prophecy of Simeon, who is waiting for the

---

[81] In Jewish tradition the name is not revealed until the circumcision.

[82] Possibly a mistake in the Greek. It is better to read "*her* purification" (καθαρισμοῦ αὐτήν), rather than "*their* purification" (καθαρισμοῦ αὐτῶν).

[83] The redemption of the firstborn (פדיון הבן/*pidiyon ha-ben*) could be accomplished anywhere; traveling to Jerusalem was not required. The parallel is to the presentation of Samuel in the temple by Hannah.

[84] The Greek καθὼς γέγραπται mimics Hebrew syntax, as in Dead Sea Scrolls 1QS 8:14: "... *as it is written*, 'In the wilderness prepare the way of the LORD'" (**כאשר** **כתוב** במדבר פנו דרך יייי).

[85] The sacrifice was for purification. Birds could be offered instead of a lamb, for those who were not wealthy. Note Lev 5:7: "And if his means do not suffice for a lamb, then he shall bring for his trespass which he has committed, *two turtle-doves, or two young pigeons*" (וְאִם-לֹא תַגִּיעַ יָדוֹ, דֵּי שֶׂה וְהֵבִיא אֶת-אֲשָׁמוֹ אֲשֶׁר חָטָא **שְׁתֵּי תֹרִים אוֹ-שְׁנֵי בְנֵי-יוֹנָה**); *Lev. R.* 3:5: "... in order that the altar be adorned with the *sacrifice of the poor*" (כְּדֵי שֶׁיְהֵא הַמִּזְבֵּחַ מְהֻדָּר בְּקָרְבָּנוֹ שֶׁל עָנִי).

"consolation of Israel." Commonly overlooked in such language is the possibility of militant redemption being referenced and a serious link to the Zealot faction.

Luke 2:25 And, **behold,**[86] there was a man in Jerusalem, whose name was Simeon; and this man was righteous and devout, **waiting for the consolation of Israel;**[87] and the **Holy Spirit** was upon him. **26** And it was revealed to him by the **Holy Spirit,**[88] that he would not see death, before he had seen the Lord's Messiah. **27** And he came by the Spirit into the temple; and when the parents brought in the child Jesus, to do for him according to the custom of the law, **28** Then he took him in his arms, and blessed God, and said: **29** Lord, now let your servant depart in peace, according to your word; **30** For my eyes have seen your salvation, **31** Which you have prepared before the face of **all people;**[89] **32** A light for revelation to the Gentiles, and the glory of your people Israel. **33** And his father and his mother marveled at the things that were spoken of him. **34 And Simeon blessed them, and said**[90] to Mary his mother: **Behold,**[91] this child is appointed for the fall and rising up of many in Israel; and for a sign which will be spoken against;

---

[86] The Greek ἰδού translates the Hebrew הִנֵּה. See Luke 1:20 n.

[87] Note Qumran Apostrophe to Zion (11Q5 22:3–4): "Generations of the pious will adorn you: they who long for the ***day of your salvation***" (דור ודור ידורו בך ודורות **חסידים תפארתך המתאוים ליום ישעך**). This could refer to messianic deliverance from Rome. John the Baptist's followers (and background) may have been even more nationalistic than John himself.

[88] See Luke 1:15. Note Dead Sea Scrolls 1QS4:21: "... cleansing from every wicked deed by a ***holy spirit***" (ולטהרו **ברוח קודש** מכול עלילות רשעה).

[89] See Luke 2:10; reflecting the universalism of the Hebrew prophets, as in Isa 2:2.

[90] "Bless and say" is not found in the Hebrew Bible; rather, a blessing involved a "prophecy." Reconstruction: "Simeon spoke a prophecy over the parents, which had special meaning for Mary."

[91] The Greek ἰδού translates the Hebrew הִנֵּה. See Luke 1:20 n.

35 And, **a sword will pierce through your own soul also**,[92] that the thoughts of many hearts may be revealed.

Scene 10:
Anna the Prophetess

The words attributed to Anna regarding "redemption in Jerusalem" betray (like Simeon's prophecy) a militant/Zealot tone.

Luke 2:36 And there was one Anna, a prophetess, the daughter of Phanuel, of the tribe of Asher; she was advanced in years, and had lived with a husband seven years from her marriage; **37** And she was a widow of about eighty-four years, who had not departed from the temple, but served God with fasting and prayers night and day. **38** And having come up at that hour, she gave thanks to the Lord, and spoke of him to all those who looked for the **redemption of Jerusalem.**[93]

Scene 11:
The Family Returns to Nazareth

"Wisdom" (חָכְמָה) and "grace"/"favor" (חֵן) are important terms and concepts in rabbinic thought and were especially prominent among ancient Hasidim.

Luke 2:39 And when they had performed all things according to the law of the Lord, they returned to Galilee, to their own city **Nazareth.**[94] **40** And the child continued to grow, and become

---

[92] D. Flusser argued (*Judaism*, 128) that the Magnificat and Benedictus appear to draw from two militant hymns known among the circles of John the Baptist, and that Luke changed only one word: "a sword will pierce *its* (Israel's) soul …" Verse 35 helps explain Heb 4:12: "For the word of God is quick, and powerful, and sharper than any two edged sword." Note *y. Ned.* 9, 41b (48): "As if he takes a sword and pierces it through his heart."

[93] See v. 25; this may indicate possible Zealot sympathies.

[94] See Luke 1:26.

strong in spirit, filled with wisdom; and the grace of God was upon him.

Scene 12:
The Boy Jesus Amazes the Scholars

One pilgrimage in a lifetime fulfilled the obligation, indicating that Jesus' parents were very observant, going to Jerusalem every year. This also indicates a level of affluence, notwithstanding that they offered, at Jesus' birth, turtledoves or pigeons since presumably they could not afford a lamb (Luke 2:24). Perhaps the text was written so as to make them appear less affluent than they were. The amazement of the teachers is similar to what Josephus wrote about his own precociousness. Jesus displays a special familiarity with God, whom he calls "my Father" (אבי), in a manner similar to the "Pious" (Hasidim).

Luke 2:41 And his parents **went to Jerusalem every year**[95] at the feast of the Passover. **42** And when he was **twelve years old,**[96] they went up to Jerusalem according to the custom of the feast. **43** And when they had **fulfilled the days,**[97] as they returned, the child Jesus remained behind in Jerusalem; and Joseph and his mother did not know of it. **44** But, supposing him to be in their company, they went a day's journey; and they sought him among their relatives and acquaintances. **45** And when they did not find him, they returned to Jerusalem, seeking him. **46 And it came to pass,**[98] that after three days they found him in the temple, sitting in the midst of the teachers, both hearing them, and asking them questions. **47** And all who heard him were **astonished at his**

---

[95] A yearly pilgrimage was not necessary; once in a lifetime was sufficient.

[96] Note Josephus *Ant*. V, 10.4, stating that Samuel began his prophetic activity at age twelve.

[97] See Deut 16:8: "Six days you shall eat unleavened bread; and on the seventh day shall be a solemn assembly to the LORD you God" (שֵׁשֶׁת יָמִים תֹּאכַל מַצּוֹת; וּבַיּוֹם הַשְּׁבִיעִי עֲצֶרֶת לַיהוָה אֱלֹהֶיךָ).

[98] The Greek καὶ ἐγένετο translates the Hebrew וַיְהִי; see Luke 1:23.

understanding and answers.[99] **48** And when they saw him, they were amazed; and his mother said to him: Son, why have you done this to us? **Behold,**[100] your father and I have been distressed seeking you. **49** And he said to them: How is it that you sought me? Did you not know that I must be about **my Father's business?**[101] **50** And they did not understand the saying that he spoke to them.

Scene 13:
Jesus Advances in Wisdom and Favor

Throughout his youth, Jesus is said to have "increased in wisdom," presumably devoting himself to Torah study, so as to amaze the scholars at the temple. This is hardly consistent with the general stereotype of an illiterate, unlearned population.

Luke 2:51 And he went down with them, and came to **Nazareth,**[102] and was subject to them; but his mother treasured all these sayings in her heart. **52** And Jesus increased in wisdom and stature, and in favor with God and men.

---

[99] Note Josephus, *Life* 9: "When I was a child, about fourteen years of age, I was commended by all for the love I had of learning; on which account the high priest and principal men of the city frequently came to me together, to know my opinion about the accurate understanding of points of the law."

[100] The Greek ἰδού translates the Hebrew הִנֵּה. See Luke 1:20 n.

[101] See note on Luke 8:44; Ps 89:27, regarding the Messiah to come: "He shall call to Me: You are **my Father**, my God, and the rock of my salvation" (הוּא יִקְרָאֵנִי, **אָבִי** אַתָּה; אֵלִי, וְצוּר יְשׁוּעָתִי). See Shmuel Safrai, "Mishnat Ḥasidim in the Literature of the Tannaim," in *In Times of Temple and Mishnah: Studies in Jewish History* (Heb.) (Jerusalem: Magnes, 1996), 2:501–17; "The Pharisees and the Ḥasidim (Heb.)," *Sidic* 10 (1977): 12–16; "The Teaching of Pietists in Mishnaic Literature," *JJS* 16 (1965): 27–31. Note the Greek phrase ἐν τοῖς τοῦ Πατρός μου ("in the [business] of my father…"). The word τοῖς (rendered "business" in the KJV) is a special idiom. It should read "my fathers house." The Hebrew בית ("house") may be understood as "temple." By saying "my father," Jesus may be saying to Joseph, "You are not my real father."

[102] See Luke 1:26.

The Baptist, the Genealogy, the Temptation and Galilee

A rguably, the source material for Luke 3–9 is the Reconstructed Text (RCT), or "Short Gospel." As with the "L" material, the construction and syntax betray a solidly Hebraic style and tone (and a possible Aramaism in Luke 3:7), and links to rabbinic and Qumranic material are abundant. The vestigial language of militancy glimpsed in the previous chapter is on full display in Chapter 3, with the introduction of John the Baptist. There is reason to suppose that John's devoted cadre of followers may have attributed to him a messianic stature, that may have anticipated the overthrow of Roman hegemony over the land of Israel. There is also a degree of syncretism between the message of John and the sternly pietistic language of the Dead Sea Scrolls. John's preaching echoes the tonality of Jewish apocalyptic. At the baptism of Jesus, a divine voice (Hebrew: *bat kol*) declares: "You are my beloved Son ... " The use of the word "son" conjures up Psalm 2:7 and suggests that Jesus is being "presented," in messianic fashion, as a newborn is "revealed." The chapter concludes with Luke's genealogy, tracing the lineage of Jesus back to Adam, so as to present him as the "second Adam," or "primordial Adam" (אדם קדמון/*Adam kadmon*)—a concept common to ancient Jewish mystical speculation. Chapter 4 of Luke is laced with rabbinic nuances that place the text squarely within the realm of ancient Jewish literature. In the account of Jesus' temptation, we find a link to the tradition that Adam in paradise had angels ministering to him, as well as the ancient folklore that the Messiah will stand on the roof of the temple. We are also reminded of

Moses fasting for forty days and the "Ten Trials of Abraham." Jesus proceeds to cast out an unclean spirit in Capernaum, commanding it to be quiet since he did not want a demon lying about him. From this incident is derived the so-called "messianic secret," repeatedly reproduced by the Gospel redactors, but incorrectly assuming that Jesus did not want his messiahship known. The "kingdom of God/heaven" concept (rabbinically understood as the present-tense divine reign) is also introduced, and we are told that Jesus proclaimed his message in "other cities also," lending credence to a possible early Judean sojourn in his proto-rabbinic mission and activity. Jesus' visit to Nazareth (Luke 4:16–30) is transposed to a time after his actions in Capernaum, which are mentioned in the Nazareth pericope as having already taken place. Jesus' "messianic" identification is underscored by the passage he reads in the synagogue of Nazareth (Isaiah 61:1), declaring that he has been "anointed," the Hebrew verb being *mashakh* (משח), of which "Messiah" is a transliteration. Luke 12:54–56 and Luke 11:29–32 (regarding "signs") have been added to the Nazareth account, as it is likely that the people would have insisted on proof of Jesus' claims (a "sign"). False signs were punished by stoning, which is how the chapter concludes, after Jesus' resounding claims that even non-Israelites were healed in the days of Elijah and Elisha.

Scene 1:
John the Baptist Prepares the Way (RCT)

This narrative (minus the introductory "L" material) represents the likely opening of the hypothetical grundschrift from which the subsequent Greek versions derived. The burden of the Reconstructed Text (RCT) appears to have been to restore chronological order to the "topical" Anthological Text (ANT). The mention of Tiberius Caesar, Pontius Pilate, Herod, Philip, Annas, and Caiaphas underscores this chronology and places what follows in a historical context, beginning with the account of John the Baptist.

Luke 3:1 Now in the fifteenth year of the reign of Tiberius Caesar, Pontius Pilate being governor of Judea, and Herod being tetrarch of Galilee, and his brother Philip tetrarch of Ituraea and of the region of Trachonitis, and Lysanias the tetrarch of Abilene, **2** Annas and Caiaphas being the high priests, the word of God came to John the son of Zechariah in the wilderness. **3** And he came into all the country about Jordan, proclaiming a **baptism of repentance**[1] for the remission of sins; **4** As it is written in the book of the words of Isaiah the prophet, saying: **The voice of one crying in the wilderness,**[2] **Prepare the way**[3] of the Lord, make his paths straight. **5** Every valley shall be filled, and every mountain and hill shall be brought low; and the crooked shall be made straight, and the rough ways shall be made smooth; **6** And all flesh shall see the salvation of God. **7** Then he said to the

---

[1] The Essenes and Morning Bathers also practiced immersion. Note Dead Sea Scrolls 1QS 3:8–9: "Through an upright and humble attitude his sin may be covered, **and by humbling himself before all God's laws** his flesh can be made clean. Only thus can he really receive the purifying waters and be purged by the cleansing flow" (ובענות נפשו לכול חוקי אל יטהר בשרו להזות במי נדה ולהתקדש במי דוכי. **ובענות נפשו לכול חוקי אל** יטהר בשרו להזות במי נדה ולהתקדש במי דוכי). This differs from traditional Judaism, in which immersion (*mikveh*) is for ritual purity only. For the Dead Sea sect and for John, the *mikveh* must be accompanied by repentance. A river was considered a "kosher" *mikveh*, consisting of "living water."

[2] See Isa 40:3: "A voice is calling: in the wilderness prepare the way of the LORD" (קוֹל קוֹרֵא--בַּמִּדְבָּר פַּנּוּ דֶּרֶךְ יְהוָה). The Hebrew text does not place the voice in the wilderness; it only decrees that "the way" must be prepared in the wilderness. Note Dead Sea Scrolls 1QS 8:13–14: "They shall separate from the session of perverse men **to go to the wilderness**, there to prepare the way of truth, as it is written, '*In the wilderness prepare the way of the LORD*, make straight in the desert a highway for our God'" (יבדלו מתוך מושב הנשי העול ללכת למדבר לפנות שם את דרך הואהא כאשר כתוב במדבר פנו דרך ייי ישרו בערבהמסלה לאלוהינו). There is no indication that John belonged to the Dead Sea sect, but he is linked to the mentality of the sect through the prominent citation of this verse as well as the linkage of the *mikveh* with repentance.

[3] The Dead Sea sect (presumably the Essenes) believed that the "good principle" walks in *the way* of good; the "evil principle" walks in *the way* of evil, i.e. "double predestination" (see Rom 9:22–23). It is argued that John the Baptist believed in "two ways," between which one must choose. See Matt 21:32; Jesus alludes to this motif. See Shmuel Safrai, "Which is the Straight Way that a Man Should Choose for Himself? (*M Ab 2.1*)," in *Judaism in the Second Temple Period* (Grand Rapids: Eerdmans, 2009), 2, 232–47.

multitudes[4] that came forth to be baptized by him, **O generation of vipers [spotted cats?]**,[5] who has warned you to flee from the wrath to come? **8 Therefore bring forth fruits worthy of repentance,**[6] and do not begin to say to yourselves: We have Abraham to our father: for I say to you, That God is able from these **stones** to raise up **children to Abraham**.[7] **9** And now also **the axe is laid to the root of the trees.**[8] Therefore every tree which does not bring forth good fruit is cut down, and cast into the fire. **10** And the people asked him, saying; What shall we do then? **11** He answered and said to them: **He who has two coats, let him give to him who has none; and he who has food, let him do likewise.**[9] **12** Then, tax collectors also came to be baptized, and said to him: Teacher, what shall we do? **13** And he said to them: **Collect no more than what has been appointed you.**[10] **14** And

---

[4] The Greek ὄχλοις is better understood as a translation of אוכלוסים ("people of the area"/"people present"), even where, as in this case, it indicates a great number. ὄχλος appears only twice in John. It is also puzzling why ὄχλος ("crowd") should appear in plural as ὄχλοις—likely since אוכלוסים is plural. Large crowds may have grown over time, but not likely at the beginning.

[5] There may have been an underlying Aramaic term "*Af'a*" (עפא), referring to a spotted cat, but misunderstood by the Greek translator as εφε ("viper" or "adder"). It was then re-rendered in the Lucan text as ἐχιδνῶν ("vipers"). The expression "brood of vipers" is not found in Hebrew or Aramaic. A viper does not symbolize hypocrisy; however, a spotted cat is attractive outwardly, but inwardly rapacious.

[6] Note the words of Eliezer ben Jacob (*m. Avot* 4:11): "**Repentance** and good deeds are a shield against punishment" (תְּשׁוּבָה וּמַעֲשִׂים טוֹבִים, כִּתְרִיס בִּפְנֵי הַפֻּרְעָנוּת).

[7] Abraham was considered the father of proselytes, who became sons of Abraham. The concept of זכות אבות/*z'chut avot*, "the merit of the fathers," is well-entrenched in Jewish tradition, but firmly rejected here. There is also a possible play on words in Hebrew: "stones" (אבנים)/"children/sons" (בנים). The parallel passage in Matthew (3:9) adds "our father" (אבינו).

[8] Note Isa 10:33: "Behold, the Lord, the LORD of hosts, shall lop the boughs with terror; and the high ones of stature shall be hewn down, and the lofty shall be laid low" (הִנֵּה הָאָדוֹן יְהוָה צְבָאוֹת, מְסָעֵף פֻּארָה בְּמַעֲרָצָה; וְרָמֵי הַקּוֹמָה גְּדוּעִים, וְהַגְּבֹהִים יִשְׁפָּלוּ).

[9] The Essenes (Dead Sea sect) taught that one had to renounce possessions while John allowed people to continue in their occupations. Sharing with the poor was enough.

[10] Tax collectors were probably dispatched from Herod Antipas, in order to build roads etc. Antipas, though a Jewish king, ruled by permission of the oppressive Romans. In telling tax collectors to collect no more than what was appointed to them, John might have expressed subtle opposition to cooperation with the authorities, whose taxation requirements were heavy and burdensome.

the **soldiers**[11] likewise asked him, saying: And what shall we do? And he said to them: Do not extort, nor accuse any falsely; **and be content with your wages.**[12] **15** And as the people were in expectation, and all the people wondered in their hearts concerning John, whether he might be the Messiah, or not; **16** John answered, saying to them all: **I indeed baptize you with water;**[13] but one mightier than I is coming, **the strap of whose sandals I am not worthy to untie.**[14] He will baptize you with the **Holy Spirit**[15] and with **fire;**[16] **17** Whose winnowing fork is in his hand, and he will thoroughly **clear his threshing floor,**[17] and will gather the wheat into his barn; but the chaff **he will burn with**[18] unquenchable fire. **18** Many other things he preached, exhorting the people. **19** But Herod the tetrarch, being reproved by him concerning **Herodias**[19]

---

[11] These were probably not Romans. There were no legions in Judea at that time; see Josephus, *Ant.* XVIII.5.1: "So Aretas made this the first occasion of his enmity between him and Herod ... So they raised armies on both sides ..."

[12] This directive is similar to Josephus' advice to his men (*Vita* 47): "I also advised them to fight with no body; nor to spoil the country: but to pitch their tents in the plain, and be content with their sustenance they had brought with them."

[13] According to John the Baptist, the body is defiled not only by contact with objects, but also through sin. Baptism cleanses the body only; repentance purifies from sin. John opposed the idea that ritual immersion (*mikveh*) miraculously cleansed from sin, a concept later adopted in Christianity.

[14] A symbol of subservience; see Mat 3:11. This may also represent an orally stated preamble to a subsequent process of the ritual purification of feet, which would have been obvious to all Jews at the time. Note *b. Kid.* 22b: "How is a non-Jewish slave acquired by force? If he unleashes his shoes for him (the buyer) or carries his baggage to the bath..."

[15] See Luke 1:15. Note Dead Sea Scrolls 1QS4:21: "... cleansing from every wicked deed by a **holy spirit**" (ולטהרו **ברוח קודש** מכול עלילות רשעה).

[16] Note *b. San.* 39a, regarding "a certain *min* (heretic)": "Rabbi Abbahu said to him: He [Moses] immersed in fire ... The heretic said to him: But is immersion in fire effective? Rabbi Abbahu said to him: On the contrary ..." See also Mat 3:11. This is typical of rabbinic denunciation of *minim* (Jewish "heretics") and their ideas.

[17] An allusion to the temple.

[18] Note the eschatological, militant tone.

[19] Herodias (daughter of Herod the Great and Miriamne I) left her husband Herod II (her half-uncle, a commoner; perhaps the same as Herod Philip) and married Herod Antipas, who wanted children who would be considered Hasmoneans. John's taunting, that this was not a legal marriage, would make the children bastards. Mark states that Herodias married Philip (perhaps the same as Herod II), though Luke drops the name Philip.

his brother **Philip's wife,**[20] and for all the evils Herod had done, **20** Added yet this to all, that he locked up John in prison.

Scene 2:
Jesus' Ritual Immersion

Having established John the Baptist's practice of ritual immersion, the narrative introduces Jesus for the first time, accompanied by miraculous signs and a divine voice.

Luke 3:21 Now **it came to pass,**[21] that all the people were baptized; **and as Jesus was also baptized,**[22] and having prayed, the heaven was opened, **22** And the **Holy Spirit**[23] descended in bodily form **like a dove**[24] upon him, **and a voice came from**

---

[20] Herod Antipas was already married to the daughter of the Nabatean monarch Haretath, and according to the Dead Sea Temple Scroll, it was unlawful for him to take a second wife while his first wife was living. While Antipas married Herodias under the law of Levirate marriage (יבום), *halakhah* was modified during this time, so that a daughter (even if there was no son) exempted the woman. Note *Sifre Deut.* 28:8: "and has no son in any case," (אין לו מכל מקום). In this case Herodias had a daughter (Salome). See Mat 22:24; Mark 6:17; Luke 9:7–9.

[21] The Greek ἐγένετο δὲ translates the Hebrew וַיְהִי.

[22] καὶ Ἰησοῦ βαπτισθέντος ("and Jesus also dipped" - aorist passive participle). This suggests the Jewish procedure at a *mikveh*, whereby a person would "dip" himself. Luke and Matthew say "dipped" but not "*by*," as in Mark 1:9: "baptized *by* John" (ἐβαπτίσθη ὑπὸ Ἰωάννου). Mark does not reflect a Hebraic construction.

[23] Note *b. Yom.* 9b: "After the last prophets Haggai, Zechariah, and Malachi died, the *Divine Spirit* of prophetic revelation departed from the Jewish people ..." (מִשֶּׁמֵּתוּ נְבִיאִים הָאַחֲרוֹנִים חַגַּי זְכַרְיָה וּמַלְאָכִי נִסְתַּלְּקָה רוּחַ הַקֹּדֶשׁ מִיִּשְׂרָאֵל).

[24] Note *b. Chag.* 15a: "'And the spirit of God hovered over the face of the waters' (Gen 1:2), *like a dove* hovering over its young without touching them" (וְרוּחַ אֱלֹהִים מְרַחֶפֶת עַל פְּנֵי הַמָּיִם **כְּיוֹנָה** שֶׁמְּרַחֶפֶת עַל בָּנֶיהָ וְאֵינָהּ נוֹגַעַת). The dove was also a symbol of Israel; note *Midrash on Song* 15; *b. San.* 95a; *Ber. R.* 39; *Yalkut* on Ps 14:7. Note *b. Ber.* 3a, quoting R. Jose: "I heard a *Heavenly voice*, like an echo of that roar of the Holy One, Blessed be He (Maharsha), cooing *like a dove* and saying: Woe to the children, due to whose sins I destroyed My house, burned My Temple, and exiled them among the nations" (שָׁמַעְתִּי **בַּת קוֹל** שֶׁמְּנַהֶמֶת **כְּיוֹנָה** וְאוֹמֶרֶת: אוֹי לְבָנִים שֶׁבַּעֲוֹנוֹתֵיהֶם הֶחֱרַבְתִּי אֶת בֵּיתִי וְשָׂרַפְתִּי אֶת הֵיכָלִי וְהִגְלֵיתִים לְבֵין הָאוּמוֹת).

heaven,[25] which said, **You are my beloved Son; in you I am well pleased.**[26]

The Genealogy of Jesus

Luke's genealogy continues the burden of placing Jesus in a historical context, tracing his lineage backwards, not only to Abraham but to Adam. Jesus is elsewhere equated with the concept of the "primordial Adam": אדם קדמון/Adam kadmon; also called אָדָם עֶלְיוֹן/Adam Elyon or אָדָם עִילָּאָה/Adam Ila'ah, "Supreme Man."

Luke 3:23 And Jesus himself began to be about **thirty years of age,**[27] being (as was supposed) the son of Joseph, who was the son of Heli, **24** Who was the son of Matthat, who was the son of Levi, who was the son of Melchi, who was the son of Jannai, who was

---

[25] A *bat kol* ("daughter of the voice") in rabbinic writing brought the testimony of heaven to perplexed rabbis. It took the place of prophecy. Note *b. Yom.* 9b: "… and they were still utilizing a ***Divine Voice***, which they heard as an echo of prophecy" (וַעֲדַיִן הָיוּ מִשְׁתַּמְּשִׁין **בְּבַת קוֹל**) Note also *b. San.* 11a: "The Sages set their eyes upon Hillel the Elder, trusting that he was the one indicated by the Divine Voice" (זכאי לכך נתנו חכמים את עיניהם בהלל הזקן); *Sotah* 33a; *y. Sot.* IX 14). See also Mat 3:17; Mark 1:9. Note *b. Ber.* 17b: "Every day a ***Divine Voice*** emerges from Mount Horeb and says: The entire world is sustained by the merit of Ḥanina ben Dosa, *my son*, and for Ḥanina, *my son*, a *kav* of carobs is sufficient to sustain him for an entire week, from one Shabbat eve to the next Shabbat eve" (בְּכָל יוֹם וְיוֹם **בַּת קוֹל** יוֹצֵאת מֵהַר חוֹרֵב וְאוֹמֶרֶת: כָּל הָעוֹלָם כּוּלּוֹ נִזּוֹנִין בִּשְׁבִיל חֲנִינָא **בְּנִי**, וַחֲנִינָא **בְּנִי** דַּי לוֹ בְּקַב חָרוּבִין מֵעֶרֶב שַׁבָּת לְעֶרֶב שַׁבָּת). Haninah ben Dosa was one of the *Hasidim* ("pious ones") of Jewish antiquity, with whom Jesus may have been associated. See Geza Vermes, "Ḥanina ben Dosa," *JJS* 23 (1972): 28–50.

[26] Note Ps 89:28–30, referencing "David My servant": "He shall call unto Me: ***You are my Father, my God***, and the rock of my salvation. I also will appoint him ***first-born***, the highest of the kings of the earth. Forever will I keep for him My mercy, and My covenant shall stand fast with him. His seed also will I make to endure forever, and his throne as the days of heaven" (הוּא יִקְרָאֵנִי, **אָבִי אַתָּה; אֵלִי** וְצוּר יְשׁוּעָתִי אַף-אָנִי, **בְּכוֹר** אֶתְּנֵהוּ; עֶלְיוֹן, לְמַלְכֵי-אָרֶץ/לְעוֹלָם, אשמור-לוֹ חַסְדִּי; וּבְרִיתִי נֶאֱמֶנֶת לוֹ/וְשַׂמְתִּי לָעַד זַרְעוֹ; וְכִסְאוֹ, כִּימֵי שָׁמָיִם). It appears that Jesus is being revealed, as a midwife reveals a child. See 2 Sam 7:14: "I will be to him *for a father*, and he shall be to Me *for a son*" (אֲנִי אֶהְיֶה-לּוֹ **לְאָב**, וְהוּא יִהְיֶה-לִּי **לְבֵן**). Note also Ps 2:7: "The LORD said to me: '***You are My son***, this day ***have I begotten you***.'" (יְהוָה, אָמַר אֵלַי **בְּנִי אַתָּה** אֲנִי הַיּוֹם **יְלִדְתִּיךָ**). "This day have I begotten you" should instead read: "**This day did I *bear* you**." The verb is feminine, depicting God as a "midwife."

[27] Note *m. Avot* 5:21: "At five years of age the study of Scripture; At ten the study of Mishnah; At thirteen subject to the commandments; At fifteen the study of Talmud; At eighteen the bridal canopy; At twenty for pursuit [of livelihood]; ***At thirty the peak of strength*** …" (בֶּן חָמֵשׁ שָׁנִים לַמִּקְרָא, בֶּן עֶשֶׂר לַמִּשְׁנָה, בֶּן שְׁלֹשׁ עֶשְׂרֵה לַמִּצְוֹת, בֶּן חֲמֵשׁ עֶשְׂרֵה לַתַּלְמוּד, בֶּן שְׁמֹנֶה עֶשְׂרֵה לַחֻפָּה, בֶּן עֶשְׂרִים לִרְדֹּף, **בֶּן שְׁלֹשִׁים לַכֹּחַ**).

the son of Joseph, **25** Who was the son of Mattathias, who was the son of Amos, who was the son of Naum, who was the son of Esli, who was the son of Nagge, **26** Who was the son of Maath, who was the son of Mattathias, who was the son of Semei, who was the son of Joseph, who was the son of Judah, **27** Who was the son of Joanna, who was the son of Rhesa, who was the son of Zerubbabel, who was the son of Salathiel, who was the son of Neri, **28** Who was the son of Melchi, who was the son of Addi, who was the son of Cosam, who was the son of Elmodam, who was the son of Er, **29** Who was the son of Jose, who was the son of Eliezer, who was the son of Jorim, who was the son of Matthat, who was the son of Levi, **30** Who was the son of Simeon, who was the son of Judah, who was the son of Joseph, who was the son of Jonan, who was the son of Eliakim, **31** Who was the son of Melea, who was the son of Menan, who was the son of Mattatha, who was the son of Nathan, who was the son of David, **32** Who was the son of Jesse, who was the son of Obed, who was the son of Booz, who was the son of Salmon, who was the son of Naasson, **33** Who was the son of Aminadab, who was the son of Aram, who was the son of Esrom, who was the son of Phares, who was the son of Juda, **34** Who was the son of Jacob, who was the son of Isaac, who was the son of Abraham, who was the son of Thara, who was the son of Nachor, **35** Who was the son of Saruch, who was the son of Ragau, who was the son of Phalec, who was the son of Heber, who was the son of Sala, **36** Who was the son of Cainan, who was the son of Arphaxad, who was the son of Sem, who was the son of Noe, who was the son of Lamech, **37** Who was the son of Methuselah, who was the son of Enoch, who was the son of Jared, who was the son of Mahalalel, who was the son of Cainan, **38** Who was the son of

Enosh, who was the son of Seth, who was the son of **Adam, who was the son of God.**[28]

Scene 3:
The Temptation of Jesus

While presented as a historical account, the narrative quickly takes on a fantastical tone, resembling that of Jewish pseudepigrapha. Reference to the "devil" (elsewhere designated as "Satan") brings to mind the linguistic shift from the term הסטן *(ha-satan/"the adversary"), as found in the Hebrew Scriptures, to the proper name "Satan"* (סטן), *as a single, malevolent power, in dualistic conflict with the God of Israel. One such reference is found in 2 Enoch 31:4: "The devil is the evil spirit of the lower places, as a fugitive he made Sotona from the heavens, as his name was Satanail; thus he became different from the angels, [but his nature] did not change [his] intelligence as far as [his] understanding of righteous and sinful [things]."*

Luke 4:1 And Jesus being full of the **Holy Spirit**[29] returned from the Jordan, and was led by the Spirit into the wilderness, **2** Being

---

[28] Philo referred to the "original man"/"heavenly man" (γενικός/οὐράνιος ἄνθρωπος). See De Allegoriis Legum, I. xii: "... as being born in the image of God, has no participation in any corruptible or earthlike essence; whereas the earthly man is made of loose material, called a lump of clay." Note *Gen. R.* 8. 1: "'You have formed me behind and before' (Ps 139:5) is to be explained 'before the first and after the last day of Creation.' For it is said, 'And the spirit of God moved upon the face of the waters,' meaning *the spirit of the Messiah* ("the spirit of Adam" in the parallel passage, Midr. Teh. to 139. 5). According to the early Sages, the spirit (רוח) of Adam was present prior to the creation of the earthly Adam and preexisted the entire creation. Note also Paul's reference to the first and second Adam; 1 Cor 15: 45–47: "*The first man Adam* was made a living soul; *the last Adam* was made a life giving spirit ... *The first man* is of the earth, earthy; *the second man* is the Lord from heaven." (Ἐγένετο ὁ *πρῶτος ἄνθρωπος* Ἀδὰμ εἰς ψυχὴν ζῶσαν. ὁ *ἔσχατος Ἀδὰμ* εἰς πνεῦμα ζωοποιοῦν ... ὁ *πρῶτος ἄνθρωπος* ἐκ γῆς, χοϊκός· ὁ *δεύτερος ἄνθρωπος*, ὁ Κύριος ἐξ οὐρανοῦ).

[29] See Luke 1:15. Note Dead Sea Scrolls 1QS4:21: "... cleansing from every wicked deed by a **holy spirit**" (ולטהרו **ברוח קודש** מכול עלילות רשעה).

forty days[30] **tempted**[31] by the **Devil.** And in those days he ate nothing: and when they had ended, he was hungry. **3** And the **devil**[32] said to him: If you are the **Son of God**,[33] command this stone to become made bread. **4** And Jesus answered him, saying: It is written, That man shall not live by bread alone, but by every word of God. **5** And the devil, taking him up into a high mountain, showed to him **all the kingdoms of the world**[34] in a moment of time. **6** And the devil said to him: I will give you all this authority, and the glory of it; for that is has been delivered to me; and to whomever I wish to give it. **7** Therefore if you will worship me, all shall be yours. **8** And Jesus answered and said to him: It is written, **You shall worship the Lord your God, and him only shall you serve.**[35] **9** And he brought him to Jerusalem, and set him on the

---

[30] Moses fasted forty days on Mt. Sinai. See Deut 9:9: "Then I abode in the mount **forty days and forty nights**; I did not eat bread or drink water" (וָאֵשֵׁב בָּהָר, **אַרְבָּעִים**). See Matt 4:2, 11; Mark 1:13. (**יוֹם וְאַרְבָּעִים לַיְלָה** לֶחֶם לֹא אָכַלְתִּי, וּמַיִם לֹא שָׁתִיתִי).

[31] Note *m. Avot* 5:3: "Ten **trials** were inflicted upon Abraham, our father, may he rest in peace, and he withstood all of them" (עֲשָׂרָה **נִסְיוֹנוֹת** נִתְנַסָּה אַבְרָהָם אָבִינוּ עָלָיו הַשָּׁלוֹם) (וְעָמַד בְּכֻלָּם).

[32] The evolution of "Satan"/the "devil" (Gr. διάβολος) from a member of the divine court ("*the* adversary/accuser" השטן), to an independent evil power (שטן, lacking the definite article ה), is well-attested in ancient sources. The latter form is evidenced in the Dead Sea Scrolls 11Q5 19:15; 11Q5 f4_5:16: "Let **Satan** have no dominion over me, nor an unclean spirit; let neither pain nor the *will to evil* rule in me" (אל תשלט בי **שטן** ורוח) (טמאה מכאוב **ויצר רע** אל ירשו). Satan is made equivalent to the "evil inclination" (יצר רע), as expressed in later rabbinic literature. In several places Luke likewise employs the term "Satan/Σατανᾶν" (see Luke 10:18, 11:18, 13:16, 22:3, 22:31) without the definite article. Here, as in one other passage (Luke 8:12), he refers to "*the* devil" (ὁ διάβολος). Luke may be hearkening back to the earlier understanding of "*the* adversary" (השטן), and Jesus may symbolically be confronting his own "evil inclination" (יצר רע).

[33] See Luke 1:32; note Dead Sea "Son of God" text.

[34] See *Apoc. Bar.* 76:3: "all the **regions of the land**." Note *Cant. R.* 8:6: "The Holy One blessed be He called to the angel of death and said, 'Although I have made you *cosmocrator over all creatures*, you have nothing to do with this nation, for they are my children'" (קָרָא הַקָּדוֹשׁ בָּרוּךְ הוּא לְמַלְאַךְ הַמָּוֶת וְאָמַר לוֹ אַף עַל פִּי שֶׁמִּנִּיתִיךְ קְפוֹקְלִיטוֹר **קוֹזְמוֹקְרָטוֹר עַל**) (**בְּרִיּוֹתַי**, אֵין לְךָ עֵסֶק בְּאֻמָּה זוֹ). "Cosmocrator" was a title of the Roman emperor ("Lord of the world"), a motif behind the temptation narrative.

[35] Note Deut. 6:13: "You shall fear the LORD your God; and Him shall you serve, and by His name shall you swear" (אֶת-יְהוָה אֱלֹהֶיךָ תִּירָא, וְאֹתוֹ תַעֲבֹד; וּבִשְׁמוֹ, תִּשָּׁבֵעַ).

pinnacle of the temple,[36] and said to him: If you are the **Son of God**,[37] **cast yourself down from here;**[38] **10** For it is written: He shall give his **angels**[39] charge over you, to keep you; **11** And in their hands they shall bear you up, lest you ever dash your foot against a stone. **12** And Jesus answering said to him: It is said, **You shall not tempt the Lord your God.**[40] **13** And when the devil had finished all the temptation, he departed from him until an opportune time.

Scene 4:
Jesus in Galilee

Luke 4:14 And Jesus returned in the power of the Spirit to **Galilee;**[41] and a report went out concerning him through all the surrounding region. **15** And he taught in their synagogues, being glorified by all.

---

[36] Note *Pesiq. Rab.* 36: "Our teachers taught at the time when the king Messiah will appear he will come and stand *on the roof of the temple*" (שנו רבותינו בשעה שמלך המשיח נגלה בא ועומד **על הגג של בית המקדש**). Jesus is tempted with messianic stature before his time came. Josephus declares (*War* VII 27–30) that Simon bar Giora "arose out of the ground [from the tunnels] at the spot where the temple formerly stood." Messianic (political) hopes surrounded the temple complex, and Jesus' temptation in this instance may involve declaring himself as a political/Zealot redeemer from Roman occupation. See Matt 4:5.

[37] See Luke 1:32; note the Dead Sea Scroll "Son of God" text.

[38] In the Acts of Peter, Pseudo-Clementines, and the Epistle of the Apostles, the magician known as Simon Magus (also referenced in Acts 8:9–24) is presented as having the ability to fly and levitate at will. See Matt 4:6.

[39] Rabbinic literature relates that in Eden angels waited on Adam and danced before him. Note *b. San.* 59b: "Rabbi Yehuda ben Teima would say: Adam, the first man, would dine in the Garden of Eden, and the *ministering angels* would roast meat for him and strain wine for him" (ר' יהודה בן תימא אומר אדם הראשון מיסב בגן עדן היה היו **מלאכי השרת** צולין לו בשר ומסננין לו יין); *PRE*, 12: "The Holy One, blessed be He, made ten wedding canopies for Adam in the garden of Eden … The *angels* were playing upon timbrels and dancing with pipes" (עשר חופות עשה הב"ה לאדם הראשון בגן עדן … והיו **המלאכים** מתופפים בתופים ומרקדין כנקבות).

[40] Note *b. Shab.* 32a: "A person should never stand in a place of danger saying that God will perform a miracle for him, lest God does not perform a miracle for him." (אל יעמוד אדם במקום סכנה לומר שעושין לו נס שמא אין עושין לו נס). See Matt 4:7.

[41] Josephus attests that Galilee was a land of rich fertility and very highly cultivated. He observes (*Wars*, III, iii, 2.3.41): "Moreover the cities lie here very thick; and the very many villages are everywhere so full of people by the richness of the soil that the very least of them contain above fifteen thousand inhabitants."

It is likely that the story of Jesus' reception in Nazareth (Luke 4:16–30) occurred later than Luke's placement since he had already been in Capernaum (Luke 4:23) and his fame had spread. See Mark 6:1–6; Matt 13:54–58.

Scene 5:
Jesus Casts Out an Unclean Spirit

Those who have attempted to cast Jesus as primarily an ethical teacher while deemphasizing his miracles must cope with the fact that the narrative presents his first public "act" as an exorcism. Notably, exorcism became a celebrated practice during the Second Jewish Commonwealth, as evidenced by the book of Tobit. Jesus' teaching "with authority" is mentioned, but no content is provided, leading to the conclusion that subtracting the "miraculous" from the historical Jesus leaves no historical Jesus.

Luke 4:31 And came down to Capernaum, a city of Galilee, and taught them on the Sabbath days. **32** And they were astonished at his teaching: for his message was with authority. **33** And in the synagogue there was a man, who had a spirit of an unclean demon, and cried out with a loud voice, **34** Saying: Let us alone; what do we have to do with you, Jesus of Nazareth? Have you come to destroy us? I know you who you are; the Holy One of God. **35** And Jesus rebuked him, saying: **Be silent,**[42] and come out of him. And when the demon had thrown him in the midst, he came out of him, and did not hurt him. **36** And they were all amazed, and spoke among themselves, saying: What a **word [thing]**[43] is this! For with authority and power he commands the unclean spirits, and they come out. **37** And the report of him spread into every place of the surrounding region.

---

[42] See 4:41, regarding the "messianic secret."

[43] Assuming a Hebrew undertext, the Greek translator rendered דבר/*davar* ("thing" or "word") as λόγος ("word"), when "thing" is indicated in the context.

Scene 6:
Peter's Mother-in-Law Healed

Acts of healing complement Jesus' work as an exorcist, and appear as a central component of the "kingdom of God/heaven" message.

Luke 4:38 And he rose up out of the synagogue, and entered into Simon's house. And Simon's mother-in-law was oppressed with a great fever; and they appealed to him for her. **39** And he stood over her, and rebuked the fever; and it left her; and immediately she arose and began to serve them.

Scene 7:
Many Healed after Sabbath Sunset

Jesus' occupation as a healer continues to be stressed, being coupled with the wrongly labeled "messianic secret" theme. Arguably, Jesus did not want demons (who understood his messianic identity) testifying about him.

Luke 4:40 Now when the sun was setting,[44] all those who had any sick with various diseases brought them to him; and he **laid his hands**[45] on each of them, and healed them. **41** And demons also came out of many, crying out, and saying: **You are the Son of**

---

[44] This suggests the close of Shabbat (מוצאי שבת/*motzei Shabbat*), when no dispute could be raised about healing on the Sabbath. See Mark 1:32: "*At evening, when the sun had set*, they brought to Him all who were sick and those who were demon-possessed"; Matt 8:16: "*When evening had come*, they brought to Him many who were demon-possessed."

[45] Note the Qumranic reference to the practice of laying on hands for healing/exorcism; 1Q20 20:28–29: "So I prayed for him, that blasphemer, **and laid my hands upon his head**. Thereupon the plague was removed from him, the evil spirit exorcised from him, and he was healed" (רצלית עלוהי מגדפא הו **וסמכת ידי על ראישה** ואתפלי מנה מכתשא ואתגערת מנה רוחא באישתא וחי).

God.[46] And rebuking them, he **did not allow them not to speak; for they knew that he was the Messiah.**[47]

Scene 8:
Jesus Preaches in Galilee and Judea

It is Jesus' healings that promote crowds. The narrative suggests that his "kingdom of God" message cannot be divorced from the healings themselves. This incident may have occurred early in Jesus' proto-rabbinic career, prior to the call of his disciples. See Luke 7:11.

Luke 4:42 And when daybreak came, he departed and went into a solitary place; and the **crowds**[48] sought him, and came to him, and detained him, that he should not leave them. **43** And he said to

---

[46] See Luke 1:32; note the Dead Sea "Son of God" text.

[47] It is theorized that Jesus said, "Be quiet!" (v. 35) in the ANT, and that the redactor of RCT adds, "Jesus did not allow the demons to speak because they knew him to be the Christ/Messiah." This becomes a theme in the Gospels (the "messianic secret"). For example, Jesus later says to a leper, "Do not say anything; go to the priest." Actually, Jesus likely silenced the demons because they are liars, and he did not want them testifying about him. See Mark 3:12; Matt 8:4; 4:30; 12:16; 17:9; Mark 1:44; 1:39; 3:12; 5:43; 7:36; 8:30; 9:9; Luke 5:14; 8:5; 9:21; 18:38. See Lindsey, *Jesus*, 211–12.

[48] The Greek ὄχλοι is better understood as a translation of אוכלוסים ("people of the area"/"people present"), even where it means a great number. ὄχλος appears only twice in John. It is also puzzling why ὄχλος ("crowd") should appear in plural as ὄχλοι - likely since אוכלוסים is plural. Large crowds may have grown over time, but not likely at the beginning.

them: I must preach the good news of the **kingdom of God**[49] to other towns also; because for this I have been sent. **44** And he preached **in the synagogues of Judea.**[50]

---

[49] Luke employs "kingdom of *God*" (βασιλεία του Θεού) as opposed to "kingdom of *heaven*" (βασιλεία τῶν οὐρανῶν, as in Matthew), the latter being used as a substitution for the Divine Name. The "kingdom of God (heaven)" was understood by the rabbinic sages not in eschatological terms, but as the present-tense divine reign. Note: *m. Ber.* 2:2: "Why, in the *mitzva* of the recitation of *Shema*, did the portion of *Shema* precede that of *VeHaya im Shamoa*? This is so that one will first accept upon himself the yoke of the **kingdom of Heaven** [the awareness of God and God's unity], and only then accept upon himself the yoke of the *mitzvot*" (לָמָּה קָדְמָה שְׁמַע לְוְהָיָה אִם שָׁמֹעַ, אֶלָּא כְדֵי שֶׁיְּקַבֵּל עָלָיו עֹל **מַלְכוּת שָׁמַיִם** תְּחִלָּה, וְאַחַר כָּךְ יְקַבֵּל עָלָיו עֹל מִצְוֹת). Note also *Mechilta* (Ex 15:18): "Yose the Galilean said, 'It is regrettable that Moses said "The Lord shall reign forever ... " for had he said, "The Lord has reigned forever," the **kingdom of heaven** would have come about immediately!'" This was the attitude of the school of Hillel. When the people repented and took on the yoke of the kingdom of heaven, the Roman yoke would vanish. No rebellion would help. This is contrary to the Zealots and Essenes, who saw the kingdom of God as a future event. D. Flusser argued that Jesus was on this issue closer to the moderate circles of the School of Hillel. See David Flusser, *Jewish Sources in Early Christianity* (New York: Adama Books, 1987), 49–54. The people should repent and avoid the threat of the temple's destruction, should rebellion erupt. The idea is the same as in Matt 19:14: "For these (children) *comprise* the **kingdom of heaven**." Note Dead Sea Scrolls CD 7:16–17: "The king is the congregation" (המלך הוא הקהל). The king was understood as the assembly. *Pesiq. Rab.* 2 links the kingdom of heaven with Zech 14:9: "And the LORD shall be King over all the earth" (וְהָיָה יְהוָה לְמֶלֶךְ עַל-כָּל-הָאָרֶץ).

[50] Some manuscripts correct to "Galilee," though perhaps the text originally read "Judea," reflecting a reference to a possible Judean sojourn.

The Judean Sojourn

Several decades ago, the American Baptist minister R.L. Lindsey, working in conjunction with Israeli scholar David Flusser, put forth the suggestion that a number of the early story units comprising a hypothetical Hebrew undertext of the Synoptic Gospels were contextually located not in Galilee, but in Judea. According to the Lucan narrative, Jesus' family were by no means strangers to Jerusalem, as evidenced by his presentation in the temple shortly after his birth, their yearly Passover pilgrimage, and Jesus' discussions with the teachers of the Law at age twelve. Lindsey theorized that in the early days of his proto-rabbinic career, prior to the calling of his disciples, Jesus was likely again to have been present in Jerusalem and its environs. There is an overt textual reference to Jesus' fame spreading "through all Judea." There are other textual hints relating to the temple and the priesthood, as well as the sacrificial system and money collection. Lindsey pointed to specific narratives that might belong in such a section of the larger Ur-text while admitting that no clear proof existed. These stories and narrative reconstructions, including relevant parables, have been collected below. Reestablishing their original order is an impossible task; however, their order of placement in the traditional Lucan account is suspect at best. The "Judean sojourn" reconstructed in this section is intended as a starting point for additional research into one aspect of the larger Synoptic Problem.

Scene 1:
The Widow of Nain (RCT)

The story of raising the son of the widow of Nain (which according to Josephus was a town in Judea) raises the overlooked possibility of a Judean sojourn during Jesus' early proto-rabbinic career.[1] The use of the term "prophet," harkening back to the Hebrew term נביא/ navi, likely carries messianic overtones often lost in English.

Luke 7:11 And it came to pass[2] the day after, that he went into a city called **Nain;**[3] and many of his disciples went with him, and a great crowd. **12** Now when he came near to the gate of the city, **behold,**[4] a dead man was being carried out, the only son of his mother, and she was a widow. And a great crowd from the town was with her. **13** And when the Lord saw her, he had compassion on her, and said to her: Do not weep. **14** And he came and touched the bier; and those who bore it stopped. And he said: Young man, I say to you, Arise. **15** And the dead man sat up, and began to speak. And he delivered him to his mother. **16** And fear seized them all; and they glorified God, saying: A great **prophet**[5] has risen up among us; and, that God **has visited**[6] his people. **17** And this report

---

[1] See David Bivin and Joshua Tilton, "Widow's Son in Nain," *Jerusalem Perspective*, May 19, 2022: https://www.jerusalemperspective.com/13167/.

[2] The Greek καὶ ἐγένετο translates the Hebrew וַיְהִי; see Luke 1:23.

[3] Note Josephus (*War* IV, 511–13), with respect to Bar-Giora's fortification of the *Judean* town near the Wadi Kelt: "At a village called Nain he erected a wall…" If this is the Nain (rather than the rabbinic town of Nain in Galilee), then this incident may have been located in Judea.

[4] The Greek ἰδοὺ is used in imitation of the Hebrew הִנֵּה.

[5] The term "prophet" could be used messianically, echoing Deut 18:15: "A **prophet** will the LORD your God raise up to you, from your midst, of your brethren, like me; to him you shall listen" (נָבִיא מִקִּרְבְּךָ מֵאַחֶיךָ כָּמֹנִי, יָקִים לְךָ יְהוָה אֱלֹהֶיךָ: אֵלָיו, תִּשְׁמָעוּן). See Luke 4:24; 13:33.

[6] The Greek Ἐπεσκέψατο ("has visited") parrots the Hebrew פקד, which carries with it the suggestion of a divine blessing, as in Gen 21:1: "And the LORD *visited* Sarah as He had said, and the LORD did to Sarah as He had spoken" (וַיהוָה פָּקַד אֶת-שָׂרָה, כַּאֲשֶׁר אָמָר; וַיַּעַשׂ יְהוָה לְשָׂרָה, כַּאֲשֶׁר דִּבֶּר).

about him went out through all **Judea,**[7] and through all the surrounding region.

Scene 2:
Jesus Cleanses a Leper

After Jesus cleanses a man afflicted with leprosy, his directive to "show yourself to the priest" for ritual purification may be indicative of a Jerusalem context. While priests were scattered across the land of Israel, the Jerusalem temple, with its complex of ritual immersion baths, well suits the setting of this pericope. In the story, we also find the reiteration of the "messianic secret" theme (earlier explained as Jesus' command to a demon to be quiet), extended by the redactor to suggest, incorrectly, that Jesus did not want his messianic identity known or proclaimed.

Luke 5:12 And it came to pass,[8] when he was in a certain city, **behold**[9] a man full of **leprosy,**[10] who seeing Jesus fell on his face, and besought him, saying: Lord, if you will, you can make me clean. **13** And he put forth his hand, and touched him, saying: I will; be clean. And immediately the leprosy departed from him. **14** And **he ordered him to tell no one:**[11] but go, and **show yourself to the priest,**[12] and offer for your cleansing, as Moses commanded, for a testimony to them. **15** But the report concerning him was spread abroad all the more, and great **multitudes**[13] came together to hear, and to be healed by him of their infirmities. **16** And he withdrew to the wilderness, and prayed.

---

[7] This may be seen as explicit evidence of an early Judean sojourn, and for that reason it has been placed first in this section.

[8] The Greek καὶ ἐγένετο translates the Hebrew וַיְהִי; see Luke 1:23.

[9] The Greek ἰδοὺ is used in imitation of the Hebrew הִנֵּה.

[10] Note Dead Sea Scrolls 11Q20 12:10; 11Q19 45:18: "No **leper** or person afflicted with a skin disease is to enter the city until purified" (וכול **צרוע** ומנוגע לוא יבואו לה עד אשר יטהרו).

[11] See Luke 4:41 regarding the so-called "messianic secret."

[12] The reference to a priest may be seen as possible evidence that the story occurred in Judea (the "certain city" being Jerusalem). See Matt 8:4.

[13] The Greek ὄχλοι translates the Hebrew אוכלוסים ("people of the area"/"people present"); see Luke 4:42. Large crowds may have grown over time, but not likely at the beginning.

Scene 3:
Jesus Forgives and Heals a Paralytic

The overt reference to "Judea and Jerusalem" helps to place this pericope in the context of the hypothetical Judean sojourn. When Jesus heals a paralytic, the audacious claim is made that he has the power to forgive sins. Is he assuming power and authority which, according to Leviticus 4, are the domain of God only? While early Judeo-Christians ascribed to Jesus much of what was ascribed to God, textual evidence of the worship of Jesus is lacking, except for a reference in the penultimate verse of the last chapter of Luke.

Luke 5:17 And it came to pass[14] on one of the days that he was teaching, that there were **Pharisees**[15] and teachers of the law sitting by, who had come out of every town of Galilee, and **Judea, and Jerusalem;**[16] and the power of the Lord was present to heal them. **18** And, **behold,**[17] men brought on a mat a man who was paralyzed; and they were seeking a means to bring him in, to place him before him. **19** And when they could not find a way to might bring him in because of the crowd, they went upon the housetop, and let him down through the tiles with his mat into the midst before Jesus. **20** And when he saw their faith, he said to him:

---

[14] The Greek καὶ ἐγένετο translates the Hebrew וַיְהִי; see Luke 1:23.

[15] The Pharisees and "teachers of the law" (a Christian designation likely added later) are here depicted, not as foes, but as actively seeking out Jesus. They are not present in the synoptic parallels (Mark 2:1; Matt 9:1), where there appears to be an agenda to depict them only in a negative light.

[16] Possible evidence of an early Judean sojourn. The reference to Galilee may be an editorial gloss.

[17] The Greek ἰδού translates the Hebrew הִנֵּה. See Luke 1:20 n.

Man,[18] **your sins are forgiven.**[19] **21** And the scribes and the
Pharisees began to reason, saying: Who is this who speaks
blasphemies? Who can forgive sins, but God alone? **22** But when
Jesus perceived their thoughts, he, answering, said to them: Why
do you reason in your hearts? **23 Which is easier,**[20] to say, Your
sins are forgiven you; or to say, Rise up and walk? **24** But that you
may know that the **Son of man**[21] has power **on earth**[22] to forgive
sins, (he said to the paralytic,) I say to you, **Arise,**[23] and take up

---

[18] The Greek Ἄνθρωπε translates the common Hebrew idiom בֶּן־אָדָם.

[19] It appears that Jesus' purpose was less about showing his power as a miracle worker and more about demonstrating the link between sin and illness. See Flusser, *Judaism*, 549–50. Note *b. Ned.* 41a: "The sick person recovers from his illness only when the heavenly court forgives him for all his sins" (אֵין הַחוֹלֶה עוֹמֵד מֵחָלְיוֹ עַד שֶׁמּוֹחֲלִין לוֹ עַל כֹּל עֲוֹנוֹתָיו). See also *b. Shab.* 55a: "There is no death without sin, and there is no suffering without iniquity" (אֵין מִיתָה בְּלֹא חֵטְא, וְאֵין יִסּוּרִין בְּלֹא עָוֹן). Note *Tos. Succah* 4:2 (attributed to the Hasidim): "Saints and pious men were dancing before them with torches, and saying words of praise; What were they saying? Happy is he who has not sinned, and whoever has sinned shall be forgiven" (חֲסִידִים וְאַנְשֵׁי מַעֲשֶׂה הָיוּ מְרַקְּדִין לִפְנֵיהֶם בַּאֲבוּקוֹת וְאוֹמְרִים לִפְנֵיהֶם). Note the saying of Hanina (דִּבְרֵי תִשְׁבָּחוֹת מֶה הָיוּ אוֹמְרִים אַשְׁרֵי מִי שֶׁלֹּא חָטָא וְכֹל מִי שֶׁחָטָא יִמָּחֵל לוֹ). ben Dosa (*b. Ber.* 33a): "It is not the serpent that kills, but the sin that kills" (אֵין עֲרָוָד מֵמִית אֶלָּא הַחֵטְא מֵמִית). See Num 21:9, regarding the "serpent." Not all illness was perceived to be caused by sin, but sin leads to illness. One who had sinned needed to be forgiven before being healed. Jesus' intent was to provoke the scribes by declaring that he had authority to grant such forgiveness. See Matt 9:2; Mark 2:5; Lev 4:26. The Greek "your sins are forgiven" (ἀφέωνταί σοι αἱ ἁμαρτίαι) easily goes back to Hebrew: וְנִסְלַח לוֹ. A Greek author would never have known this expression. In Leviticus it is clear that only God can forgive sin. While the people forgive each other, only God can use this language. The priest did the atoning; God did the forgiving. See also Lev 4:31, 35; 5:10, 16. It is noted, however, that in Jesus' day "to heal," "to expel demons," and "to forgive sins" were often interchangeable. While early Judeo-Christians ascribed to Jesus much of what was ascribed to God, there is no indication that they actually worshipped Jesus.

[20] Jesus, in rabbinic fashion, frequently answers a question with a question. Obviously, it is easier to say "Your sins are forgiven," and in that sense an ironic sense of humor is present.

[21] Note Dan 7:13: "I saw in the night visions, and, behold, there came with the clouds of heaven one like unto a *son of man*, and he came even to the Ancient of days, and he was brought near before Him." (חָזֵה הֲוֵית בְּחֶזְוֵי לֵילְיָא, וַאֲרוּ עִם־עֲנָנֵי שְׁמַיָּא, **כְּבַר אֱנָשׁ אָתֵה** הֲוָא; וְעַד־עַתִּיק יוֹמַיָּא מְטָה, וּקְדָמוֹהִי הַקְרְבוּהִי). The theme of the passage is divine authority. Jesus appears to equate himself with a supernatural judge at the end of days.

[22] "On earth" (Heb. ארץ) is in contrast to the heavenly theme. Note the statement of the Sages to Honi the Circle Drawer, *b. Taan.* 23a: "'You shall also decree a matter'; you, Honi, decree from below, and the Holy One, Blessed be He, fulfills your statement from above." (אַתָּה גָּזַרְתָּ מִלְּמַטָּה וְהַקָּדוֹשׁ בָּרוּךְ הוּא מְקַיֵּים מַאֲמָרְךָ מִלְמַעְלָה). Therefore, the idea that a hasid could decree God's decisions *on earth* was not foreign to ancient Judaism.

[23] Jesus does not say "In the name of God…" when healing or casting out demons.

your mat, and go into your house. **25** And immediately he rose up before them, and took up that on which he was lying, and departed to his own house, glorifying God. **26** And they were all amazed, and they **glorified God,**[24] and were filled with fear, saying: We have seen remarkable things today.

Scene 4:
A Man with Dropsy
Healed On the Sabbath (ANT)

Jesus was said to have begun his proto-rabbinic career with healings, prior to the call of his disciples, and this passage suits those early days, which may contextually have occurred in Judea. It is commonly assumed that Judaism forbade healing on the Sabbath. Such characterizations have furthered the "straw man" argument that Jewish law is by nature strict, rigid, and inflexible. However, there was no single Judaism in the second Jewish commonwealth, but rather, multiple "Judaisms." Jesus' larger dispute appears not to have been with the Pharisees but with the Dead Sea sect, who forbade rescuing an animal who had fallen into a pit on the Sabbath.[25]

Luke 14:1 And it came to pass,[26] as he went into the house of one of the chief Pharisees to eat bread on a Sabbath day, that they watched him. **2** And, **behold,**[27] there was a certain man before him

---

[24] Possible blessing recited by the crowd, *b. Ber.* 58a: "One who sees the Sages of Israel recites: Blessed… who has shared of His wisdom with those who revere Him" (הָרוֹאֶה חַכְמֵי יִשְׂרָאֵל, אוֹמֵר "בָּרוּךְ ... שֶׁחָלַק מֵחָכְמָתוֹ לִירֵאָיו"). See also Biblical Antiquities of Pseudo-Philo 26:6: "Blessed is He who has given of His power to flesh and blood." See Matt 9:8. Note Dead Sea Scrolls *Prayer of Nabonidus,* (*4QPrNab*) in which a Jewish exorcist pardons a Babylonian king's sins and cures him of seven years of illness. 4Q242 f1_3:4–5: "An exorcist—a Jew, in fact, a member of the community of exiles—came to me and said, 'Declare and write down this story, and so ***ascribe glory and greatness to the name of God Most High***'" (גזר והוא יהודי מן בני גלותא על לי ואמר החוי **וכתב למעבד יקר ורבו** **לשם אלהא עליא**).

[25] See John P. Meier, *A Marginal Jew: Rethinking the Historical Jesus, Vol. 5* (New Haven, CT: Yale University Press, 2009), 244.

[26] The Greek καὶ ἐγένετο translates the Hebrew וַיְהִי; see Luke 1:23.

[27] The Greek ἰδοὺ is used in imitation of the Hebrew הִנֵּה.

who had dropsy. **3** And Jesus, answering, spoke to the lawyers and Pharisees, saying: **Is it lawful to heal on the Sabbath day?**[28] **4** And they held their peace. And he took him, and healed him, and let him go; **5** And he answered them, saying: **Which of you, whose son or ox has fallen into a pit, will not immediately pull him out on the Sabbath day?**[29] **6** And they were not able to answer these things.

The Wedding Feast

Jesus' admonition to take the lowly place is reminiscent of Hillel's saying: "My humiliation is my exaltation and my exaltation, and my exaltation is my humiliation." Jesus' meekness, like Hillel's, was rooted in his strength, and in his exalted view of himself.[30] Jesus was voicing a social protest, congruent in some ways with the Essene sect. Yet, he takes aim at the Dead Sea sect or its ideology in referencing the lame and the blind (bidden to the supper), whereas the Dead Sea Scrolls exclude such individuals from entering the assembly.

Luke 14:7 Then he put forth a parable to those who were invited, remarking how **they chose out the first places;**[31] saying to them:

---

[28] Note *m. Yoma* 8:6: "And a case of uncertainty concerning a life-threatening situation overrides Shabbat" (וְכָל סְפֵק נְפָשׁוֹת דּוֹחֶה אֶת הַשַּׁבָּת); see Luke 13:17.

[29] Note Dead Sea Scrolls (CD 11:13–14): "No one should help an animal give birth on the Sabbath; and if it falls into a well or a pit, he may not lift it out on the Sabbath" (אל יילד איש בהמה ביום השבת ואם תפול אל בור ואל פחת אל יקימה בשבת). Note *Mekh.* 31:13: "R. Akiva says: If the saving of a life overrides the sacrificial service, which overrides the Sabbath, how much more so does the saving of a life override the Sabbath!" (רבי עקיבא אומר, אם דוחה [רציחה] את העבודה שהיא דוחה שבת, קל וחומר לפקוח נפש שדוחה שבת). Note also *y. Bez.* 63a (34), where R. Judah and R. Meir permitted healing on the Sabbath. See also *b. Shab.* 128b: "One may help domesticated animals, non-domesticated animals, and fowl walk in the courtyard on Shabbat" (מְדַדִּין בְּהֵמָה חַיָּה וָעוֹף בֶּחָצֵר). See Matt 12:11.

[30] See Flusser, *Judaism*, 509, 512.

[31] The Pharisees taking places of honor at the table is reminiscent of the "messianic banquet" tradition. Note Dead Sea Scrolls (1QSa 2:14–15): "Then the Messiah of Israel may enter, and the heads of the thousands of Israel are to sit before him by rank…" (ואחר ישב משיח ישראל וישבו לפניו ראשי אלפי ישראל איש לפי כבודו). Note also 1 Cor 11:21: "For in eating, each one takes his own supper ahead of others."

8 When you are invited by anyone to a **wedding,**[32] do not recline in **the first place,**[33] lest one more honorable than you be invited by him; **9** And he who invited you and him will come and say to you: Give this one your place; and then you should begin with shame to take the last place. **10** But when you are invited, go and recline in the last place; so that when the one who invited you comes, he may say to you: **Friend, come up higher.**[34] Then you will have glory in the presence of all those **reclining**[35] with you. **11** For whoever exalts himself will be humbled; and **he who humbles himself will**

---

[32] Note Rev 19:9: "Blessed are those who are called to the ***marriage supper*** of the Lamb."

[33] In Talmudic tradition, the middle couch at a banquet was for the three worthiest. The second worthiest sat on the left, the third on the right. The Greeks and Romans had up to four per couch, also arranged by rank. Note Theophrastus, *Characters* 21:2: "A vain person looks for the seat next to the host."

[34] The Greek φίλε ("friend") translates the Hebrew חבר, possibly a reference to the meals of the Pharisaic *haverim* (חברים). Some have compared the Dead Sea sect (who called themselves the *yahad*) with the *havurah* (חבורה) of early rabbinic literature. See also Luke 12:4. Note *Lev. R.* 1:5: "Rabbi Yehoshua of Sikhnin [said]: Do not exalt yourself in the king's presents, and do not claim a place among great men; it is better for him to say to you, '**Come up here**' than for him to humiliate you before a nobleman. (Prov 25:7). R. Akiva taught … "Move two or three places lower and there sit down. Move down so that you will be told '**Move up**'…'" רַבִּי יְהוֹשֻׁעַ דְּסֻכְנִין בְּשֵׁם רַבִּי לֵוִי פָּתַר קְרָא: כִּי טוֹב אֲמָר לְךָ **עֲלֵה הֵנָּה** מֵהַשְׁפִּילְךָ לִפְנֵי נָדִיב וגו', רַבִּי עֲקִיבָא מַתְנֵי לָהּ בְּשֵׁם רַבִּי שִׁמְעוֹן בֶּן עַזַּאי, רְחַק מִמְּקוֹמְךָ **שְׁנַיִם וּשְׁלֹשָׁה מוֹשָׁבוֹת וְשֵׁב עַד שֶׁיֹּאמְרוּ לְךָ עֲלֵה**).

[35] "Reclining" (Greek συνανακειμένων; Hebrew מְסֻבִּים, as in the Haggadah) evokes the image of Passover. It is a theme echoed prominently in the Lucan account, from the Transfiguration (Luke 9:31), which depicts Jesus speaking of his "departure" (ἔξοδον) from Jerusalem, to the Last Supper.

be exalted.[36] **12** Then he also said to those who invited him: When you make a dinner or a supper, do not call your friends, or your brothers, or your relatives, or your rich neighbors; lest they also invite you in return, in order to recompense to you. **13** But when you make a feast, call **the poor,**[37] the crippled, the lame, the blind; **14** And you will be blessed; for they cannot repay you; for you will be recompensed at the resurrection of the righteous. **15** And when one of them that **reclined**[38] with him heard these things, he said to him: **Blessed** is he **who will eat bread**[39] **in the kingdom of God.**[40]

---

[36] Note *b. Er.* 13b; *b. San.* 17a: "This is to teach you that anyone who *humbles* himself, the Holy One, Blessed be He, *exalts* him, and anyone who *exalts* himself, the Holy One, Blessed be He, *humbles* him" (לְלַמֶּדְךָ שֶׁכָּל הַמַּשְׁפִּיל עַצְמוֹ – הַקָּדוֹשׁ בָּרוּךְ הוּא מַגְבִּיהוֹ, וְכָל הַמַּגְבִּיהַּ עַצְמוֹ – הַקָּדוֹשׁ בָּרוּךְ הוּא מַשְׁפִּילוֹ). Note also *Lev. R.* 1:5 on Prov 25:6–7: "And so Hillel used to say, 'My *humiliation* is my exaltation and my *exaltation*, and my *exaltation* is my *humiliation*.' What is the proof? 'He who raises himself is to be made to sit down, he who **abases** himself is to be raised up so that he is seen (Ps 113:5–6).'" (וְכֵן הָלֵל אוֹמֵר הַשְׁפָּלָתִי הִיא הַגְבָּהָתִי, הַגְבָּהָתִי הִיא הַשְׁפָּלָתִי, מַה טַעַם: הַמַּגְבִּיהִי לָשֶׁבֶת הַמַּשְׁפִּילִי לִרְאוֹת). Hillel's meekness was said to derive from his strength. There is no evidence that the rabbis borrowed from Christian tradition; therefore, this was already a rabbinic saying. Note also *b. B.M.* 85b: "Anyone who *humbles* himself over matters of Torah in this world becomes **great** in the World-to-Come; and anyone who establishes himself as a servant over matters of Torah in this world becomes free in the World-to-Come" (כל המקטין עצמו על דברי תורה בעוה"ז נעשה **גדול** לעוה"ב וכל המשים עצמו כעבד על דברי תורה בעוה"ז נעשה חפשי לעוה"ב). Note that the slave becomes free. Note also Qumran *Thanksgiving Scroll* (1QHa 17:25): "The contempt of my enemies has become a glorious crown for me, and my stumbling, eternal strength" (ובוז צרי לי לכליל כבוד וכשלוני לגבורת). See also Matt 18:4; Luke 18:14; James 4:10.

[37] Note the possible sectarian/"Essene" reference to "the poor." Note the Qumran *War Scroll*, 1QM 13:14: "Your mighty hand is with the *oppressed/poor*" (אביונים יד גבורתכה); 1QM 14:7: "Among the *poor in spirit* [there is power] over the hard of heart" (ובענוי רוח] רשות -- [סם לבב קושי). Jesus may be contrasting the Pharisaic *haverim* (חברים), referenced in 14:7 with the "poor" of his own sect. See also Matt 19:21.

[38] "Reclined" (as in 14:10, above) evokes Passover imagery.

[39] The reflexive Greek verb φάγεται ("eats/will eat") translates the Hebrew imperfect יאכל, which can equally be understood in the present tense: "eats." This is significant if the Kingdom of God is understood in the present.

[40] Rather than conveying an eschatological concept, it is a declaration of how good it is to sit together in the present tense divine "reign" ("kingdom of heaven/God"). Note the "messianic banquet" tradition (14:7). The Beatitudes (Luke 6:20–26) may belong here (immediately after the statement "*Blessed* is he who eats bread ...") as a response by Jesus.

The Beatitudes (RCT)

The "Beatitudes"/"Blesseds" may represent a response to the declaration about eating bread in the kingdom of God. The Beatitudes and "woes" may have been originally in a more developed context, echoing the Testaments of Twelve Patriarchs. Matthew's version of the Beatitudes (Matt 5:3–11) and the entire "Sermon on the Mount" is more developed and detailed, and in that sense preferable to Luke, who relied on the edited and truncated version found in RCT (unknown to Matthew).[41]

Luke 6:20 And he [lifted up his eyes on his disciples and][42] said: Blessed are you poor: for yours is the kingdom of God.[43] **21 Blessed are you who hunger now: for you shall be filled. Blessed are you who weep now: for you will laugh.**[44]

Jesus Pronounces Woes

Jesus may have intended to demonstrate what his message had in common with Essenism, as a "social protest." Note that Luke has four "blesseds" and four "woes," and that three "blesseds" are Matthew's. He created a fourth from Matthew's ninth (from a different context). This indicates the work of the redactor of the "short Gospel" (RCT).

---

[41] See Lindsey, *Jesus*, 112.

[42] Possibly an editorial gloss to place these "Beatitudes" in another context. Theoretically, during the "Judean sojourn," the disciples had not yet been called.

[43] This may represent an abbreviation of an original text, later recorded in Matt 5:6–10. A better understanding might be: "… for they *make up* the kingdom of heaven."

[44] Verse 21b is the only beatitude not found in Matthew. The total number should be ten, paralleled in the "woes." Note *b. Shab.* 104a: "The bent *nun* (נ) and the straight *nun* (ן) at the end of a word refer to a faithful person who is bent [*ne'eman kafuf*] and is modest now, who will ultimately become a well-known faithful person [*ne'eman pashut*]" (נו"ן כְּפוּפָה, נו"ן פְּשׁוּטָה—נֶאֱמָן כָּפוּף, נֶאֱמָן פָּשׁוּט). Note also *Ecc. Rab.* 30, citing Ben Zoma (an unmarried mystic): "So Ben Zoma used to say and explain: if you were ashamed in this world, you will not be ashamed of the Holy One, who is a consuming fire, in the coming world" (וְכֵן הָיָה בֶּן זוֹמָא אוֹמֵר וְדוֹרֵשׁ נִתְבַּיַּשְׁתָ בָּעוֹלָם הַזֶּה אֵין אַתָּה מִתְבַּיֵּשׁ מִן הַקָּדוֹשׁ בָּרוּךְ הוּא לְעוֹלָם הַבָּא שֶׁהוּא אֵשׁ אֹכְלָה).

24 But **woe**[45] **to you who are rich!**[46]

    for you are receiving your consolation.

25 Woe[47] to you who are full!

    for you will hunger.

Woe[48] to you who laugh now!

    for you will mourn and weep.

26 Woe[49] to you, when all men speak well of you!

    for so did their fathers to the false prophets.

Scene 5:
The Rich Young Ruler (ANT)

Luke 18:18–30 may be added here, continuing the narrative and teaching regarding riches and the poor. The "rich young ruler" may well have been in attendance at the house of one of the Pharisees, during the Sabbath meal referenced above.[50]

---

[45] The Greek Οὐαί is used in the Septuagint chiefly for הוֹי and אוֹי.

[46] See Enoch 94:6–11, containing "woes" against the rich and hope for the righteous poor. The Beatitudes and "woes" may have originally been redacted in a larger, more elaborate form. Note *Test. Judah* 25:4–5: "And they who have died in grief shall arise in joy, And they who were poor for the Lord's sake shall be made rich, And they who are put to death for the Lord's sake shall awake to life. And the hearts of Jacob shall run in joyfulness" (וכל אשר ביגון מתו בשמחה יקומו: והמתים למען יי לחיים יקיצו: וצבאי יעקב בשמחה ירוצו).

[47] The Greek Οὐαί is used in the Septuagint chiefly for הוֹי and אוֹי.

[48] The Greek Οὐαί is used in the Septuagint chiefly for הוֹי and אוֹי.

[49] The Greek Οὐαί is used in the Septuagint chiefly for הוֹי and אוֹי.

[50] See Lindsey, *Jesus*, 80.

Luke 18:18 And a certain ruler asked him, saying: **Good Teacher,**[51] **what shall I do to inherit eternal life?**[52] **19** And Jesus said to him: Why do you call you me **good?**[53] No one is good, except God alone. **20** You know the commandments, Do not commit adultery, Do not kill, Do not steal, Do not bear false witness, Honor your father and your mother. **21** And he said: All these I have kept from my youth. **22** Now when Jesus heard these things, he said to him: Yet one thing you lack. Sell all that you have, and **distribute to the poor,**[54] and you will have **treasure in heaven.**[55] And come, follow me. **23** And when he heard this, he was very sorrowful; for he was very rich.

---

[51] The phrase "Good teacher/rabbi" (Heb. רבי הטוב) is not Hebraic. Matt 19:16 is better: "Teacher, what good thing must I do to get eternal life?" The NU-Text omits "good": "What [good] thing shall I do …?"

[52] Typical of the "calculating Pharisee"; note *m. Avot* 2:7 (attributed to Hillel): "He who has acquired for himself things of the Torah has acquired for himself *life in the world to come*" (קָנָה לוֹ דִבְרֵי תוֹרָה, קָנָה לוֹ **חַיֵּי הָעוֹלָם הַבָּא**). Note also *b. Ber.* 28b: "When Rabbi Eliezer fell ill, his students entered to visit him. They said to him: Teach us paths of life, guidelines by which to live, and we will thereby merit the *life of the World-to-Come*. He said to them: Be vigilant in the honor of your counterparts, and prevent your children from logic when studying verses that tend toward heresy (*ge'onim*), and place your children, while they are still young, between the knees of Torah scholars, and when you pray, know before Whom you stand. For doing that, you will merit the *life of the World-to-Come*" (כְּשֶׁחָלָה רַבִּי אֱלִיעֶזֶר נִכְנְסוּ תַּלְמִידָיו לְבַקְּרוֹ. אָמְרוּ לוֹ: רַבֵּינוּ לַמְּדֵנוּ אוֹרְחוֹת חַיִּים וְנִזְכֶּה בָּהֶן לְחַיֵּי **הָעוֹלָם הַבָּא**. אָמַר לָהֶם: הִזָּהֲרוּ בִּכְבוֹד חַבְרֵיכֶם, וּמִנְעוּ בְּנֵיכֶם מִן הַהִגָּיוֹן, וְהוֹשִׁיבוּם בֵּין בִּרְכֵּי תַּלְמִידֵי חֲכָמִים, וּכְשֶׁאַתֶּם מִתְפַּלְּלִים—דְּעוּ לִפְנֵי מִי אַתֶּם עוֹמְדִים. וּבִשְׁבִיל כָּךְ תִּזְכּוּ לְחַיֵּי **הָעוֹלָם הַבָּא**).

[53] Matt 19:17 is better; the NU-Text reads: "Why do you ask me about what is good?"

[54] The early followers of Jesus, like the Dead Sea sect, appear to have handed all their possessions over to the community, euphemistically known as "the poor" (Heb. אביונים; Greek τέλειος/τέλειοι). Jesus may possibly be commending such a lifestyle in order to experience the "kingdom of heaven/God" in the present. Perhaps Luke 14:13 ("invite the poor") carries a double, "sectarian" meaning, referencing the sectarians of his own movement. Note the Qumran *War Scroll*, 1QM 13:12, 14: "But we, in the lot of Your truth, rejoice in Your mighty hand … Your mighty hand is with the **oppressed/poor**" (ואנו יד גבורתכה; בגורל אמתכה נשמחה ביד גבורתכה ... **אביונים**); 1QM 14:7: "Among the **poor in spirit** [there is power] over the hard of heart/and by the **perfect of the way** all the nations of wickedness have come to an end" (ובענוי רוח[רשות -- סם לבב קושי. ובתמימי דרך יתמו כול] גויי רשעה). See also Matt 5:3 ("Blessed are the *poor* in spirit"). The Qumran sect also called themselves the "perfect"; CD 20:7: "the men of holy *perfection*" (אנשי תמים הקדש). Note also, that according to Jewish law (*b. Ket.* 50a) one should not give away more than one-fifth of one's possessions during one's lifetime.

[55] Note Ben Sira 29:11: "Dispose of your treasure according to the commandments of the Most High, and that will profit you more than the gold" (NABRE).

With God All Things Are Possible

The "incident" described above would theoretically have been followed by this subsequent teaching and thereafter by two parables.

Luke 18:24 And when Jesus saw that he was very sorrowful, he said, How hard shall it be for those who have riches to enter into the kingdom of God! **25** For it is easier for a camel to go through the **eye of a needle**[56] than for a rich man to enter into the **kingdom of God.**[57] **26** And those who heard it said: Who then can be saved? **27** And he said: The things that are impossible with men are possible with God. **28** Then Peter said: **Behold,**[58] we have left all, and followed you. **29** And he said to them: **Truly**[59] I say to you, There is no one who has left **house, or parents, or brothers, or**

---

[56] Note *Cant. R.* 5:3: "The Holy One, blessed be He, said to Israel: My children, make for Me an opening of repentance no bigger than the point of a needle, and I will widen it for you into openings through which wagons and carriages can pass" (אָמַר הַקָּדוֹשׁ בָּרוּךְ הוּא לְיִשְׂרָאֵל, בָּנַי, פִּתְחוּ לִי פֶּתַח אֶחָד שֶׁל תְּשׁוּבָה כְּחֻדָּהּ שֶׁל מַחַט, וַאֲנִי פּוֹתֵחַ לָכֶם פְּתָחִים שֶׁיִּהְיוּ עֲגָלוֹת וּקְרוֹנִיּוֹת נִכְנָסוֹת בּוֹ); see also *Pes. K.* 24:12. See Matt 19:24; Mark 10:25.

[57] The rich man asks about eternal life, but Jesus speaks of the "kingdom of God/heaven" in the present tense. There is arguably a degree of humor in Jesus' statement.

[58] The Greek ἰδού is used in imitation of the Hebrew הִנֵּה.

[59] The Greek ἀμὴν transliterates the Hebrew אָמֵן. This follows and emphasizes the previous statement: "Behold, we have left all, and followed you." See Luke 18:17; Jer 28:6; Num 5:22; See Luke 4:24; Matt 5:18.

wife, or children,[60] for the sake of the kingdom of God, **30** Who shall not receive manifold more in this present time, and in the world to come eternal life.

Two parables (building on the theme of the "kingdom of God")
theoretically belong here.

Parable 1: The Mustard Seed

The following parables of the mustard seed and the leaven (= Matt
13:31–33; Mark 4:30–32) work together to illustrate the gradual
growth of the "Kingdom of God." They should not be taken as
eschatological/referring to the end of days but to the present tense
growth of divine agency.[61]

Luke 13:18 Then he said: To what is the kingdom of God like?
And **to what shall I liken it?**[62] **19** It is like a grain of **mustard**

---

[60] The Hebrew word "house" (בית) is here rendered literally. "To leave house" means "to leave home," including family. Therefore, "or parents or brothers or wife or children" is added. This is preferable to Mark 10:29–30, which expands on Luke's wording, as if attempting to explain the word "house": "There is no man that has left house, or brothers, or sisters, or father, or mother, or wife, or children, or lands, for my sake, and the gospel's, but he shall receive a hundredfold now in this time, houses, and brothers, and sisters, and mothers, and children, and lands, with persecutions; and in the world to come eternal life." Luke's Jesus is not in the habit of promising physical rewards for dedication to his movement, as opposed to Mark. He does not indicate what "more" will be received in this time. Hypothetical reconstruction by R. Lindsey: "There is no one who has left home for the sake of the kingdom of God who shall not receive much more in this time, and in the age to come everlasting life." Following a sage meant total commitment, i.e. leaving home; see Matt 9:9. Note *m. Peah* 1:1: "The following are the things for which a man enjoys the fruits in this world while the principal remains for him in the world to come: *Honoring one's father and mother*; The performance of righteous deeds; And the making of peace between a person and his friend; *And the study of the torah is equal to them all*" (אֵלּוּ דְבָרִים שֶׁאָדָם אוֹכֵל פֵּרוֹתֵיהֶן בָּעוֹלָם הַזֶּה וְהַקֶּרֶן קַיֶּמֶת לוֹ לָעוֹלָם הַבָּא. **כִּבּוּד אָב וָאֵם**, וּגְמִילוּת חֲסָדִים, וַהֲבָאַת שָׁלוֹם בֵּין אָדָם לַחֲבֵרוֹ, **וְתַלְמוּד תּוֹרָה כְּנֶגֶד כֻּלָּם**).

[61] See Lindsey, *Jesus*, 104.

[62] Luke (vs. Matt) echoes a "rabbinic" introduction to the parable: למה הדבר דומה? ("To what is this comparable?").

seed,[63] which a man took, and cast **into his garden;**[64] and it grew, and **became a tree; and the birds of the air lodged in its branches.**[65]

Parable 2: The Leaven

The sages often linked "leaven" to the "evil inclination." However, the amoraic sage Ḥiyya bar Abba compared the study of Torah to the action of leaven.

Luke 13:20 And again he said: To what shall I liken the kingdom of God? **21 It is like leaven,**[66] which a woman took and hid in three measures of meal, until it was all leavened.

---

[63] Hypothetical Hebrew reconstruction by Brad Young, *Jesus and His Jewish Parables: Rediscovering the Roots of Jesus' Teaching* (New York: Paulist Press, 1989), 209: למה דומה מלכות שמים? דומה לגרגר של חרדל. נטלו אדם ושם אותו בשדהו וצמח והיה לעץ ועוף. השמים שרנו בענפיו. Note *b. Ket.* 111b: "There was an incident which occurred in the village of Shiḥin, in Eretz Yisrael, involving one whose father had left him three branches of **mustard**, one of which broke. And they discovered on this one branch alone nine *kav* of **mustard**. And with the wood of its large branches they roofed a booth for artisans" מעשה בשיחין באחד שהניח לו אביו שלשה בדי חרדל ונפשח אחד מהן ונמצאו בו תשעה קבין חרדל ועציו סיככו בו (סוכת יוצרין).

[64] Note *m. Kil.* 3:2, which prohibits planting mustard seeds in a garden: "They may not sow different species of seeds in one bed, but they may sow different species of vegetables in one bed. **Mustard** and small polished peas are a species of seed; large peas are a species of vegetable" כָּל מִין זְרָעִים אֵין זוֹרְעִים בַּעֲרוּגָה, וְכָל מִין יְרָקוֹת זוֹרְעִין בַּעֲרוּגָה. חַרְדָּל (וַאֲפוּנִים הַשּׁוּפִין, מִין זְרָעִים. אֲפוּנִים הַגַּמְלוֹנִים, מִין יָרָק). The parallel in Matt reads "in his field," while Mark reads "upon the ground"—a better rendering.

[65] Note *Cant. R.* 6.1: "Just as if you had a sack of nuts, you can still put in it plenty of sesame grains and mustard seeds, so many proselytes have come and added themselves to Israel." However, this verse should not necessarily be taken a reference to proselytes. The tree is a metaphor for a righteous person. See Ps 1:3; *m. Avot* 3:17: "But one whose deeds exceed his wisdom, to what may he be compared? *To a tree whose branches are few but roots are many*, so that even if all the winds in the world come and blow upon it, they cannot move it out of its place" אֲבָל כָּל שֶׁמַּעֲשָׂיו מְרֻבִּין מֵחָכְמָתוֹ, לְמָה הוּא דוֹמֶה. **לְאִילָן שֶׁעֲנָפָיו מֻעָטִין וְשָׁרָשָׁיו מְרֻבִּין**, שֶׁאֲפִלּוּ כָל הָרוּחוֹת שֶׁבָּעוֹלָם בָּאוֹת וְנוֹשְׁבוֹת בּוֹ אֵין מְזִיזִין אוֹתוֹ מִמְּקוֹמוֹ). It is significant that Jesus may be compared to the early *Hasidim*, who stressed good deeds over study. Note that the tree metaphor is also used negatively; see Ezek 17:2–24; 31:3–13. Note also Dan 4:18: "... *and upon whose branches* the fowls of the heaven had their habitation" (וּבְעַנְפוֹהִי יְשְׁכְּנָן צִפֲּרֵי שְׁמַיָּא).

[66] Ḥiyya bar Abba declared that if Israel abandons God, yet studies the Torah, its leaven will bring them back; see *y. Chag.* 76c (chap. 1). See also *Pereq ha-Shalom* (beginning), citing Joshua b. Levi: "Peace is to the earth as leaven to dough." Hypothetical Hebrew reconstruction by Brad Young, *Jesus and His Jewish Parables*, 212: לשאור שנטלה אשה וטמנה בשלש שאים של קמח עד שחמץ כלו.

Scene 6:
The Cost of Discipleship

The message of leaving "house, or parents, or brothers, or wife, or children" (18:29) is continued here, and for this reason, is also included in the "Judean sojourn" section.

Luke 14:25 And there went great crowds with him. And he turned, and said to them: **26** If anyone comes to me, and **does not hate his father, and mother,**[67] and wife, and children, and brothers, and sisters, yes, and even his own life, he cannot be my disciple. **27** And whoever does not **carry his cross**[68] and come after me cannot be my disciple. **28** For which of you, intending to build a tower, does not **sit down first, and count the cost,**[69] whether he has sufficient to finish it? **29** Thus, after he has laid the foundation, and is not able to finish it, all who see it may begin to mock him, **30** Saying: This man began to build, and was not able to finish. **31** Or what king, going to make war against another king, does not sit down first and take counsel, whether he is able with ten thousand to meet the one who comes against him with twenty thousand? **32** Or else, while the other is still far away, he sends an embassy, and asks for peace. **33** So likewise, whoever of you who does not forsake all that he has, cannot be my disciple.

---

[67] Note *m. B.M.* 2:11: "If one finds his *father's* lost item and his *teacher's* lost item, tending to his teacher's lost item takes precedence, as his *father* brought him into this world, and his *teacher*, who taught him the wisdom of Torah, brings him to life in the World-to-Come" (אֲבֵדַת **אָבִיו** וַאֲבֵדַת **רַבּוֹ**, שֶׁל רַבּוֹ קוֹדֶמֶת. שֶׁ**אָבִיו** הֱבִיאוֹ לָעוֹלָם הַזֶּה, וְ**רַבּוֹ** שֶׁלִּמְּדוֹ חָכְמָה מְבִיאוֹ לְחַיֵּי הָעוֹלָם הַבָּא). See Matt 10:37: "He who loves his *father or mother* more than me is not worthy of me."

[68] Note Gen 22:6: "And Abraham took the wood of the burnt-offering, and laid it upon Isaac his son" (וַיִּקַּח אַבְרָהָם אֶת-עֲצֵי הָעֹלָה וַיָּשֶׂם עַל-יִצְחָק בְּנוֹ).

[69] Note *b. Tam.* 32a: "Who is truly worthy of being called wise? They said to him, citing a tradition (see *m. Avot* 2:9): 'Who is the wise person? The one who sees and anticipates the consequences of his behavior'" (אידין מתקרי חכים אמרו ליה איזהו חכם הרואה את הנולד).

Scene 7:
A Spirit of Infirmity

The contextual theme of the Sabbath finds additional narrative content here, in "one of the synagogues" that may have been located in Judea. With no mention of disciples, we may suggest that it occurred early in Jesus' proto-rabbinic career.[70] The "kingdom of God/heaven" is again witnessed in the healing of a woman with a "spirit of infirmity." The Genesis Apocryphon contains a reference to the practice of the "laying on of hands," later adopted for rabbinic ordination. We next see Jesus accepting the liberal rabbinic position regarding the humane treatment of animals on the Sabbath, to which he likens the healing of human beings.

Luke 13:10 And he was teaching in one of the synagogues on the Sabbath. **11** And, **behold,**[71] there was a woman who had a spirit of infirmity eighteen years, and was bent over, and could not lift herself up. **12** And when Jesus saw her, he called her to him, and said to her: Woman, you are freed from your infirmity. **13** And he **laid his hands**[72] on her; and immediately she was made straight, and glorified God. **14** And the ruler of the synagogue answered with indignation, because Jesus had **healed on the Sabbath day,**[73]

---

[70] See Lindsey, *Jesus*, 49–50.

[71] The Greek ἰδοὺ is used in imitation of the Hebrew הִנֵּה.

[72] The Greek ἐπέθηκεν τὰς χεῖρας ("laid the hands") reproduces the Hebrew סמך ידים. Note Genesis Apocryphon (1Q20 20:28–29), relating that Abram prayed for Pharaoh: "So I prayed for him, that blasphemer, and **laid my hands** upon his head. Thereupon the plague was removed from him, the evil spirit exorcised from him, and he was healed" (וצלית עלוהי מגדפא הו **וסמכת ידי** על ראישה. ואתפלי מנה מכתשא ואתגערת מנה רוחא באישתא וחי). This provides evidence that the laying on of hands was practiced among ancient Jews. Rabbinic literature uses the root סמך for ordination. See also Mark 6:5; 7:32; Luke 4:40; Acts 6:6; 28:8.

[73] Note *m. Yoma* 8:6: "And a case of uncertainty concerning a life-threatening situation overrides Shabbat" (וְכָל סָפֵק נְפָשׁוֹת דּוֹחֶה אֶת הַשַּׁבָּת); *Mekh. Ex.* 31:13: "Whence is it derived that the saving of a life overrides the Sabbath? ... How much more so does the saving of life override the Sabbath!" (מנין לפקוח נפש שדוחה את השבת ... קל וחומר לפקוח נפש שדוחה את השבת). Note also *y. Bez.* 63a (34): "R. Judah and R. Meir permitted healing on the Sabbath"; *y. Shab.* 15:16 (134).

and said to the people: There are six days in which men ought to work; in these therefore come and be healed, and not on the Sabbath day. **15** The Lord then answered him, and said: You hypocrite, does not each one of you **untie his ox or his donkey from the stall on the Sabbath, and lead him away to watering?**[74] **16** Now, should not this woman, being a daughter of Abraham, whom Satan has bound eighteen years, **be loosed from this bond on the Sabbath day?**[75] **17** And when he had said these things, all his adversaries were ashamed; and all the people rejoiced for all the glorious things that were done by him.[76]

Scene 8:
Lord of the Sabbath (RCT)

Luke 6:1–5 may derive from the hypothetical Judean sojourn since it continues the Sabbath discussion and since there is an overt reference to David (from Bethlehem of Judea) and the Jerusalem temple. While generic "disciples" are mentioned, the traditional placement in Luke precedes the calling of the twelve. The incident occurred in the early part of Jesus' proto-rabbinic career and may have taken place in the vicinity of Jerusalem.[77] Contrary to the notion that Jesus was relaxing Sabbath law, he appears to agree with the early Sages, that preserving life is paramount. Passing

---

[74] I.e. "loosen the knots." Note *m. Shab.* 5:1–2: "With what may an animal go out into the public domain on Shabbat…? A camel may go out on Shabbat with an *afsar*, and a *naka* may go out with a *ḥatam*, and a *luvdekim* may go out with a *perumbiya*. And a horse may go out with a chain around its neck. And, in general, all animals that typically have a chain around their necks when they go out to the public domain may go out with a chain on Shabbat and may be pulled by the chain… A donkey may go out on Shabbat with a saddlecloth… Rabbi Yosei prohibits the animals from going out with all of these items" בַּמֶּה בְּהֵמָה יוֹצְאָה וּבַמֶּה אֵינָהּ יוֹצְאָה. יוֹצֵא הַגָּמָל בְּאַפְסָר, וְנָאקָה בַחֲטָם, וְלַבְדְּקִיס בִּפְרֻמְבְּיָא, וְסוּס) (בְּשֵׁיר, וְכָל בַּעֲלֵי הַשֵּׁיר יוֹצְאִים בַּשֵּׁיר וְנִמְשָׁכִים בַּשֵּׁיר … חֲמוֹר יוֹצֵא בְמַרְדַּעַת…רַבִּי יוֹסֵי אוֹסֵר בְּכֻלָּן). Jesus adopts the liberal rabbinic position, likening the humane treatment of animals on the Sabbath to human healing.

[75] A rabbinic methodology: "light and heavy" (קַל וָחוֹמֶר); See Matt 7:9 ff. However, it might be argued to the contrary that this case was not an emergency.

[76] Theorized to have been part of an early Judean sojourn. It may have occurred early in Jesus' "proto-rabbinic" career, prior to the call of his disciples.

[77] See Lindsey, *Jesus*, 49.

through an already harvested barley field, the disciples see grain heads still on the ground and rub. Only some Pharisees object. The disciples were not poor or about to die, but Jesus argues pikuakh nefesh, i.e. "the saving of a life," which supersedes the Sabbath.

Luke 6:1 And it came to pass[78] **on the second Sabbath after the first,**[79] that he went through the grain fields; and his disciples **plucked the ears of grain**, and **rubbed** them in their hands. **2** And **certain of the Pharisees** said to them: Why do you do what is not lawful to do on the Sabbath day? **3** And Jesus answering them said, Have you not read what **David did, when he himself was hungry,**[80] and those who were with him; **4** How he entered the house of God, and took and ate the showbread, and also gave to those who were with him; that which is not lawful to eat except for the priests alone? **5** And he said to them, The Son of man is Lord of the Sabbath.

---

[78] The Greek ἐγένετο δὲ translates the Hebrew וַיְהִי.

[79] The Greek ἐν σαββάτῳ δευτεροπρώτῳ appears to be attempting to render the Hebrew "the second Sabbath of the counting of the Omer" (ביום השבת השנית לספירת העומר). Later copyists deleted the term δευτεροπρώτῳ ("second"), likely because they did not understand the counting of the Omer (see Lev 23:15).

[80] According to Leviticus 23, the new crop of barley could not be harvested or eaten until the *Omer* had been offered in the temple on the second day of Passover (16 *Nisan*). Sometimes it was difficult to find a ripe sheaf because it was not yet harvest time. The poor entered the field immediately after the harvesters left, but did not pick up every last head of grain. Luke relates that the disciples "plucked and rubbed." Matthew and Mark only say "plucked." The hypothetical undertext would have said only "rubbed." Most sages prohibited rubbing, but *b. Shab.* 128a states: "One may rub and eat" (וּמוֹלֵל וְאוֹכֵל). Note *M. Peah* 8:1: "From when are all people permitted to take gleanings, [forgotten sheaves and peah]? After the old ones of the poor have gone." (מֵאֵימָתַי כָּל אָדָם מֻתָּרִין בְּלֶקֶט. מִשֶּׁיֵּלְכוּ הַנָּמוֹשׁוֹת). According to Deut 23:25 one may pluck in a neighbor's field: "When you come into your neighbor's vineyard, then you may eat grapes until you have enough at your own pleasure" (כִּי תָבֹא בְּכֶרֶם רֵעֶךָ, וְאָכַלְתָּ עֲנָבִים כְּנַפְשְׁךָ שָׂבְעֶךָ). However, *m. Bab. Metz.* 7:2–5 declares that this refers to the laborer, not the passerby. Luke 6:1–5 may be interpreted as follows: Passing through an already harvested barley field, the disciples see grain heads still on the ground and rub. Only *some* Pharisees object. The disciples are not poor or about to die, but Jesus argues the principle of *pikuakh nefesh* (the saving of a life supersedes all). Note *Seder Eliyahu Rab.* 14 (preserving ancient hasidic overtones): "I do not know which comes first - some say the Torah is first; I would say the holy children of Israel are first" (איני יודע איזה מהם קודם אמרתי לו בני דרכן של בני אדם אומרים התורה קדמה... אבל אני אומר ישראל קדמו). See Mark 2:27.

Scene 9:
Healing on the Sabbath

The reference to the Sabbath fits contextually with the other narrative units presumed to comprise Jesus' Judean sojourn. There is no mention of the disciples (evidence of early placement in the assumed grundschrift), and the presence of "scribes" lends credence to a Jerusalem setting.

Luke 6:6 And it came to pass,[81] **on another Sabbath,** that he entered into the synagogue and taught: **and there was a man whose right hand was withered. 7 And the scribes and Pharisees**[82] **watched him, whether he would heal on the Sabbath; that they might find an accusation against him.**[83] **8** But he knew their thoughts, and said to the man who had the withered hand, Rise up, and stand in the midst. And he rose and stood. **9** Then Jesus said to them, I will ask you one thing; Is it lawful on the Sabbath to do good, or to do evil? To save life, or to destroy it? **10** And looking round about on them all, he said to the man, Stretch out your hand. And he did so: and **his hand was**

---

[81] The Greek ἐγένετο δὲ translates the Hebrew וַיְהִי.

[82] The term "Pharisees" does not appear at this point in the parallel passages in Matthew or Mark. While Jesus harshly criticizes the Pharisees in Luke, they are not depicted in conspiratorial fashion.

[83] From the mid-second century BCE through the second century CE, textual evidence suggests that the Jewish Sages permitted healing on the Sabbath, notwithstanding its apparent prohibition by Torah law. The teaching of Jesus on this subject derives from the arguments of Rabbi Eleazar ben Azariah, Rabbi Akiva and especially Rabbi Ishmael, who was the first to be associated with the term *pikuakh nefesh*, which he likely coined for any act that saved life, even at the expense of Jewish law. Note *b. Yom.* 85b: "Rabbi Elazar ben Azarya answered and said: Just as the mitzva of circumcision, which rectifies only one of the 248 limbs of the body, overrides Shabbat, so too, *a fortiori*, saving one's whole body, which is entirely involved in mitzvot, overrides Shabbat" (נَעֲנָה רַבִּי אֶלְעָזָר וְאָמַר: וּמָה מִילָה שֶׁהִיא אֶחָד מִמָּאתַיִם וְאַרְבָּעִים וּשְׁמוֹנָה אֵיבָרִים שֶׁבָּאָדָם דּוֹחָה שַׁבָּת — קַל וָחוֹמֶר לְכָל גּוּפוֹ שֶׁדּוֹחֶה אֶת הַשַּׁבָּת). Mark is much more inflammatory than Luke, alleging a murderous plot: "Then the Pharisees went out and immediately took counsel with the Herodians against Him…" (Mark 3:6).

restored.[84] **11** And they were filled with rage; and discussed with one another **what they might do to Jesus.**[85]

Scene 10:
A House Divided Cannot Stand (ANT)

This pericope (11:14–26) may be included in the theorized Judean sojourn, if any weight is given to Mark's assertion (3:22) that the "scribes" (identified with the Jerusalem temple) were involved. After Jesus casts out a demon, the text relates that some in the crowd accuse him of utilizing the power of Beelzebub. Interestingly, when Mark's Gospel relates the story, the scribes make the accusation, and in Matthew's Gospel, it is the Pharisees. From such narratives developed the stereotype that the Jewish leadership, and hence all of Judaism, rejected Jesus and was in some way responsible for his death. Helpful here is the theory of the primacy of Luke, which singles out neither scribes nor Pharisees nor any of the Jewish leadership as antagonists of Jesus. Importantly, the act of casting out demons is depicted as evidence that the kingdom of God has arrived. The specific term, "finger of God," links with Exodus 8:15.

Luke 11:14 And he was casting out a demon, and it was mute. **And it came to pass,**[86] when the demon had gone out, the mute

---

[84] Jesus does not physically touch the man, obviating the charge that he is performing work on the Sabbath.

[85] Here the opponents discuss "what they might do" with Jesus, as opposed to Mark and Matthew, who report that they plot against Jesus, "how they might destroy him." See *b. Taan.* 23a, regarding Honi HaMe'aggel ("the Circle-Drawer") demanded of Heaven that rain be sent: "Shimon ben Shetakh relayed to Honi HaMe'aggel: If you were not Honi, I would have decreed ostracism upon you … However, **what can I do to you**, as you nag God and He does your bidding, like a son who nags his father and his father does his bidding?" (שָׁלַח לוֹ שִׁמְעוֹן בֶּן שָׁטַח אִלְמָלֵא חוֹנִי אַתָּה גּוֹזְרַנִי עָלֶיךָ … אֲבָל **מָה אֶעֱשֶׂה לְךָ שֶׁאַתָּה** שֶׁמִּתְחַטֵּא לִפְנֵי הַמָּקוֹם וְעוֹשֶׂה לְךָ רְצוֹנְךָ כְּבֵן שֶׁמִּתְחַטֵּא עַל אָבִיו וְעוֹשֶׂה לוֹ רְצוֹנוֹ). The response to Honi is not more severe than: "What can I do to you?" Even a "ban" (excommunication/ "ostracism") is not contemplated.

[86] The Greek ἐγένετο δὲ translates the Hebrew וַיְהִי.

man spoke; and the crowds marveled. **15** But **some of them**[87] said: **He casts out demons through Beelzebub**[88] the prince of the demons. **16** And others, testing him, sought from him a sign from heaven. **17** But he, knowing their thoughts, said to them: **Every kingdom divided against itself is brought to desolation;**[89] and a house divided against a house falls. **18** Now, if Satan is also divided against himself, how will his kingdom stand? For you say that I cast out demons through **Beelzebub**. **19** Now, if I cast out demons **by Beelzebub,**[90] by whom do your sons cast them out? Therefore they shall be your judges. **20 But if I cast out demons by the finger of God,**[91] then the kingdom of God has come upon you. **21** When an armed **strong man**[92] guards his house, his possessions are in peace: **22** But when one stronger than he comes upon him, and overcomes him, he takes from him all his armor in

---

[87] Luke recounts that "some" in the crowd accused Jesus while Mark (3:22) says it was the "teachers of the law" (scribes) and Matthew (9:34) says it was the Pharisees (see also Matt 12:24). This progressive identification of the Pharisees was first noticed by Bultmann, who failed to see that this demolishes Markan priority. Mark also includes the charge that Jesus "has Beelzebub." It has been argued that the original story ("Q text"), as reproduced in Luke, did not include the charge of demon possession, which may have been a Markan "pickup" from the charge against John the Baptist (Luke 7:33; Matt 11:18).

[88] Note *b. San.* 107b: "Jesus *performed sorcery*, incited Jews to engage in idolatry, and led Israel astray" (יש"ו **כישף** והסית והדיח את ישראל). Note also *b. Sot.* 47a: "Jesus the Nazarene *performed sorcery*, and he incited the masses, and subverted the masses, and caused the Jewish people to sin" (**כישף** והסית והדיח והחטיא את ישראל [יש"ו]). The root *ZBL* in Ugaritic means "prince," and could be equated with the Hebrew *Baal* (בַּעַל). The Hebrew זְבֶל refers to "dung."

[89] Note *Sifrei* Num 42; *Gen. R.* 38: "'Ephraim has bound himself (in friendship to serve) idols — Let him be.' But when they were *divided* among themselves, what is written of them? 'Their hearts are divided — Now they will be laid waste!'" (חָבוּר עֲצַבִּים אֶפְרַיִם הַנַּח לוֹ, אֲבָל מִשֶּׁנֶּחְלְקוּ מַה הוּא אוֹמֵר: חָלַק לִבָּם עַתָּה יֶאְשָׁמוּ). The term נחלק is a Hebrew term, referring to a difference of opinion. See Matt 12:25; Mark 3:25.

[90] Greek: ἐν Βεελζεβοὺλ. "ἐν" mimics the Hebrew preposition בּ.

[91] The action of casting out demons is expressed as "proof" of the kingdom of God. See Deut 9:10: "And the LORD delivered to me the two tables of stone written with the *finger of God*" (וַיִּתֵּן יְהוָה אֵלַי אֶת-שְׁנֵי לוּחֹת הָאֲבָנִים כְּתֻבִים בְּאֶצְבַּע אֱלֹהִים). In context, Jesus is suggesting that while even the pagan magicians recognized God's power, you have not. See also Exod 8:15: "Then the magicians said to Pharaoh: 'This is the *finger of God*'" (וַיֹּאמְרוּ הַחַרְטֻמִּם אֶל-פַּרְעֹה אֶצְבַּע אֱלֹהִים הִוא); Ex 31:18: "...the two tables of the testimony, tables of stone, written with the *finger of God*" (שְׁנֵי לֻחֹת הָעֵדֻת לֻחֹת אֶבֶן כְּתֻבִים בְּאֶצְבַּע אֱלֹהִים); *Test. Levi* 18:12: "And Beliar shall be bound by him, and he shall give power to his children to tread upon evil spirits."

[92] Note *Pss. Sol.* 5:4: "For no man takes the spoil from a mighty man."

which he trusted, and divides his spoils. **23 The one who is not with me is against me,**[93] and **the one who does not gather with me scatters.**[94]

When an Unclean Spirit Returns

Demons were frequently referenced in rabbinic literature and were said to inhabit desolate, dry places. One of the divine punishments on the city of Jerusalem was said to be habitation by demons.

Luke 11:24 When an unclean spirit has gone out of a man, **it passes through dry places,**[95] seeking rest; and finding none, it says: I will return to **my house**[96] from which I came out. **25** And having come, it finds it swept and in order. **26** Then it goes, and takes seven other spirits more evil than itself; and having entered, they dwell there; and the last state of that man is worse than the first.

---

[93] Note *m. Avot* 1:14, citing Hillel: "If I am not for myself, who is for me?" (אִם אֵין אֲנִי לִי, מִי לִי).

[94] Note *Sifre Zuta*, Pinchas ed., 316–17, citing Hillel: "In a time when men scatter, gather; when there is no demand, buy then; and in a place where there are no men, be a man" (וּבְמָקוֹם שֶׁאֵין אֲנָשִׁים, הִשְׁתַּדֵּל לִהְיוֹת אִישׁ). It has been argued that Jesus had a similar sense of self-awareness as Hillel, or the Dead Sea sect's "Teacher of Righteousness." In the Lucan context, a moment of revival had begun in Israel, though it needed to be centered on Jesus; separate initiatives would not "gather" but "scatter."

[95] Note *b. Ber.* 3b: "The Sages taught, for three reasons one may not enter a ruin: Because of suspicion of prostitution, because the ruin is liable to collapse, and because of demons" (תָּנוּ רַבָּנָן, מִפְּנֵי שְׁלֹשָׁה דְּבָרִים אֵין נִכְנָסִין לְחוּרְבָּה: מִפְּנֵי חָשָׁד, מִפְּנֵי הַמַּפּוֹלֶת, וּמִפְּנֵי הַמַּזִּיקִין); Baruch 4:33–35, regarding Jerusalem: "For just as she rejoiced at your fall and was glad for your ruin, so she will be grieved at her own desolation … For fire will come upon her from the Everlasting for many days, and for a long time she will be inhabited by demons."

[96] Note *b. Hul.* 105b: "There was a certain man who was pursued by the ministering angel of poverty but could not prevail… He subsequently heard the ministering angel of poverty say: Woe is me, as that man has removed me *from my house*" (ההוא גברא דהוה מהדר עליה שרא דעניותא ולא הוה יכיל ליה … שמעיה דקאמר ווי דאפקיה ההוא *גברא מביתיה*); *b. Git.* 52a: "He then heard Satan say: Woe, that Rabbi Meir removed that man, Satan, from *his house*" (שמעיה דקאמר ווי דאפקיה להההוא גברא ר' מאיר *מביתיה*).

Scene 11:
The Lawyer's Question and the Good Samaritan

The Good Samaritan account makes no mention of disciples, and for this reason it may have taken place in the unhurried atmosphere of the early period of Jesus' proto-rabbinic career, perhaps in Judea.[97]

Luke 10:25 And, **behold,**[98] a certain **lawyer**[99] stood up, and tested him, saying: **Teacher,**[100] what shall I do to inherit **eternal life?**[101] **26** He said to him: What is written in the law? How do you read it? **27** And he, answering, said: **You shall love the Lord your God with all your heart, and with all your soul, and with all your strength, and with all your mind; and your neighbor as**

---

[97] See Lindsey, *Jesus*, 65. See also Brad Young, *The Parables: Jewish Tradition and Christian Interpretation* (Grand Rapids: Baker Academic, 1998), 101–18.

[98] The Greek ἰδοὺ is used in imitation of the Hebrew הִנֵּה.

[99] The Greek νομικός suggests the Hebrew חכם; i.e. a student of the Torah.

[100] The Greek Διδάσκαλε ("Teacher") translates the Hebrew רבי ("Rabbi"), in its early, pre-tannaitic meaning, before it came to be used as a title.

[101] Note *m. Avot* 2:7: "If one acquires for himself knowledge of Torah, he has acquired life in the world to come" (קָנָה לוֹ חַיֵּי הָעוֹלָם הַבָּא).

yourself.[102] **28** And he said to him: You have answered correctly; do this, and you shall live.

Jesus' View of the Torah

Given that the lawyer quotes Scripture, D. Flusser theorized that Jesus' lengthy discussion of his view of the Torah (from Matthew's "Sermon on the Mount"), leading to the question of who is one's neighbor, belongs here.[103]

---

[102] See Deut 6:5: "And you shall love the LORD you God with all your heart, and with all you soul, and with all your might" (וְאָהַבְתָּ, אֵת יְהוָה אֱלֹהֶיךָ, בְּכָל-לְבָבְךָ וּבְכָל-נַפְשְׁךָ, וּבְכָל-מְאֹדֶךָ). "With all your *mind* (διανοίᾳ)" is added, as if to explain the meaning of the Hebrew word "heart" (לב), which, to an ancient audience, was synonymous with the thinking process. See also Lev 19:18: "You shall love your neighbor as yourself" (וְאָהַבְתָּ לְרֵעֲךָ כָּמוֹךָ). "Love" here is followed by the unusual construction ל (as in לעזור ל/"to help"). This expression is used rarely, e.g. Lev 19:34 (loving the stranger as oneself); 1 Kings 5:1,15 (Hiram always loved David); 2 Chron 18:28–19:2 (The prophet says to Jehoshaphat: "Should you help the wicked and love those who hate the Lord?") In this construction "love" means "help." Therefore, one should be helpful to one's neighbor as one is to oneself. One is not commanded to feel but to do. See Matt 22:37–40; Mark 12:29–31; Luke 10:27. The first text where these two commandments are mentioned together is Jub. 36:9: "… that you will fear Him and worship Him. And that each will love his brother with affection and righteousness" (כי תיראו אותו ותכבדוהו וכי תאהבו איש את אחיו ברחמים ובאמת). Note *ARN* Ver. B 26 - "Rabbi Hanina, the Prefect of the Priests, says: An oath from Mount Sinai has been sworn on this saying ('Love your neighbor as yourself') upon which the whole world depends" (רבי חנינה סגן הכהנים אומר דבר שכל העולם כולו תלוי בו נאמר עליו מהר סיני). Note also *ARN* 16: *Hatred of Others*. How so? This teaches that a person should not say: Love the sages, but hate the scholars; or: Love the scholars, but hate the common people. Rather, love all of them, but hate the heretics, the enticers, the bad influences, and the traitors" (ושנאת הבריות כיצד מלמד שלא יכוין אדם לומר אהוב את החכמים ושנוא את התלמידים אהוב את התלמידים ושנוא את עמי הארץ [אלא אהוב את כולם] ושנוא את האפיקורסין והמסיתים ומדיחין וכן המסורות). See also *Test. Iss.* 5:2: "But love the Lord and your neighbor, Have compassion on the poor and weak." (ואהבו את־יי ואיש את־קרובו ועל־דל ועל־חולה תחמלו).

[103] See Lindsey, *Jesus*, 66.

Matthew 5:17 Do not think that **I have come**[104] to **destroy**[105] the **Law**[106] or the **Prophets.**[107] I have not come to destroy but to **fulfill.**[108] **18** For truly [Amen] **I say to you,**[109] till **heaven and earth pass away,**[110] **one** *iota/yod* **or one tittle will by no means pass from the law**[111] till all is fulfilled. **19** Whoever therefore

---

[104] The Greek aorist tense (ἦλθον) should be translated "I came," and does not convey the Hebrew (באתי), "I have come."

[105] The semitic undertext may have read להפר ("to end"), but more likely לבתל ("to cancel," i.e. "interpret incorrectly"), or לעקור ("to uproot"), cf. Ecc 3:2: "and a time to uproot that which is planted" (ועת לעקור נטוע).

[106] Compare Rom 3:31: "Do we then overthrow the law by this faith? By no means! On the contrary, we uphold the law."

[107] The "Writings" are omitted. Perhaps the "Writings" were not canonized until 65–140 CE. They are cited in an anti-sectarian passage in *b. Shab.* 116b.

[108] The semitic undertext may have read למלא ("to fill"), but more likely לקיים ("to establish," i.e. "interpret rightly"). Note the dichotomy here. Compare vv. 17–28 to the Didache: "There are two ways in the world, one of life and one of death, one of light and one of darkness." The Didache likely rests on a Hebrew source, similar to the Qumran Community Rule; see 1QS 4:2: "Upon earth their operations are these…" (ואלה דרכיהן בתבל), i.e. of the "two spirits." Note *m. Avot* 2:8–9: "Which is the right way to which a man should cleave?" (אֵיזוֹהִי דֶרֶךְ יְשָׁרָה שֶׁיִּדְבַּק בָּהּ הָאָדָם). See Flusser, *Judaism*, 499.

[109] Amen/"assuredly" (Heb. אמן) was commonly added after a strong statement. Note Jer 28:6: "***Amen!*** The Lord do so; the Lord perform your words which you have prophesied…" (אָמֵן, כֵּן יַעֲשֶׂה יְהוָה יָקֵם יְהוָה, אֶת-דְּבָרֶיךָ אֲשֶׁר נִבֵּאתָ). See Luke 4:24.

[110] Even the smallest portion of the Torah preserves the world, and therefore cannot be discarded. Note *Lev. R.* 19:2: "Should all the nations of the world unite ***to uproot one word of the Torah***, they would be unable to do so… The guilt of one who **destroys one letter** is so great that if done [all the world would be destroyed]." (אִם מִתְכַּנְּסִים כָּל אֻמּוֹת הָעוֹלָם **לַעֲקֹר דָּבָר אֶחָד מֵהַתּוֹרָה** אֵינָן יְכוֹלִין … עַל יְדֵי שֶׁבִּקֵּשׁ **לַעֲקֹר אוֹת אַחַת מִן הַתּוֹרָה** עָלָה קַטֵּיגוֹרוֹ). See Luke 16:17.

[111] Note *y. San.* 20c chap. 2, *Ex. Rab.* 6:1, in which Shimon b. Yochai said: "Solomon ***cancelled*** the Torah by deleting the לא and changing the negative commandments to positive ones. Who knows? Today he has ***abolished*** one letter; tomorrow he will ***abolish*** another, until the whole Torah will be nullified? God responded: Solomon and a thousand like him will pass away, but the ***smallest tittle*** will not be canceled from you." Note also *Gen. R.* 10:1: "The heavens and earth have their end; only one thing is excepted which has no end, and that is the Law." Note Philo, *Life of Moses*, 2:3: "The Law is immortal, as long as the sun and moon and whole universe exist"; *Ex. R.* 6:1: "Not a letter shall be abolished from the Law forever"; *b. Men.* 34b: "The Law had to be taught in respect to the ***tittle*** of the *yod.*"

breaks one of the **least of these commandments,**[112] and teaches men so, shall be called least in the kingdom of heaven; but **whoever does**[113] and teaches them, he shall be called **great**[114] in the kingdom of heaven. **20** For I say to you, that unless your **righteousness**[115] exceeds that of the scribes and Pharisees, you **will by no means enter [are not entering]**[116] the kingdom of heaven.

Murder Begins in the Heart

21 You have **heard**[117] that it was said to those of old: You shall not murder, and whoever murders will be in danger of the judgment. **22** But I say to you that whoever is **angry**[118] with his brother without a cause shall be in danger of the **judgment.**[119] And

---

[112] This echoes the rabbinic expression, "In the end, there will be no great or small commandments." Note the humorous play on words, in that whoever does not take the small commandments seriously (i.e. חמור) will himself be small—whoever makes little of the commandments will be little. Note *m. Avot* 2:1: "And be careful with a light commandment as with a *grave* one" (וֶהֱוֵי זָהִיר בְּמִצְוָה קַלָּה כְּבַחֲמוּרָה); *m. Avot* 4:2: "Be quick in performing a minor commandment as in the case of a *major* one" (הֱוֵי רָץ לְמִצְוָה קַלָּה כְּבַחֲמוּרָה). Three themes present themselves in the following verses: 1) the least of the commandments 2) the angry face judgment 3) lust. This parallels three themes found in Didache 3:1–6 1) flee anything resembling evil 2) anger leads to murder 3) covetousness leads to adultery. The Didache appears to rest on sources which underly the Sermon on the Mount. Both are linked to the second half of the Decalogue, e.g. Matt 22:37–40; Rom 13:9. See Flusser, *Judaism*, 494–508.

[113] Note the stress on *doing*.

[114] I.e. חמור.

[115] "Righteousness"; the Greek δικαιοσύνη translates the Hebrew צדקה. While the original meaning was "salvation," or "redemptive plan," it came to mean "almsgiving." See Job 29:14–16. Jesus' intent is that one must grasp the earlier, redemptive meaning of "righteousness" in order to experience the present-tense "kingdom of heaven."

[116] The future tense of the Greek μη εισέλθετε does not translate the hypothetical Hebrew original לא תבואו, which can suggest a present tense meaning: "You do not enter/are not entering...."

[117] The text does not say "It is written," but "You have heard," mimicking how the following proclamation comes out of the mouth of every observant Jew.

[118] Note *Tos. Derech Eretz* (edit. Higger, 312): "He who hates his neighbor is considered a murderer"; *Sifre Deut.* 186–7: "R. Eliezer said, 'He who hates his brother belongs to the shedders of blood!'" Note also *b. B.M.* 58b: "Anyone who humiliates another in public, it is as though he were spilling blood" (כל המלבין פני חבירו ברבים כאילו שופך דמים).

[119] In rabbinic times, "judgment" was determined by the *Bet Din*, a local body consisting of three members.

whoever says to his brother: **Raca!**[120] shall be in danger of the **council.**[121] But whoever says: You **fool!**[122] shall be in danger of hell fire. **23** Therefore if you bring your gift to the altar, and there remember that your brother has something against you, **24 leave your gift there before the altar,**[123] and go your way. First be reconciled to your brother, and then come and offer your gift. **25** Agree with your adversary quickly, while you are on the way with him, lest your adversary deliver you to the judge, the judge hand you over to the officer, and you be thrown into prison. **26** Truly, [**Amen.**][124] I say to you, you will by no means get out of there till you have paid the last penny.

Adultery in the Heart

Jesus, in rabbinic fashion, "builds a fence around the Torah," taking a stringent position. Anger leads to murder; lust leads to adultery.

27 You have heard that it was said to those of old: **You shall not commit adultery.**[125] **28** But I say to you that whoever looks at a woman to lust for her has already committed adultery with her in

---

[120] A semitism: רקא. In Hebrew ריק ("empty"). This was considered slander.

[121] Each town of over 150 inhabitants had a Sanhedrin. The small Sanhedrin was comprised of 23 members; the large 71.

[122] Note Ps 14:1: "The *fool* has said in his heart: 'There is no God'" (אָמַר נָבָל בְּלִבּוֹ, אֵין אֱלֹהִים). There is a progression here. Anger without cause leads to the *Bet Din*; slander leads to the Sanhedrin; but saying "fool" (נבל) means that the offender has usurped God in judgment, and is worthy of Gehenna.

[123] There are two categories of sin in Judaism: בין אדם למוקם ("between man and God") and בין אדם לאדם ("between man and man"). Sacrifice atones for the former, but even Yom Kippur does not atone for the latter unless the aggrieved party has been pacified and has agreed to forgive the wrongdoer.

[124] "Amen"/"assuredly" (Heb. אמן) was commonly added after a strong statement. Note Jer 28:6: "**Amen**! The Lord do so; the Lord perform your words which you have prophesied …" (אָמֵן, כֵּן יַעֲשֶׂה יְהוָה יָקֵם יְהוָה אֶת-דְּבָרֶיךָ אֲשֶׁר נִבֵּאתָ). See Luke 4:24.

[125] Heb. לא תנאף. The Sages noted that תנאף is spelled with four letters since adultery is committed with the *eyes*, the *hands*, the *heart*, and the *feet*; cf. Mark 9:45.

his **heart.**[126] **29** If your right **eye** causes you to sin, pluck it out and cast it from you; for it is more profitable for you that one of your members should perish, than for your whole body to be cast into hell. **30** And if your right **hand**[127] causes you to sin, cut it off and cast it from you; for it is more profitable for you that one of your members should perish, than for your whole body to be cast into hell.

On Divorce

Jesus appears to enter the Shammai-Hillel controversy, only allowing "fornication" as just cause for divorce.

31 It has been said: Whoever divorces his wife, let him give her a certificate of divorce. **32** But I say to you that whoever divorces his wife for any reason except for **fornication (sexual immorality)**[128] causes her to commit adultery; and whoever marries a woman who is divorced commits adultery.

On Oaths

Note the similarity to the teaching of the Dead Sea sect, who deemed God's Name too holy to swear by it.

33 Again you have heard that it was said to those of old: **You shall not swear falsely,**[129] but shall perform your oaths to the Lord.

---

[126] Note *Num. R.* 8:5: "Shall commit (Num 5:6). This is to teach that the moment a man contemplates sin it is as though he has committed a trespass …" Note also *Test. Benj.* 8:2: "He who has a pure **heart** in love looks not on a woman with thoughts of fornication"; *Lev. R.* 23:12 (attributed to Reish Lakish): "If he commits adultery with his *eyes* ... he is also an adulterer."

[127] This could be a subtle reference to the penis; cf. Isa 57:8: "You have loved their bed, Where you saw their *hand* [חזית יד/nudity]." Note *b. Ned.* 13b: "My mouth shall be forbidden with regard to my speech, or: My *hands* shall be forbidden with regard to their work, or: My feet should be forbidden with regard to their walking" (יֵאָסֵר פִּי לְדִיבּוּרִי). (יָדַי לְמַעֲשֵׂיהֶם רַגְלַי לְהִילוּכָן).

[128] See Luke 16:18.

[129] See Matt 23:16–20.

34 But I say to you, do not swear at all: neither by heaven, for it is God's throne; **35** nor by the earth, for it is his footstool; nor by Jerusalem, for it is the city of the great king. **36** Nor shall you **swear by [the life of] your head,**[130] because **you cannot make one hair white or black.**[131] **37** But **let your Yes be Yes, and your No, No.**[132] For whatever is more than these is from the evil one.

Eye for Eye, Tooth for Tooth

Rather than a blanket statement of pacifism, Jesus appears to be loosely quoting Psalm 37:7–11. Evildoers will be no more, and the humble will "inherit the earth." If by extension the Romans are divinely "cut off," there will be no need to engage or resist them.

38 You have heard that it was said: An eye for an eye and a tooth for a tooth. **39** But I tell you **not to resist evil.**[133]

---

[130] Note *m. Ned.* 2:2: "Vow *by the life of your head.*" The Greek text appears to have shortened the saying.

[131] Note *Lev. R.* 19:2: "If the nations gather to make *white* one wing of a raven, they would not be able to accomplish it."

[132] *Ruth R.* 3:4 says of the *Tzadikim* ("righteous") that their word is "Yes, yes; No, no." (הן הן לא לא). Note *b. Shav.* 36a: "But from where do we derive the fact that *yes* can be an oath? It is based on logical reasoning; from the fact that *no* can be an oath, *yes* too can be an oath. Rava said: And where one said *no, no,* two times, or where one said *yes, yes,* two times" (אלא הן שבועה מנא לן סברא הוא מדלאו שבועה הן נמי שבועה אמר רבא והוא דאמר לאו לאו תרי זימני והוא דאמר הן הן תרי זימני). See James 5:12, which is perhaps the earlier version: "But above all, my brethren, do not swear, either by heaven or by earth or with any other oath, but let your yes be yes and your no be no, that you may not fall under condemnation." Note B. Sira 23:9: "Do not accustom your mouth to swearing." See also Slav. Enoch 49:1–2. Some ultra-orthodox continue in the tradition of saying בלי נדר ("without an oath").

[133] Note Ps 37:7–11: "Resign yourself to the Lord, and wait patiently for Him; do not fret because of him who prospers in his way, because of the man who brings wicked devices to pass. Cease from anger, and forsake wrath; do no fret, it tends only to evil-doing. For evil-doers shall be cut off; but those that wait for the Lord shall inherit the earth. And yet a little while, and the wicked is no more; yea, you will look well at his place, and he is not. But the humble will inherit the earth, and delight themselves in abundance of peace" (דּוֹם לַיהוָה וְהִתְחוֹלֵל-לוֹ אַל-תִּתְחַר בְּמַצְלִיחַ דַּרְכּוֹ; בְּאִישׁ עֹשֶׂה מְזִמּוֹת. הֶרֶף מֵאַף וַעֲזֹב חֵמָה; אַל-תִּתְחַר אַךְ-לְהָרֵעַ. כִּי-מְרֵעִים יִכָּרֵתוּן; וְקֹוֵי יְהוָה הֵמָּה יִירְשׁוּ-אָרֶץ. וְעוֹד מְעַט וְאֵין רָשָׁע; וְהִתְבּוֹנַנְתָּ עַל-מְקוֹמוֹ וְאֵינֶנּוּ. וַעֲנָוִים יִירְשׁוּ-אָרֶץ; וְהִתְעַנְּגוּ עַל-רֹב שָׁלוֹם). See Matt 5:5.

Love Your Enemies (= Matthew 5:39–48) (RCT)

Jesus' teaching of love for one's enemies suggests that one should not seek vengeance; it is not an endorsement of pacifism. Like the Sages, he advised against exercising the prerogative of revenge: "He who is yielding, who ignores a slight or wrong, has all his sins forgiven" (b. Yoma 23a).

Luke 6:27 And I say to you who hear, Love your enemies, do good to those who hate you, **28** Bless those who curse you, and pray for those who despitefully use you. **29 And to him who strikes you on the one cheek offer also the other;**[134] and him who takes away your cloak **forbid not to take your coat**[135] also. **30 Give to every one who asks of you;/and of him who takes away your goods do not ask him again.**[136] **31 And as you wish**

---

[134] Rather than an overt endorsement of pacifism, this suggests that one should not seek vengeance. Note *m. B.K.* 8:1: "One who injures another is liable to pay compensation for that injury due to five types of indemnity: He must pay for damage, for pain, for medical costs, for loss of livelihood, and for humiliation" (הַחוֹבֵל בַּחֲבֵרוֹ חַיָּב עָלָיו מִשּׁוּם חֲמִשָּׁה דְבָרִים, בְּנֶזֶק, בְּצַעַר, בְּרִפּוּי, בְּשֶׁבֶת, וּבְבֹשֶׁת). In cases involving a private wrong, it was up to the injured to demand monetary payment. Jesus, like the Sages, advised against exercising the prerogative. Note *b. Yoma* 23a: "With regard to whoever forgoes his reckonings with others for injustices done to him, the heavenly court in turn forgoes punishment for all his sins" (כָּל הַמַּעֲבִיר עַל מִדּוֹתָיו — מַעֲבִירִין לוֹ עַל כָּל פְּשָׁעָיו). See also *m. B.K.* 8:6, indicating that a slap is more insulting than a punch: "***One who strikes another*** must give him a *sela*. Rabbi Yehuda says in the name of Rabbi Yosei HaGelili that he must give him one hundred dinars. If he ***slapped another on the cheek***, he must give him two hundred dinars. If he ***slapped him on the cheek with the back of his hand***, which is more degrading than a slap with the palm, he must give him four hundred dinars" (הַתּוֹקֵעַ לַחֲבֵרוֹ, נוֹתֵן לוֹ סֶלַע. רַבִּי יְהוּדָה אוֹמֵר מִשּׁוּם רַבִּי יוֹסֵי הַגְּלִילִי, מָנֶה. ***סְטָרוֹ***, נוֹתֵן לוֹ מָאתַיִם זוּז. ***לְאַחַר יָדוֹ***, נוֹתֵן לוֹ אַרְבַּע מֵאוֹת זוּז). See also y. *B.K.* 9:29: "If you are **struck** you must forgive the offender, even though he does not ask for your forgiveness." Note *Amidah* prayer: "May my soul be dust to all" (ונפשי כעפר לכל תהיה).

[135] Similar to the teaching of John the Baptist (Luke 3:10). Note the concept of sharing, as opposed to the Essene/Dead Sea sect doctrine of asceticism.

[136] Note the Hebrew *parallelism/poetry*. The Hebrew verb שאל means "to ask," or, in this case "to borrow." The admonition is not to get even with one who has wronged that person by refusing him a loan. Note *Sira* 20:15: "Today he lends and tomorrow he asks it back; such a one is hateful to God and humans."

that men should do to you, likewise do also to them.[137] **32** For if you love those who love you, what thanks do you have? for sinners also love those who love them. **33** And if you do good to those who do good to you, what thanks do you have? for sinners also do the same. **34** And if you lend to those of whom you hope to receive, what thanks do you have? for sinners also lend to sinners, to receive as much again. **35 But love your enemies, and do good, and lend, hoping for nothing again;**[138] and your reward shall be great, and you shall be the children of the Highest: for he is kind to the unthankful and to the evil. **36 Be therefore merciful, as your Father**[139] **also is merciful.**[140]

The Good Samaritan (ANT)

Jesus now returns to the issue of identifying the "neighbor" of the lawyer in Luke 10:27. The story ("parable") of the good Samaritan is a perfect expression of the rabbinic precept of saving a life (pikuakh nefesh), which supersedes every other Jewish law. The crowd expects the hero of the story to be a Pharisee since the Pharisee party actively advanced such early rabbinic precepts. The

---

[137] Note *b. Shab.* 31a (attributed to Hillel): "***That which is hateful to you do not do to another;*** that is the entire Torah, and the rest is its interpretation. Go study" (דַּעֲלָךְ סְנֵי לְחַבְרָךְ לָא תַעֲבֵיד—זוֹ הִיא כָּל הַתּוֹרָה כּוּלָּהּ, וְאִידַךְ פֵּירוּשָׁהּ הוּא, זִיל גְּמוֹר). See also Tobit 4:15: "And that which you hate, do not do to man"; Didache 1:2: "The way of life is this: first you shall love the God who made you... and whatever you would not have done to yourself, do not do to another."

[138] Likely added later, as the same is said earlier; vv. 27, 30.

[139] See Matt 5:48.

[140] A Hebraic play on words (active/הָיוּ רַחֲמִים/"be merciful" vs. passive/רַחוּם/"is merciful"). Note *Mekh. Ex.* 15:2: "Abba Shaul says: 'I will liken myself to Him' (i.e. *"ve'anvehu"* read as *"ani ve'hu"*/"I and He") ***Just as He is merciful and gracious, you, too, be merciful and gracious***" (אבא שאול אומר אדמה לו מה הוא רחום וחנון אף אתה רחום וחנון). Note also an anonymous exegete on Deut 10:12: "How can a man be called by the Name of God? As God is called merciful, you too must be merciful. The Holy One Blessed Be He is called gracious, so you too must be gracious ... and give presents *freely* (see Luke 11:13; Matt 10:8). See also *Sifre Deut.* 11:22: "God is called righteous, so you too must be called hasid." Note *Targum Ps. Jon.* on Lev 22:28: "As you father is merciful in heaven, so you must be merciful on earth." See Matt 6:10.

surprise is that a despised Samaritan behaves as if he were a Pharisee.[141]

Luke 10:29 But he, wanting to justify himself, said to Jesus: And who is my **neighbor?**[142] **30** And Jesus, answering, said: A certain man went down from Jerusalem to Jericho, and fell among thieves, who **stripped(1)** him of his clothes, and **wounded(2)** him, and **departed(3)**, leaving him **half dead(4)**.[143] **31** Now, by chance a certain **priest** came down on that road; and when he saw him, he passed by on the other side. **32** And likewise a **Levite**,[144] when he had come to the place, looked at him, and passed by on the other side. **33** But a certain **Samaritan**,[145] as he journeyed, came to where he was; and when he saw him, he had compassion on him, **34** And went to him, and **bound up his wounds(1), pouring on oil and wine(2)**, and set him on his own beast, and **brought him to an inn(3)**, and **took care of him(4)**.[146] **35** And on the next day, he

---

[141] See Young, *Jesus and His Jewish Parables*, 239–41.

[142] In Lev 19:18 the word "neighbor" (רֵעֶךָ) strictly means "someone near," not an "enemy." The Samaritan was regarded as an enemy, and not considered Jewish. Jesus therefore expands the meaning of "neighbor" to include enemies.

[143] In the story, the Samaritan reversed the actions of the bandits, who 1) stripped him; 2) beat him; 3) abandoned him 4) left him for dead.

[144] The Levite and priest were both Sadducees, who, like the Samaritans, rejected the Oral Law. They emphasized ritual purity, especially after serving in Jerusalem. They did not want to go through the process of ritual cleansing. Note the term "half-dead" (Heb. גוסס) and the rabbinic discussion (*b.* Gittin 28b) regarding who died and who was about to die. The rabbis were concerned that a dying person (גוסס) would not receive adequate care. Note *m. Sem.* 1:11: "A dying man is regarded as a living entity in respect of all matters in the world" (הגוסס הרי הוא כחי לכל דבר לעולם). All means must be used to save his life. Legal functions may be performed on his behalf (e.g. will and testaments). Any Torah law may be broken to save a life. In this case obeying the written law (Lev 21:11) would violate the Oral Law, which taught that even the high priest is required to become unclean to bury an abandoned corpse. See *m. Nazir* 7:1: "A High Priest and a Nazirite may not become ritually impure even to bury their deceased relatives. However, they become impure to bury a corpse with no one to bury it [*met mitzvah*]" (כֹּהֵן גָּדוֹל וְנָזִיר אֵינָן מִטַּמְּאִין לִקְרוֹבֵיהֶן, אֲבָל מִטַּמְּאִין לְמֵת מִצְוָה. הָיוּ מְהַלְּכִין בַּדֶּרֶךְ וּמָצְאוּ מֵת מִצְוָה). The expectation is for a Pharisee (following the Oral Torah) to be the hero; but the Samaritan is the true "neighbor." The message is: "Love your *enemy* as yourself."

[145] It has been suggested that instead of "Samaritan," the earliest text may have read "one of the people of the land" (עם הארץ). This of course would dilute the larger message of the parable.

[146] The Samaritan, not knowing to which sect he belonged 1) bound his wounds; 2) poured oil and wine on him; 3) took him to the inn; 4) paid his bills.

took out two denarii, and gave them to the innkeeper, and said to him: Take care of him; and whatever more you spend, when I come again, I will repay you. **36** Which now of these three, do you think was a neighbor to him who fell among the thieves? **37** And he said: The one who showed compassion on him. Then Jesus said to him: Go, and do likewise.

Scene 12:
Levi the Tax Collector (RCT)

Luke appears to have copied the story of Levi, the tax collector, from the reconstructed text (RCT). It may originally have been followed by the Parable of Lost Sheep and the Lost Coin (Luke 15:4–10), which were taken from the anthological text (ANT). The following reconstruction may belong to the Judean sojourn since the Lost Sheep parable references "scribes," who were connected with the Jerusalem temple. The narrative also appears to have been early since the twelve have yet to be called.[147]

Luke 5:27 And after these things he went forth, and saw a tax collector, named Levi, sitting at the tax booth; and he said to him: Follow me. **28** And he left all, rose up, and followed him. **29** And Levi made him a great banquet in his own house: and there was a great crowd of tax collectors and of others who sat down with them. **30** But the scribes and Pharisees murmured against his disciples, saying: Why do you eat and drink with tax collectors and sinners? **31** And Jesus answering said to them: **Those who are**

---

[147] See Lindsey, *Jesus*, 79.

whole have no *need* of a physician,[148] but those who are sick. **32** I came not to call the *righteous*, but *sinners* to *repentance*.[149]

Parable 1: The Lost Sheep[150] (ANT)

Luke 15:1–10 possibly belongs here. Following the call of Matthew, two parables (each containing unmistakable links to rabbinic thought and expression) have been transposed from Luke 15. As noted, it is theorized that in the hypothetical Hebraic grundschrift (prior to its "topical" reordering), an incident in the narrative would have been followed by a short teaching and two parables. In this case, Matthew's calling was followed by a teaching regarding repentance and the parables (from ANT) of the lost sheep and the lost coin.

Luke 15:1 Then all the tax collectors and sinners drew near to him to hear him. **2** And the Pharisees and **scribes**[151] murmured, saying: This man **receives sinners, and eats with them.**[152]   **3** And he spoke this parable to them, saying: **4** What man of you, having a hundred sheep, having lost one of them, does not leave the ninety-nine in the open field, and **go after the one that is lost, until he**

---

[148] Those who are "well" are the self-righteous. The banquet's "sinners" vs. the "righteous" is the context for the sheep and lost coin parables. God cares more for one who is aware of his spiritual condition (in Jewish terms not Torah observant) than for ninety-nine self-righteous. The words *need, righteous*, and *sinners* are linguistic links to the parables that follow.

[149] Note the subsequent repetition of the words "need," "righteous ones," "sinners," and "repentance/repents," (Luke 5:31–32; 15:7, 10) suggesting that these passages originally comprised a single story unit. See Lindsey, *Jesus*, 80.

[150] The shepherd motif is also present in the Dead Sea Scrolls CD13:9, regarding the Overseer of the community: "... he should care for them as a father does his children, taking care of all their problems as a shepherd does for his flock. " (וירחם עליהם כאב לבניו וישקה לכל מדהובם כרועה עדרו).

[151] The presence of scribes might suggest that verses 1–10 derive from a hypothetical early Judean sojourn (prior to the call of the disciples) since they are linked to the temple.

[152] Note *Mekh. Ex.* 18:1:2: "Let one not befriend an *evildoer*, even to draw him close to Torah" (אל יתחבר אדם לרשע אפילו לקרבו לתורה). See Luke 5:30–32.

finds it?[153] **5** And when he has found it, he lays it on his shoulders, rejoicing. **6** And when he comes home, he calls together his friends and neighbors, saying to them: Rejoice with me; for I have found my sheep that was lost. **7** I say to you, that likewise there will be joy in heaven over one ***sinner*** who repents, more than over ninety-nine ***righteous ones***, who ***need*** no ***repentance***.[154]

Parable 2: The Lost Coin

The "lost sheep" finds a parallel in the "lost coin," which echoes a saying in Canticles Rabba: "If a man loses a coin in his house he kindles many lights, and seeks until he finds it." The last part of Chapter 5 (verses 33–39) has been transposed to a later section of the book, as Lindsey and Flusser theorized.

Luke 15:8 Or what woman having ten drachmas, if she should **lose one drachma,**[155] does not light a candle, and sweep the house, and seek diligently until she finds it? **9** And when she has found it, she calls her friends and her neighbors together, saying: Rejoice with me; for I have found the drachma that I lost. **10** Likewise, I say to

---

[153] Note *Ex. Rab.* 2:2: "Once, while Moses our Teacher was tending [his father-in-law] Yitro's sheep, one of the sheep ran away. Moses ran after it... He then put the lamb on his shoulders and carried him back. The Holy One said, 'Since you tend the sheep of human beings with such overwhelming love - by your life, I swear you shall be the shepherd of My sheep, Israel.'" (כְּשֶׁהָיָה מֹשֶׁה רַבֵּינוּ עָלָיו הַשָּׁלוֹם רוֹעֶה צֹאנוֹ שֶׁל יִתְרוֹ בַּמִּדְבָּר, בָּרַח מִמֶּנּוּ גְּדִי, וְרָץ אַחֲרָיו ... הִרְכִּיבוֹ עַל כְּתֵפוֹ וְהָיָה מְהַלֵּךְ. אָמַר הַקָּדוֹשׁ בָּרוּךְ הוּא, יֵשׁ לְךָ רַחֲמִים לִנְהֹג צֹאנוֹ שֶׁל בָּשָׂר וָדָם כָּךְ חַיֶּיךָ אַתָּה תִּרְעֶה צֹאנִי יִשְׂרָאֵל, הֲוֵי: וּמֹשֶׁה הָיָה רוֹעֶה).

[154] Note the repetition of the words "need," "righteous ones," "sinners," and "repentance/repents," (Luke 5:31–32; 15:7, 10) suggesting that these passages originally comprised a single story unit.

[155] Note *Cant. R.* 1:9: "If a man **loses a coin** in his house he **kindles many lights**, and seeks until he finds it. If for something which affords only and hour's life in this world a man kindles many lights and searches until he finds it, how much more should you dig as for hidden treasure after the words of the Law, which gives both life in this world and in the world to come" (מְשַׁל לְאָדָם אִם **מְאַבֵּד סֶלַע** אוֹ כִילָרִין בְּתוֹךְ בֵּיתוֹ, הוּא **מַדְלִיק כַּמָּה נֵרוֹת**, כַּמָּה פְּתִילוֹת, עַד שֶׁיַּעֲמֹד עֲלֵיהֶם. וַהֲרֵי דְּבָרִים קַל וָחֹמֶר, וּמָה אֵלּוּ שֶׁהֵם חַיֵּי שָׁעָה שֶׁל עוֹלָם הַזֶּה אָדָם מַדְלִיק כַּמָּה נֵרוֹת וְכַמָּה פְּתִילוֹת עַד שֶׁיַּעֲמֹד עֲלֵיהֶם וְיִמְצָאֵם, דִּבְרֵי תוֹרָה שֶׁהֵם חַיֵּי הָעוֹלָם הַזֶּה וְחַיֵּי הָעוֹלָם הַבָּא).

you, there is joy before the angels of God over one *sinner* **who repents**.[156]

Scene 13:
Mary and Martha

The story of Mary and Martha underscores an early rabbinic teaching found in the Mishnah, that one's house should be a meeting place for the wise and that one should sit in the dust of their feet, drinking in their words. John's Gospel identifies their house as being located in Bethany, which would place this incident during Jesus' Judean sojourn (or perhaps after his final triumphant arrival in Jerusalem). In the following reconstruction, the initial "incident" is supplemented by a teaching "doublet" concerning "the ravens" and "the lilies" (Luke 12:22–31). These are followed by two parables, "The Rich Fool" (Luke 12:16–20) and "The Rich Man and Lazarus" (Luke 16:19–31), in which Jesus takes aim at the Sadducees, who (unlike the Pharisees) were his natural adversaries. Rejecting the notion of the hereafter (Gehimon), they will not believe "Moses and the prophets" (who for Sadducees were their only authority). In a rabbinic kal v'khomer ("light and heavy"/a fortiori) argument, they will not be persuaded even if one were to rise from the dead.

Luke 10:38 Now, as they went, he entered into a certain village; and a certain woman named **Martha**[157] received him **into her house**.[158] **39** And she had a sister called Mary, who also **sat at**

---

[156] Note the repetition of the words "need," "righteous ones," "sinners," and "repentance/repents," (Luke 5:31–32; 15:7, 10) suggesting that these passages originally comprised a single story unit.

[157] Feminine form of מר/*Mar*, meaning "madam," "lady," "mistress."

[158] Note *m. Avot* 1:4: "May your house be a meeting house for Sages, roll in the dust of their feet and drink their words thirstily" (יְהִי בֵיתְךָ בֵית וַעַד לַחֲכָמִים, וֶהֱוֵי מִתְאַבֵּק בַּעֲפַר רַגְלֵיהֶם, וֶהֱוֵי שׁוֹתֶה בְצָמָא אֶת דִּבְרֵיהֶם). If one followed a rabbi, one would become "dusty" from the road.

Jesus' **feet**,[159] and **heard his word.**[160] **40** But Martha was distracted about much serving, and came to him, and said: Lord, do you not care that my sister has left me to serve alone? Speak to her, therefore, that she might help me. **41** And Jesus answered and said to her: Martha, Martha, you are **worried**[161] and troubled about many things; **42** But one thing is necessary, and Mary has chosen **the good portion,**[162] which will not be taken away from her.

Consider the Ravens

The Mary and Martha story is theorized to be followed by Luke 12:22–31 (= Matt 6:25–34), Luke 12:13–20, and Luke 16:19–31, producing one of the longer Gospel accounts. The expression "how much more" is typical of rabbinic discourse.

Luke 12:22 And he said to his disciples: Therefore I say to you, **Do not be anxious**[163] for your **life,**[164] what you should eat; neither for your body, what you should put on. **23** For life is more than food, and the body is more than clothing. **24** Consider the **ravens,**[165] for they neither sow nor reap; who have neither a storehouse nor a **barn;**[166] and God feeds them. **How much**

---

[159] The Greek παρακαθεσθεῖσα πρὸς τοὺς πόδας translates the Hebrew expression ישבה לרגליו.

[160] The Greek ἤκουεν τὸν λόγον αὐτοῦ translates the Hebrew שמעה את דבריו, producing a rhyming parallelism with ישבה לרגליו. Mary's attentiveness exemplifies the occasional place of women as scholars and sages in Jewish society. In rabbinic literature the wife of Rabbi Meir, Bruriah, who was admired for her breadth of knowledge. According to Rashi, she made light of the Talmudic assertion (*b. Shab.* 33b.) that "women are light-minded" (נָשִׁים דַּעְתָּן קַלָּה עֲלֵיהֶן).

[161] The theme of "worry" ties this passage to Luke 12:22–31 (= Matt 6:25–34).

[162] Note *b. Qid.* 42a: "If orphans came to divide their father's property, the court appoints a steward for them, and they select for them *a fine portion*" יתומים שבאו (לחלוק בנכסי אביהם בית דין מעמידים להם אפוטרופוס ובוררים להם **חלק יפה**).

[163] Connects the story to Martha; Luke 10:41.

[164] Greek ψυχῇ ("soul"); Hebrew נפש. This links Luke 12:22–31 ("Consider the Ravens") to Luke 12:16–21 ("The Rich Fool").

[165] "Raven" vs. Matt 6:26 "birds." Ravens, being unclean, may sharpen the point; cf. Ps. 147:9: "He gives to the beast his food, and to the young ravens who cry" (נוֹתֵן לִבְהֵמָה לַחְמָהּ לִבְנֵי עֹרֵב אֲשֶׁר יִקְרָאוּ).

[166] The word "barn" links this section to Luke 12:18 ("store"). See Lindsey, *Jesus,* 89.

more[167] valuable are you than the birds? **25** And which of you, being anxious, can add one hour to his lifespan? **26** If, then, you are not able to do even the least thing, why are you anxious about the rest?

Consider the Lillies

Luke 12:27 Consider the lilies, how they grow. They do not toil, nor do they spin; and yet I say to you, that Solomon in all his glory was not arrayed like one of these. **28** If, then, God so clothes the grass, which today is in the field, and tomorrow is thrown into the oven; **how much more**[168] will he clothe you, O you of little faith? **29** And do not seek what you might eat, or what you might drink, nor be of doubtful mind. **30** For all the nations of the world seek after these things. Now, your Father knows that you have need of these things. **31** But **seek**[169] his kingdom, and all these things will be added to you.

Parable 1: The Rich Fool

The addition of Luke 12:13–21 provides the first of two parables (linked to v. 24 by the word "barn") to complete the narrative unit. Rabbinic teaching does not eschew material things but does not make them the goal of life.

Luke 12:13 And one from the crowd said to him: Teacher, speak to my brother, that he divide the inheritance with me. 14 And he said to him: Man, who made me a judge or a partitioner over you?[170] **15** And he said to them: Take heed, and

---

[167] A rabbinic methodology: "light and heavy" (קַל וָחוֹמֶר); in Latin *a fortiori* ("from the stronger case").

[168] A rabbinic methodology: "light and heavy" (קַל וָחוֹמֶר).

[169] See Matt 6:33; Job; 29:16: "I *was* a father to the poor, And I **searched** out the case that I did not know" (אָב אָנֹכִי לָאֶבְיוֹנִים וְרִב לֹא-יָדַעְתִּי **אֶחְקָרֵהוּ**).

[170] vv. 13–14 likely represent an editorial emendation, to place the parable which follows in a different location.

beware of covetousness; for one's **life does not consist of the abundance of the things**[171] which he possesses. **16** And he spoke a parable to them, saying: The ground of **a certain rich man**[172] brought forth abundantly: **17** And he thought to himself, saying: What shall I do, because I have no place to store my fruits? **18** And he said: I will do this. I will tear down my **barns,**[173] and build larger; and there will I store all my grain and my produce. **19** And I will say **to my soul:**[174] Soul, you have **many goods**[175] laid up for many years; be at ease, eat, drink, and be merry. **20** But God said to him: You fool, this night your soul shall be required of you; then **whose shall those things be, which you have prepared?**[176] **21** So is he who stores up treasure for himself, but is not rich toward God.

Parable 2: The Rich Man and Lazarus

The addition of Luke 16:19–31 continues the warning about riches and completes the narrative unit with a second parable.

Luke 16:19 There was **a certain rich man,**[177] who was clothed in purple and fine linen, and made good cheer every day. **20** And

---

[171] Note *b. San.* 29b, suggesting that human nature is never satisfied: "A person is prone to make false statements so as not to make himself appear sated" (אדם עשוי שלא להשביע את עצמו).

[172] This language links the parable to Luke 16:19 ("The Rich Man and Lazarus").

[173] The first part of the teaching ("Consider the Ravens") is theoretically linked to "The Parable of the Rich Fool" by the words "barn" (Luke 12:24) and "barns" (Luke 12:18).

[174] Hebraism: לנפשי. The word "soul" ($\psi\nu\chi\tilde{\eta}$/נפש) unites the second and third fragments. Two "doublets" ("ravens"/"birds" and "lillies") belong to the main body; two parables ("The Rich Fool" and "The Rich Man and Lazarus") conclude it.

[175] The words "many goods" ($\pi o\lambda\lambda\grave{\alpha}\ \grave{\alpha}\gamma\alpha\theta\grave{\alpha}$) links this passage to Luke 16:25: "your good things" ($\tau\grave{\alpha}\ \grave{\alpha}\gamma\alpha\theta\acute{\alpha}\ \sigma o\upsilon$).

[176] Note Sir. 11:18–19: "Some become rich through a miser's life, and this is their allotted reward: When they say: 'I have found rest, now I will feast on my goods,' They do not know how long it will be till they die and leave them to others."

[177] Perhaps a Sadducee. This language links the story to Luke 12:16 (the "Rich Fool" parable).

there was a certain poor man named **Lazarus,**[178] who was laid at his gate, full of sores, **21** And desiring to be **fed with that which fell from the rich man's table.**[179] But even the dogs came and licked his sores. **22 And it came to pass,**[180] that the poor man died, and was **carried by the angels into Abraham's bosom.**[181] The rich man also died, and was buried; **23** And **in Hades he lifted up his eyes, being in torment,**[182] and seeing Abraham from afar, and Lazarus in his bosom. **24** And he cried and said: Father Abraham, have mercy on me, and send Lazarus, **that he might dip the tip of his finger in water,**[183] and cool my tongue; for I am suffering in

---

[178] Shortened form of Eliezer (אליעזר); a slurring of the guttural, common among Galileans.

[179] Note *b. Bez.* 32b: "The Sages taught: There are three whose lives are not lives, and they are as follows: One who *looks to the table of others* for his sustenance; and one whose wife rules over him; and *one whose body is ruled by suffering*" (תָּנוּ רַבָּנַן שְׁלֹשָׁה חַיֵּיהֶן אֵינָם חַיִּים וְאֵלּוּ הֵן הַמְצַפֶּה לְשֻׁלְחַן חֲבֵירוֹ וּמִי שֶׁאִשְׁתּוֹ מוֹשֶׁלֶת עָלָיו וּמִי שֶׁיִּסּוּרִין מוֹשְׁלִין בְּגוּפוֹ).

[180] The Greek ἐγένετο δὲ translates the Hebrew וַיְהִי.

[181] Note *Test. Asher* 6:4–6: "For the latter ends of men do show righteousness when they meet the **angels** of the Lord and of Satan. For when the soul departs troubled, it is tormented by an evil spirit… But if he is peaceful with joy, he meets the **angel** of peace."

[182] If the rich man were a Sadducee, he would now be aware of the error of disbelief in the hereafter. Note *Mid. Ps.* 28:3 (115a); *y. Hag.* 2, 77d (38): "Woe to him who takes his portion with the wicked … The wicked have but a single hour. They eat what is theirs … then … go down to **Gehinom.**" *Gehinom* fits the context better, being a place of fiery torment. Jeremias notes that the Greek ᾅδη can also translate *Gehinom*.

[183] Note *y. Hag.* 2, 77d: "Two godly men lived in Ashkelon… One of them died, and kindness was not shown to him [i.e. no one came to his funeral]. The son of Mayan, a tax collector, died, and the whole city stopped work… The [surviving] pious man complained… He saw a vision, and one said to him, 'Do not despise the children of the Lord. The one [the pious] had committed one sin and departed in it [i.e. his funeral canceled it], and the other [the wealthy publican] had performed one good deed and departed in it [i.e. his splendid funeral canceled it]…' After some days the pious man saw in a dream his companion walking in the Garden… And he saw the tax collector, and his tongue **sought to drink at the brink of a river; he tried to reach the water, but he could not.**" Note also *Ruth R.* 3:3, regarding two men who died: "One repented of evil before his death, while the other did not. The former stands in the company of the righteous, while his fellow in the company of the wicked and beholding him he says, 'Woe is me!' … And they [the angels] say to him, 'You fool! You were despicable *after your death and lay for three days*, and did they not drag you to your grave with ropes?… Do you know that this world is like the Sabbath and the world from which you came is like the eve of the Sabbath? If a man does not prepare a meal on the eve of the Sabbath, what shall we eat on the Sabbath?'" (אֶחָד מֵהֶן עָשָׂה תְשׁוּבָה לִפְנֵי מוֹתוֹ וְאֶחָד לֹא עָשָׂה תְשׁוּבָה, נִמְצָא זֶה עוֹמֵד בַּחֲבוּרַת הַצַּדִּיקִים, וְזֶה עוֹמֵד בַּחֲבוּרַת הָרְשָׁעִים, וְהוּא רוֹאֶה אוֹתוֹ וְאוֹמֵר אוֹי לִי… וְאוֹמְרִין לוֹ, שׁוֹטֶה שֶׁבְּעוֹלָם. מְנֻוָּל הָיִיתָ וּמֻשְׁלָךְ לְאַחַר מִיתָתְךָ שְׁלֹשֶׁת יָמִים וְלֹא בַּחֲבָלִים גְּרָרוּךְ לַקֶּבֶר… אֵין אַתָּה יוֹדֵעַ שֶׁעוֹלָם שֶׁבָּעוֹלָם, זֶה דוֹמֶה לְשַׁבָּת וְעוֹלָם שֶׁבָּאתָ מִמֶּנּוּ דוֹמֶה לְעֶרֶב שַׁבָּת, אִם אֵין אָדָם מְתַקֵּן בְּעֶרֶב שַׁבָּת מַה יֹּאכַל בְּשַׁבָּת).

this flame. **25** But Abraham said: Son, remember that you in your lifetime you received **your good things,**[184] and likewise Lazarus evil things. But now he is comforted, and you are suffering. **26** And besides all this, between us and you a **great chasm has been fixed;**[185] so that those desiring to pass from here to you cannot; nor can they pass from there to us. **27** Then he said: I implore you, then, Father, that you would send him to my father's house: **28** For I have **five brothers;**[186] so that he might warn them, that they also might not come to this place of torment. **29** Abraham said to him: They have Moses and the prophets; let them hear them. **30** And he said: No, Father Abraham: but if one went to them from the dead, they will repent. **31** And he said to him: If they do not hear **Moses and the prophets,**[187] neither will they be persuaded, even if one should rise from the dead.

Scene 14:
A Sinful Woman Forgiven (RCT)

When Jesus forgives the sinful woman at the house of the Pharisee, he assumes an almost Godlike authority in his declaration that her sins are forgiven. The Hebraic sense of the passage easily connects with Leviticus 4:26 ("… and the priest shall make atonement for him as concerning his sin, and he shall be forgiven - וְנִסְלַח לוֹ"). In John 12, this story appears six days before Passover, also at the home of Simon the Leper. However, Luke's chronology may be correct, and the story may have taken place during one of Jesus' earlier trips to Jerusalem (if one accepts John's references to earlier visits). Luke may not have been concerned with the exact geographic location. It has been theorized (by Yigael Yadin) that

---

[184] The words "your good things" (τὰ ἀγαθά σου) links this passage to Luke 12:19: "many goods" (πολλὰ ἀγαθὰ).

[185] Note 1 En. 22:9: "And this **division** has bas been made for the spirits of the righteous."

[186] Representing the five books of Moses.

[187] If the rich man were a **Sadducee**, Moses and the prophets would be his only authority.

Jesus deliberately made himself unclean prior to entering Jerusalem in order to show his displeasure with rigid purification ordinances (as evident among the Dead Sea sectarians).

Luke 7:36 Now one of the Pharisees[188] was asking him to eat with him. **And he went into the Pharisee's house,**[189] and reclined. **37** And, **behold,**[190] there was a woman in **the city,**[191] who was a **sinner,**[192] and when she knew that Jesus had reclined in the Pharisee's house, brought an alabaster flask of fragrant oil, **38** And stood at his feet behind him weeping, **and began to wash his feet with tears, and wiped them with the hairs of her head, and kissed his feet, and anointed them with the fragrant oil.**[193] **39** Now when the Pharisee who had invited him saw this, he spoke within himself, saying: This man, if he were a **prophet,**[194] would have known who and what this woman is who touches him; for she is a sinner. **40** And Jesus answered and said to him: Simon, I have something to say to you. And he said: Teacher, say it. **41** There was

---

[188] Sometimes identified as Simon the Pharisee, perhaps Shimon ben Gamliel.

[189] Travelers entering a house in Jerusalem or any of the outlying villages might have been expected to undergo a number of forms of ritual purification. Such rituals included the washing and anointing of feet to rid them of impurities derived from the road.

[190] The Greek ἰδού is used in imitation of the Hebrew הִנֵּה.

[191] Identified as Bethany in John, Mark and Matthew.

[192] Perhaps an unchaste woman, who did not keep her hair covered as a sign of immodesty.

[193] Contrary to the claims of many scholars, the anointing of Jesus' feet would not have been out of place in first century Jerusalem. The woman is apparently a member of the household. That the oil was perfumed and therefore expensive indicates that the household was well off. The tears symbolically represent a preliminary washing of feet with water that would have been done before any oil was applied. At Suba, near Ein Kerem, a stone installation was found that was used for the cultic anointing of feet with oil, inside a cave, perhaps used by followers of John the Baptist. See Shmuel Gibson, *The Cave of John the Baptist: The First Archaeological Evidence of the Truth of the Gospel Story* (London: Century, 2004).

[194] Early Greek manuscripts contain the definite article for the word "prophet": ("*the* prophet"/ὁ προφήτης). Note also Dead Sea Scrolls 1QS 9:10–11, which relates that the men of holiness "… shall govern themselves using the original precepts by which the men of the Yahad began to be instructed, doing so until there come the **Prophet** and the Messiahs of Aaron and Israel" (ונשפטו במשפטים הרשונים אשר החלו אנשי היחד לתיסר בם עד בוא נביא ומשיחי אהרון וישראל). The Qumran sectarians apparently expected three leading men at the end of days. Cave 4 *Messianic Anthology* also links the *prophet* with Deut 18 and the messiahs with Num 24:15–17 and Deut 3:8–11.

a certain creditor who had two debtors; one owed five hundred denarii, and the other fifty. **42** And when they had nothing to pay, he forgave them both. Which of them, therefore, will love him most? **43** Simon answered and said: I suppose he to whom he forgave most. And he said to him: You have rightly judged **44** And he turned to the woman, and said to Simon: Do you see this woman? I entered into your house, you gave me no water for my feet; but she has washed my feet with tears, and wiped them with the hair of her head. **45** You gave me no kiss; but this woman from the time I came in has not ceased kissing my feet. **46** You did not anoint my head with oil; but this woman has anointed my feet with fragrant oil. **47** Therefore I say to you: **Her sins, which are many, have been forgiven;**[195] for she loved much; but to whom little is forgiven, he loves little. **48** And he said to her: Your sins are forgiven. **49** And those reclining with him began to say within themselves: Who is this who even forgives sins? **50** And he said to the woman: Your faith has saved you; go in peace.

---

[195] See Luke 5:20; Lev 4:26. Greek "sins are forgiven" easily goes back to Hebrew: נסלחו לו.

The Return to Galilee

The Lucan narrative places Jesus in his hometown, Nazareth, following his immersion by John and the temptation in the Judean wilderness. This placement, however, seems too early. It is easily assumed that Jesus began his proto-rabbinic career as a healer, in Capernaum and its vicinity. It is likely that crowds began to gather, though not yet the "multitudes" often imagined, and which possibly did develop as his fame later grew. Nor had he called his twelve disciples, though we are told that he healed Simon's (Peter's) mother-in-law. For some time he continued healing and teaching in Galilee, though we are told thereafter that "he preached in the synagogues of Judea" (Luke 4:44). It is difficult to imagine that no record of such a "Judean sojourn" would have survived, and for this reason, a significant number of narrative units, traditionally viewed as being located in Galilee, have been transposed to this point in the hypothetical Ur-text (*grundschrift*). It is after this theorized Judean sojourn that he presumably returned to Nazareth, where the comment in Luke 4:23 now makes sense, chronologically: "Whatever we have heard done in Capernaum, do also here in your hometown." Subsequently, having called his disciples, it appears that Galilee became the "hub" of Jesus' activity and that his travels through the region culminated in his decision to return to Jerusalem for Passover and for what would become his final days. As for Galilee itself, it is arguably the case that the whole notion of an illiterate, pastoral, poverty-stricken population of peasants, desperate for societal reform, needs to be reconsidered. Josephus attests that Galilee was a land of rich fertility and very highly cultivated. He observes:

"Moreover the cities lie here very thick; and the very many villages are everywhere so full of people by the richness of the soil that the very least of them contain above 15,000 inhabitants" (*War*, III, iii, 2). As a region, it was well-suited for the work and "mission" of Jesus. While the exact order of the original narrative units cannot be known with certainty, the following represents an attempt to reconstruct a plausible sequence.

Scene 1:
Jesus' Reception in Nazareth (RCT)

In Luke, the placement of this pericope immediately follows the account of Jesus' temptation and before he arrived in Capernaum. It is suggested, however, that the Nazareth story likely took place at a later time since, according to Luke 4:23, Jesus had he had already been in Capernaum. In this reconstruction, it is placed after his hypothetical Judean sojourn. Luke preserves a highly Hebraic and much longer account than Mark and Matthew. Combining it with other story units allows for a more "original" narrative.[1]

Luke 4:16 And he came to Nazareth, where he had been brought up; and, as his custom was, he went into the synagogue on the Sabbath day, and **stood up for to read.**[2] **17** And there was given to him the scroll of the prophet Isaiah. And when he had opened the scroll, he found the place where it was written: **18** The Spirit of the Lord is upon me, because he has **anointed**[3] me to proclaim good news to the poor; he has sent me **[to heal the brokenhearted], to**

---

[1] See Lindsey, *Jesus*, 38–43.

[2] Jesus acts as a traditional Jewish religious itinerant preacher, later known as a *magid* (מַגִּיד).

[3] Reading a passage from the Prophets came to be standard synagogue practice after the reading of the weekly Torah portion. Isa 61:1: "The spirit of the Lord GOD is upon me; because the LORD has *anointed* [*mashakh*] me" (רוּחַ אֲדֹנָי יְהוִה, עָלָי--יַעַן מָשַׁח יְהוָה אֹתִי). Jesus is presented as applying this to himself, and is understood as declaring his messianic identity, as the "anointed one" (מָשִׁיחַ).

proclaim deliverance to the captives,[4] and the **recovery of sight to the blind,**[5] to set at liberty those who are oppressed, **19** To proclaim **the year of the Lord's favor.**[6] **20** And he rolled up the scroll, and gave it again to the **attendant,**[7] and sat down. And the eyes of all who were in the synagogue were fixed on him. **21** And he began to say to them, This day is this scripture fulfilled in your hearing. **22** And all **bore witness,**[8] and marveled at the **gracious [disgraceful] words**[9] that proceeded out of his mouth. And they said: **Is not this Joseph's son?**[10]

Discern the Time (ANT)

It is likely that the people would have insisted on proof of Jesus' claims, and since Deuteronomy 13 decrees stoning as the punishment for those who lead Israel astray through false signs, it is likely that Jesus' statements regarding "signs" belong here. Luke 12:54–59 and Luke 11:29–32 have been added at this point.[11]

---

[4] Quoting Isa 61:1, the Hebrew reads: "***To bring good tidings to the humble He has sent me***; to bind up the broken-hearted, to proclaim liberty to the captives …" (לְבַשֵּׂר עֲנָוִים שְׁלָחַנִי, לַחֲבֹשׁ לְנִשְׁבְּרֵי-לֵב, לִקְרֹא לִשְׁבוּיִם דְּרוֹר). Jesus omits "bind up the brokenhearted" (as apparent in the NU-Text) and proceeds to "deliverance/liberty to the captives." Note Dead Sea Scrolls 11Q13 2:4: "[the interpretation] is that it applies to the Last Days and concerns ***the captives*** [just as Isaiah said …]" (פשרו]לאחרית הימים על **השבויים** אשר).

[5] The Hebrew text reads לַאֲסוּרִים פְּקַח-קוֹחַ, often understood as "the opening of the prison to those who are bound," but here taken as "the opening of the eyes of the blind" (also permissible from the Hebrew). This is more consistent with his prophetic vocation as a healer.

[6] Note Dead Sea Scrolls 11Q13 2:9: "This is the time decreed for 'the ***year of Melchizedek's favor***' and for his hosts, together with the holy ones of God, for a kingdom of judgment" (הואה הקץ **לשנת הרצון למלכי צדק** ולצבאיו עם קדושי אל לממשלת משפט).

[7] In Greek ὑπηρέτῃ, the ancient equivalent of a *gabbai* (גבאי), also known as *shamash* (שמש)—a person who assists in the running of synagogue services.

[8] In Hebrew "bearing witness" means testifying against; note 1 Kgs 21:10: "… and let them bear witness against him" (וִיעִדֻהוּ).

[9] The Greek χάριτος ("grace") translates the Hebrew חסד, which can also mean "disgrace," e.g. Lev 20:17; Prov 14:34. The Lucan text may be understood as saying that they all spoke critically of him and were astonished at the words of apostasy coming from his mouth.

[10] As a translation of the Greek negative, the underlying Hebrew text (הלא זה הוא בן יוסף) could also be read: "After all this is Joseph son!" It is not an expression of surprise, but horror.

[11] See Lindsey, *Jesus*, 46.

Luke 12:54 And he said also to the crowds: When you see a cloud rise out of the west, immediately you say: A shower is coming; and so it is. **55** And when you see the south wind blow, you say: There will be heat; and it comes to pass. **56** You hypocrites, you can discern the face of the sky and of the earth; but how is it that you do not discern this time? **57** "Yes, and why, even of yourselves, do you not judge what is right? **58** When you go with your adversary to the magistrate, **make every effort along the way to settle with him,**[12] lest he drag you to the **judge,**[13] the judge deliver you to the officer, and the officer throw you into prison. **59** I tell you, you shall not depart from there till you have paid the very last mite (lepton)."

Seeking a Sign

In the Lucan context, the people did not want a "sign" as proof that Jesus was the Messiah, but a sign of final "salvation."

Luke 11:29 Now, when the people were pressed together, he began to say: **This is an evil generation: it seeks after a sign; but no sign will be given to it, but the sign of Jonah**[14] [the prophet]. **30** For as Jonah was a sign to the Ninevites, so also will the **Son of**

---

[12] Note *b. Yoma* 23a: "Whoever forgoes his reckonings [with others for injustices done to him, the heavenly court] forgoes [punishment] for all his sins?" (כָּל הַמַּעֲבִיר עַל מִדּוֹתָיו מַעֲבִירִין לוֹ עַל כָּל פְּשָׁעָיו).

[13] In rabbinic times, the *Bet Din*, a local body consisting of three members.

[14] Hebraic reconstruction: "This evil generation seeks a sign, but no sign shall be given to it but the sign of Jonah" (הדור הרע הזה מבקש אות ואות לא אלה לו ינתן לא אלה אות של יונה). See Mark 8:31; Matt 12:41, where the message is amended to focus on "three days and three nights." The preaching of Jonah was a call to repent, and Jonah himself became a "sign." Isaiah and his children became "*signs* and portents in Israel" (אֹתוֹת וּלְמוֹפְתִים, בְּיִשְׂרָאֵל; Isa 8:18). Note Ezek 12:8: "I have set you for a *sign* to the house of Israel" (כִּי מוֹפֵת נְתַתִּיךָ לְבֵית יִשְׂרָאֵל). Note *b. San.* 98a: "Rabbi Yosei ben Kisma's students asked him: When will the son of David come? Rabbi Yosei ben Kisma said: I am hesitant to answer you, lest you request from me a *sign* to corroborate my statement ... The students said to him: Our rabbi, give us a *sign*" (שאלו תלמידיו את רבי יוסי בן קיסמא אימתי בן דוד בא אמר מתיירא אני שמא תבקשו ממני **אות** ... אמרו לו רבינו תן לנו **אות**). Note also Josephus, *War* VI.235, relating that a false prophet told the people to go up to the top of the temple to receive three *signs* of salvation. According to Ben Sira, Enoch (who walked with God in Gen 5:22, 24) was a "sign of knowledge to all generations." See Flusser, *Judaism*, 528.

Man[15] be to this generation. **31** The queen of the **south**[16] will rise up in the judgment with the men of this generation, and condemn them. For she came from the ends of the earth to hear the wisdom of Solomon; and, **behold,**[17] a **greater than Solomon**[18] is here. **32** The men of Nineveh will rise up in the judgment with this generation, and will condemn it. For they repented at the preaching of Jonah; and, **behold,**[19] a **greater than Jonah**[20] is here.

"Physician, heal yourself" (RCT)

The statement from the crowd, "Whatever we have heard done in Capernaum, do also here in your hometown," is key in placing the Nazareth episode later than its traditional position, immediately after the temptation sequence. Significantly, the two examples Jesus brings (the widow of Zarephath and Naaman the Syrian) are both Gentiles. Jesus is effectively issuing a grave insult, declaring that even Gentiles are better than these Israelites.

Luke 4:23 And he said to them: You will surely say to me this proverb, **Physician, heal yourself; whatever we have heard done in Capernaum, do also here in your hometown.**[21] **24** And he

---

[15] The Aramaic בר אנוש ("son of man") links to Dan 7:13; authority being the theme.

[16] In the Lucan context, Jesus is likewise a "sign" and will rise in judgment with the Queen of the South. Josephus references her as the Queen of Egypt and Ethiopia. However, in ancient cartography "south" was to the "right" (Heb. ימין), a derivative of which was תימן (Yemen).

[17] The Greek ἰδού is used in imitation of the Hebrew הִנֵּה.

[18] The Testament of Solomon (chap. 8) refers to Solomon as having power over demons, having put them to work building the temple. It may be asked whether the "greater than" mentioned by Jesus refers to himself or the main emphasis of his teaching, the kingdom of God.

[19] The Greek ἰδού is used in imitation of the Hebrew הִנֵּה.

[20] See Matt 12:41; Heb 1:5, implying that Jesus is greater than the angels.

[21] Note *Gen. Rab.* 23:4: "Physician, physician, heal your own limp!" (Aramaic: אסיא אסי חיגרתך); i.e. charity begins at home (in this case Nazareth). Also note Euripides, frag. 1086: "a physician for others but himself." Note also *b. B.M.* 107b, commenting on Deut 7:15: "And the LORD will take away from you all sickness" (וְהֵסִיר יְהוָה מִמְּךָ כָּל-חֹלִי).

said: **Truly I say to you,**[22] **No prophet is accepted in his own hometown.**[23] **25** But I tell you in truth, many widows were in Israel in the days of Elijah, when the heaven was shut up for **three years and six months,**[24] when great famine was throughout all the land; **26** But to none of them was Elijah sent, except to Zarephath, a city of **Sidon, to a woman who was a widow.**[25] **27** And many lepers were in Israel in the time of Elisha the prophet; and none of them was cleansed, except **Naaman the Syrian.**[26] **28** And all in the synagogue were filled with anger when they heard these things, **29** And rose up, and **cast him out of the city,**[27] and **led him to the brow of the hill on which their town was built, in order to throw him down.**[28] **30** But he, passing through the midst of them, went away.

---

[22] The word "Amen" (Ἀμὴν = אמן) would conclude a statement, not begin it. Jesus patterns his use of "Amen" after Jer 28:5–7, in which the significant statement of the false prophet Hanania is followed by "Amen" (here used in irony). Note Jer 28:6: "The prophet Jeremiah said: '*Amen*! the LORD do so! the LORD perform Your words which You have prophesied'" (וַיֹּאמֶר, יִרְמְיָה הַנָּבִיא, **אָמֵן**, כֵּן יַעֲשֶׂה יְהוָה; יָקֵם יְהוָה, אֶת-דְּבָרֶיךָ, אֲשֶׁר נִבֵּאתָ). Next, Jeremiah says: "Nevertheless hear now this word that *I speak* in your ears, and in the ears of all the people ..." (אַךְ-שְׁמַע-נָא הַדָּבָר הַזֶּה, אֲשֶׁר **אָנֹכִי דֹבֵר** בְּאָזְנֶיךָ, וּבְאָזְנֵי, כָּל-הָעָם). Jesus' use of "*I say*" (אני אומר) recalls **אָנֹכִי דֹבֵר**. See also Num 5:22: (אמן אמן); also Matt 5:18, 26; 6:5; Luke 12:37, 18:17.

[23] The Greek translator tried to imitate the Hebrew expression (as recorded in early medieval rabbinic literature): "There is no prophet in his [own] city" (אין נביא בעירו).

[24] See 1 Kgs 18:1: "... the word of the LORD came to Elijah, in the third year, saying: 'Go, show yourself to Ahab, and I will send rain upon the land.'" Here, "three years and six months" represents a stereotyped length of distress (see *Apoc. Bar.* 1.4); also the length of the persecution under Antiochus IV (see Dan 7:25, 12:7; Rev 11:2; 12:6, 14.

[25] The widow was a Gentile; see 1 Kgs 17:8–16.

[26] Naaman was also a Gentile; see 2 Kgs 5:1–4.

[27] Perhaps a ritual of excommunication; Hebrew חרם (*kherem*), a "ban," i.e. the total exclusion of a person from the Jewish community.

[28] Though Nazareth was not situated on a cliff, the procedure bears resemblance to the accusation against Naboth (1 Kgs 21:10), who was accused of cursing God and his king: "And then carry him out, and stone him, that he die" (וְהוֹצִיאֻהוּ וְסִקְלֻהוּ, וְיָמֹת). In Talmudic law, a person would be thrown down and incapacitated, whereupon heavy stone, which several must lift, would be used to crush him.

Scene 2:
First Disciples Called (RCT)

We find depicted here the Jewish practice of an Israelite sage gathering a select group of disciples (תלמידים), for the specific purpose of advancing the teaching of the master, in this case, the "kingdom of God/kingdom of heaven" movement. It hardly needs emphasizing that this movement of religious renewal was directed at Israelites only. Simon's (Peter's) declaration that he is a sinful man, understood Hebraically, means that he is not observant of Jewish law/halakha. Nonetheless, Galilee was known historically as a region of deep piety, as well as Jewish nationalism, and even "simple men" were well-versed in the Torah. The fact that they would leave everything to follow the sage Jesus is another indicator of the degree to which religious zeal had penetrated the local population.

Luke 5:1 And it came to pass,[29] that, as the people pressed upon him to hear the word of God, he stood by the lake of Gennesaret, **2** And saw two boats standing by the lake; but the fishermen were gone from them, and were washing their nets. **3** And he entered into one of the boats, which was Simon's, and asked him to pull out a little from the land. And he sat down, and taught the people from the boat. **4** Now when he had finished speaking, he said to Simon: Launch out into the deep water, and let down your nets for a catch. **5** And Simon answering said to him: **Master,**[30] we have toiled all night, and have taken nothing; nevertheless at your word I will let down the net. **6** And when they had done this, they enclosed a multitude of fish; and their nets were breaking. **7** And they called to their partners, who were in the other boat, that they should come and help them. And they came, and filled both the boats, so that they began to sink. **8** When Simon Peter saw it, he fell down at Jesus' knees, saying: **Depart from me; for I am a**

---

[29] The Greek ἐγένετο δὲ translates the Hebrew וַיְהִי.
[30] The Greek Ἐπιστάτα translates the Hebrew "rabbi" (רבי).

sinful man,[31] O Lord. **9** For he was astonished, and all who were with him, at the catch of the fish they had taken. **10** And so also were James, and John, the sons of **Zebedee,**[32] who were partners with Simon. **And** Jesus **said**[33] to Simon: Do not fear; from now on you will be catching men. **11** And when they had brought their boats to land, **they left all, and followed him.**[34]

Scene 3:
The Twelve Apostles

Luke 5:11–39 likely belong to the "Judean sojourn" and have been moved accordingly. With regard to the twelve disciples, it is speculated that after Joseph died, his brother Alpheus took his place, fathering children by Mary in accordance with the law of yibum (brother-in-law marriage). One of his sons was named Matthew, though he was also given the name Joseph (Joses), in honor of his deceased brother. Jesus' brothers may therefore have been among his closest followers.[35]

---

[31] The Hebrew word for "sin" is חֵטְא and literally means "to miss the mark," closely translated by the Greek ἁμαρτία. It involves not being halakhically observant of Jewish law, both written and oral. Note 2 Kgs 18:14: "Then Hezekiah king of Judah sent to the king of Assyria at Lachish, saying, '*I have sinned*; *turn away from me*; whatever you impose on me I will bear'" (**שׁוּב**, **חָטָאתִי**, לֵאמֹר לְכִישָׁה אֶל-מֶלֶךְ-אַשּׁוּר אֶל-מֶלֶךְ-יְהוּדָה חִזְקִיָּה וַיִּשְׁלַח (**מֵעָלַי** אֵת אֲשֶׁר-תִּתֵּן עָלַי, אֶשָּׂא).

[32] The possible priestly connections of Zebedee (Heb. זְבַדְיָה, "endowment of God") have been a subject of much speculation, given his mention as the father of John. See Acts 4:6: "Annas the high priest was there, and so were Caiaphas, *John*, Alexander and others of the high priest's family ..." See also John 18:15: "Simon Peter and another disciple (*John the Beloved*) were following Jesus. Because this disciple was known to the high priest ..."

[33] The Greek Καὶ εἶπεν ("And said ...") translates the Hebrew וַיֹּאמֶר.

[34] Note Dead Sea Scrolls 1QS 5:1–2: "This is the rule for the men of the *Yahad* who volunteer to repent from all evil and to hold fast to all that He, by His good will, has commanded. They are to separate from the congregation of perverse men ..." (וזה הסרך). See also (לאנשי היחד המתנדבים לשוב מכול רע ולהחזיק בכול אשר צוה לרצונו להבדל מעדת אנשי העול). Dead Sea Scrolls CD 1:7–9: "And they perceived their iniquity and recognized that they were guilty men; yet for twenty years they were like blind men, groping for the way" (ויבינו בעונם וידעו כי אנשים אשימים הם. וַיִּהְיוּ כעורים וכי מגששים דרך); CD 1:11: "So He raised up for them a teacher of righteousness to guide them in the way of His heart" (ויקם להם מורה צדק להדריכם בדרך לבו).

[35] See Tabor, *The Jesus Dynasty*, 79.

Luke 6:12 And it came to pass[36] in those days, that he went out to a mountain to pray, and continued all night in prayer to God. **13** And when it was day, he called his disciples to him: and of those he chose twelve, whom he also named apostles; **14** Simon, (whom he also named **Peter**,[37]) and Andrew his brother, James and John, Philip and **Bartholomew**,[38] **15 Matthew** and Thomas, **James** the son of **Alphaeus**, and **Simon**[39] called the Zealot, **16** And **Judas** the brother of James, and Judas **Iscariot, was who also the traitor.**[40]

Scene 4:
Jesus Heals a Great Multitude

Having already sojourned in Judea, it is not difficult to imagine that Jesus' fame would have spread and that many from Judea and Jerusalem would have traveled to see him. Though perhaps not a "multitude," at least yet, the crowds may well have grown in number.

Luke 6:17 And he came down with them, and stood in the plain, and the company of his disciples, and a great multitude of people out of all Judea and Jerusalem, and from the sea coast of Tyre and Sidon, who came to hear him, and to be healed of their diseases;

---

[36] The Greek ἐγένετο δὲ translates the Hebrew וַיְהִי.

[37] In conferring on Simon (Heb. שִׁמְעוֹן) a "nickname," Jesus used the Aramaic term "Rock" (כיפה), rendered Πέτρον in Greek. No one else in Scripture is called "Peter."

[38] "Son of Ptolemy" (בר תלמי) in Aramaic. Jews had always thought better of the Ptolemies and (during the Maccabean revolt) allied with the pretender Alexander Balas against Seleucid King Demetrius I.

[39] Matthew was also known as Levi and called the son of Alpheus (Mark 2:14). **Matthew** was arguably the same as **Joses**. Note Mark 6:3: "Jesus ... the brother of **James** and **Joses** and **Judas** and **Simon**." Jesus' brothers may have been among his disciples.

[40] It is commonly assumed that "Iscariot" refers to his hometown, Kerioth (קְרִיּוֹת). A possible play on words may exist in the hypothetical Hebrew undertext: "Iscariot"/"man of Kerioth" (איש קריות) /"betrayed him" (הסגיר אותו). "Iscariot" has also been theorized to indicate a "man of the Sicarii" (Hebrew: סיקריים), who carried daggers (*sica* = a Roman short sword) under their robes. See Hugh H. Schonfield, *The Original New Testament* (San Francisco: Harper & Row, 1985), 11. An alternate understanding involves the Aramaic שקריה (*sheqarya*), meaning "false one"/"liar."

18 And those who were afflicted with unclean spirits: and they were healed. **19** And the whole multitude sought to touch him: for virtue went out of him, and healed them all.

Do Not Judge

Jesus' admonition not to judge is reminiscent of Hillel: "Judge not your fellow man until you have come to his place." The essence of his teaching appears to be Pharisaic, as evidenced by the parallels with rabbinic literature. Luke 6:20b–36 have been transposed to the "Judean Sojourn" section.

Luke 6:20 And he lifted up his eyes on his disciples and said: **Luke 6:37 Judge not/and you shall not be judged:**[41] **condemn not/and you shall not be condemned:**[42] **forgive/and you shall be forgiven:**[43] **38 Give/and it shall be given to you;**[44] good measure, pressed down, and shaken together, and running over, shall men give into your bosom. For **with the same measure that you**

---

[41] Abbreviated in Mark 4:25; Matt 7:2. Hebrew parallelism; play on words (active vs. passive), reconstructed as: אל תשפטו ולא תשפטו. Note *m. Avot* 1:6, attributed to Joshua ben Perahiah: "Judge all men with the scale weighted in his favor" (וֶהֱוֵי דָן אֶת כָּל הָאָדָם לְכַף זְכוּת); *m. Avot* 2:4, attributed to Hillel: "Do not judge your fellow man until you have reached his place" (וְאַל תָּדִין אֶת חֲבֵרְךָ עַד שֶׁתַּגִּיעַ לִמְקוֹמוֹ). See also *b. R.H.* 16b, attributed to Rabbi Avin: "Anyone who passes a case against another to God is punished first" (כָּל הַמּוֹסֵר דִּין עַל חֲבֵירוֹ הוּא נֶעֱנָשׁ תְּחִלָּה); *b. B.K.* 93a, attributed to Rabbi Ḥanan: "One who passes the judgment of another to Heaven is punished first" (דין על חבירו הוא נענש תחילה).

[42] Hebrew parallelism; play on words (active vs. passive), reconstructed as: אל תחיבו ולא תחויבו.

[43] Hebrew parallelism; play on words (active vs. passive), reconstructed as: נקו ותינקו.

[44] Hebrew parallelism; play on words (active vs. passive), reconstructed as: תנו ותנתן לכם.

measure it shall be measured to you again.[45] **39** And he spoke a parable to them: Can the blind lead the blind? shall they not both fall into the ditch? **40** The disciple is not above his master: but everyone who is perfect shall be as his master. **41** And why do you observe the beam that is in your brother's eye, but do not perceive the beam that is in your own eye? **42** How can you say to your brother, Brother, let me pull out the beam that is in your eye, when you yourself do not see the beam that is in your own eye? You hypocrite, **first cast out the beam out of your own eye, and then shall you see clearly to pull out the beam that is in your brother's eye.**[46]

A Tree Is Known by Its Fruit

The term "Lord" (Hebrew אדון) was Jesus' preferred self-designation and could be used as a messianic moniker.

Luke 6:43 For a good tree does not bring forth corrupt fruit; neither does a corrupt tree bring forth good fruit. **44** For every tree is known by its own fruit. For men do not gather figs from thorns, nor do they gather grapes from a bramble bush. **45** A good man **out**

---

[45] See Matt 7:2. Note *m. Sotah* 1:7: "With the measure that a person measures, he is measured with it" (בַּמִּדָּה שֶׁאָדָם מוֹדֵד, בָּהּ מוֹדְדִין לוֹ); *m. Sotah* 1:8: "Samson followed his eyes, therefore he was punished measure for measure, as the Philistines gouged out his eyes, as it is stated: 'And the Philistines laid hold on him, and put out his eyes.' Absalom was excessively proud of his hair, and therefore he was hanged by his hair" (שִׁמְשׁוֹן הָלַךְ אַחַר עֵינָיו, לְפִיכָךְ נִקְּרוּ פְלִשְׁתִּים אֶת עֵינָיו, שֶׁנֶּאֱמַר וַיֹּאחֲזוּהוּ פְלִשְׁתִּים וַיְנַקְּרוּ אֶת עֵינָיו. אַבְשָׁלוֹם נִתְגָּאֶה בִּשְׂעָרוֹ, לְפִיכָךְ נִתְלָה בִשְׂעָרוֹ). Note *b. Meg.* 28a, attributed to Rava: "Anyone who overlooks exacting a measure of retribution against those who wronged him, all his transgressions are removed from him" (כָּל הַמַּעֲבִיר עַל מִדּוֹתָיו מַעֲבִירִין מִמֶּנּוּ כָּל פְּשָׁעָיו). Note also *m. Gen. R.* 9:13: "R. Simeon b. Abba said: 'All the measures have ceased [i.e. modes of execution] yet the rule of measure for measure has not ceased'" (שִׁמְעוֹן בַּר אַבָּא, כָּל הַמִּדּוֹת בָּטְלוּ, מִדָּה כְנֶגֶד מִדָּה לֹא בָטְלָה); *b. Sot.* 11a: "In the pot in which they cooked, they themselves cooked" (בקדירה שבישלו בה נתבשלו).

[46] Note *b. B.B.* 15b: "If a judge would say to the defendant standing before him: **Remove the splinter from between your eyes**, meaning rid yourself of some minor infraction, the defendant would say to him: **Remove the beam from between your eyes**" (אוֹמֵר לוֹ **טוֹל קֵיסָם מִבֵּין עֵינֶיךָ** אוֹמֵר לוֹ **טוֹל קוֹרָה מִבֵּין עֵינֶיךָ**). However, there is arguably a degree of humor in Jesus' statement.

of the good treasure of his heart[47] brings forth that which is good; and an evil man out of the evil treasure of his heart brings forth that which is evil: for of the abundance of the heart his mouth speaks. **46** And why do you call me, **Lord, Lord,**[48] and **do not the things that I say?**[49]

Scene 5:
The Model Prayer (ANT)

The prayer offered by Jesus and referenced below is classically Hebraic, containing phrases equivalent to specific sections of the morning prayer in Jewish tradition: "and do not lead us into the hands of sin, or into the hands of wrath or transgression, or into the hands of temptation, or into the hands of malice…" The words, "and do not lead us into temptation" remind us of another expression found in the same Hebrew prayer: "and may the evil inclination not rule over us…" The words "hallowed be your name" remind us of the Hebrew Kaddish prayer: "may your great name be magnified and sanctified." Jesus is instructing his disciples regarding the minimum prayer that would be required of his followers. It appears to have occurred after the call of the disciples, and it is reasonable to assume that it took place early in the narrative since John the Baptist is still in mind.

---

[47] Note *Eccl. Rab.* 7:2 §1: "If the **heart** has not revealed it to the mouth, to whom does the mouth reveal it?"

[48] The Greek Κύριε translates the Hebrew אדון, which could be used as a messianic designation.

[49] See parallel; Matt 7:21. Note *b. Kiddushin* 40b: "Rabbi Tarfon and the Elders were reclining in the loft of the house of Nit'za in Lod, when this question was asked of them: Is study greater or is action greater? Rabbi Tarfon answered and said: **Action is greater**" (רבי טרפון וזקנים מסובין בעלית בית נתזה בלוד נשאלה זו בפניהם תלמוד גדול או מעשה נענה רבי טרפון ואמר **מעשה גדול**). See Luke 4:43, where Jesus declares that to enter the kingdom of heaven (understood rabbinically as the rule/reign of God), one must also keep the commandments. The Sages (b. Korha) taught that keeping the Commandments should not be mechanical; therefore, one must first commit to the kingdom of heaven, by reciting the *Shema*. (Deut 6:4).

Luke 11:1 And it came to pass,[50] that, as he was praying in a certain place, when he ceased, one of his disciples said to him: Lord, **teach us to pray,**[51] as John also taught his disciples. **2** And he said to them: When you pray, say, **Our Father [who is in heaven]**[52] **Hallowed be your name.**[53] **May your kingdom come.**[54] May your will be done, **in heaven and on earth.**[55] **3** Give us day by day our **daily**[56] **bread.**[57] **4** And **forgive us of our sins;**[58]

---

[50] The Greek καὶ ἐγένετο translates the Hebrew וַיְהִי; see Luke 1:23.

[51] The disciples may be understood as asking what is the minimum number of benedictions to fulfill the obligation to pray. Rabbinic Judaism later specified eighteen (שמונה עשרה) such benedictions, comprising the *Amidah* (עמידה). The Mishnah discusses the shortest prayer permissible in a time of imminent danger. See Lindsey, *Jesus*, 95.

[52] Greek: Πάτερ ἡμῶν ("Our Father") translates the Hebrew אבינו, a common address in Jewish prayer. It is likely that the phrase "who is in heaven" (Greek ὁ ἐν τοῖς οὐρανοῖς; Hebrew שבשמים) was not present in the earliest recension of the Greek text because it conjured up the "abode of Zeus" in the Greek mind. However, some Jewish communities include the expression after the evening *Shema*: "Our God *in heaven*, hallow [unify] your name, and establish your kingdom forever, and rule over us for ever and ever" (אֱלֹהֵינוּ שֶׁבַּשָׁמַיִם יַחֵד שִׁמְךָ וְקַיֵּם מַלְכוּתְךָ תָּמִיד וּמְלֹךְ עָלֵינוּ לְעוֹלָם וָעֶד).

[53] Parallels the *Kaddish* prayer: "Exalted and *hallowed* be His great *Name*" (יִתְגַּדַּל וְיִתְקַדַּשׁ שְׁמֵהּ רַבָּא).

[54] This should not be confused with the messianic age. The "kingdom of God/heaven" concept was rabbinically understood as the present-tense divine reign; see Luke 4:43. The Greek ἐπιούσιον ("come") is an imperative. However, a hypothetical Hebrew reconstruction might read: "May your kingdom *reign*" (תמליך מלכותך).

[55] An early Greek text reads: "in heaven and on earth" (ἐν οὐρανῷ καὶ ἐπὶ τῆς γῆς), equating to the Hebrew בשמים ובארץ—a genuinely Hebraic idea and expression.

[56] Note Ps 68: 20: "Blessed be the Lord, *day by day* He bears our burden" (בָּרוּךְ אֲדֹנָי יוֹם יוֹם: יַעֲמָס-לָנוּ). The Greek ἐπιούσιον ("daily") has sometimes been understood as a future pronouncement: "bread for tomorrow," referencing the "messianic banquet" at the end of days. This, however, contradicts the present tense understanding of the kingdom of God/heaven.

[57] Note Prov 30:8: "feed me with my *allotted bread*" (הַטְרִיפֵנִי לֶחֶם חֻקִּי).

[58] The sense of obligation here is akin to the petition in the *Kol Nidre* for absolution from rash vows. "We regret having made them; may they all be permitted, forgiven, eradicated and nullified" (בְּכֻלְּהוֹן אִחֲרַטְנָא בְהוֹן כֻּלְּהוֹן יְהוֹן שָׁרָן שְׁבִיקִין, שְׁבִיתִין בְּטֵלִין וּמְבֻטָּלִין). Note Deut 15:2 "And this is the manner of the release: every creditor shall release that which he has lent to his neighbor; he shall not exact it of his neighbor and his brother; because the LORD'S release has been proclaimed" (וְזֶה, דְּבַר הַשְּׁמִטָּה—שָׁמוֹט כָּל-בַּעַל) (מַשֵּׁה יָדוֹ אֲשֶׁר יַשֶּׁה בְּרֵעֵהוּ: לֹא-יִגֹּשׂ אֶת-רֵעֵהוּ וְאֶת-אָחִיו כִּי-קָרָא שְׁמִטָּה לַיהוָה).

for we also forgive everyone who is indebted to us. **And do not lead us into temptation;**[59] but deliver us from **evil.**[60]

Asking, Seeking, Knocking

The "Model Prayer" is theorized to be followed by a teaching regarding persistent prayer (Luke 11:9–13), which is in turn followed by the parable of the persistent friend (Luke 11:5–8) and the parable of the persistent widow (Luke 18:1–8). This is consistent with the theory that an event (a disciple asking Jesus to "teach us to pray") would then be followed by a teaching ("ask," "seek," "knock") and two parables.[61]

Luke 11:9 And I say to you, Ask, and it shall be given to you; seek, and you shall find; knock, and it shall be opened to you. **10** For everyone who asks receives; and the one who seeks finds; and to the one who knocks it shall be opened. **11** If a son asks bread of any of you who is a father, will he give him a stone? Or if he asks for a fish, will he give him a serpent instead of a fish? **12** Or if he asks for an egg, will he give him a scorpion? **13** If you, then, **being evil,**[62] know how to give good gifts to your children: **how much more**[63] shall your **heavenly Father**[64] give the Spirit to those who ask him?

---

[59] Note the Hebrew morning prayer: "**And do not lead us** into the hands of sin, or into the hands of wrath or transgression, or into the hands of **temptation**, or into the hands of malice ..." (**ואל תביאנו** לא לידי חטא ולא לידי עברה ועון ולא לידי **נסיון** ולא לידי בזיון ...). See 1 Cor 10:13: "God is faithful, who will not allow you to be tempted beyond what you are able ..."

[60] Note the Hebrew morning prayer: "And may the **evil inclination** not rule over us ..." (... ואל ישלוט בנו **יצר הרע**).

[61] See Lindsey, *Jesus*, 98–99.

[62] That is, possessing an "evil inclination" (in Hebrew יֵצֶר רַע). See Luke 6:35–36: "He is kind to the unthankful and *evil*. Therefore be merciful, just as your Father also is merciful."

[63] A rabbinic methodology: "light and heavy" (קַל וָחוֹמֶר). See Matt 7:9 ff.

[64] Rabbinic literature has many examples of a son making requests of a father, e.g. *Pesikta d-Rav Kahana* [PRK] 3:1, where the "spoiled son" represents Israel in the wilderness.

Parable 1: A Persistent Friend Comes at Midnight

The message of persistence is reminiscent of the ancient hasid, Honi HaMe'aggel, who was said to "nag God."

Luke 11:5 And he said to them: Who among you will have a friend, and go to him at midnight, and say to him, Friend, lend me three loaves; **6** For a friend of mine has come to me during his journey, and I have nothing to set before him? **7** And he from within will answer and say, Do not trouble me; for the door is already shut, and my children are with me in bed; I cannot rise and give you. **8** I say to you, If he will not even rise and give to him, because he is his friend, yet because of **his persistence**[65] he will rise and give him as much as he needs.

Parable 2: The Persistent Widow

Luke 18:1 And he spoke a parable to them to this end, about how always to pray, and not to lose heart; **2** Saying: There was in a certain city **a judge, who did not fear God, nor regarded man. 3 And there was a widow in that city;**[66] and she came to him, saying: Avenge me of my adversary. **4** And he would not for a while; but afterward he said to himself: Though I do not fear God, nor regard man; **5** Yet because this widow **troubles me, I will**

---

[65] The Greek word for "persistence" (ἀναίδειαν) indicates boldness (as in the Hebrew *chutzpah* חוצפה ["his arrogance" חצופו]).

[66] Note Ben Sira 35:15–18: "Do not rely on a dishonest sacrifice; for the Lord is the *judge*, and with him there is no partiality… He will not ignore the supplication of the orphan, or the *widow* when she pours out her complaint." The judge represents divine authority on earth; see 2 Chron 19:5–7: "And he set *judges* in the land throughout all the fortified cities of Judah, city by city. and said to the *judges*: 'Consider what you do; for you *judge* not for man, but for the LORD; and [He is] with you in giving *judgment*. Now therefore let the fear of the LORD be upon you; take heed and do it; for there is no iniquity with the LORD our God, nor respect of persons, nor taking of bribes.'" (וַיַּעֲמֵד

שֹׁפְטִים בָּאָרֶץ, בְּכָל-עָרֵי יְהוּדָה הַבְּצֻרוֹת--לְעִיר וָעִיר. וַיֹּאמֶר אֶל-**הַשֹּׁפְטִים**, רְאוּ מָה-אַתֶּם עֹשִׂים--כִּי לֹא לְאָדָם **תִּשְׁפְּטוּ**, כִּי לַיהוָה; וְעִמָּכֶם, בִּדְבַר **מִשְׁפָּט**. וְעַתָּה, יְהִי פַחַד-יְהוָה עֲלֵיכֶם: שִׁמְרוּ וַעֲשׂוּ--כִּי-אֵין עִם-יְהוָה אֱלֹהֵינוּ עַוְלָה וּמַשֹּׂא פָנִים, וּמִקַּח-שֹׁחַד.)

avenge her, so that her continual coming may not exhaust me.[67]
6 And the Lord said: Hear what the unrighteous judge says. **7** And
shall not God avenge **his own elect, who cry day and night**[68] to
him, though he defer long to them? **8** I tell you that he will avenge
them speedily. Nevertheless, when the Son of Man comes, will he
find **faith**[69] on the earth?[70]

Scene 6:
A Centurion's Servant (RCT)

The narrative now presumably shifts back to Capernaum—the first
mention of the town since Jesus' return from his Judean sojourn.
The story of the Roman centurion highlights the fact that Jews,
including Jesus, generally avoided dealings with non-Jews,
refusing even to enter an un-kosher home. Only when the disciples
convince Jesus that this is a "God-fearer" (a class in antiquity
who embraced Judaism without formal conversion) did he deign to
speak to the man, healing his servant from a distance.[71]

---

[67] Note *b. Taan.* 25b: "To what is this matter comparable? To a situation where
there is a slave who requests a reward from his master, and the master says to his
ministers: Give him what he asks for and let me not hear his voice … To what is this
matter comparable? To a situation where there is a slave who requests a reward from his
master, and the master says to his ministers: Wait until he pines away and suffers, and
afterward give it to him" (לָמָה הַדָּבָר דּוֹמֶה לְעֶבֶד שֶׁמְּבַקֵּשׁ פְּרָס מֵרַבּוֹ וְאָמַר לָהֶם הַמְתִּינוּ לוֹ עַד
שֶׁיִּתְמַקְמַק וְיִצְטַעֵר וְאַחַר כָּךְ תְּנוּ לוֹ … לָמָה הַדָּבָר דּוֹמֶה לְעֶבֶד שֶׁמְּבַקֵּשׁ פְּרָס מֵרַבּוֹ אָמַר לָהֶם תְּנוּ לוֹ וְאַל
אֶשְׁמַע קוֹלוֹ); *b. San.* 105a: "Rav Naḥman says: **Impudence** is effective even toward
Heaven" (אמר רב נחמן **חוצפא** אפילו כלפי שמיא מהני). Note also *y. Hag.* 2, 77d (attributed to R.
Eliezer): "There was a man who had two daughters; one tenacious and the other gracious.
When the tenacious one wanted something she went to her *father to ask for it. He would
say, 'Give her what she wants so she will get out of here.'*" See *y. Ber.* 9.1 (11) 13b: "A
man has a patron, if he **bothers** him too much, he says 'I will forget him …' But God is
not so. However much you importune Him, He receives you."

[68] Note Ps 1:1: "And in His law does he meditate *day and night*" (וּבְתוֹרָתוֹ יֶהְגֶּה
יוֹמָם וָלָיְלָה); the passage involves a "light and heavy" (קַל וָחוֹמֶר), *a fortiori* argument. There
is arguably a degree of humor humor in the parable.

[69] Note the word "faith" in Luke 8:48, Mark 5:34, Matt 9:22.

[70] This pessimistic verse is inconsistent with the tone of the passage, which is
positive toward his "elect" and not eschatological. It may represent an editorial gloss.

[71] See Flusser, *Judaism*, 556.

Luke 7:7 And when he had completed all of his sayings in the hearing of the people, he entered Capernaum. **2** And a certain centurion's servant, whom he highly valued, was sick, and about to die. **3** And when he heard of Jesus, **he sent to him the elders of the Jews, begging him to come and heal his servant.**[72] **4** And when they came to Jesus, they begged him earnestly, saying, that he was worthy for whom he should do this: **5** For **he loves our nation, and he has built us a synagogue.**[73] **6** Then Jesus went with them. And when he was not far from the house, the centurion sent friends to him, saying to him, Lord, do not trouble yourself: for **I am not worthy that you should enter under my roof:**[74] **7** Therefore I never thought myself worthy to come to you: but say the word, and my servant shall be healed. **8** For I **am also a man under authority,**[75] having soldiers under me, and I say to this one, "Go," and he goes; and to another, "Come," and he comes; and to my servant, "Do this," and he does it. **9** When Jesus heard these things, he marveled at him, and turned around, and said to the people who followed him, "I say to you, I have not found so great

---

[72] Note *b. B.B.* 116a, attributed to Rabbi Pineḥas bar Ḥama: "Anyone who has a sick person in his home should go to a sage, and the sage will ask for mercy on the sick person's behalf" (כָּל שֶׁיֵּשׁ לוֹ חוֹלֶה בְּתוֹךְ בֵּיתוֹ יֵלֵךְ אֵצֶל חָכָם וִיבַקֵּשׁ עָלָיו רַחֲמִים).

[73] Although there is no record of the Roman military being stationed in Galilee at the time, and while some have questioned whether a non-Jewish centurion would have built a synagogue, the story accurately reflects relations between Jews and non-Jews. The disciples argue that Jesus should agree to speak with him since he is a "God-fearer." Known in Hebrew as "fearers of Heaven"/*yirei shamayim* (ירא שמים) in Greek as "fearers of God"/*phovoumenoi ton Theon* (φοβούμενοι τὸν Θεόν), and in Latin *metuens*, they were said to have numbered in the tens of thousands or even upwards of one million. Such individuals were closely associated with the Jewish faith, but, for whatever reason, resisted formal conversion to Judaism.

[74] The centurion understands that Jesus will not enter the unclean, un-kosher home of a non-Jew.

[75] Note Josephus, *War* II.195, with regard to the Roman legate Petronius, who supported the Jews when Caligula ordered that his statue be installed in the temple: "And when they insisted on their law, and the custom of their country, and how it was not only not permitted them to make either an image of God, or indeed of a man, and to put it in any despicable part of their country, much less in the temple itself, Petronius replied, 'And am not I also,' said he, 'bound to keep the law of my own lord? For if I transgress it, and spare you, it is but just that I perish; while he that sent me, and not I, will commence a war against you; for *I am under command/authority as well as you.*'"

faith, not even in Israel. **10** And those who were sent, having returned to the house, **found the servant in good health.**[76]

Scene 7:
John the Baptist Sends Messengers to Jesus

That John the Baptist sends messengers to inquire whether Jesus is the promised one or whether he should look for another betrays the fact that John was never an active follower of Jesus, whose kingdom of God/heaven movement was very different from John's message of fiery judgment.

Luke 7:18 And the disciples of John brought word to him of all these things. **19** And John, calling near two of his disciples, sent them to Jesus, saying: Are you the one who will come? Or are we to look for another? **20** When the men had come to him, they said: John Baptist has sent us to you, saying, **Are you the one who will come? Or are we to look for another?**[77] **21** And that very hour he cured many of their infirmities and afflictions, and evil spirits; and he gave sight to many who were blind. **22** Then Jesus answered and said to them: Go your way, and tell John what you have seen and heard; how that **the blind receive sight, the lame walk, the**

---

[76] Note *b. Ber.* 34b: "It happened that the son of R. Gamaliel was ill. He sent two disciples of the sages to R. Hanina b. Dosa to pray on his behalf. When he saw them, he assumed to an upper chamber and prayed on his behalf. On descending he said to them, 'Go, the fever has left him.' They said to him, 'Are you a prophet?' He replied, 'I am no prophet nor a prophet's son (Amos 7:14); but so is my tradition: If my prayer is fluent in my mouth I know that it is accepted; but if not, I know that it is rejected.' They sat down and wrote and noted the time. When they came to R. Gamliel, he said to them, 'By the temple service! You have neither overstated nor understated the time. But thus it happened; at that very hour the fever left him.' And he asked for water to drink" (תָּנוּ רַבָּנָן:

מַעֲשֶׂה שֶׁחָלָה בְּנוֹ שֶׁל רַבָּן גַּמְלִיאֵל. שִׁגֵּר שְׁנֵי תַּלְמִידֵי חֲכָמִים אֵצֶל רַבִּי חֲנִינָא בֶּן דּוֹסָא לְבַקֵּשׁ עָלָיו רַחֲמִים. כֵּיוָן שֶׁרָאָה אוֹתָם, עָלָה לַעֲלִיָּיה, וּבִקֵּשׁ עָלָיו רַחֲמִים. בִּירִידָתוֹ אָמַר לָהֶם: לְכוּ, שֶׁחֲלָצַתּוּ חַמָּה. אָמְרוּ לוֹ: וְכִי נָבִיא אַתָּה?! אָמַר לָהֶם: לֹא נָבִיא אָנֹכִי וְלֹא בֶן נָבִיא אָנֹכִי, אֶלָּא כָּךְ מְקוּבְּלַנִי: אִם שְׁגוּרָה תְּפִלָּתִי בְּפִי — יוֹדֵעַ אֲנִי שֶׁהוּא מְקוּבָּל, וְאִם לָאו — יוֹדֵעַ אֲנִי שֶׁהוּא מְטוֹרָף. יָשְׁבוּ וְכָתְבוּ וְכִוּוְנוּ אוֹתָהּ שָׁעָה. וּכְשֶׁבָּאוּ אֵצֶל רַבָּן גַּמְלִיאֵל, אָמַר לָהֶן: הָעֲבוֹדָה, לֹא חִסַּרְתֶּם וְלֹא הוֹתַרְתֶּם, אֶלָּא כָּךְ הָיָה מַעֲשֶׂה בְּאוֹתָהּ שָׁעָה חֲלָצַתּוּ חַמָּה וְשָׁאַל לָנוּ מַיִם לִשְׁתּוֹת).

[77] John was apparently not certain that Jesus was the "anointed one" since his message regarding the kingdom of God/heaven was quite unlike and in contrast with John's eschatological message of approaching judgment.

lepers are cleansed, the deaf hear, the dead are raised, the poor hear the good news.[78] 23 And blessed is whoever shall not be offended in me.[79] 24 And when the messengers of John had departed, he began to speak to the people concerning John: **What have you gone out into the wilderness to see? A reed shaken by the wind?**[80] **25 But what have you gone out to see? A man dressed in fine clothing?**[81] **Behold,**[82] those who are splendidly clothed, and live luxuriously, are in palaces. 26 But what have you gone out to see? A prophet? Yea, I say to you, and one more excellent than a prophet. 27 This is he, of whom it is written: Behold, I send my messenger before your face, who shall prepare your way before you. 28 For I say to you, Among those that are born of women there is no greater prophet than John the Baptist: but he who is least in the **kingdom of God**[83] is greater than he. 29 And all the people who heard him, even the tax collectors, justified God, having been baptized with the baptism of John. 30 But the Pharisees and lawyers rejected the counsel of God against themselves, having not been baptized by him.

Luke 7:31–50 has been transposed to the "Judean Sojourn" section.

---

[78] While traditional Jewish texts do not reference the Messiah as a worker of miracles, the restoration of those who are afflicted is consistent with the kingdom of God/ heaven message, at the heart of Jesus' self-proclaimed mission. This is the meaning of hearing the "good news"—lit. being *gospelized* (εὐαγγελίζονται), in Hebrew הַבְּשׂוֹרָה. The term evokes Isa 40:9: "O you who *tell good tidings* to Zion, get up into the high mountain …" (עַל הַר־גָּבֹהַּ עֲלִי־לָךְ, **מְבַשֶּׂרֶת צִיּוֹן**). See also Isa 26:19; 29:18; 35:5–6; 42:18; 61:1.

[79] Note Isa 8:14: "And He shall be as a sanctuary; but as a stone of stumbling and as a rock of *offense* to both the houses of Israel" (וְהָיָה לְמִקְדָּשׁ; וּלְאֶבֶן נֶגֶף וּלְצוּר **מִכְשׁוֹל** לִשְׁנֵי בָתֵּי יִשְׂרָאֵל).

[80] A possible play on words. The Hebrew for "reed" is קנה, which may also be read as "Zealot." There may be a reference to to Aesop's fable about the oak and the reeds. The reed bends in the wind, but the oak fights the wind. Likewise, John fought. His imprisonment may have been motivated by fear of political unrest; witness the militancy of Luke 2:25–38, etc.

[81] Note the Hebrew *parallelism/poetry*.

[82] The Greek ἰδού is used in imitation of the Hebrew הִנֵּה.

[83] John is viewed as the last prophet of the biblical period, though not taking part in the kingdom of God/heaven movement. There is no indication that he was ever an active follower of Jesus.

Scene 8:
Many Women Attend to Jesus and Disciples

Luke chapter 8 references several women who were apparently important supporters of Jesus, including the wife of the manager of King Herod's estate. It is logically followed by Jesus' mother and brothers coming to him.

Luke 8:1 And it came to pass[84] soon afterward, that he went throughout every city and village, preaching and showing the good news of the kingdom of God: and the twelve were with him, **2** And certain women, who had been healed of evil spirits and infirmities, Mary called Magdalene, from whom seven demons went out, **3** And Joanna the wife of Chuza Herod's **steward,**[85] and Susanna, and many others, who ministered to them of their own means.

Scene 9:
Jesus' Mother and Brothers Come to Him

This passage (Luke 8:19–21) is theorized to be the beginning of a complete story unit about God's word, perhaps being followed by Luke 23:29 ("Blessed are the barren, and the wombs that never bore"). It is likely the original context of Luke 11:27–28 ("Blessed is the womb that bore you …"), which echoes the concept of hearing the word and doing it. This is followed by Luke 8:5–8 (the Parable of the Sower and its interpretation) and a second parable: the House on the Rock (Luke 6:47–49; Matt 7:24–27).

Luke 8:19 Then his mother and his brothers came to him, and could not reach him because of the crowd. **20** And it was told him: Your mother and your brothers are standing outside, wanting to see

---

[84] The Greek καὶ ἐγένετο translates the Hebrew וַיְהִי; see Luke 1:23.
[85] Probably the manager of the estate.

you. **21** And he answered and said to them: My mother and my brothers are those **who hear the word of God, and do it.**[86]
Luke 23:29 For, **behold,**[87] the days are coming, in the which they will say, **Blessed are the barren, and the wombs that never bore,**[88] and the breasts that never nursed.[89]

"Blessed is the womb that bore you" (ANT)

We also see Jesus as one who rejected a "cult of personality," when a woman in the crowd calls out: "Blessed is the womb that bore you." In Hebraic fashion, Jesus responds: "Rather, blessed are those who hear the word of God, and keep it." This saying is a literary "doublet" of the saying we find in Luke 8:21, in which Jesus declares: "My mother and my brothers are those who hear the word of God, and do it."[90] Jesus "de-centers" himself, emphasizing the Torah and observing the commandments.

Luke 11:27 And it came to pass,[91] as he spoke these things, that a certain woman from the crowd lifted up her voice, and said to him: **Blessed is the womb that bore you,**[92] and the breasts at which

---

[86] Note Deut 5:23: "You shall speak to us all that the LORD our God may speak to you; and ***we will hear it and do it***" (וְאַתְּ תְּדַבֵּר אֵלֵינוּ, אֵת כָּל־אֲשֶׁר יְדַבֵּר יְהוָה אֱלֹהֵינוּ אֵלֶיךָ **וְשָׁמַעְנוּ וְעָשִׂינוּ**).

[87] The Greek ἰδοὺ is used in imitation of the Hebrew הִנֵּה.

[88] Blessing of Luke 1:42 is reversed. Note the lamentation composed over the destruction of the temple: "Blessed is he who was not born, Or he, who having been born, has died. But as for us who live, woe unto us, Because we see the afflictions of Zion ... And, ye women, pray not that ye may bear ... Or why, again, should mankind have sons?" (2 Bar. 10:6–16).

[89] This saying has been transposed from the later description of Jesus carrying his cross to the place of his execution. It is theoretically followed by the declaration of the woman in the crowd: "Blessed is the womb that bore you ..."

[90] Flusser (*Judaism*, 291–92) notes that the woman's blessing and Jesus' sharp rejoinder does not appear to be a "redactional invention." See Lindsey, *Jesus*, 202.

[91] The Greek ἐγένετο δὲ translates the Hebrew וַיְהִי.

[92] Mimics Luke 1:42.

you nursed. **28** But he said: **No, rather, blessed are those who hear the word of God, and keep it**.[93]

Parable 1: The Sower[94] (RCT)

The Parable of the Sower should well be called the Parable of the Soils since it is about how the message is received.[95] We also find a clear parallel with Mishnah Avot.

Luke 8:4 And when a great crowd were gathered together, having come to him from each town, he spoke by a parable: **5** A sower went out to sow his seed; and as he sowed, some fell along the roadside; and it was trampled upon, and the birds of the air devoured it. **6** And some fell upon a rock; and as soon as it had sprung up, it withered away, because it lacked moisture.**7** And some fell among thorns; and the thorns sprang up with it, and choked it. **8** And other fell on good ground, and sprang up, and bore fruit a hundredfold. And when he had said these things, he cried: He who has ears to hear, let him hear. **9** And his disciples asked him: What might this parable be?

The Parable of the Sower Explained

Jesus' words are not in this case allegorical. A disciple with a "good heart" seeks first the "kingdom of God."

---

[93] This saying is a literary "doublet" of one we find sandwiched in an earlier Lucan context (8:15), in which Jesus, having been told that his mother and brothers are waiting to see him, declares: "My mother and brothers are those who hear God's word and put it into practice." Jesus rejected a "cult of personality," deflecting personal attention, in a traditionally Jewish way, to the performance of *mitzvot*.

[94] Note *m. Avot* 5:15: "There are four types among those who sit before the sages: a sponge, a funnel, a strainer and a sieve. A sponge, soaks up everything; A funnel, takes in at one end and lets out at the other; A strainer, which lets out the wine and retains the lees; A sieve, which lets out the coarse meal and retains the choice flour" (אַרְבַּע מִדּוֹת בְּיוֹשְׁבִים לִפְנֵי חֲכָמִים. סְפוֹג, וּמַשְׁפֵּךְ, מְשַׁמֶּרֶת, וְנָפָה. סְפוֹג, שֶׁהוּא סוֹפֵג אֶת הַכֹּל. מַשְׁפֵּךְ, שֶׁמַּכְנִיס בְּזוֹ וּמוֹצִיא בְּזוֹ. מְשַׁמֶּרֶת, שֶׁמּוֹצִיאָה אֶת הַיַּיִן וְקוֹלֶטֶת אֶת הַשְּׁמָרִים. וְנָפָה, שֶׁמּוֹצִיאָה אֶת הַקֶּמַח וְקוֹלֶטֶת אֶת הַסֹּלֶת). Note also *ARN* 24:5: "Words of Torah are as difficult to acquire as golden vessels. And they are as easy to lose as glass vessels" (קשין דברי תורה לקנותם ככלי זהבים. ונוחין לאבדם ככלי זכוכית).

[95] See Young, *Jesus and His Jewish Parables*, 7–10.

Luke 8:11 Now the parable is this: The seed is the word of God. **12** Those by the roadside are those who hear; then comes the devil, and takes away the word from their hearts, lest they believe and be **saved.**[96] **13** Those on the rock are those, who, when they hear, receive the word with joy; and these **have no root,**[97] having for a time believed, and in time of testing fall away. **14** And that which fell among thorns are those, who, having heard, go forth, and are choked with cares and riches and pleasures of life, and do not mature. **15** But that on the **good soil are those who in an honest and good heart,**[98] having **heard the word, keep it,**[99] and bring forth fruit by perseverance.

Parable 2: The House on the Rock

In the ancient rabbinic debate over whether study or good deeds take precedence, Jesus appears to favor good deeds, which ultimately became the minority opinion.

Luke 6:47 Whoever comes to me, and hears my sayings, and does them, I will show you to whom he is like: **48** He is like a man who built a house, and dug deep, and laid the foundation on a rock: and when the flood came, the stream beat vehemently upon that house, and could not shake it: for it was founded upon a rock. **49** But he who hears, and does not do, is **like a man who built a house upon**

---

[96] Greek: σωθῶσιν. "Saved" in Hebrew derives from the root ישע, and indicates being delivered from enemies or physically healed. It does not refer to the hereafter, but is related to the word ישועה/"salvation," from which is derived the name "Jesus" (ישוע).

[97] Note Ben Sira 40:15: "The children of the ungodly put out few branches; they are unhealthy roots on sheer rock."

[98] Note *m. Avot* 2:9: "He [Rabban Yohanan ben Zakkai] said unto them: go forth and observe which is the right way to which a man should cleave? Rabbi Eliezer said, a good eye; Rabbi Joshua said, a good companion; Rabbi Yose said, a good neighbor; Rabbi Shimon said, foresight; Rabbi Elazar said, *a good heart*" (אָמַר לָהֶם, צְאוּ וּרְאוּ אֵיזוֹהִי דֶרֶךְ יְשָׁרָה שֶׁיִּדְבַּק בָּהּ הָאָדָם. רַבִּי אֱלִיעֶזֶר אוֹמֵר, עַיִן טוֹבָה. רַבִּי יְהוֹשֻׁעַ אוֹמֵר, חָבֵר טוֹב. רַבִּי יוֹסֵי אוֹמֵר, שָׁכֵן טוֹב. רַבִּי שִׁמְעוֹן אוֹמֵר, הָרוֹאֶה אֶת הַנּוֹלָד. רַבִּי אֶלְעָזָר אוֹמֵר, **לֵב טוֹב**). See Matt 13:10–23; Mark 4:10–20. See also 2 Esd. 8:41: "Just as a farmer sows many seeds on the land, but in time not all seeds that are sown will be saved nor will all the planted things take root, so also not all of those who are sown in the world will be saved."

[99] The words "having heard the word, keep it" link the passage to Luke 11:28.

the earth without a foundation;[100] against which the stream beat vehemently, and immediately it fell; and the ruin of that house was great.

Luke 8:16 No one, having lit a lamp, covers it with a vessel, or puts it under a bed; but puts it on a lamp stand, so that those entering may see the light.[101] **17** For nothing is secret, that shall not become manifest; nor anything hidden, that shall not be known and come to light. **18** Take heed therefore how you hear: for whoever has, to him shall be given; and whoever has not, from him shall be taken even what he seems to have.

Luke 8:16 is a "doublet," repeated in Luke 11:33. This may be explained by the assumption that Luke relied on two hypothetical sources, an Anthological Text (ANT) and a Reconstructed Text (RCT).

The Lamp of the Body (ANT)

In Hebrew, a "good eye" is a euphemism for generosity while an "evil eye" suggests miserliness. Jesus' emphasis is characteristically on good deeds.

Luke 11:33 No man, when he has lit a candle, puts it in a secret place, nor under a bushel, but on a lamp stand, that those entering may see the light. 34 The lamp of the body is the eye: **therefore**

---

[100] Note *m. Avot* 3:17, attributed to Rabbi Elazar ben Azariah: "One whose wisdom exceeds his deeds, to what may he be compared? To a tree whose branches are numerous but whose roots are few, so that when the wind comes, it uproots it and overturns it" (וְהָרוּחַ, וְשָׁרָשָׁיו מְעַטִּין, שֶׁעֲנָפָיו מְרֻבִּין לְאִילָן, דּוֹמֶה הוּא לְמַה מִמַּעֲשָׂיו, מְרֻבָּה שֶׁחָכְמָתוֹ כָּל פָּנָיו עַל וְהוֹפַכְתּוֹ וְעוֹקַרְתּוֹ בָּאָה).

[101] Note *Sifre Num* 93: "What was Moses like at that time? Like a **lamp placed upon a menorah**, from which many lamps are lighted without the first losing any of its light. So, the wisdom of Moses was in no way diminished thereby" (באותה דומה משה למה של חכמתו היתה לא כך כלום; אורו חסר ולא הרבה נרות ממנו ודלקו מנורה, גבי על שמונה לנר—?שעה כלום חסרה משה). The Torah ("wisdom of Moses") is here equated with light. See also Mid. Hallel, Ps. 113: "If a man has a dwelling which is ten cubits square, where does he set a lamp? ... In the middle of the dining room." See also Matt 5:15.

when your eye is clear, your whole body is also full of light;[102] but when your **eye is evil,**[103] your body is also full of darkness. **35** Take heed, therefore, that the light that is in you is not darkness. **36** If your whole body, therefore, is full of light, having no dark part, it will all be full of light, as when the bright shining of a lamp might light you.

Scene 10:
Wind and Waves Rebuked (RCT)

Continuing with Luke Chapter 8, when Jesus is said to rebuke the wind and the waves, he is using a technical Hebrew term for subduing evil, indicating the present tense arrival of the kingdom of God/heaven.

Luke 8:22 Now it came to pass[104] on a certain day, that he went into a boat with his disciples: and he said to them: Let us go over to the other side of the lake. And they launched out. **23** But as they sailed he fell asleep; and there **a storm of wind came down on the lake;**[105] and they were being swamped, and were in danger. **24** And they came to him, and awoke him, saying: Master, master, we are perishing. Then he arose, and **rebuked the wind and the**

---

[102] The Greek "good/clear eye" (ὀφθαλμός ἁπλοῦς) refers to generosity. See Matt 6:22; note *m. Avot* 5:19: "A *good eye*, a humble spirit and a moderate appetite he is of the disciples of Abraham, our father" (עַיִן טוֹבָה, וְרוּחַ נְמוּכָה, וְנֶפֶשׁ שְׁפָלָה, מִתַּלְמִידָיו שֶׁל אַבְרָהָם אָבִינוּ). Note also Prov 22:9: "He who has a *good eye* shall be blessed; for he gives of his bread to the poor." (טוֹב-עַיִן הוּא יְבֹרָךְ: כִּי-נָתַן מִלַּחְמוֹ לַדָּל).

[103] Note Deut 15:9: "... and your *eye is evil* against your needy brother, and you give him nothing; and he cries to the Lord against you, it will be a sin in you" (וְרָעָה עֵינְךָ בְּאָחִיךָ הָאֶבְיוֹן וְלֹא תִתֵּן לוֹ, וְקָרָא עָלֶיךָ אֶל-יְהוָה, וְהָיָה בְךָ חֵטְא); Prov 28:22: "He who has an *evil eye* hastens after riches" (נִבְהָל לַהוֹן אִישׁ רַע עָיִן); Ben Sira 14:10: "An *evil eye* is towards evil things: and he shall not have his fill of bread, but shall be needy and pensive at his own table."

[104] The Greek ἐγένετο δὲ translates the Hebrew וַיְהִי.

[105] Note the parallel with the book of Jonah (1:4): "... there was a mighty storm in the sea" (וַיְהִי סַעַר גָּדוֹל, בַּיָּם).

raging of the water: and they ceased,[106] and there was a calm.
25 And he said to them: Where is your faith? And being afraid,
they marveled, saying one to another: Who then is this? For he
commands even the winds and water, and they obey him.

Scene 11:
A Demon-Possessed Man Healed

*When Jesus exorcises a demon-possessed man, he is engaging in a
practice not uncommon in ancient Judaism, as attested in
apocryphal literature and in Josephus. Beyond the miracle
account, an underlying meaning involves the subduing of the
power of evil, as a sign that the kingdom of God/heaven had
arrived.*

Luke 8:26 And they sailed down to the region of the
Gadarenes,[107] which is opposite Galilee. **27** And when he went
forth to land, a certain man from the city met him, who had
demons for a long time, and **wore no clothes, nor lived in any**

---

[106] The Greek ἐπετίμησεν ("rebuked") translates the Hebrew גער—a technical
term for rebuking a demon. Note *b. B.M.* 59b: "And even Rabban Gamliel was coming
on a boat at the time, and a large wave swelled over him and threatened to drown him.
Rabban Gamliel said: It seems to me that this is only for the sake of Rabbi Eliezer ben
Hyrcanus. Rabban Gamliel stood on his feet and said: Master of the Universe, it is
revealed and known before You that neither was it for my honor that I acted when
ostracizing him, nor was it for the honor of the house of my father that I acted; rather, it
was for Your honor, so that disputes will not proliferate in Israel. In response, *the sea
calmed from its raging*" (ואף ר"ג היה בא בספינה עמד עליו נחשול לטבעו אמר כמדומה לי שאין זה
אלא בשביל ר"א בן הורקנוס עמד על רגליו ואמר רבונו של עולם גלוי וידוע לפניך שלא לכבודי עשיתי ולא
לכבוד בית אבא אלא לכבודך שלא ירבו מחלוקות בישראל **נח הים מזעפו**). Note the Talmudic
anecdote: "A ship, belonging to a heathen owner, was one sailing over the sea, one of the
passengers being a Jewish boy. A great storm arose … The boy immediately stood up and
called with all his heart upon God, Who hearkened to his prayer, and the sea became
calm" (*y. Ber.* 13b).

[107] Gedara was predominantly Greek; a city of the Decapolis (Josephus, *Ant.*
XVII.11.4), located five miles southeast of the Sea of Galilee. Variants: Gerasa, Gergasa.
The Greek population accounts for the swine. The tombs, being unclean, were suitable
for demons.

house, but in the tombs.[108] **28** When he saw Jesus, he cried out, and fell down before him, and with a loud voice said: What have I to do with you, Jesus, you **Son of God most high God?**[109] I implore you not to torment me. **29** (For **he was commanding the unclean spirit to come out of the man.**[110] For many times it had seized him; and he was kept bound with chains and in shackles; and he broke the chains, and was driven by the demon into the deserts.) **30** And Jesus asked him: What is your name? And he said, Legion; because many demons had entered into him. **31** And they begged him not to command them to go out into the Abyss. **32** And there was there a herd of many pigs feeding in the mountain: and they begged him that he would allow them to enter into them. And he allowed them. **33 Then the demons went out of the man, and entered into the pigs:**[111] and the herd rushed down a steep bank into the lake, and were drowned. **34** When those who fed them saw what had taken place, they fled, and reported it to the city and to the country. **35** Then they went out to see what had taken place, and came to Jesus, and found the man, from whom the demons had gone out, sitting at the feet of Jesus, clothed, and in his

---

[108] Similar to an "imbecile," as in *y. Git.* 7.1 (48c): "Who is considered to be an imbecile? He who goes alone at night and he who spends the night on a cemetery and he that tears his garments." Hanina ben Dosa was said to have encountered the queen of the demons (*b. Pes.* 112b): "Agrat, daughter of Maḥalat, she and 180,000 angels of destruction go out at these times. And as each and every one of them has permission to destroy by itself …'" אָגְרַת בַּת מָחֲלַת, הִיא וּשְׁמוֹנָה עֶשְׂרֵה רִבּוֹא שֶׁל מַלְאֲכֵי חַבָּלָה יוֹצְאִין, וְכָל אֶחָד וְאֶחָד); "I decree upon you that you should never travel through inhabited places" (יֵשׁ לוֹ רְשׁוּת לְחַבֵּל בִּפְנֵי עַצְמוֹ). (גּוֹזֵר אֲנִי עָלַיִךְ שֶׁלֹּא תַעֲבוֹרִי בַּיִּשׁוּב לְעוֹלָם).

[109] See Luke 1:32 n.; Note Dead Sea "Son of God" text.

[110] See Judg 11:12; 1 Kgs 17:18; 2 Kgs 16:10. Exorcism was not uncommon in ancient Judaism. See Josephus, *Ant.* XVIII.2.5: "… and God granted [Solomon] knowledge of the art used against demons for the benefit and healing of men. He also composed incantations … and left behind exorcism … A certain Eleazar … in the presence of Vespasian … put to the nose of a possessed man a ring which had … one of the roots prescribed by Solomon … drew out the demons through the nostrils … The man fell down … adjured the demon never to come back." Note also *b. B.M.* 17b: "The demon ben Temalyon went before them and ascended into the emperor's daughter and possessed her. When Rabbi Shimon ben Yoḥai arrived there, the emperor's palace, he said: Ben Temalyon, emerge! Ben Temalyon, emerge! And once Rabbi Shimon called to him, ben Temalyon emerged and left" (קְדֵים הוּא עַל בִּבְרַתֵּיהּ דְּקֵיסָר כִּי מְטָא הָתָם אֲמַר בֶּן תְּמַלְיוֹן צֵא בֶּן תְּמַלְיוֹן צֵא וְכֵיוָן דִּקְרוֹ לֵיהּ נְפַק אֲזַל). See also Luke 11:31.

[111] Since pigs were unclean, it was proper for Jesus to send the demons into them.

right mind: and they were afraid. **36** Those who saw it related to them how the one who was possessed by demons was healed. **37** Then the whole multitude of the surrounding region of the Gadarenes asked him to depart from them; for they were seized with great fear: and he entered into the boat, and returned back again. **38** However, the man from whom the demons had gone out begged to be with him; but Jesus sent him away, saying: **39** Return to your own house, and relate all that **God**[112] has done for you. And he went his way, proclaiming throughout the whole city all that Jesus had done for him.

Scene 12:
A Woman Healed and a Girl Revived

When the hemorrhagic woman touches the border of his garment, we understand that Jesus likely wore tzitzit ("tassels"). When he raises the dead, it is often viewed as a display of his divinity; however, we find similar examples of raising the dead with Elijah and Elisha. It may well be that comatose individuals were often incorrectly presumed to be dead.

Luke 8:40 And it came to pass,[113] that, when Jesus returned, the people gladly received him; for they were all looking for him. **41** And, **behold,**[114] there came a man named Jairus; and he was a ruler of the synagogue: and he fell down at Jesus' feet, and begged him to come to his house: **42** For he had only one daughter, about twelve years old, and she lay dying. But as he went, the crowds pressed in on him. **43** And a woman having a flux of blood for twelve years, who had spent all her living on physicians, but could not be healed of any, **44** came behind him, and touched the **fringe**

---

[112] Mark 5:19 reads Κύριος ("Lord"), possibly translating הָאָדוֹן, a messianic designation for Jesus.

[113] The Greek καὶ ἐγένετο translates the Hebrew וַיְהִי; see Luke 1:23.

[114] The Greek ἰδού is used in imitation of the Hebrew הִנֵּה.

of his cloak:[115] and immediately her flux of blood stopped. **45** And Jesus said: Who touched me? When all denied it, Peter and those who were with him said: Master, the people are surrounding you and pressing in on you; and you say, Who touched me? **46** And Jesus said: Somebody has touched me: for I know that power has gone out for me. **47** And when the woman saw that she was not hidden, she came trembling, and falling down before him, she declared to him before all the people how she had touched him, and how she was healed immediately. **48** And he said to her: Daughter, your faith has healed you; go in peace. **49** While he was still speaking, one of the synagogue rulers came, saying: Your daughter is dead; do not trouble the teacher. **50** But when Jesus heard this, he answered him: Do not fear; only believe, and she will be made whole. **51** And when he came into the house, he did not allow anyone to go in with him, except Peter, and James, and John, and the father and the mother of the child. **52** And all were weeping, and mourning for her: but he said: **Do not weep; she is not dead, but is only sleeping.**[116] **53 And they were laughing at**

---

[115] The Greek κράσπεδον translates the Hebrew צִיצִית ("fringe/tassel"). See Num 15:38: "... that they make fringes on the corners of their garments" (וְעָשׂוּ לָהֶם צִיצִת עַל כַּנְפֵי בִגְדֵיהֶם). This represents evidence of Jesus' clothing. See also Matt 14:36: "... and begged him that they might only touch the hem of his garment;" Mark 6:56. Note *b.Taan.* 23b: "Ḥanan HaNeḥba was the son of Ḥoni HaMe'aggel's daughter. When the world was in need of rain, the Sages would send schoolchildren to him, and they would grab him *by the hem of his cloak* and say to him: *Father, Father*, give us rain. He said before the Holy One, Blessed be He: Master of the Universe, act on behalf of these children, who cannot distinguish between their *Father in Heaven*, Who can provide rain, and the *father* who cannot provide rain" (חָנָן הַנֶּחְבָּא בַּר בְּרַתֵּיה דְּחוֹנִי הַמְעַגֵּל הֲוָה כִּי מִצְטַרְיךְ עָלְמָא לְמִיטְרָא הֲווּ מְשַׁדְּרִי רַבָּנַן יָנוּקֵי דְּבֵי רַב לְגַבֵּיה וְנָקְטִי לֵיה **בְּשִׁיפּוּלֵי גְלִימֵיה** וַאֲמְרוּ לֵיה **אַבָּא אַבָּא** הַב לַן מִיטְרָא אָמַר לִפְנֵי הַקָּדוֹשׁ בָּרוּךְ הוּא רִבּוֹנוֹ שֶׁל עוֹלָם עֲשֵׂה בִּשְׁבִיל אֵלּוּ שֶׁאֵין מַכִּירִין בֵּין **אַבָּא** דְּיָהֵיב מִיטְרָא לְ**אַבָּא** דְּלָא יָהֵיב מִיטְרָא). The link with Ḥoni HaMe'aggel and the use of the word "Father" (אַבָּא) further identifies Jesus with the ancient *Hasidim*. Jesus displays a special familiarity with God, whom he calls "my Father" (אבי), in a manner similar to the "Pious" (*Hasidim*). Shmuel Safrai distinguished between the *Hasidim* of the Maccabean revolt and the later breed, to whom Jesus was presumably related. The former stressed purification, the latter good deeds. Note John 17:1: "Jesus spoke these words, lifted up His eyes to heaven, and said: 'Father, the hour has come. Glorify Your Son, that Your Son also may glorify You …'"

[116] In antiquity, comatose people were sometimes incorrectly presumed dead.

him,[117] knowing that she was dead. **54** And he took her by the hand, and called out: **Child, arise.**[118] **55** And her spirit returned, and she arose immediately: and he directed that she be given food. **56** And her parents were astonished: but **he instructed them to tell no one what had happened.**[119]

Scene 13:
Herod Seeks to See Jesus

Repeated reference is made by Luke to the prophet Elijah, who is associated with the appearance of the Messiah and who ascended to heaven without experiencing death. When the disciples report the saying that one of the prophets of old has risen, the reference is not necessarily to one rising from the dead but to the messianic phrase in Deuteronomy 18:18, "I will raise up a prophet from among your brethren." The very term prophet has messianic overtones, and Jesus is presented as the prophet of whom Moses spoke.

Luke 9:7 Now Herod the tetrarch heard of all that was done by him; and he was perplexed, because that it was said by some, that John had risen from the dead; **8** And by some, that **Elijah had appeared; and by others, that one of the old prophets had risen**

---

[117] The Greek καὶ κατεγέλων translates the Hebrew וישחקו ("laughs"/ "ridicules"). It is a humorous word play apparent only in the hypothetical Hebrew *grundschrift*. See Mark 5:39; Matt 9:24. The Elijah and Elisha stories are seen as examples of the dead rising; see Mark 6:15. See also *Lev. R.* 10:4; *b. A.Z.* 10b; *b. Meg.* 7b.

[118] Likely a "pickup" from Acts 9:40: "But Peter sent them all out, and kneeled down, and prayed; and turning him to the body said, **Tabitha, arise.**" The Aramaic for "young girl" is *talita.*

[119] See Luke 4:41–42, where Jesus silenced the demons because he did not want them testifying about him. This idea becomes a subsequent "theme" in Luke's telling, developed as the "messianic secret."

again.[120] **9** And Herod said, **I have beheaded John: but who is this, of whom I hear such things?**[121] And he desired to see him.

Scene 14:
Feeding the Five Thousand

The account of the miraculous feeding of the multitude serves as a prelude to Peter's declaration that Jesus is the Messiah. He is not declaring his "discovery" of Jesus' true identity, but rather producing a "motto," similar to the Shema of Deuteronomy 6:4 ("Hear O Israel, the Lord our God, the Lord is One").

Luke 9:10 And the apostles, when they had returned, told him all that they had done. And having taken them, he went by himself into a town called Bethsaida. **11** And the **people,**[122] when they knew it, followed him: and he received them, and spoke to them of the kingdom of God, and healed those in need of healing. **12** And when the day began to wear on, the twelve came, and said to him:

---

[120] The Elijah and Elisha stories were seen as examples of the dead rising. See *Lev. R.* 10:4. The phrase "one of the old prophets had risen" does not refer to a dead prophet coming forth, but instead references Deut 18:18: "I will raise them up a ***prophet*** from among their brethren" (נָבִיא אָקִים לָהֶם מִקֶּרֶב אֲחֵיהֶם). The Dead Sea Scrolls may reflect belief in a form of reincarnation, especially regarding the Teacher of Righteousness. See 1QS 9:10–11, stating that the men of holiness "shall govern themselves using the original precepts … until there come the ***Prophet*** and the Messiahs of Aaron and Israel" (ונשפטו במשפטים הרשונים … עד בוא נביא ומשיחי אהרון וישראל). It therefore appears that three individuals were expected to usher in the last days. See Cave 4 Messianic Anthology, which also links the "prophet" with Deut 18 and the messiahs with Num 24:15–17 and Deut 3:8–11. See also Luke 7:16, 39; 9:19 (= Matt 16:14); 22:64; Mark 6:15; Jn 6:14; 7:40; Acts 7:37.

[121] Herod was already married to the daughter of the Nabatean monarch Haretath, and according to the Temple Scroll, it was unlawful to take a second wife while the first was living. Also, Antipas married Philip's wife, Herodias, under the law of *yibum* (Levirate marriage). However, Jewish law was modified during this time, so that a daughter (even if there was no son) exempted the woman (*Sifre* Deut 288: "…had no son —in any case" (אין לו - מכל מקום). In this case Herodias had a daughter (Salome). See Matt 14:3; 22:24; Mark 6:17.

[122] Greek ὄχλοι better understood as a translation of אוכלוסים ("people of the area"/"people present"), even where, as in this case, it indicates a great number. ὄχλος appears only twice in John. It is also puzzling why ὄχλος ("crowd") should appear in plural as ὄχλοι—likely since אוכלוסים is plural. Large crowds may have grown over time, but not likely at the beginning.

Send the **crowd**[123] away, that they may go into the surrounding villages and countryside, and lodge, and find provisions: for we are here in a desolate place. **13** But he said to them: Give them to eat. And they said: We have no more than five loaves and two fish; unless we should buy food for all these people. **14** They were about five thousand men. And he said to his disciples: Make them sit down in groups of about fifty. **15** And they did so, and made them all sit down. **16** Then he took the five loaves and the two fish, and looking up to heaven, **he blessed**[124] them, and broke, and gave them to the disciples to set before the crowd. **17** And they ate, and were all filled: and the fragments that remained were taken up, amounting to twelve **baskets.**[125] **18 And it came to pass,**[126] as he was alone praying, his disciples being with him, and he asked them, saying: Who do the people say that I am? **19** They answering said: **John the Baptist; but some say, Elijah;**[127] and others say, that one of the **old prophets has risen again.**[128] **20** He said to them: But who do you say that I am? Peter answering said: **The Anointed One (Messiah) of God.**[129]

---

[123] ὄχλῳ; see v. 11.

[124] Note Matt 26:26, where the Greek does not say "blessed it" (referring to the bread) because Jesus would have said a traditional Hebrew blessing based on Deut 8:10: "And you shall eat and be satisfied, and bless the LORD your God ..." (וְאָכַלְתָּ וְשָׂבָעְתָּ וּבֵרַכְתָּ אֶת יְהוָה אֱלֹהֶיךָ). From this the rabbis justified saying a blessing before and after a meal. One Greek text for Luke 9:16 reads "blessed for them," not "blessed them," as this was not a blessing for "holy objects."

[125] Reminiscent of the twelve tribes of Israel. Note Juvenal, *Sat* vi. 542: "A gypsy Jewess whispers in your ear—Her goods a *basket*, and old *hay* her bed ..."; *Sat* iii. 13: "... Jews, a wretched, wandering train, Whose wealth is but a *basket* stuff'd with hay." See Matt 14:20; Mark 6:43.

[126] The Greek καὶ ἐγένετο translates the Hebrew וַיְהִי; see Luke 1:23.

[127] Some considered John the Baptist to be the "deliverer." Note Mal 3:23: "Behold, I will send you ***Elijah*** the prophet before the coming of the great and terrible day of the LORD" (הִנֵּה אָנֹכִי שֹׁלֵחַ לָכֶם אֵת אֵלִיָּה הַנָּבִיא לִפְנֵי בּוֹא יוֹם יְהוָה הַגָּדוֹל וְהַנּוֹרָא).

[128] See Luke 9:8.

[129] Peter does not "discover" that Jesus is the Messiah; he produces a "motto," akin to the *Shema* (Deut 6:4). Answering Jesus' question regarding what people are saying about him, Peter declares, "the Messiah of God" (Χριστὸν τοῦ Θεοῦ, in Hebrew משיח אל). This is awkward, as 1 Sam 26:9 reads "anointed of the Lord" (מְשִׁיחַ יְהוָה). However, the Dead Sea Scrolls combine a noun with the word "God" (אל) frequently. This is the first use of the term "Messiah" by Peter. There is no mention here, as in Matt 16:18, of the "Church."

Jesus Predicts His Death and Resurrection

When Jesus predicts his death and resurrection, he is possibly echoing concepts found in the so-called Gabriel Revelation, best described as a Dead Sea Scroll in stone. It contains the phrase, "In three days, live…"

Luke 9:21 And he sternly warned them, and commanded them **to tell no one of this;**[130] **22** Saying: The **Son of Man**[131] must suffer many things, and be rejected of the elders and chief priests and scribes, and **be slain, and be raised the third day.**[132]

The Call to Follow

The editor likely added the idea of the coming of the Son of Man. Note Luke 12:9, which does not contain a reference to the parousia. The reference to "taking up his cross" may either be a later editorial gloss or a further link to the Gabriel Revelation and the Messiah son of Joseph tradition.

---

[130] See Luke 4:41–42, where Jesus silenced the demons because he did not want them testifying about him. This idea becomes a subsequent "theme" in Luke's telling, developed as the "messianic secret."

[131] The Aramaic בר אנוש ("son of man") links to Dan 7:13; authority being the theme.

[132] See note on Luke 4:41. Verse 22 may have been added by later redactor. However, consider the Hebrew inscription (ink on stone) known as the "Gabriel Revelation." Its provenance and textual reading is in dispute, but its contents are potentially of great significance. In lines 16–17, God addresses David as follows: "My servant David, ask Ephraim…" (עבדי דוד בקש מן לפני אפרים). Ephraim is the son of Joseph, setting up an equivalence between David and Ephraim and the Talmudic "Messiah Son of David" and the "Messiah Son of Joseph." It suggests that the Messiah Son of Joseph was already a known figure at the end of the first century BCE. A disputed reconstruction of another passage (lines 19–21) reads: "***In three days, live***, I, Gabriel, command you" (לשלושת ימים חייה אני גבריאל גוזר עליך). The archangel is ordering someone to rise from the dead within three days. In the revolt of 4 BCE the most prominent rebel was Simon, who operated from Transjordan. He declared himself king, wore a crown, and was perceived as king by his followers, who (though he was slain by a commander in the Herodian army) hung messianic hopes on him. If the Gabriel Revelation dates to the end of the first century BCE, there were possibly people in Jesus' day who believed that the death of the Messiah was an integral part of the salvation process. The slain messianic leader would be resurrected within three days, and, like Elijah, rise to heaven in a chariot. See Knohl, *Messiahs and Resurrection*, 35.

Luke 9:23 And he said to them all: If anyone will come after me, **let him deny himself, and take up his cross daily, and follow me.**[133] **24** For whoever desires to save his life will lose it: but whoever will lose his life for my sake will save it.[134] **25** For what is a man profited, if he gains the whole world, and loses himself, or is cast away? **26** For **whoever is ashamed of me and of my words, of him will the Son of Man**[135] be ashamed **when he shall come in his glory, and in his Father's, and of the holy angels.**[136] **27** Now I tell you truthfully, there are some standing here, who shall not taste of death, till they **see the kingdom of God.**[137]

Scene 15:
The Transfiguration (ANT)

When Jesus is transfigured on the mount, there is an obvious connection with Moses, whose exalted status links Jesus to the Messiah, and with Passover since the crucifixion is interpreted as the "exodus" of Jesus from Jerusalem. At this point, the hypothetical Reconstructed Text ends and the Anthological Text begins.

Luke 9:28 It came to pass about **eight days**[138] after these sayings, he took Peter and John and James, and went up to a mountain to pray. **29 And it came to pass**[139] as he prayed, **the appearance of**

---

[133] Reminiscent of the call to Abraham; see Genesis 12:1: "Get out of your country, and from your kindred, and from your father's house, to the land that I will show you" (לֶךְ-לְךָ מֵאַרְצְךָ וּמִמּוֹלַדְתְּךָ וּמִבֵּית אָבִיךָ אֶל-הָאָרֶץ אֲשֶׁר אַרְאֶךָּ).

[134] Doublet, Luke 17:33. The Greek "will save it" (σώσει αὐτήν) translates the Hebrew יושיענה, referring to the "soul" (feminine in Hebrew: נפש), in Greek ψυχὴν.

[135] Aramaic בר אנוש links to Dan 7, the theme of which is authority.

[136] Doublet, Luke 12:8–9.

[137] The writer/redactor picked up the idea of "seeing" because of the way the editor revised Luke 21:31. He reads Luke 21:32 ("this generation …") as referring to the *parousia* (wrongly equated with the kingdom of God), when it is actually about the destruction of Jerusalem. See Mark 9:1; Matt 16:28.

[138] Reminiscent of circumcision, on the eighth day.

[139] The Greek καὶ ἐγένετο translates the Hebrew וַיְהִי; see Luke 1:23.

his countenance was altered,[140] and his clothing was white and dazzling. **30** And, **behold,**[141] there talked with him two men, who were **Moses and Elijah;**[142] **31** who appeared in glory, and spoke **of his departure which he would accomplish at Jerusalem**.[143] **32** But Peter and those who were with him were heavy with sleep; and when they were awake, they saw his glory, and the two men who stood with him. **33 And it came to pass,**[144] as they left him, Peter said to Jesus: Master, it is good for us to be here; and let us make three tabernacles; one for you, and one for Moses, and one for Elijah; not knowing what he said. **34** As he was speaking, **there came a cloud, and overshadowed them;**[145] and they feared as they entered into the cloud. **35** And **a voice**[146] **came out of the**

---

[140] Jesus is likened to Moses, suggesting an exalted view of the Messiah. See Exod 34:29: "When he came down from the mount, Moses did not know that the skin of **his face sent forth beams** while He talked with him" (בְּרִדְתּוֹ מִן-הָהָר וּמֹשֶׁה לֹא יָדַע כִּי **קָרַן עוֹר** פָּנָיו בְּדַבְּרוֹ אִתּוֹ). The text may also be appealing to the concept of the archetypal "heavenly Messiah." Note 1 En. 46:3: "This is the Son of Man to whom belongs righteousness and with whom righteousness dwells." The Son of Man is depicted as a heavenly being, who, though he appears as a human being, is a supernatural entity, in a special proximity to God.

[141] The Greek ἰδοὺ is used in imitation of the Hebrew הִנֵּה.

[142] Perhaps suggesting the Torah and the Prophets. See Bivin and Blizzard, 158–59.

[143] In Greek ἔξοδον αὐτοῦ ("his departure/exodus") translates the Hebrew צאתו. As Passover commemorates the exodus from Egypt, the crucifixion is interpreted as the "exodus" of Jesus from Jerusalem ("Egypt"). This perhaps echoes the sentiments of the Dead Sea (Essene) sect, who perceived Jerusalem as corrupt and defiled, and who made and "exodus" of their own into the desert. Note Rev 11:8: "And their dead bodies will lie in the street of the great city which spiritually is called Sodom and Egypt, where also our Lord was crucified."

[144] The Greek καὶ ἐγένετο translates the Hebrew וַיְהִי; see Luke 1:23.

[145] Reminiscent of Moses disappearing into a cloud on Mount Sinai. Exod 33:9: "And it came to pass, when Moses entered into the Tent, **the pillar of cloud descended,** and stood at the door of the Tent; and [the LORD] spoke with Moses" (וְהָיָה, כְּבֹא מֹשֶׁה הָאֹהֱלָה, **יֵרֵד עַמּוּד הֶעָנָן**, וְעָמַד פֶּתַח הָאֹהֶל; וְדִבֶּר, עִם-מֹשֶׁה).

[146] The Greek φωνὴν translates the Hebrew קול, as in בת קול ("daughter of the voice"), which in rabbinic writing conveyed the testimony of heaven. See Luke 3:23.

cloud, saying: **This is my chosen Son;**[147] **listen to him**.[148] **36** And when the voice was heard, Jesus was found alone. And they were silent, and told no one in those days anything which they had seen.

Scene 16:
A Boy Is Healed

When Jesus is depicted as delivering a boy afflicted with a demon, he is again displaying the nature of his essential message, that the Kingdom of God/heaven has arrived, in the present tense.

Luke 9:37 And it came to pass,[149] that on the next day, when they had come down from the hill, a great crowd met him. **38** And, **behold,**[150] a man from the crowd cried out, saying: Teacher, I implore you, look upon my son; for he is my only child. **39** And, **behold,**[151] a spirit takes him, and he suddenly cries out; and he is convulsed with foaming, and it departs from him with great difficulty, bruising him. **40** And I begged your disciples to cast it out; and **they could not.**[152] **41** And Jesus answering said: O faithless and perverse generation, how long shall I be with you, and bear with you? Bring your son here. **42** And while he was still coming, the demon threw him down and into convulsions. And

---

[147] The passive participle Greek term (ἐκλελεγμένος), rendered "chosen," is better translated "whom I have chosen" and reflects the Hebrew בחירי ("my chosen one"). It evokes the second of 2 Isaiah's so-called "servant songs" (Isa 42:1): "This is My servant, whom I uphold, My chosen one, in room I delight. I have put My Spirit upon him, He shall teach the true way to the nations" (הֵן עַבְדִּי אֶתְמָךְ בּוֹ **בְּחִירִי** רָצְתָה נַפְשִׁי; נָתַתִּי רוּחִי עָלָיו מִשְׁפָּט לַגּוֹיִם יוֹצִיא). The word "son" in the verse (υἱός) evokes the declaration of Psalm 2, also understood messianically in the Gospel narrative (Ps 2:7): "The Lord has said to Me, 'You are My Son, Today I have begotten You'" (יְהוָה אָמַר אֵלַי **בְּנִי אַתָּה** אֲנִי הַיּוֹם יְלִדְתִּיךָ).

[148] The Greek (αὐτοῦ ἀκούετε) parrots the last words of Deuteronomy 18:15: "… to him you shall hearken" (אֵלָיו תִּשְׁמָעוּן). Jesus is presented here as the "prophet" like Moses. The first part of the verse is a reference to the sacrifice of the "beloved son" Isaac; the second to the eschatological prophet of Deuteronomy.

[149] The Greek ἐγένετο δὲ translates the Hebrew וַיְהִי.

[150] The Greek ἰδοὺ is used in imitation of the Hebrew הִנֵּה.

[151] The Greek ἰδοὺ is used in imitation of the Hebrew הִנֵּה.

[152] This could be a parallel to 2 Kgs 4:31, in which Gehazi (servant of Elisha) is unable to revive the dead.

Jesus rebuked the unclean spirit, and healed the body, and delivered him again to his father.

Jesus Again Predicts His Death[153]

Luke 9:43 And they were all amazed at the mighty power of God. But while they all marveled at all the things that Jesus did, he said to his disciples, **44 Let these sayings sink down into your ears:**[154] for the **Son of Man**[155] shall be betrayed into the hands of men. **45** But they did not understand this saying, and it was hidden from them, so that they would not perceive it; and they feared to ask him about that saying.

Who Is the Greatest?

The emphasis on humility is a rabbinic/Talmudic concept, reminiscent of Hillel.

Luke 9:46 Then there arose an argument among them, about which of them should be the greatest. **47** And Jesus, perceiving the thought of their hearts, took a child, and set him by his side, **48** And said to them: Whoever receives this child in my name receives me: and whoever receives me receives the One who sent me: for **whoever is least among you all shall be great.**[156]

---

[153] Compare Luke 18:31–34.

[154] The Greek (θέσθε ὑμεῖς εἰς τὰ ὦτα ὑμῶν τοὺς λόγους τούτους) parrots the Hebrew: שימו באזניכם ("place in your ears/pay attention"). See Bivin and Blizzard, 160–63.

[155] The Aramaic בר אנוש ("son of man") links to Dan 7:13; authority being the theme.

[156] See Luke 18:9; note *b. San.* 17a: "This is to teach you that anyone who *humbles* himself, the Holy One, Blessed be He, *exalts* him, and anyone who *exalts* himself, the Holy One, Blessed be He, *humbles* him" (לְלַמֶּדְךָ שֶׁכָּל הַ**מַּשְׁפִּיל** עַצְמוֹ—הַקָּדוֹשׁ בָּרוּךְ הוּא **מַגְבִּיהוֹ**, וְכָל הַ**מַּגְבִּיהַּ** עַצְמוֹ—הַקָּדוֹשׁ בָּרוּךְ הוּא **מַשְׁפִּילוֹ**).

Jesus Forbids Sectarianism

Jesus' emphasis on the "kingdom of God" is advanced by anyone bringing about healing, wholeness or deliverance.

Luke 9:49 And John answered and said: Master, we saw one casting out demons in your name; and we forbade him, because he does not follow us. **50** And Jesus said to him: Do not forbid him; for **whoever is not against us is for us.**[157]

Luke 9:51–62, relating Jesus' resolution to travel to Jerusalem and Samaritan opposition, has been transposed to the beginning of the next "Act": "Up to Jerusalem."

Scene 17:
Sending Out the Twelve (RCT)

Note the sending of disciples in two passages: Luke 9:1–6 and 10:1–12. This double sending indicates that Luke was relying on two sources. Consequently, Jesus' directives to his disciples may be gleaned from either "sending." In Jesus' sending of the twelve, he may be mimicking practices found among the Essenes, who Josephus says took nothing with them in their travels since they would be provided for by members of the sect in other towns.

Luke 9:1 Then he called his twelve disciples together, and gave them power and authority over all demons, and to heal diseases. **2** And he sent them to proclaim the **kingdom of God,**[158] and to heal the sick. **3** And he said to them, **Take nothing for your**

---

[157] Rather than fostering a "cult of personality," he "de-centers" himself.
[158] See Matt 10:7.

journey,[159] neither **staff**[160], nor bag, nor bread, nor money; neither have two tunics apiece. **4** And whatever house you enter, remain there, and go forth from there. **5** And whoever will not receive you, when you go out of that city, shake off the dust from your feet as a testimony against them. **6** And they departed, and went through the villages, proclaiming the good news, and healing everywhere.

Scene 18:
The Seventy Sent Out (ANT)

The "double sending" of disciples (Luke 9:1–6; 10:1–12) is due to two sources. The instructions may have been taken from either account.

Luke 10:1 After these things the Lord **also**[161] appointed seventy others and sent them **two by two**[162] **before his face**[163] into every city and place, where he himself was about to go. **2** Therefore he said to them: **The harvest is indeed great, but the workers are few;**[164] pray therefore to the Lord of the harvest, that he would send forth workers into his harvest. **3** Go; **behold,**[165] I send you forth as lambs in the midst of wolves. **4** Carry neither purse, nor

---

[159] According to Josephus the Essenes carried no provisions with them since other Essene groups had stores in various cities. *Wars* 2:125 (II.8.4): "They have no one certain city, but many of them dwell in every city; and if any of their sect come from other places, what they have lies open for them, just as if it were their own; and they go in to such as they never knew before, as if they had been ever so long acquainted with them." Jesus likewise sends his disciples out, insisting that people in the towns they enter will provide for them. However, he adopts John the Baptist's approach, not accepting the full community of property.

[160] Note *y. Shev.* 8.1, 36c (bot.): "… the proselyte who comes with nothing but his staff and traveling bag."

[161] It is likely that "also" (καὶ) is an editorial gloss and should be deleted.

[162] Note the ancient Jewish concept of "pairs" of ancient Sages, known as the *zugot* (זוּגוֹת).

[163] The Greek πρὸ προσώπου αὐτοῦ translates the Hebrew idiom: לִפְנֵי פָנָיו.

[164] Compare *m. Avot* 2:15: "Rabbi Tarfon said: the day is short, and the work is plentiful, and the laborers are indolent, and the reward is great, and the master of the house is insistent" (רַבִּי טַרְפוֹן אוֹמֵר, הַיּוֹם קָצֵר וְהַמְּלָאכָה מְרֻבָּה, וְהַפּוֹעֲלִים עֲצֵלִים, וְהַשָּׂכָר הַרְבֵּה, וּבַעַל הַבַּיִת דּוֹחֵק). This refers to study, whereas Jesus references the kingdom of God movement. Note Hippocrates (5th century BCE): "The day is short and the task is great."

[165] The Greek ἰδοὺ is used in imitation of the Hebrew הִנֵּה.

bag, nor sandals; and greet no one on the road. **5** And whatever house you enter, first say: Peace to this house. **6** And **if a son of peace is there, your peace shall rest upon him.**[166] If not, however, **it shall turn to you again.**[167] **7** Remain in the same house, eating and drinking whatever they supply: for the workman is worthy of his wages. Do not go from house to house. **8** And into whatever city you might enter, when they receive you, eat the things set before you; **9** And heal the sick who are there, and say to them: The kingdom of God **has come near to you.** **10** But whatever city you enter, if they do not receive you, go out into the streets, and say: **11** Even the dust of your city, which clings to us, we wipe off against you; but know this, that the kingdom of God **has come near to you.**[168] **12** But I say to you, that it shall be more tolerable in that day for Sodom, than for that city.

Woe to the Unrepentant Cities

We again witness Jesus' stringent level of Jewish piety, as he employs a classic Kal v-khomer ("light and heavy") reasoning technique, saying that if it will be bad for Tyre and Sidon (Gentile cities which Jesus would not visit) on the day of judgment, it will be even worse for "you" (Chorazin and Bethsaida).

Luke 10:13 Woe to you, Chorazin! **woe**[169] to you, Bethsaida! for if the mighty works had been done in **Tyre and Sidon,**[170] which have been done in you, they would have long ago repented, sitting in sackcloth and ashes. **14** But it shall be more tolerable for Tyre and Sidon at the judgment, than for you. **15** And you, Capernaum, will

---

[166] Note the rabbinic blessing: "Shalom to you, shalom to your house (i.e. family) and shalom to everything you own." See Bivin and Blizzard, 167–69.

[167] I.e. the blessing will not take effect.

[168] S The Greek ἤγγικεν means "about to appear" or "almost here." It translates the Hebrew קרב ("has arrived"). The concept is spatial, not temporal, and used to suggest physical intimacy. See Gen 20:4; Lev 18:6,14, 20:16, Deut 22:14; Isa 8:3; Ezek 18:6.

[169] The Greek Οὐαί is used in the Septuagint chiefly for הוי and אוֹי.

[170] See Matt 11:21. Cities of the gentiles where Jesus did not speak.

not be exalted to heaven, but will be brought down to **Hades**.[171] **16** He who hears you hears me; and he who despises you despises me; and he who despises me despises the One who sent me.

Scene 19:
The Seventy Return with Joy

Jesus goes on to express the immediacy of his kingdom of God/ heaven message, as we understand him saying, not, "I saw Satan fall like lightning," but "I am seeing (present tense) Satan fall like lightning." His meaning is that whenever demons are expelled, the reign of God is displayed.

Luke 10:17 And the seventy returned with joy, saying: Lord, even the demons are subject to us through your name. **18** And he said to them: **I beheld Satan fall as lightning**[172] from heaven. **19 Behold,**[173] I give to you power to tread on serpents and scorpions, and over all the power of the enemy; and **nothing shall by any means hurt you.**[174] **20** Yet, do not rejoice in this, that the spirits are subject to you; but rather rejoice, that **your names are written in heaven.**[175]

---

[171] The Greek ᾅδου is the equivalent of the Hebrew שאול (Sheol; see Isa 14:9, 11) or גהינום (Gehenna; see Jer 7:31; 19:2–6), the latter being the destination of the wicked in rabbinic literature. Note *b. Sotah* 4b: "… this transgression of adultery will entrap him into the judgment of Gehenna" (היא תצודנו לדינה של גיהנם).

[172] Before the messianic age, Satan is to be vanquished; see *Test. Dan.* 5; *Test. Zev.* 9. Jesus is essentially saying, "I have just been watching Satan fall like lightning …" The expulsion of demons is evidence of the present tense appearance of the kingdom of God.

[173] The Greek ἰδού is used in imitation of the Hebrew הִנֵּה.

[174] Note *b. Pes.* 8b: "Those on the path to perform a mitzvah are not susceptible to harm" (שְׁלוּחֵי מִצְוָה אֵינָן נִזּוֹקִין).

[175] Note *m. Avot* 2:16: "And know that the grant of reward unto the righteous is in the age to come" (וְדַע מַתַּן שְׂכָרָן שֶׁל צַדִּיקִים לֶעָתִיד לָבֹא).

Jesus Rejoices in the Spirit

We also see Jesus mimicking the language of the Dead Sea Psalms Scroll, which regularly employs the Hebrew expression "I thank you."[176] We see Jesus echoing ancient Jewish concepts later reflected in the Babylonian Talmud, that prophecy was taken away from prophets and given to fools and children.

Luke 10:21 In that hour he rejoiced in the **Holy Spirit**,[177] and said: **I thank you, O Father, Lord of heaven and earth, that you have hidden these things**[178] **from the wise and intelligent, and have revealed them to little children.**[179] Even so, Father; for so it seemed good before you. **22** All things have been delivered to me by **my Father**: and no one knows who **the Son is, but the Father**; and who the **Father** is, but the **Son**, and he to whom the **Son**[180] will reveal him. **23** And he turned him to his disciples, and said privately: **Blessed are the eyes which see what you see:**[181] **24** For

---

[176] See Flusser, *Jewish Sources*, 41.

[177] See Luke 1:15. Note Dead Sea Scrolls 1QS4:21: "… cleansing from every wicked deed by a ***holy spirit***" (ולטהרו ברוח קודש מכול עלילות רשעה).

[178] The Dead Sea Scrolls frequently reference "secrets"/"hidden things." Note 1Q27 f1i:3 "But they did not know the ***secret of the way things are*** nor did they understand the things of old" (ולוא ידעו רז נהיה ובקדמוניות).

[179] See Matt 11:25. Jesus speaks in the style of the Dead Sea Thanksgiving Hymns, most of which being with the words "I thank You" (אודך). The idea that the deepest truth is closed to some but open to the "simple" possibly expresses the anti-intellectualism of the Essenes and Hasidim. Note *b. B.B.* 12b: "From the day that the Temple was destroyed, prophecy was taken from the prophets and ***given to imbeciles and children***" (מיום שֶׁחֲרַב בֵּית הַמִּקְדָּשׁ נִטְּלָה נְבוּאָה מִן הַנְּבִיאִים וְנִיתְּנָה לַשּׁוֹטִים וְלַתִּינוֹקוֹת).

[180] See Luke 2:49. The language here is fairly "generic," as if to say: "No one knows a father like a son." Note Ezek 18:4: "The soul of the father as well as the soul of the son is Mine" (כְּנֶפֶשׁ הָאָב וּכְנֶפֶשׁ הַבֵּן הַבֵּן לִי).

[181] Note Luke 1:42: "Blessed are you among women …" Note *b. San.* 99a: "All the prophets prophesied only about the messianic era, but with regard to the World-to-Come the reward is not quantifiable, as it states: '***No eye has seen it***, God, aside from You, Who will do for those who await Him'" (כל הנביאים כולן לא נתנבאו אלא לימות המשיח אבל לעולם הבא עין לא ראתה אלהים זולתך (אלהים) יעשה למחכה לו).

I tell you, that **many prophets and kings have desired to see**[182] what you see, and have not seen them; and to hear what you hear, and have not heard them.

Luke 8:10 may be added at this point. Jesus may be understood as saying that the disciples do not need parables since they inherently understand the divine power of God's kingdom. They see what prophets and kings have wished to see.

Mysteries of the Kingdom (RCT)

Luke 8:10 And he said: To you it is given to know the **mysteries of the kingdom of God:**[183] but **to the rest in parables;**[184] that **seeing they might not see,**[185] and hearing they might not understand.

---

[182] Note Mekh. Ex. 15:2: "Whence is it derived that a maid-servant *beheld* at the Red Sea *what was not beheld* by Ezekiel and the other prophets, of whom it is written (Hos. 12:11) 'By the ministry of the prophets have I used similitudes'" (מנין אתה אומר); שראתה שפחה על הים מה שלא ראו ישעיה ויחזקאל שנ' וביד הנביאים אדמה). Note Matt 13:17, where Jesus declares that from John's day, the kingdom is "breaking forth." Jesus apparently saw history in three dispensations: the Law and the Prophets; the kingdom of heaven; and the world to come. See also Luke 7:20.

[183] According to the earliest manuscript evidence, read "secrets of God" (רזי אל) as opposed to "secrets of the kingdom of God." Note Dead Sea Scrolls CD 2:14–15: "So now, my children, listen to me that I may uncover your eyes to see and to understand the *deeds of God*' (מעשי אל); 1QS3:22–23: "All their sins, iniquities, shameful and rebellious deeds are at his prompting, a situation *God in His mysteries* allows to continue until His era dawns." (וכל חטאתם ועונותם ואשמתם ופשעי); ועתה בנים שמעו לי ואגלה עיניכם לראות ולהבין במעשי אל) מעשיהם בממשלתו לפי רזי אל עד קצו); 1QM 3:8–9: "On the trumpets of ambush they shall write, '*Mysteries of God* to wipe out wickedness'" (ועל חצוצרות המארב יכתובו רזי אל לשחת) רשעה).

[184] The disciples do not need parables because they are privy to the mysteries of God. This is contrary to the notion that the parables are meant to obscure rather than clarify. This verse better suits the description of blessings greater than prophets rather than its traditional context.

[185] Note *Gen. R.* 91:6: "Since the day Joseph was stolen, the Holy Spirit departed from [Jacob] so that *he saw yet did not see*, heard yet did not hear" (מיום שנגנב יוסף נסתלקה רוח הקדש ממנו ורואה ואינו רואה, ושומע ואינו שומע).

Scene 20:
Woe to the Pharisees and Lawyers (ANT)

When Jesus dines with "a certain Pharisee," it is appropriate to ask why the cup is mentioned with reference to washing hands. The Mishnah reveals a first century understanding that not only must food be clean but also the utensils.

Luke 11:37 And as he spoke, a certain Pharisee asked him to dine with him; and he went in, and reclined. **38** And when the Pharisee saw it, he marveled that **he had not first washed before dinner.**[186] **39** And the Lord said to him: **Now, you Pharisees make the outside of the cup clean and the dish; but the inside of you is full of plundering and wickedness.**[187] **40** You fools, did not the one who made that the outside also make the inside? **41** But rather give alms of the things you have; and, **behold,**[188] all things are clean to you. **42** But **woe** to you, Pharisees! For you tithe mint and rue and every herb, and pass by the justice and the love of God. These ought you to have done, and not leave the other undone. **43 Woe** to you, Pharisees, for you love the first seats in the synagogues, and the greetings in the marketplaces. **44 Woe**[189]

---

[186] See Mark 7:2; Matt 23:25. A primary concern in the first century was eating food in a state of ritual purity. However, *halakhah* regarding this was still in flux at this time. It has also been suggested (by Simon Gibson, *The Final Days of Jesus*) that Jesus initiated a movement with alternative purification rituals, including anointing with oil and immersion.

[187] See Mark 7:1–8. The House of Shammai maintained that one must clean the outside first while the House of Hillel ruled that the inside must be cleaned first. In the Lucan context Jesus agrees with the House of Hillel and is therefore closer to traditional rabbinic law: if the inside is unclean, so is the outside; but if the outside is unclean, the inside (if originally pure) is uncontaminated. If an unclean cup is cleansed from the outside, it is not pure. It must be cleansed on the inside first.

[188] The Greek ἰδού is used in imitation of the Hebrew הִנֵּה.

[189] The Greek Οὐαί is used in the Septuagint chiefly for הוֹי and אוֹי.

to you, scribes and Pharisees, **hypocrites!**[190] For you are **as unmarked graves,**[191] and the men who walk over them are not aware of them. **45** Then one of the lawyers answered, and said to him: Teacher, in saying these things you insult us also. **46** And he said: **Woe** also to you lawyers! For you load men with burdens too heavy to bear, and you yourselves do not touch the burdens with one of your fingers. **47 Woe**[192] to you! For you build the tombs of the prophets; yet, your fathers killed them. **48** Truly, you bear witness that you consent to the works of your fathers; for they indeed killed them, and you build their tombs. **49** Therefore, the Wisdom of God also said: I will send them prophets and **apostles,**[193] and some of them they will kill and persecute; **50** That the blood of all the prophets, which was shed from the foundation of the world, may be required of this generation. **51** From the blood of Abel to the blood of **Zechariah**[194] who perished between

---

[190] See also Matt 23:27. The Greek word for "hypocrites" (ὑποκριταί) is related to the word for "judge," the Hebrew word is צבועים/צבוע/צבועין ("colored ones"). Bearing this in mind, the passage need not be seen as a blanket condemnation of the Pharisees. Note *b. Sot.* 22b: "King Yannai said to his wife before he died: Do not be afraid of the *Pharisees* [*perushin*], and neither should you fear from those who are not *Pharisees*, i.e., the Sadducees; rather, beware of the *hypocrites* who appear like *Pharisees*, as their actions are like the act of the wicked Zimri and they request a reward like that of the righteous Pinehas" (אמר לה ינאי מלכא לדביתיה אל תתיראי מן **הפרושין** ולא ממי שאינן **פרושין** אלא מן **הצבועין** שדומין **לפרושין** שמעשיהן כמעשה זמרי ומבקשין שכר כפנחס). Note also *b. Sot.* 41b: "Any person who has *flattery* [a form of hypocrisy] in him falls into Gehenna" (כל אדם שיש בו **חנופה** נופל בגיהנם); *b. Sot.* 42a: "Four classes of people will not greet the Divine Presence: The class of cynics, and the class of *flatterers* [a form of hypocrisy], and the class of liars, and the class of slanderers." (ארבע כיתות אין מקבלות פני שכינה כת ליצים וכת **חניפים** וכת שקרים וכת מספרי לשון הר). Matthew repeatedly appends the words "hypocrites" to "Pharisees" while there is no such continuous usage in Luke. This suggests that the source material for both did not contain "hypocrites."

[191] That is, becoming accidentally defiled by contact. Matt 23:27 substitutes "whitewashed." A rolling stone was whitewashed after a body was interred, to warn off defilement.

[192] The Greek Οὐαί is used in the Septuagint chiefly for הוי and אוי.

[193] A better understanding of the Greek ἀποστέλλω is provided by the Hebrew "seekers of Torah" (דורשי תורה). Note Matt 23:34: "Therefore, indeed, I send you prophets, wise men, and scribes …"

[194] Not the prophet Zechariah, but a reference to the martyred son of the High Priest in the times of Ahaziah and Joash (2 Chron 24:20).

the altar and the **house;**[195] **truly I say to you,**[196] It will be required of this generation. **52 Woe**[197] to you, lawyers, for you have taken away the key of knowledge. You did not enter yourselves, and those who were entering you hindered. **53** And as he said these things to them, the scribes and the Pharisees began to press upon him urgently, and to provoke him to speak about many things; **54** watching him, to catch him in something out of his mouth.

Scene 21:
Beware of Hypocrisy

Hypocrisy is a major concern of Jesus' kingdom of God/heaven message. Rather than a full-throated attack on the Pharisees, who were the upholders of the Judaism of the day, Jesus may be better understood as condemning "leaven," which rabbinically represents the "evil inclination." This is what gives rise to hypocrisy. In Luke 12 we also find several statements that are more suited to post-resurrection appearances of Jesus, such as the admonition not to fear those who kill the body. The Lucan editor likely transposed these sayings to an earlier period in Jesus' life and teaching. Vv.4–12 and 35–48 have accordingly been moved to the "Post-Resurrection" section.

Luke 12:1 In the meantime, when a great multitude of people were gathered together, inasmuch as they trampled one another, he

---

[195] The Greek οἴκου translates the Hebrew בית (a euphemism for the temple).

[196] "Amen"/"assuredly" (Heb. אמן) was commonly added after a strong statement. Note Jer 28:6: "*Amen*! The Lord do so; the Lord perform your words which you have prophesied ..." - (אָמֵן, כֵּן יַעֲשֶׂה יְהוָה יָקֵם יְהוָה אֶת-דְּבָרֶיךָ אֲשֶׁר נִבֵּאתָ). See Luke 4:24; Matt 5:18.

[197] The Greek Οὐαί is used in the Septuagint chiefly for הוֹי and אוֹי.

began to say to his disciples: First of all, beware of the **leaven**[198] of the Pharisees, which is hypocrisy. **2 For there is nothing covered, that will not be revealed/nor hidden, that will not be known.**[199] **3** Therefore whatever you have spoken in darkness will be heard in the light; and that which you have spoken into the ear in the inner rooms will be proclaimed upon the housetops.

Luke 12:13–31 have been moved to follow Luke 10:42.

Do Not Worry

The message not to fear is consistent with rabbinic teaching, specifically with the ancient Hasidim. If the "kingdom" is understood in the present tense, it is about the divine reign on earth, in addition to the promise of the world to come. The key is again the performance of good deeds.

Luke 12:32 Do not fear, little flock; for it is your Father's good pleasure to give you the kingdom. **33** Sell what you have, and **give alms;**[200] make yourselves bags which do not grow old, **a treasure**

---

[198] Leaven is said to represent the evil inclination; eg. *b. Ber.* 17a: "Master of the Universe, it is revealed and known before You that our will is to perform Your will, and what prevents us? On the one hand, *the yeast in the dough*, the evil inclination that is within every person" (שְׂאוֹר—?רְבּוֹן הָעוֹלָמִים, גָּלוּי וְיָדוּעַ לְפָנֶיךָ שֶׁרְצוֹנֵנוּ לַעֲשׂוֹת רְצוֹנֶךָ, וּמִי מְעַכֵּב שֶׁבָּעִיסָה); *Gen. R.* 34: "Abba Jose the potter said: How terrible must be the *leaven* when he who created it testifies that it is bad, as it is written 'For He knows *our inclinations*, it is remembered that we are dust' (Ps 103:14)" (אַבָּא יוֹסֵי הַתּוֹרְתִי אוֹמֵר עָלוּב הוּא הַשְּׂאוֹר, שֶׁמִּי שֶׁבְּרָאוֹ אוֹתוֹ מֵעִיד עָלָיו שֶׁהוּא רַע, שֶׁנֶּאֱמַר תהלים קג, יד: כִּי הוּא יָדַע יִצְרֵנוּ זָכוּר כִּי עָפָר אֲנָחְנוּ).

[199] Note the Hebraic *parallelism/poetry*. This represents the original context of the saying found in Matt 10:26. Note *Targ. Koh.* 12:13: "Every word which is done in the world in secret will ultimately be publicized and announced to all of mankind" (סוֹף פִּתְגָם דְּאִתְעֲבִיד בְּעַלְמָא בְּצִנְעָא כּוֹלָא עָתִיד לְאִתְפַּרְסָמָא וּלְאִשְׁתְּמָעָא לְכָל בְּנֵי אֱנָשָׁא); *m. Avot* 4:4 "Whoever profanes the name of heaven in secret, he shall be punished in the open" (כָּל הַמְחַלֵּל שֵׁם שָׁמַיִם בַּסֵּתֶר, נִפְרָעִין מִמֶּנּוּ בְּגָלוּי).

[200] See Matt 19:21: "If you will be perfect, go and sell that you have, and give to the poor."

in the heavens[201] that does not fail, where no thief approaches, nor where moth destroys. **34** For where your treasure is, there will your heart be also.

Luke 12:49–53 has been moved to the "Up to Jerusalem" section. Luke 12:54–59 has been moved to follow Luke 4:22

Scene 22:
Repent or Perish

Here we find reference to the activities of the Zealots in Galilee, which was a hotbed of resistance to Roman occupation. There may well have been attempts to incite Jesus to lead a revolt against Rome and say something against Pilate. Jesus resists all such temptations; however, the tone of the passage may serve as a segue to Jesus' final trip to Jerusalem. Luke 13:18–21 have been placed after Luke 18:30.

Luke 13:1 There were present at that time some who told him of the **Galileans,**[202] **whose blood Pilate had mingled with their**

---

[201] See Matt 6:20: "Lay up for yourselves treasures in heaven." Note *m. Peah* 1:1 "The following are the things for which a man enjoys the fruits in this world while *the principal remains for him in the world to come*: Honoring one's father and mother; The performance of righteous deeds; And the making of peace between a person and his friend" (אֵלוּ דְבָרִים שֶׁאָדָם אוֹכֵל פֵּרוֹתֵיהֶן בָּעוֹלָם הַזֶּה וְהַקֶּרֶן קַיֶּמֶת לוֹ לָעוֹלָם הַבָּא. כִּבּוּד אָב וָאֵם, וּגְמִילוּת חֲסָדִים, וַהֲבָאַת שָׁלוֹם בֵּין אָדָם לַחֲבֵרוֹ); *b. B.B.* 11a, citing King Monobazus (of Adiabene), who used up the storehouses of his fathers in a time of scarcity: "My ancestors stored up below, whereas I am storing above … My ancestors stored up treasures in a place where the human hand can reach, and so their treasures could have been robbed, whereas I am storing up treasures in a place where the human hand cannot reach" (אֲבוֹתַי גָּנְזוּ לְמַטָּה וַאֲנִי גָּנַזְתִּי לְמַעְלָה … אֲבוֹתַי גָּנְזוּ בְּמָקוֹם שֶׁהַיָּד שׁוֹלֶטֶת בּוֹ וַאֲנִי גָּנַזְתִּי בְּמָקוֹם שֶׁאֵין הַיָּד שׁוֹלֶטֶת בּוֹ). In the Talmudic context there is an emphasis is on charity and a play on words (no fruits/fruit; money/soul; others/myself; this world/future world); rather than otherworldly dualism. Note also Tobit 4:7–9: "Do not be afraid to give sparingly to **charity** … for then you will lay up for yourselves a good **treasure** against the day of adversity;" Tobit 12:8 "It is better to give **charity** than to lay up gold …"

[202] These may have been Galilean revolutionaries, perhaps intending to incite Jesus to lead a revolt against Rome and/or say something against Pilate.

sacrifices.[203] **2** And Jesus answering said to them: Do you suppose that these Galileans were sinners beyond all the Galileans, because they suffered such things? **3** I tell you, No; but, unless you repent, you will all likewise perish. **4** Or those eighteen, **upon whom the tower in Siloam fell, and killed them;**[204] do you think that they were sinners beyond all men who dwelt in Jerusalem? **5** I tell you, No; but, unless you repent, you will all likewise perish.

---

[203] See Mark 15:7; Pilate's main objective was always to prevent unrest, which meant executing revolutionaries. He was later prepared to release Jesus not because he respected him, but because he knew that Barabbas was quite possibly a leader of the Zealots.

[204] At the southeast corner of the city walls of Jerusalem; perhaps they were undermining Pilate's operations to improve the water supply to the city. See Josephus, *Ant.* XVIII, 60.

Up to Jerusalem

Following the "centerpiece" of Jesus' proto-rabbinic career in Galilee, the focus progressively shifts to Jerusalem, where the final scenes in the narrative will transpire. Traveling south, the region of Samaria is situated en route, and the passages dealing with this part of the journey have been transposed from earlier in Luke (chap. 9) to this point. They are supplemented by two parables from Matthew. The chronological reconstruction continues with additional teaching and parables as he journeys toward Jerusalem. The predictions of his death and resurrection are appropriate in this part of the narrative, and may build on a tradition found in the "Gabriel Revelation" (mentioned earlier as a text engraved in stone, and dated to the end of the first century BCE): "In three days, live, I, Gabriel, command you." Jesus' lament over Jerusalem connects him to the prophetic tradition, and while most scholars argue that it is a later emendation, David Flusser suggested that it may well predate the destruction of the temple.[1] In the story of Zacchaeus the tax collector, a linguistic link is hidden, given that his name in Hebrew means "worthy one." The "unworthy" becomes "worthy." When Jesus declares that he has come "to seek and to save," he is arguably appropriating authority that belongs only to God. His message relates not to the world to come, but to the present tense kingdom of God/heaven. As with later Talmudic teaching, he saw history divided into three dispensations: the Law and the Prophets, the kingdom of God/ heaven, and the world to come. In its original context, the parable

---

דוד פלוסר, *יהדות ומקורות הנצרות* (ישראל: ספרית הפועלים, 1982), 30: "באוונגליון לוקס ¹ אין אנו מוצאים שום הוכחה שנכתב לאחר ימי הבית."

of the Pharisee and the tax collector (transposed from Luke 18) may have followed the encounter with Zaccheus. Jesus' declaration that those who exalt themselves will be brought down and that those who humble themselves will be raised up is reminiscent of the sayings of both Akivah and Hillel. The "triumphal entry" into Jerusalem is followed by another Matthean passage, the "woman caught in adultery," which bears linguistic hallmarks of having originally been part of the ANT. It may have been dropped from Luke at some point, though preserved in Matthew's narrative. Jesus' "cleansing of the temple" is likely to have been the determinative factor in his subsequent arrest and trial for promoting insurrection. Jesus' attitude toward the temple and the sacrificial system remains a central question in contemporary scholarly debate.

Scene 1:
Rejection by a Samaritan Village (ANT)

Jesus' determination to travel to Jerusalem for Passover provides an "incident" (rejection by a Samaritan village) as the background for a "teaching" (that division rather than peace will result from his message; transposing Luke 12:49–53), followed by two parables, imported from Matthew's Gospel (the Wheat and the Tares, and its "companion," the Dragnet).[2]

Luke 9:51 And it came to pass,[3] when the time had come[4] for him to be taken up, he **steadfastly set his face to go[5]** to Jerusalem, **52** And sent messengers **before his face:[6]** and they went, and

---

[2] See Lindsey, *Jesus*, 131–34.

[3] The Greek καὶ ἐγένετο translates the Hebrew וַיְהִי; see Luke 1:23.

[4] The Greek here ἐν τῷ συμπληροῦσθαι τὰς ἡμέρας ("in the fulfilling of the days") mimics the Hebrew expression מְלֹאת הַיָּמִים ("when the days were fulfilled"), as in 1 Sam 18:26: "And the days were not expired" (וְלֹא מָלְאוּ הַיָּמִים).

[5] The Greek τὸ πρόσωπον ἐστήρισεν translates the Hebrew וַיָּשֶׂם אֶת פָּנָיו לָלֶכֶת ("and put/set his face to go").

[6] The Greek πρὸ προσώπου αὐτοῦ translates the Hebrew לְפָנָיו ("before his face").

entered into **a village of the Samaritans,**[7] to make ready for him. **53** And they did not receive him, because **his face**[8] was going to Jerusalem. **54** And when his disciples James and John saw this, they said: Lord, will you allow us to command **fire to come down from heaven,**[9] and consume them, even as Elijah did? **55** But he turned, and rebuked them, and said: You do not know of what spirit you are. **56** For the **Son of Man**[10] did not come to destroy men's lives, but to save them. And they went to another village.

Scene 2:
The Cost of Discipleship

Luke 9:57 And as they went along the road, a certain man said to him, Lord, I will follow you wherever you go. **58** And Jesus said to him: **Foxes have holes, and birds of the air have nests;**[11] but the **Son of Man**[12] has nowhere to lay his head. **59** And he said to another: Follow me. But he said: Lord, **allow me first to go and bury my father.**[13] **60** Jesus said to him: **Let the dead bury their own dead;**[14] but you go and declare the kingdom of God. **61** And another also said: Lord, I will follow you; but let me first bid farewell to those who are at my house. **62** And Jesus said to him: No one, having laid his hand to the plow, and looking back, is fit for the kingdom of God.

---

[7] Likely, Beth-Shean.

[8] The Greek προσώπου αὐτοῦ translates the Hebrew פניו ("his face").

[9] The attitude of James and John ("sons of thunder") is typical of the Zealots. In this case it recalls the divine judgment on Sodom and Gomorrah.

[10] The Aramaic בר אנוש ("son of man") links to Dan 7:13; authority being the theme.

[11] In the Book of Enoch "foxes" are symbolic of the Ammonites, here perhaps Edomite interlopers. "Birds" represent the Romans. In other words, everyone is at home in Israel except Israelites.

[12] The Aramaic בר אנוש ("son of man") links to Dan 7:13; authority being the theme.

[13] Rabbinic literature refers to the Pharisee who knocks his feet together, i.e., finds excuses to delay and avoid doing good deeds.

[14] Perhaps the translator (under later Aramaic influence) read למקבר (in Hebrew "*l'meqaber*" - "to the undertaker") as "*l'maqbar*" (Aramaic "to bury"). Perhaps better read as: "Leave the dead to the undertaker …" Possible reconstruction: הנח מתים למקבר.

Not Peace, but Division

Luke 12:49–53 is added here. Jesus' statement that he comes to send fire on the earth should be understood as a reluctant recognition of the division that may result from his message, but when he adds that he wishes it were already kindled, we see him emphasizing that the kingdom of God/heaven is not about judgment, but present tense wholeness, healing, and abundance.

Luke 12:49 "I have come to send fire on the earth;[15] and how I wish that it were already kindled?[16] **50** But I have a baptism to be baptized with [with which to baptize];[17] and how am I distressed until it is accomplished![18] **51** Do you suppose that I have come to give peace on the earth? I tell you, No; **but rather division.**[19] **52** For from now on, there will be five in one house divided, three against two, and two against three. **53 The father will be divided against the son, and the son against the father; the mother against the daughter, and the daughter against the mother; the mother-in-law against her daughter-in-law, and the daughter-in-law against her mother-in-law.**[20]

Parable 1: The Wheat and the Tares

Adding Matt 13:24–30; 13:47–50 preserves the theorized pattern of a teaching followed by two parables. The "kingdom of heaven"

---

[15] Links Jesus with supernatural power.

[16] Jesus arguably would have preferred to postpone judgment indefinitely. See Bivin and Blizzard, 126–42.

[17] A hypothetical Hebrew reconstruction would read: יש לי טבילה לטבול. This may be also be understood as "a baptism with which to baptize [others]." The saying then becomes parallel with the first: "to send fire on the earth."

[18] Note the Hebraic *parallelism/poetry*.

[19] See Matt 10:34, which reads "sword" (μάχαιραν) rather than "division" (διαμερισμόν). The Messiah was expected to bring peace; see Isa 9:6–7; 11:1–9.

[20] Note *b. Sot.* 49b: "In the times of the approach of the Messiah, impudence will increase ... A son will disgrace a father; a daughter will rise up against her mother, a daughter-in-law against her mother-in-law. A man's enemies will be the members of his household" (בעקבות משיחא חוצפא יסגא ויוקר יאמיר ... בן מנוול אב בת קמה באמה כלה בחמותה אויבי (איש אנשי ביתו).

suggests a present tense reality while the parable here should be understood eschatologically.

Matthew 13:24 Another parable put he forth to them, saying, The **kingdom of heaven**[21] is like a man who sowed good seed in his field: **25** But while men slept, his enemy came and sowed **weeds**[22] among the wheat, and went his way. **26** But when the plants had sprung up, and brought forth fruit, the weeds also appeared. **27** So the servants of the master of the house came and said to him, Sir, did you not sow good seed in your field? How then does it have weeds? **28** And he said to them: An enemy has done this. And the servants said to him, Do you then wish that we go and gather them up? **29** But he said: No; lest while you gather up the weeds, you also root up the wheat with them. **30** Let both grow together until the harvest; and in the time of the harvest I will say to the harvesters: Gather together first the weeds, and bind them in bundles to burn them; but gather the wheat into my barn.

Parable 2: The Dragnet

The "net" refers to the removal of the wicked at the end of days.

---

[21] "Kingdom of heaven" was likely added in the Greek text, as a "proliferation" of the term. The original language might have read something to the effect of "Consider ..." as in other parables.

[22] The Greek ζιζάνια translates the Hebrew זון ("weeds"), which closely resembles wheat, being left in then fields until the harvest. The rabbis looked at it as a degenerative form of wheat as a product of sexual excess in the plant world prior to the flood. They (fancifully) derived its meaning from the Hebrew זנה (to fornicate).

Matthew 13:47 Again, the **kingdom of heaven**[23] is like a **net,**[24] that was cast into the sea, and gathered every kind; **48** Which, when it was full, they drew to shore, and sat down, and gathered the good into vessels, but **cast the bad away.**[25] **49** So shall it be at the end of the world; the angels shall come forth, and divide the **wicked**[26] from among the righteous, **50** And shall cast them into the furnace of fire; there shall be weeping and gnashing of teeth.

Scene 3:
The Narrow Gate (ANT)

Jesus' transit through various "cities and villages" en route to Jerusalem provides the "incident" that frames a teaching about the "narrow gate" and a message about Jerusalem's coming destruction. In response to the transposed question about the imminence of the end of the age (Luke 19:11), two parables follow.

Luke 13:22 And he went through the cities and villages, teaching, and journeying toward Jerusalem. **23** Then one said to him: Lord, are there few that are being saved? And he said to them: **24** Strive to enter in through the narrow gate; **for many, I say to you, will seek to enter in, and will not be able.**[27] **25** For once the master of the house has risen up, and has shut the door, and you begin to stand outside, and knock at the door, saying: Lord, open to us. And

---

[23] The original language might have read something to the effect of "Consider…" as in other parables.

[24] The comparison is to the "wheat and tares" (vv. 24–30), an eschatological judgment. Note *b. A.Z.* 3b, in which the Israelites are compared to fish, swimming in the Torah, where alone they can live: "Why are people compared to the fish of the sea? This serves to say to you: Just as with regard to the fish of the sea, once they arise onto dry land they die immediately; so too, with regard to people, once they separate themselves from studying words of Torah and performing the mitzvot, they die immediately" (למה נמשלו בני אדם כדגי הים לומר לך מה דגים שבים כיון שעולין ליבשה מיד מתים אף בני אדם כיון שפורשין מדברי תורה ומן המצות מיד מתים דבר אחר מה דגים שבים כיון שקדרה עליהם חמה מיד מתים).

[25] Catfish, for example, are not kosher and would be cast away.

[26] Note Ps 140:5: "Keep me, O LORD, from the hands of the **wicked**" (שָׁמְרֵנִי יְהוָה, מִידֵי רָשָׁע).

[27] Note 4 Ezra 8:3: "Many have been created, but **few shall be saved**"; Apoc. Bar. (Syr.) 44:15: "There are more who perish than shall be saved."

he will answer and say to you: I do not know you, from where you are. [**26** Then you will begin to say: We have eaten and drunk in your presence, and you have taught in our streets. **27** But he will say: I tell you, I do not know from where you come. Depart from me, all you workers of iniquity. **28** There will be weeping and gnashing of teeth, when you see **Abraham, and Isaac, and Jacob, and all the prophets, in the kingdom of God, and you yourselves thrust out. 29 And they will come from the east, and from the west, and from the north, and from the south, and will recline in the kingdom of God.**[28] **30** And, behold,[29] there are last who will be first, and there are first who will be last.][30]

Scene 4:
Lament over Jerusalem

If the Pharisees were part of a conspiratorial plot to have Jesus killed, it is odd that they would warn him of Herod's murderous intentions. Jesus again speaks of the "third day" in a manner reminiscent of the Gabriel Revelation; see Luke 9:22.

Luke 13:31 The same hour there came certain of the Pharisees, saying to him: Get out, and depart from here; for Herod seeks to kill you. **32** And he said to them: Go and tell that **fox,**[31] **Behold,**[32] I cast out demons, and I do cures today and tomorrow, and **the third**

---

[28] Note Secrets of Enoch 42:5: "At the last coming they will lead forth Adam and *our forefathers* ... that they may rejoice, as a man calls those whom he loves to *feast with him*." See also Matt 8:11.

[29] The Greek ἰδού is used in imitation of the Hebrew הִנֵּה.

[30] vv. 26–30 likely represent a strong redaction from a fragment of "Q" (the theorized "sayings" section of ANT). The passage reads better in Matt 7:21–22: "Not everyone who says to me: Lord, Lord, shall enter the kingdom of heaven; but he who does the will of my Father who is in heaven. Many will say to me in that day: Lord, Lord, have we not prophesied in your name? and in your name cast out demons? And in your name done many wonderful works?" See Flusser, *Judaism*, 555–56.

[31] A "fox" is a euphemism for one who is inferior or double-dealing.

[32] The Greek ἰδού is used in imitation of the Hebrew הִנֵּה.

day I will be perfected.[33] **33** Nevertheless I must walk **today, and tomorrow,**[34] and the day **following;**[35] for it cannot be for a **prophet**[36] to perish outside of Jerusalem. **34 O Jerusalem, Jerusalem,**[37] who kills the prophets and **stones those who are sent to you;**[38] how often would I have gathered your children together, **as a hen gathers her brood under her wings,**[39] and you were not willing! **35 Behold,**[40] your **house**[41] is left to you desolate. I say now to you, you shall not see me, until the time comes when you say: Blessed is he who comes in the name of the Lord.

Parable 1: The Minas/Talents (RCT)

The parable of the minas/talents is the twin of the parable of the unjust steward (in Luke 16) and is echoed in rabbinic literature, in a story about a king who goes away and leaves his estate to two servants.[42] Luke's language ("We will not have this man reign over us") reflects the slaughter by the Roman ethnarch Archelaus of those who refused his rule.

---

[33] See Luke 9:22. Note the "Gabriel Revelation": "In three days, live, I, Gabriel, command you" (לשלושת ימים חייה אני גבריאל גוזר עליך). A slain messianic leader would be resurrected within three days, and rise to heaven in a chariot.

[34] Meaning, a short time; the "third day."

[35] Note the Hebrew equivalent: מחרתיים ("the day after").

[36] Note Deut 18:15: "A ***prophet*** will the LORD your God raise up to you, from the midst of you, of your brethren, like to me; to him you shall hearken" (נָבִיא מִקִּרְבְּךָ מֵאַחֶיךָ כָּמֹנִי יָקִים לְךָ יְהוָה אֱלֹהֶיךָ: אֵלָיו תִּשְׁמָעוּן).

[37] This reference connects Jesus to the prophetic tradition; see Matt 23.37.

[38] A few decades earlier Honi HaMe'agel was stoned outside of Jerusalem. Yohanan b. Zakkai also prophesied the temple's destruction.

[39] Note *Lev. R.* 25: "**The hen, when her chicks are young, gathers them together and places them under her wings** and warms them and digs up the earth before them. But when they grow bigger, if one of them wants to come near to her as she pecks him on the head and says to him, 'Dig in your own dirt!'" (הָדָא תַּרְנְגוֹלְתָּא כַּד אָפְרוֹחֶיהָ דַּקִּיקִין הִיא מְכַבְּשָׁא לְהוֹן וַיַהֲבַת לְהוֹן תְּחוֹת אֲגַפַּיָּא וּמְשַׁחֲנָה לְהוֹן וּמַעֲדַרְנָה קֳדָמֵיהוֹן, וְכַד אִינּוּן רַבְיָה חַד מִנְהוֹן בָּעֵי לְמִקְרַב לְוָתֵיהּ וְהִיא נָקְרָה לֵיהּ בְּגוֹ רֵישֵׁיהּ, וַאֲמְרַת לֵיהּ זִיל עֲדוֹר בְּקוּקַלְתָּךְ). *Lev. R.* 2 speaks of how proselytes come "***under the wings*** of the *Shekhinah*" (תַּחַת כַּנְפֵי הַשְּׁכִינָה).

[40] The Greek ἰδοὺ is used in imitation of the Hebrew הִנֵּה.

[41] The Hebrew בית ("house") may be understood as "temple."

[42] See Lindsey, *Jesus*, 214–15.

Luke 19:11 And as they heard these things, he added and spoke a parable, because he was nearing Jerusalem, and because they thought that the kingdom of God should immediately appear. **12** He said therefore: **A certain nobleman went into a distant country**[43] to receive for himself a kingdom, and to return. **13** And he called his ten servants, and delivered to them ten **minas,**[44] and said to them: **Occupy**[45] until I come. **14** But his citizens hated him, and sent a delegation after him, saying: **We will not have this man reign over us.**[46] **15 And it came to pass,**[47] that when he had returned, having received the kingdom, he then commanded these servants, to whom he had given the money, to be called to him, so that he might know how much each had gained by trading. **16** Then came the first, saying: Lord, your mina has gained ten more minas. **17** And he said to him: Well done, good servant. Because you have been faithful in very little, you have authority over ten cities. **18** And the second came, saying: Lord, your mina

---

[43] Note *Yal.* 837: "What is the distinction between Love and fear? It may be illustrated by means of a parable. To what may the matter be compared? One loved the king and feared him. The other feared the king but did not love him. *The king went into a far country.* The servant who loved the king and feared him rose up to plant gardens, orchard and all varieties of fruit. The servant who feared the king remained inactive and did nothing at all. Upon returning from the far country, the king saw the gardens, orchards and many varieties of fruits arranged before him according to the design of the servant who loved him … But when the king entered the domain of the servant who feared him but did not love him, he saw all the desolate grounds which lay before him. He was greatly distressed in accordance with the anger of the king.... Hence you learn that the reward of the one who loved [the king] was a double portion while the reward of the one who feared the king was only a single portion." מה בין אהבה ליראה, משלו משל למה הדבר דומה למלך שהיו לו שני עבדים אחד אוהב את המלך ומתירא ממנו ואחד מתירא ממנו ואין אוהבו, **הלך המלך למדינת הים** האוהב את המלך ומתירא ממנו עמד ונטע גנות ופרדסין וכל מיני מגדים, והירא ואינו אוהבו יש לו ולא עשה כלום, כיון שבא המלך ממדינת הים ראה גנות ופרדסים וכל מיני מגדים סדורים לפניו כנגד דעתו של אובה... והירא ממנו ואינו אוהבו כיון שנכנס המלך לביתו ראה כל_מי חרבות כולם סדורים לפניו ... נזדעזע דעתו כנגד קצפו של מלך ... הא למדת ששכר האוהב שני חלקים ושכר הירא חלק אחד). See also *Seder Elijah* (25) 26 (*Seder Eliyahu Rabbah*).

[44] The *mina* (מנה) was an ancient Near Eastern unit of weight, divided into fifty shekels; also a unit of currency; plural: *minot* (מנות), perhaps a wordplay with the Hebrew for "kingdoms" (מדינות) recalling v. 12.

[45] The Greek "do business" (πραγματεύσασθε) suggests engaging in state business.

[46] See Matt 25:14–30; influenced by the history of Archelaus, who went to Rome to be confirmed by Augustus, but his people sent a delegation to oppose him (Josephus, *War* II, V, 80–85).

[47] The Greek καὶ ἐγένετο translates the Hebrew וַיְהִי; see Luke 1:23.

has gained five more minas. **19** And he said likewise to him: And you also are to be over five cities. **20** And another came, saying: Lord, **behold,**[48] here is your mina, which I have kept laid away in a piece of cloth: **21** For I feared you, because you are a harsh man. You take up what you did not lay down, and you reap what you did not sow. **22** And he said to him: Out of your own mouth I will judge you, you wicked servant. You knew that I was a harsh man, taking up what I did not lay not down, and reaping what I did not sow. **23** Why, then, did you not give my money to the bank, so that at my coming I might have received my own with interest? **24** And he said to them who stood by: Take from him the mina, and give it to the one who has ten minas. **25** And they said to him, Master, he has ten minas. **26** For I say to you, that to everyone who has, more will be given; and from the one who has not, even what he has will be taken away from him. **27** [But[49] **those who are my enemies, who are not willing for me to reign over them, bring them here, and slay them before me.**][50]

Parable 2: The Unjust Steward (ANT)

The parable of the unjust manager ("steward") is the "twin" of the parable of the talents (Luke 19:11–27; Matt 25:14–30) and was possibly aimed against the Dead Sea Sect. Jesus often creates amoral and immoral characters, emphasizing clever behavior.

Luke 16:1 And he also said to his disciples: There was a certain rich man, who had a manager ("steward"); and he accused him of having wasted his possessions. **2** And he called him, and said to him: What is this that I hear of you? Give an account of your

---

48 The Greek ἰδού is used in imitation of the Hebrew הִנֵּה.
49 "But" added in Greek (πλήν).
50 Archelaus' "enemies" were slaughtered. This section was likely redacted later than the Matthean parallel, as it deals with the problem of the delayed *parousia*. The historical events around Archelaus were the catalyst for the revision, which impairs the moral implications of the parable. The "enemies" of v. 27 are *not* the Jews. This statement is not found in Matthew. See Young, *Jesus and His Jewish Parables*, 169.

stewardship; for you may no longer be a manager. **3** Then the manager said to himself: What shall I do? For my master is taking away from me the management. I cannot dig; I am ashamed to beg. **4** I know what I will do; so that, when I am removed from the management, they may receive me into their homes. **5** So he called every one of his master's debtors to him, and said to the first: How much do you owe to my master? **6** And he said, A hundred baths of oil. And he said to him, Take your bill, and sit down quickly, and write fifty. **7** Then said he to another: And how much do you owe? And he said: A hundred measures of wheat. And he said to him: Take your bill, and write eighty. **8** And the master commended the unjust manager, because he had acted wisely; **for the sons of this age are in their generation wiser than the sons of light.**[51] **9** And I say to you: Make to yourselves friends of the **wealth ("mammon") of unrighteousness;**[52] that, when it fails, they may receive you into eternal dwellings. **10 The one who is faithful with very little is faithful also with much/and the one who is unjust in the least is also unjust in much.**[53] **11** If therefore you have not been **faithful in the unrighteous wealth ("mammon"),**[54] who will entrust to you **true riches?**[55] **12** And if you have not been faithful in that which is another's, who will give you that which is

---

[51] Possibly a backhanded reference to the Dead Sea sect, who referred to themselves as "sons of light" (בני אור) and who rejected financial undertakings with outsiders. See 1 Thess 5:5: "You are all *sons of light* and sons of the day." See Flusser, *Judaism*, 150–52.

[52] Note the Dead Sea Scrolls terminology: הון הרשעה and הון אנשי רמיה (CD 6:14; 1QS 9:8); also הון חמס 1QS 10:14). The Greek ἐκ ("by") is too literal. The text should be understood as saying "from" (מן): "Make friends *from* (not *by*) the mammon of unrighteousness." Hypothetical Hebrew reconstruction: עשו לכם ידידים מממון החמס. Jesus is not telling his disciples to give alms, but to pursue dealings "*out of* economic contact with the world at large." See Flusser, *Judaism*, 152–54.

[53] Note the Hebraic *parallelism/poetry*.

[54] If one is faithful in a small matter, one can be trusted with a major one. The larger context involves "deposits" entrusted by "unbelievers." Note Pliny's *Letter X* 96:7 which presents three arguments: a small matter, "*unrighteous mammon*," and what belongs to another, admonishing to be trustworthy with the "deposits" of others.

[55] "True wealth" is seen here as spiritual wealth, which is offered to others. If one shares material goods, one should also share spiritual things. Note *m. Avot* 3:16: "Everything is given against a pledge, and a net is spread out over all the living; the store is open and the storekeeper allows credit" (הַחֲנוּת. הַכֹּל נָתוּן בָּעֵרָבוֹן, וּמְצוּדָה פְרוּסָה עַל כָּל הַחַיִּים פְּתוּחָה, וְהַחֶנְוָנִי מַקִּיף).

yours? **13** No servant can **serve two masters;**[56] for either he will hate the one, and love the other; or else he will be devoted to the one, and despise the other. You cannot serve God and money ("mammon"). **14** And the **Pharisees,**[57] being lovers of money, heard all these things; and they derided him. **15** And he said to them: You are those who **justify**[58] yourselves before men; but **God knows your hearts. For that which is highly esteemed among men**[59] is an abomination before God. **16** The law and the prophets were until John. Since that time the **kingdom of God**[60] is proclaimed, and every man forces his way into it. **17 It is easier for heaven and earth to pass, than one stroke of the law to**

---

[56] Note *Test. Jud.* 18:2, 6: "Beware, therefore, my children, of fornication, and the love of money ... For he is *a slave to two contrary passions*, And cannot obey God, Because they have blinded his soul, And he walks in the day as in the night." (וְעַל־כֵּן) השמרו בני מן־הזנות ומאהבת־כסף ... כי הוא **לשני יצרים יעבד** ולא יוכל לשמע בקול אלהים כי החשיכו (את־נפשו וביום כבלילה יהלך); *m. Git.* 4:5: "In the case of one who is a half-slave half-freeman because only one of his two owners emancipated him, *he serves his master one day and serves himself one day*; this is the statement of Beit Hillel. Beit Shammai say: Through such an arrangement you have remedied his master, as his master loses nothing through this. However, you have not remedied the slave himself, as the slave himself remains in an unsustainable situation. It is not possible for him to marry a maidservant because he is already a half-freeman, as it is prohibited for a freeman to marry a maidservant" (מִי שֶׁחֶצְיוֹ עֶבֶד וְחֶצְיוֹ בֶּן חוֹרִין, **עוֹבֵד אֶת רַבּוֹ יוֹם אֶחָד וְאֶת עַצְמוֹ יוֹם אֶחָד**, דִּבְרֵי בֵּית הִלֵּל. אָמְרוּ לָהֶם בֵּית שַׁמַּאי, תִּקַּנְתֶּם אֶת רַבּוֹ, וְאֶת עַצְמוֹ לֹא תִקַּנְתֶּם. לִשָּׂא שִׁפְחָה אִי אֶפְשָׁר, שֶׁכְּבָר חֶצְיוֹ בֶּן חוֹרִין). Jesus is closer to Shammai in this case. Note also Plato, *Rep.* VIII, 555c: "It is impossible for the citizens of a state to order wealth and at the same time acquire a proper amount of temperance"; Persius, *Sat.* 5.154: "... torn between avarice and extravagance: 'You have hooks pulling you in *two different ways*....'" See Matt 6:24.

[57] This is a troublesome reading since the Sadducees (not the Pharisees) were doubtless the wealthy class, being more elitist and aristocratic. Passages such as this undoubtedly contributed to the stereotype of the "money-grubbing Jew." "Sadducees" might be a better reading, being a play on words with "justify" in the following verse.

[58] Assuming a Hebraic *grundschrift*, "Sadducees" (in Hebrew צדוקים) would be a play on words with "*justify* (מצדיקים) yourselves."

[59] Note *Mek. Ex.* 20:18: "And all who are *haughty of heart* cause the land to be defiled and the Shechinah to depart" (וכל שהוא **גבה לב**—גורם ליטמא את הארץ ולסלק את השכינה).

[60] See Matt 11:11–12: "Among those born of women there has not risen one greater than John the Baptist; but he who is least in the kingdom of heaven is greater than he. And from the days of John the Baptist until now the kingdom of heaven suffers violence, and the violent take it by force." John is viewed as the last prophet of the biblical period, though not in the kingdom of God/heaven movement and never an active follower of Jesus. See Bivin and Blizzard, 123–25; R. S. Notley, "The Kingdom of Heaven Forcefully Advances," in *The Interpretation of Scripture in Early Judaism and Christianity: Studies in Language and Tradition*, C. A. Evans, ed. (Sheffield: Sheffield Academic Press, 2000), 279–311.

fail.[61] **18** Whoever **puts away his wife, and marries another, commits adultery: and whoever marries her who has been put away from her husband commits adultery.**[62]

Scene 5:
Jesus Warns of Stumbling Blocks

As Jesus warns of "offenses," the theory of a Hebraic undertext becomes essential to understanding the passage. While the Greek involves a mental process of "being offended," the hypothetical Hebrew original amounts to a midrash on Isaiah 8:14, revolving around the word מִכְשׁוֹל/"offense." Those who do not recognize or

---

[61] Even the smallest portion of the Torah preserves the world, and therefore cannot be discarded. Note *Lev. R.* 19:2: "Should all the nations of the world unite **to uproot one word of the Torah**, they would be unable to do so... The guilt of one who **destroys one letter** is so great that if done [all the world would be destroyed]." (אִם מִתְכַּנְּסִים כָּל אֻמּוֹת הָעוֹלָם לַעֲקֹר דָּבָר אֶחָד מֵהַתּוֹרָה אֵינָן יְכוֹלִין ... עַל יְדֵי שֶׁבִּקֵּשׁ לַעֲקֹר אוֹת אַחַת מִן הַתּוֹרָה עָלָה קַטֵּיגוֹרוֹ). See Matt 5:18.

[62] In Matt 5:32 (also Matt 19:6) Jesus appears to enter the Shammai-Hillel controversy, only allowing "fornication" as just cause for divorce. A certificate stating that the bride was a virgin was required. "Fornication" would invalidate the *Ketubah*. See *m. Git.* 9:10: "Beit Shammai say: A man may not divorce his wife unless he finds out about her having engaged in *a matter of forbidden sexual intercourse [devar erva]*, i.e., she committed adultery or is suspected of doing so, as it is stated: 'Because he has found *some unseemly matter [ervat davar]* in her, and he writes her a scroll of severance' (Deuteronomy 24:1). And Beit Hillel say: He may divorce her *even due to a minor issue, e.g., because she burned or over-salted his dish*, as it is stated: 'Because he has found some unseemly matter in her,' meaning that he found any type of shortcoming in her. Rabbi Akiva says: He may divorce her even if he found another woman who is better looking than her and wishes to marry her, as it is stated in that verse: 'And it comes to pass, *if she finds no favor in his eyes*'" (בֵּית שַׁמַּאי אוֹמְרִים, לֹא יְגָרֵשׁ אָדָם אֶת אִשְׁתּוֹ אֶלָּא אִם כֵּן מָצָא בָהּ דְּבַר עֶרְוָה, שֶׁנֶּאֱמַר (דברים כד). כִּי מָצָא בָהּ עֶרְוַת דָּבָר. וּבֵית הִלֵּל אוֹמְרִים, אֲפִלּוּ הִקְדִּיחָה תַבְשִׁילוֹ, שֶׁנֶּאֱמַר (שם), כִּי מָצָא בָהּ עֶרְוַת דָּבָר. רַבִּי עֲקִיבָא אוֹמֵר, אֲפִלּוּ מָצָא אַחֶרֶת נָאָה הֵימֶנָּה, שֶׁנֶּאֱמַר (שם), וְהָיָה אִם לֹא תִמְצָא חֵן בְּעֵינָיו). The term עֶרְוַת דָּבָר of Deut 24:1 is interpreted by Shammai as adultery, by Hillel as something displeasing, and by Akivah as failure to satisfy sexually. Luke 16:18 may be a better reading than Mark 10:11–12. In Luke "divorce" and "marry" are in the present tense in Greek, as opposed to the subjunctive tense in Mark. The verse should be understood as: "Every one who divorces his wife *[in order] to marry another* commits adultery." See *m. Sot.* 5:1, which states that a woman who divorced *because of an adulterous relationship* is not allowed to marry her paramour. It appears that Jesus does not prohibit divorce; he simply states that one cannot divorce in order to marry another. Note Qumran Temple Scroll (11Q19 57:17–18): "[The king] shall take no wife in addition to her for she alone will be with him all the days of her life" (ולוא יקח עליה אשה אחרת כי היאה לבדה תהיה עמו כול ימי חייה). What is required of the king is more than what is required of others.

who are unsure of his messianic stature are, in Isaiah's words, "stumbling blocks." Examples might include John the Baptist in Matthew 11:6 and Peter in Matthew 16:23.

Luke 17:1 Then he said to the disciples: It is impossible that **stumbling blocks**[63] will not come; but **woe**[64] to him, through whom they come! **2** It is **better for him if a millstone were hung around his neck,**[65] and he be cast into the sea, than that he should cause one of these little ones to stumble. **3** Take heed to yourselves: If your brother sins against you, rebuke him; and if he repents, forgive him. **4** And if he sins against you seven times in a day, and seven times in a day returns to you, saying: I repent; you shall forgive him.

Faith and Duty

With regard to faith "as a grain of mustard seed," we find Talmudic reference to "twigs of mustard," the timber of which was sufficient to cover a potter's hut. Elsewhere in the Talmud, we find a declaration that a carob tree should be moved, "and it was." In the Mishnah there is the admonition not to ascribe merit to oneself, paralleling Jesus' directive.

---

[63] Note Isa 8:14: "And He shall be for a sanctuary; but for a *stone of stumbling* and for a rock of offense to both the houses of Israel" (וְהָיָה, לְמִקְדָּשׁ; וּלְאֶבֶן נֶגֶף וּלְצוּר מִכְשׁוֹל לִשְׁנֵי בָתֵּי יִשְׂרָאֵל). Jesus makes a *midrash* on this passage, using the term "stumbling block" (צוּר מִכְשׁוֹל) messianically, referring to those who do not recognize the Messiah. Matt 11:6 suggests the differences between Jesus and John: "Blessed is anyone who does not *stumble* on account of me." In Matt 16:23 Peter is the מכשׁול: "Get behind Me, Satan! You are an *offense* to Me." In Mark 14:27–29 Jesus refers to denying him as a מכשׁול: "All of you will be made to *stumble* because of Me this night." Peter declares that he will never "stumble." The Greek σκάνδαλον suggests a mental process of "being offended"/ "scandalized." The Hebrew makes it clear that it is a "stumbling," a "falling." See Matt 18:7. Rom 9:33; 1 Cor 1:23; 1 Pet 2:8.

[64] The Greek Οὐαί is used in the Septuagint chiefly for הוֹי and אוֹי.

[65] Note *b. Ket.* 67b: "It is *preferable for a person to deliver himself into a fiery furnace* so that he not whiten the face of, i.e., embarrass, his friend in public" (נוח לו לאדם שימסור עצמו לתוך כבשן האש ואל ילבין פני חברו ברבים).

Luke 17:5 And the apostles said to the Lord: Increase our faith. **6** And the Lord said: If you had faith as a grain of **mustard seed,**[66] you might say to **this mulberry tree, Be uprooted,**[67] and be planted in the sea; and it would obey you. **7** But which of you, having a servant plowing or feeding cattle, will say to him immediately, when he has come from the field: Go and recline? **8** And will not rather say to him: Make ready what I may eat, and gird yourself, and serve me, till I have eaten and drunk; and afterward you shall eat and drink? **9** Does he not thank that servant because he did the things that were commanded? **10** So likewise you, when you will have done all those things that were commanded you, say: **We are unworthy servants; we have done that which was our duty**[68] to do.

Scene 6:
Ten Lepers Cleansed

The cleansing of the ten lepers may include an error by the Greek redactor, as it involves Samaria along with Galilee, taking pains to point out that one of the lepers was a Samaritan. Jesus would not have commanded a Samaritan to present himself to a Jewish priest. It makes more sense that the incident occurred solely in Galilee, without reference to Samaria or Samaritans. The redactor appears to have been wanting to expand the mission of Jesus beyond Israelites.

---

[66] Note *b. Ket.* 111b: "There was an incident which occurred in the village of Shiḥin, in Eretz Yisrael, involving one whose father had left him three branches of **mustard**, one of which broke. And they discovered on this one branch alone nine *kav* of mustard. And with the wood of its large branches they roofed a booth for artisans" (מעשה בשיחין באחד שהניח לו אביו שלשה בדי **חרדל** ונפשח אחד מהן ונמצאו בו תשעה קבין חרדל ועציו סיככו בו סוכת יוצרין).

[67] Note *b. B.M.* 59b: "Rabbi Eliezer said to them: If the *halakha* is in accordance with my opinion, this carob tree will prove it. *The carob tree was uprooted from its place* one hundred cubits, and some say four hundred cubits" (אמר להם אם הלכה כמותי חרוב זה יוכיח **נעקר חרוב ממקומו** מאה אמה ואמרי לה ארבע מאות אמה).

[68] Note *m. Avot* 2:8: "if you have learned much Torah, *do not claim credit for yourself,* because for such a purpose were you created" (אם לָמַדְתָּ תּוֹרָה הַרְבֵּה, **אַל תַּחֲזִיק טוֹבָה** לְעַצְמְךָ, כִּי לְכָךְ נוֹצָרְתָּ).

Luke 17:11 And it came to pass,[69] as he went to Jerusalem, that he passed through the midst of **Samaria**[70] and Galilee. **12** And as he entered into a certain village, he was met by ten leprous men, who stood afar off. **13** And they lifted up their voices, and said: Jesus, Master, have compassion on us. **14** And when he saw them, he said to them: Go **show yourselves to the priests.**[71] **And it came to pass,**[72] that, as they went, they were cleansed. **15** And one of them, when he saw that he was healed, turned back, and with a loud voice glorified God, **16** And fell down on his face at his feet, giving him thanks; and he was a Samaritan. **17** And Jesus answering said: Were there not ten cleansed? But where are the nine? **18** None was found there who returned to give glory to God, except this foreigner. **19** And he said to him, Arise, go your way. Your faith has made you whole.

The Kingdom of God is in the Midst of You

The saying, "The kingdom of God is within you" appears to be a redactional misunderstanding. The saying is better understood as "The kingdom of God is among you," suggesting a community of observant followers. It is paralleled by the Talmudic passage: "Is the Lord among us or not?... If we think our thoughts and He knows what we think, then we will serve him" (b. Pes. 28a).

[Luke 17:20 And when he was asked of the Pharisees, **when the kingdom of God should come,**[73] he answered them and said: The kingdom of God does not come with observation. 21 Neither shall

---

[69] The Greek καὶ ἐγένετο translates the Hebrew וַיְהִי; see Luke 1:23.
[70] Galilee, not Samaria, would have been the original context; a Lucan redaction.
[71] Luke's redactional error. Why would a Samaritan present himself to the priests, unless to Samaritan priests? Moreover, why would Jesus command this?
[72] The Greek καὶ ἐγένετο translates the Hebrew וַיְהִי; see Luke 1:23.
[73] Often missed is that little or no sign of the *parousia* is given. Reflective of Gen 18.

they say, **Behold** it is here! or, **Behold** it is there! For, **behold,**[74] **the kingdom of God is in the midst of you.**[75]]

The last section of Luke 17 (vv. 22–37, dealing with the parousia) is theorized to comprise post-resurrection sayings, which belong after Luke 24:51/Acts 1:3.[76] Jesus in his lifetime was focused not on eschatology but on the present.

Scene 7:
Jesus Blesses the Children

Note that the purity of children is stressed in rabbinic literature. The study of Scripture would begin with Leviticus, dealing with laws of ritual purity.

Luke 18:15 And they brought to him also **infants, that he might touch them.**[77] But when his disciples saw it, they rebuked them. **16** But Jesus called them to him, and said: Permit the little **children**[78] to come to me, and do not forbid them; for of such is

---

[74] The Greek ἰδοὺ is used in imitation of the Hebrew הִנֵּה.

[75] vv. 20–21 were likely added by the Lucan redactor. This section says much the same thing as the verses which follow (though Luke equates the coming of the Son of Man with the "kingdom of God"). "The kingdom of God is within you" is nonsense; it is better read "among you."

[76] See Lindsey, *Jesus*, 188–91.

[77] Gen 48:14 depicts the laying on of hands as an act accompanying a blessing: "And Israel stretched out his right hand, and laid it upon Ephraim's head" (וַיִּשְׁלַח יִשְׂרָאֵל אֶת-יְמִינוֹ וַיָּשֶׁת עַל-רֹאשׁ אֶפְרַיִם). The Greek βρέφη ("infants") translates the Hebrew תִּינוֹקוֹת ("infants"/"young children"). The sense here is "young children." See Matt 19:13–15.

[78] Note *m. Avot* 5:21: (attributed to Judah ben Tema): "At five years of age the study of Scripture; At ten the study of Mishnah; At thirteen subject to the commandments; At fifteen the study of Talmud; At eighteen the bridal canopy; At twenty for pursuit [of livelihood]; At thirty the peak of strength" (בֶּן חָמֵשׁ שָׁנִים לַמִּקְרָא, בֶּן עֶשֶׂר לַמִּשְׁנָה, בֶּן שְׁלֹשׁ עֶשְׂרֵה לַמִּצְוֹת, בֶּן חֲמֵשׁ עֶשְׂרֵה לַתַּלְמוּד, בֶּן שְׁמֹנֶה עֶשְׂרֵה לַחֻפָּה, בֶּן עֶשְׂרִים לִרְדּוֹף, בֶּן שְׁלֹשִׁים לַכֹּחַ).

the kingdom of God. **17 Truly**[79] **I say to you,**[80] Whoever does not receive the kingdom of God as a little child will by no means enter into it.

vv. 18–30 should be transposed to precede Luke 19:25

Jesus a Third Time Predicts His Death and Resurrection

Either such predictions represent later interpolations, or reference is being made to an established tradition, that a messianic leader would be slain, only to return alive (as in the "Gabriel Revelation").

Luke 18:31 Then he took aside the twelve, and said to them: **Behold,**[81] we go up to Jerusalem, and all things that are written by the prophets concerning the **Son of Man**[82] will be accomplished. **32** For he will be delivered to the Gentiles, and will be mocked, and insulted, and spit upon. **33** And they will scourge him, and put him to death; and **on the third day he will rise again.**[83] **34** And they understood none of these things; and this saying was hidden from them. Neither did they know the things that were spoken.

---

[79] In Greek ἀμὴν (Hebrew אמן). This ends the previous statement, "… for of such is the kingdom of God." "Amen"/"assuredly" (אמן) is added after a strong statement, e.g. Jer 28:6: "The prophet Jeremiah said: '**Amen**! The Lord do so; the Lord perform your words which you have prophesied …'" (וַיֹּאמֶר יִרְמְיָה הַנָּבִיא, **אָמֵן**, כֵּן יַעֲשֶׂה יְהוָה; יָקֵם יְהוָה אֶת-דְּבָרֶיךָ). The significant statement of the false prophet Hanania is followed by "amen" (used in irony). Jesus patterns his use of the word "amen" after this. See also Num 5:22: "… and the woman shall say: '**Amen, Amen**.'" (וְאָמְרָה הָאִשָּׁה, **אָמֵן אָמֵן**).

[80] Jesus' use of the phrase "I say to you" (Heb. אני אומר) recalls Jer 28:7, where Jeremiah says to Hanania: "Nevertheless hear now this word that **I speak** in your ears" (אַךְ-שְׁמַע-נָא הַדָּבָר הַזֶּה אֲשֶׁר **אָנֹכִי דֹבֵר** בְּאָזְנֶיךָ).

[81] The Greek ἰδοὺ is used in imitation of the Hebrew הִנֵּה.

[82] The Aramaic בר אנוש ("son of man") links to Dan 7:13; authority being the theme.

[83] See Luke 9:22. The prophecy of rising again was possibly added by later redactor. However, consider the "Gabriel Revelation": לשלושת ימים חייה אני גבריאל גוזר עליך ("In three days, live, I, Gabriel, command you"). A slain messianic leader would be resurrected within three days, and rise to heaven in a chariot.

Scene 8:
A Blind Man Receives His Sight

The Jewish sense of "faith" is steadfastness and perseverance, especially in keeping the commandments. Here, the afflicted man continues to entreat Jesus for healing despite being rebuked for being boisterous. This is consistent with the parable of the persistent widow (Luke 18:1–8).

Luke 18:35 And it came to pass,[84] that as he was approaching Jericho, a certain blind man sat by the road begging. **36** And hearing a crowd pass by, he asked what it meant. **37** And they told him, that Jesus of Nazareth is passing by. **38** And he cried, saying: Jesus, **son of David, have mercy on me.**[85] **39** And **those who went before rebuked him, that he should hold his peace.**[86] But he cried so much more: Son of David, have mercy on me. **40** And Jesus stopped, and commanded that he be brought to him. And when he had come near, he asked him, **41** Saying: What do you desire me to do for you? And he said: Lord, that I may receive my sight. **42** And Jesus said to him: **Receive your sight: your faith has healed you.**[87] **43** And immediately he received his sight, and followed him, glorifying God. And all the people, when they saw it, gave praise to God.

---

[84] The Greek ἐγένετο δὲ translates the Hebrew וַיְהִי.

[85] The Greek υἱὲ Δαυίδ (son of David) translates the Hebrew בֶּן-דָּוִד, a messianic designation which was politically inflammatory. See 2 Sam 7:16 (regarding David): "And your house and your kingdom shall be made sure for ever before you; your throne shall be established forever" (וְנֶאְמַן בֵּיתְךָ וּמַמְלַכְתְּךָ עַד-עוֹלָם לְפָנֶיךָ: כִּסְאֲךָ, יִהְיֶה נָכוֹן עַד-עוֹלָם).

[86] The crowd silences the blind man, but Jesus does not rebuke him. See Luke 4:41–42. Jesus silenced the demons because he knew they are liars, and did not want them testifying about him. Here, he allows the testimony, contrary to the "messianic secret" concept.

[87] A rabbinic *a fortiori* ("light and heavy"/וְחוֹמֶר קַל) argument: if the blind recognizes him, how much more should those who see (Mark 10:46 ff.; Matt 9:27).

Scene 9:
Jesus Comes to Zacchaeus' House (RCT)

The story of Zacchaeus likely occurred immediately prior to Jesus'
triumphal entry to Jerusalem, as large numbers of pilgrims from
Galilee were passing through Jericho.[88]

Luke 19:1 And Jesus entered and passed through Jericho. **2** And,
behold,[89] there was a man named **Zacchaeus,**[90] who was the chief
among the tax collectors, and he was rich. **3** And he sought to see
Jesus, who he was; and could not because of the crowd, since he
was small in stature. **4** And he ran before, and climbed up into a
sycamore tree to see him; for he was about to pass that way. **5** And
when Jesus came to the place, he looked up, and saw him, and said
to him: Zacchaeus, hurry, and come down; for today I must stay at
your house. **6** And hurrying, he came down, and received him
joyfully. **7** And when they saw it, they all grumbled, saying: He
has gone to be guest with a man who is a sinner. **8** And Zacchaeus
stood, and said to the Lord: **Behold,**[91] Lord, half of my goods I
give to the poor; and if I have taken anything from anyone by
fraud, I restore him **fourfold.**[92] **9** And **Jesus said to him: This day
salvation**[93] has come to this house, because he is also a son of

---

[88] See Lindsey, *Jesus,* 75–76.

[89] The Greek ἰδοὺ is used in imitation of the Hebrew הִנֵּה.

[90] In Hebrew Zakkai (זכּי—"worthy one"). The irony is that the "unworthy" tax
collector becomes "worthy." Emil Schurer theorized that he may have come from the
same family as Yohanan ben Zakkai (GJV 1:478). Note Neh 7:14: "The children of
Zakkai, seven hundred and threescore" (בְּנֵי זַכָּי, שְׁבַע מֵאוֹת וְשִׁשִּׁים).

[91] The Greek ἰδοὺ is used in imitation of the Hebrew הִנֵּה.

[92] Zakkai considers that he has acquired his wealth illegally (the law of theft).
One caught stealing essential items without remorse was to make fourfold recompense.
See Exod 21:37: "If a man steal an ox, or a sheep, and kill it, or sell it, he shall pay five
oxen for an ox, and ***four*** sheep for a sheep" (,כִּי יִגְנֹב-אִישׁ שׁוֹר אוֹ-שֶׂה, וּטְבָחוֹ אוֹ מְכָרוֹ--חֲמִשָּׁה בָקָר
יְשַׁלֵּם תַּחַת הַשּׁוֹר, וְאַרְבַּע-צֹאן, תַּחַת הַשֶּׂה); 2 Sam 12:6: "... and he shall restore the lamb
fourfold" (וְאֶת-הַכִּבְשָׂה יְשַׁלֵּם אַרְבַּעְתָּיִם). Zakkai by his own volition determined to make the
entire restitution for such "theft."

[93] A Hebraic wordplay, absent in Greek: "Salvation" (Greek σωτηρία; Hebrew
ישועה)/"Jesus" (Greek Ἰησοῦς; Hebrew ישוע) has come to this house (see Luke 2:30; Matt
1:21).

Abraham. **10** For the **Son of Man**[94] **has come to seek and to save that which was lost.**[95]/[96]

At this point, the formula of an event, followed by a teaching ("The Son of Man has come to seek and to save...") and two parables may be reconstructed. The parables of the Pharisee and the Tax Collector and the Great Supper are transposed accordingly.

Parable 1: The Pharisee and the Tax Collector (ANT)

Luke 18:9 Now he spoke this parable to some who **trusted in themselves**[97] that they were righteous, and despising others. **10** Two men went up into the **temple to pray,**[98] one a Pharisee and the other a tax collector. **11** The Pharisee stood and prayed thus **toward himself:**[99] God, **I thank you, that I am not as other men**

---

[94] The Aramaic בר אנוש ("son of man") links to Dan 7:13; authority being the theme.

[95] One of the "dominical sayings" thought to have been composed later. However, the Greek aorist tense (ἦλθεν/"came") does not convey the Hebrew בא, which also means "comes"/"has come."

[96] Followed by Luke 18:9–14 (the self-righteous Pharisee). Note Ezek 34:12: "As a shepherd **seeks out** his flock on the day he is among his scattered sheep, so **will I seek out** My sheep and **deliver** them ..." (כְּבַקָּרַת **רֹעֶה** עֶדְרוֹ בְּיוֹם הֱיוֹתוֹ בְתוֹךְ צֹאנוֹ נִפְרָשׁוֹת כֵּן, אֲבַקֵּר אֶת צֹאנִי וְהִצַּלְתִּי אֶתְהֶם). Jesus, as an ancient Hasid, is doing what only God is said do: "to seek and to save." Ezek 34:23 links the messiah with the earlier statement: "I will establish one **shepherd** over them, and **he shall feed** them—My **servant** David" (וַהֲקִמֹתִי עֲלֵיהֶם **רֹעֶה** אֶחָד **וְרָעָה** אֶתְהֶן אֵת **עַבְדִּי** דָוִד). Jesus apparently saw history in three dispensations: the Law and the Prophets, the Kingdom of heaven (messianic era), and the world to come. See *b. San.* 99a: "Rabbi Yoḥanan says: In their prophecies with regard to redemption and the end of days, all the **prophets** prophesied only about the **messianic era**, but with regard to the **World-to-Come** the reward is not quantifiable, as it states: 'No eye has seen it, God, aside from You, Who will do for those who await Him' (Isaiah 64:3)" (א"ר יוחנן כל **הנביאים** כולן לא נתנבאו אלא **לימות המשיח** אבל **לעולם הבא**).

[97] Note *m. Avot* 2:4: "**Do not trust in yourself** until the day of your death" (וְאַל תַּאֲמִין בְּעַצְמְךָ עַד יוֹם מוֹתְךָ).

[98] The temple, not the synagogue, was the place of prayer.

[99] Note the Hebrew expression: "between him and between himself" (בינו ובין עצמו).

are,[100] swindlers, unrighteous, adulterers, or even as this tax collector. **12** I fast twice a week, I give **tithes**[101] of all that I possess. **13** And the tax collector, standing afar off, would not so much as lift up his eyes to heaven, but struck his breast, saying: God be merciful to me, a sinner. **14** I tell you, this man went down to his house justified rather than the other. For **everyone that exalts himself shall be humbled; but he who humbles himself shall be exalted.**[102]

Parable 2: The Great Supper

Luke 14:16 Then he said to him: A certain man made **a great supper,**[103] and invited many; **17** And sent his servant at the hour of the **supper**[104] to say to them who were invited: Come; for all

---

[100] Note *b. Ber.* 28b: "Rabbi Neḥunya ben Hakana would recite a brief prayer upon his entrance into the study hall and upon his exit. They said to him: What room is there for this prayer? He said to them: Upon my entrance, I pray that no mishap will transpire caused by me in the study hall. And upon my exit, *I give thanks* for my portion" (רַבִּי נְחוּנְיָא בֶּן הַקָּנָה הָיָה מִתְפַּלֵּל בִּכְנִיסָתוֹ לְבֵית הַמִּדְרָשׁ וּבִיצִיאָתוֹ תְּפִלָּה קְצָרָה. אָמְרוּ לוֹ: מָה מָקוֹם לִתְפִלָּה זוֹ? אָמַר לָהֶם: בִּכְנִיסָתִי אֲנִי מִתְפַּלֵּל שֶׁלֹּא יֶאֱרַע דְּבַר תַּקָּלָה עַל יָדִי. וּבִיצִיאָתִי **אֲנִי נוֹתֵן הוֹדָאָה** עַל חָלְקִי).

[101] The word Pharisees (פרושים) derives from the Hebrew פרוש (*parush*), meaning "separated." They were understood to have separated themselves for a life of purity. They may also have been involved at their inception in the separation of tithes required by Mosaic law. Note *T. San.* 2:6, depicting Rabban Gamliel and the elders writing to Galilee and the diaspora: "I inform you that the time for the removal has come, to *separate* the **tithes** from the olive vats."

[102] See Luke 14:11; Note *Lev. R.* 1:5: "Rabbi Yehoshua of Sikhnin [said]: Do not exalt yourself in the king's presents, and do not claim a place among great men; it is better for him to say to you, '*Come up here*' than for him to humiliate you before a nobleman. (Prov 25:7). R. Akiva taught … Move two or three places lower and there sit down. Move down so that you will be told '*Move up*'…" (רַבִּי יְהוֹשֻׁעַ דְּסַכְנִין בְּשֵׁם רַבִּי לֵוִי פָּתַר: כִּי טוֹב אֲמַר לָךְ **עֲלֵה הֵנָּה** מֵהַשְׁפִּילְךָ לִפְנֵי נָדִיב וגו', רַבִּי עֲקִיבָא מַתְנֵי לָהּ … רְחַק מִמְּקוֹמְךָ שְׁנַיִם וּשְׁלֹשָׁה מוֹשָׁבוֹת וְשֵׁב עַד שֶׁיֹּאמְרוּ לָךְ **עֲלֵה**). Hillel's meekness is rooted in his strength, his exalted view of himself: "And so Hillel used to say, 'My **humiliation** is my exaltation and my *exaltation*, and my *exaltation* is my *humiliation*.' What is the proof? 'He who raises himself is to be made to sit down, he who **abases** himself is to be raised up so that he is seen (Ps 113:5–6)." (וְכֵן הִלֵּל אוֹמֵר **הַשְׁפָּלָתִי** הִיא **הַגְבָּהָתִי**, **הַגְבָּהָתִי** הִיא **הַשְׁפָּלָתִי**, מַה טַעַם: הַמַּגְבִּיהִי **לְרָאוֹת**, **הַמַּשְׁפִּילִי** לְרָאוֹת). Note also *b. Er.* 13b; *b. San.* 17a: "This is to teach you that anyone who **humbles** himself, the Holy One, Blessed be He, *exalts* him, and anyone who *exalts* himself, the Holy One, Blessed be He, **humbles** him" (לְלַמֶּדְךָ שֶׁכָּל **הַמַּשְׁפִּיל** עַצְמוֹ—הַקָּדוֹשׁ בָּרוּךְ הוּא **מַגְבִּיהוֹ**, וְכָל **הַמַּגְבִּיהַּ** עַצְמוֹ—הַקָּדוֹשׁ בָּרוּךְ הוּא **מַשְׁפִּילוֹ**).

[103] See parallel: Matt 22:1–14; the Lucan version is superior.

[104] Note *m. Avot* 3:16 (attributed to R. Akiva): "… the judgment is a righteous judgment, and everything is prepared for the **banquet**" (וְהַדִּין דִּין אֱמֶת. וְהַכֹּל מְתֻקָּן לַ**סְּעוּדָה**).

things are now ready. **18** And they all with one accord began to make **excuses**.[105] The first said to him: I have bought a field, and I need to go and see it. I beg you to excuse me. **19** And another said: I have bought five yoke of oxen, and I am going to prove them. I beg you to excuse me. **20** And another said: I have married a wife, and therefore I cannot come. **21** So that servant came, and reported to his master these things. Then the master of the house, being angry, said to his servant, Go out quickly into the streets and lanes of the city, and bring in **the poor**,[106] and the crippled, and the **blind, and the lame**.[107] **22** And the servant said: Lord, it has been done as you have commanded, and still there is room. **23** And the lord said to the servant, Go out into the highways and hedges,[108] and compel them to come in, that my house may be filled. **24** For I say to you, that none of those men who were invited will taste of my supper.

---

[105] Compare *Sifre Deut.* 192, regarding excuses for those not allowed to retreat in war: "As Rabban Yochanan ben Zakai has said: Come and see how G-d cares for human dignity. When one [soldier] returns, the others would say 'maybe he has just built a house' or 'maybe he has betrothed a woman.' All had to bring proof besides the fearful one whose situation was evident" (כדברי ר' יוחנן בן זכאי, בוא וראה כמה חס המקום על כבוד הבריות, מפני היראה ורך הלבב. כשהוא חוזר, יאמרו "שמא בנה בית", "שמא ארש אשה". וכולם היו צריכים להביא עדותן חוץ מן היריא ורך הלבב, שעדיו עמו). In the Lucan narrative, the absurdity of the excuses is intended to be humorous.

[106] Another possible "Essene" reference to "the *poor*." Note the Qumran *War Scroll*, 1QM 13:14: "Your mighty hand is with the **oppressed/poor**" (אביונים יד גבורתכה); see Luke 14:13; Matt 19:21. Note also the story of the tax collector Bar Ma'jan (*y. Sanh.* 6.23c par. *y. Hagh.* 2.77d): "Ma'jan had arranged a banquet to which he invited the city councilors—unsurprisingly, they refused to attend and eat with a tax-gatherer, and so, to show his contempt for them, Ma'jan invited all the *poor*, sick and beggars of the city to attend instead."

[107] Note Dead Sea Scrolls 1QSa 2:5–8: "No man with a physical handicap—*crippled* in both legs or hands, *lame, blind*, deaf, dumb, or possessed of a visible blemish in his flesh—or a doddering old man unable to do his share in the congregation—may enter to take a place in the congregation of the men of reputation" (וכול מנוגע בבשרו נכאה רגלים או ידים פסח או עור או חרש או אלם או מום מנוגע בבשרו לראות עינים או איש זקן כושל לבלתי התחזק בתוך העדה. אל יבואו אלה להתיצב בתוך עדת אנושי השם).

[108] Note the Semitic parallelism: "Streets"/"lanes"; "poor"/"maimed"; "lame"/ "blind"; "highways"/"hedges." Not in Matthew.

Scene 10:
The Triumphal Entry (RCT)

When Jesus triumphantly enters Jerusalem, there is an obvious reference to the prophet Zechariah, who declares that Israel's Messiah will come on the foal of a donkey. There are rabbinic parallels in which people spread their garments before Moses, who is proclaimed King of Kush, and myrtle was strewn on the street before Mordecai, the willow being called "hosanna."

Luke 19:28 And when he had spoken these things, he went ahead, going up to Jerusalem. **29 And it came to pass,**[109] when he had come near to Bethphage and Bethany, at the mount called the Mount of Olives, he sent two of his disciples, **30** Saying: Go into the village ahead of you; in which, upon entering, you will find a **colt**[110] tied, on which no man ever sat. Untie him, and bring him here. **31** And if anyone asks you: Why do you untie him? Thus you will say to him: Because the Lord has need of him. **32** And those who were sent went their way, and found it just as he had said to them. **33** And as they were untying the colt, its **owner[s]**[111] said to them: Why are you untying the colt? **34** And they said: The Lord has need of him. **35** And they brought him to Jesus: and they cast their garments on the colt, and they set Jesus upon him. **36** And as

---

[109] The Greek καὶ ἐγένετο translates the Hebrew וַיְהִי; see Luke 1:23.

[110] See Zechariah 9:9: "Rejoice greatly, O daughter of Zion, shout, O daughter of Jerusalem; behold, your king comes to you, he is triumphant, and victorious, lowly, and riding on a donkey, even on a **colt** the foal of a donkey" (גִּילִי מְאֹד בַּת-צִיּוֹן, הָרִיעִי בַּת יְרוּשָׁלַ‍ִם, הִנֵּה מַלְכֵּךְ יָבוֹא לָךְ, צַדִּיק וְנוֹשָׁע הוּא; עָנִי וְרֹכֵב עַל-חֲמוֹר, וְעַל-**עַיִר** בֶּן-אֲתֹנוֹת.).

[111] The Greek κύριοι ("owners") translates the Hebrew בעליו, which can mean either "owners" or "owner." The context here suggests the singular.

he went, **they spread their clothes on the road.**[112] **37** And when he had come near, already at the descent of the Mount of Olives, the whole multitude of the disciples began to rejoice and praise God with a loud voice for all the mighty works which they had seen; **38** Saying: Blessed is the King who comes in the name of the Lord: **peace in heaven, and glory in the highest.**[113] **39** And some of the Pharisees from among the multitude said to him: Teacher, rebuke your disciples. **40** And he answered and said to them: I tell you that, if these should hold their peace, **the stones would immediately cry out.**[114]

The account of Jesus weeping over Jerusalem (Luke 19:41–44) likely belongs in a later context, after Luke 23:31.[115]

Scene 11:
Jesus Cleanses the Temple (RCT)

The short Lucan passage in which Jesus cleanses the temple is laden with meaning. While some have suggested that he was symbolically destroying the temple, there is no such sense in Luke's

---

[112] See 2 Kgs 9:13, where the people spread their garments under Jehu. Note *Yal.* 168, which relates that when Moses was proclaimed the king of Cush, the people spread their garments on the ground; *b. Ket.* 66b: "They said about Nakdimon ben Guryon that when he would leave his home to go to the study hall, there were *fine woolen garments his attendants would spread underneath him*" (אמרו עליו על נקדימון בן גוריון כשהיה יוצא מביתו לבית המדרש **כלי מילת היו מציעין תחתיו**). Note also *Lam. R.*, Intro. #25, which relates that a carpet was spread for the high priest, from his house to the Temple; and *Targ. Esther* 1:5, relating that myrtle was strewn in the street when Mordechai came out of the king's gate.

[113] See Mark 11:9–10 ("hosanna in the highest"); Matt 21:9 ("hosanna to the Son of David"); note *b. Suk.* 30b–31a: "And let the merchants acquire a myrtle branch with a change of name that it underwent, as initially it was called a myrtle branch, and now it is called *hoshana,*" (וְלִיקְנְיֻּה בְּשִׁינּוּי הַשֵּׁם, דְּמֵעִיקָרָא הֲוָה לֵיהּ אַסָא וְהַשְׁתָּא **הוֹשַׁעְנָא**). See also Luke 2:14.

[114] Recalling Hab 2:11: "For *the stone shall cry* out of the wall …" (כִּי **אֶבֶן** מִקִּיר תִּזְעָק). Used similarly in rabbinic literature; see *b. Hag.* 16a; *b. Ta'an* 11a: "The *stones* of a person's house and the beams of a person's house will testify against him, as it is stated: 'For a *stone* shall *cry out* from the wall, and a beam out of the timber shall answer it' (Habakkuk 2:11)" (**אַבְנֵי** בֵיתוֹ שֶׁל אָדָם וְקוֹרוֹת בֵּיתוֹ שֶׁל אָדָם מְעִידִים בּוֹ שֶׁנֶּאֱמַר כִּי **אֶבֶן** מִקִּיר תִּזְעָק); וְכָפִיס מֵעֵץ יַעֲנֶנָּה); *Mid. R.* Ps 73:3.

[115] See Lindsey, *Jesus*, 170.

account, where we are told afterward that he taught daily in the temple. Although this incident certainly contributed to the later charge of insurrection, Luke takes pains to assert that it was the chief priests and scribes who felt threatened. There is no sense that the Pharisees or anyone else conspired to turn Jesus over to the Roman authorities.

Luke 19:45 And he went into the temple, and began to cast out **those who sold there,**[116] **46** saying to them: It is written, **My house is the house of prayer;**[117] but you have made it a **den of thieves.**[118]

---

[116] See *m. Ket.* 1:7: "There was an incident where the price of nests stood in Jerusalem at one gold dinar. Rabban Shimon ben Gamliel said: I swear by this abode of the Divine Presence that I will not lie down tonight until the price of nests will be in silver dinars" (לֹא, הַזֶּה הַמָּעוֹן גַּמְלִיאֵל, בֶּן שִׁמְעוֹן רַבָּן אָמַר זָהָב. בְּדִינָרֵי בִּירוּשָׁלַיִם קִנִּים שֶׁעָמְדוּ מַעֲשֶׂה בְּדִינָרִין שֶׁיְּהוּ עַד הַלַּיְלָה, אָלִין). Money changers were called by the term κολλυβιστες (Hebrew: שולחני—"one who sits at table"). Exod 30:11 requires a half-shekel "temple tax." In Second Temple times, this was paid in Tyrian silver coins. Tables were set up, first in the provinces, later in Jerusalem. Jesus paid this tax, for himself and for Peter (Matt 17:24). It is likely that the collectors were priests. See *b. Men.* 108a: "Where would this premium [*kalbon*] go? It would be added to the shekels themselves; this is the statement of Rabbi Meir. Rabbi Eliezer says: It would be used for communal gift offerings" (לנדבה אומר אליעזר ר' מאיר ר' דברי לשקלים הולך זה קלבון להיכן). The outer court of the Temple was used for the sale of sacrificial birds and beasts, and for the exchange of heathen coinage for that of the sanctuary. Since the chief priests benefitted from the mart, the people called it "Annas' Bazaar."

[117] See Isa 56:7: "My house shall be called *a house of prayer* for all peoples." (לְכָל-הָעַמִּים יִקָּרֵא תְפִלָּה בֵּית, בֵּיתִי); 2 Sam 7:10: "And I will appoint a *place* for my people Israel" (לְיִשְׂרָאֵל לְעַמִּי מָקוֹם וְשַׂמְתִּי); 2 Sam 7:11: "For the LORD will make you a *house*" (כִּי הוּא יְהוָה לְךָ יַעֲשֶׂה בַּיִת); 2 Sam 7:13: "He shall build a *house* for my name" (לִשְׁמִי בַּיִת יִבְנֶה הוּא).

[118] Note Dead Sea Scrolls eschatalogical midrashim (4Q174 f1_2i:3–6), based on 2 Sam 7:10: "'A temple of the Lord are you to prepare with your hands; the Lord will reign forever and ever' (Exod 15:17–18). This passage describes the temple that no man with a permanent fleshly defect shall enter, nor Ammonite, Moabite, bastard, foreigner or alien, forevermore. Surely His holiness shall be revealed there; eternal glory shall ever be apparent there. ***Strangers shall not again defile it, as they formerly defiled the Temple of Israel through their sins***" (יבוא לוא אשר הבית הואה ועד. עולם ימלוך יהוה ידיכה כוננו אדני מקדש שמה ... יראה עליו תמיד עולם ... שם קדושי כיא עולם עד ונכר בן וממזר ומואבי ועמוני עולם עד ... שמה ולא **בחטאתמה ישראל מקדש את בראישונה השמו כאשר זרים עוד ישמוהו**).

Scene 12:
A Woman Caught in Adultery

It is suggested that a passage in John 8, relating that Jesus went to the Mount of Olives, belongs in this immediate context. This passage utilizes the same vocabulary as found in the Lucan text. It was likely dropped from Luke by an early copyist and inserted in John's Gospel. When Jesus arrives in Jerusalem, this is his first encounter with the "scribes," representing the Sadducean temple authorities.[119]

John 8:1 Jesus went to the Mount of Olives. **2** And early in the morning he came again into the temple, and all the people came to him. And he sat down, and taught them. **3** And the scribes **[and Pharisees]**[120] brought to him a woman caught in adultery. And when they had set her in the midst, **4** they said to him: Teacher, this woman was caught in adultery, in the very act. **5 Now Moses in the law commanded us, that such should be stoned;**[121] but what do you say? **6** This they said, testing him, so that they might have grounds to accuse him. But Jesus stooped down, and with his finger wrote on the ground. **7** However, when they continued asking him, he lifted himself up, and said to them: The one among

---

[119] See Lindsey, *Jesus*, 142–43.

[120] The term "scribes and Pharisees" appears repeatedly in Luke's Gospel, in an almost "stylized" fashion. The scribes are never mentioned alone. In Luke 20:39 they appear along with the Sadducees and commend Jesus on his answer regarding resurrection. Elsewhere (Luke 9:22; 20:1), the scribes are mentioned, not with the Pharisees, but with the elders and chief priests, with whom they would have been much more inclined to associate. In Luke 20:19 and 22:1, 66 they are referenced along with the chief priests, and in Luke 19:47 with the chief priests and "chiefs of the people." It may have been that the writer/redactor of Luke was not inclined to reference the scribes without including the Pharisees, as a matter of "literary convention." The presence of Pharisees is arguably an editorial gloss, perhaps by a later hand (subsequent to its deletion from Luke) since it is unlikely that they would have collaborated here with the Sadducee-oriented scribes. Contextually, it might be better to read: "And the scribes and *Sadducees* brought to him a woman caught in adultery."

[121] The condemnation of the woman conflicts with what became rabbinic *halakha*, which requires witnesses and a judicial procedure (known in rabbinic literature as a דין בית/*Bet Din*). It is doubtful that the Pharisees would have assented to such a stoning procedure.

you who is without sin, let him cast the first stone at her. **8** And again he stooped down, and wrote on the ground. **9** And those who heard it, being convicted by their own conscience, went out one by one, beginning at the eldest, until the last. And Jesus was left alone, with the woman standing in the midst. **10** When Jesus had lifted himself up, and saw no one but the woman, he said to her: Woman, where are those who accuse you? Has no one condemned you? **11** She said: No one, Sir. And Jesus said to her: Neither do I condemn you. Go, and sin no more.

Luke 19:47 And he taught daily in the temple. But the chief priests and the scribes and the chiefs of the people sought to destroy him, **48** And could not find what they might do. For all the people were very attentive to hear him.

Temple to Tomb

The "final days" of Jesus transpire against the backdrop of the city of Jerusalem, with the brooding image of the temple as its centerpiece. Jesus is no stranger to the temple, having been presented there shortly after his birth, and having reappeared there at the age of twelve. His hypothetical Judean sojourn would certainly have brought him back to Jerusalem and the sacred shrine. At this point, however, following his triumphal entry to the city for the last time, the focus of the narrative shifts to direct confrontation with the chief priests, scribes, and elders. Understanding this antagonism is vital in reframing Jesus' conflict, not with the Pharisees and certainly not with "Judaism" per se, but with the Sadducee-dominated "temple committee." The events leading to the crucifixion are of course central to Christian thought, theology, and religious tradition, but it is possible to re-create several narrative units, based on the notion that certain "incidents" recounted in the hypothetical Hebrew *grundschrift* would have been supplemented by a short teaching, followed by two parables. Rearranging the Lucan account is key to this endeavor, as is the integration of specific sections of the Matthean narrative. The Parable of the Two Sons (Matthew 21:28–32) finds a parallel in the Parable of the Lost Son (Luke 15:11–32). The Parable of the Barren Fig Tree (Luke 13:6–9) is transposed to this part of the narrative, to be paralleled by the parable of the Wicked Vinedressers/"Only Son" (Luke 20:9–16). The so-called "Last Supper" also comes into focus, having become a central sacrament in traditional Christianity. In a Hebraic context, there is serious discussion over its possible connection with the Passover Seder (greatly in dispute) and with the "messianic banquet" of Qumranic literature. The order of the wine and bread, concerning Qumranic and traditional Jewish practice, is of particular interest, especially in connection with Paul's reworking of the narrative in a sacramental fashion. Following Jesus' arrest in Gethsemane, the trial before Pilate becomes another central element in understanding the complex issues relating to who may have been "responsible" for his execution. The repercussions of this "blame" have impacted Jewish-Christian relations down to the present and could not be more important to scholarly discourse.

Scene 1:
Jesus' Authority Questioned (RCT)

Jesus is questioned by the chief priests, scribes, and elders, comprising the temple committee, representing Sadducean elements (not the Pharisees) who are his natural adversaries. The multitude are depicted as supportive of both Jesus and John.

Luke 20:1 And it came to pass,[1] that on one of those days, as **he taught the people in the temple**[2] and proclaimed the **gospel**,[3] the **chief priests** and the **scribes**[4] came to him with the **elders,**[5] **2 And** spoke to him, saying: Tell us, by what authority do you do these things? Or who is the one who has given you this authority? **3 And**

---

[1] The Greek καὶ ἐγένετο translates the Hebrew וַיְהִי; see Luke 1:23.

[2] Note *b. Pes.* 26a: "They said about Rabban Yoḥanan ben Zakkai that *he would sit in the shade of the Sanctuary and expound to a large number of people* all day long" (אָמְרוּ עָלָיו עַל רַבָּן יוֹחָנָן בֶּן זַכַּאי **שֶׁהָיָה יוֹשֵׁב בְּצִילוֹ שֶׁל הֵיכָל, וְדוֹרֵשׁ** כָּל הַיּוֹם כּוּלוֹ).

[3] See Luke 7:22. The Hebrew term בְּשׂוֹרָה, rendered "gospel" in Greek, evokes Isa 40:9: "O you who *tell good tidings* to Zion, get up into the high mountain..." (עַל הַר-גָּבֹהַּ עֲלִי-לָךְ, **מְבַשֶּׂרֶת צִיּוֹן**).

[4] i.e. "temple secretaries."

[5] i.e. "elders of the temple." The *chief priests, scribes,* and *elders* comprised the "temple committee." There were no Pharisees, and this was not the Sanhedrin. David Flusser and Dan Barag, "The Ossuary of Yehohanah Granddaughter of the High Priest Theophilus," *Israel Exploration Journal* 36, no. 1–2 (1986): 39–44, highlight the involvement of a single priestly family (Annas, Caiaphas, John and Alexander) in Jesus' interrogation.

he answered and said to them: **I will also ask you one thing;**[6] and answer me. **4** The baptism of John, was it from **heaven**[7] or from men? **5** And they reasoned among themselves, saying: If we say, From heaven, he will say: Why then did you not believe him? **6** But if we say, Of men, **all the people will stone us; for they are persuaded that John was a prophet.**[8] **7** And they answered, that they did not know from where it was. **8** And Jesus said to them: Neither will I tell you by what authority I do these things.

Scene 2:
Jesus Is Questioned About Fasting

Luke 5:33–39 (Matthew 9:15–20) is added here, as this passage complements the narrative of the "temple committee" questioning Jesus. Regarding fasting, it should not be construed that Jesus disregarded traditional Jewish fast days, but rather that he did not observe special fast days, unique to the Pharisees and John the Baptist.[9] Jesus' statement concerning new wine in old wineskins should be understood as a desire to reinvigorate (not replace) Judaism.

Luke 5:33 And they said to him: **Why do the disciples of John fast often, and make prayers, and likewise the disciples of the Pharisees; but yours eat and drink?**[10] **34** And he said to them: Can you make the **children of the bride chamber**[11] fast, while the bridegroom is with them? **35** But the days will come, when the

---

[6] A rabbinic technique of answering a question with a question.

[7] The Greek οὐρανοῦ translates the Hebrew שמים, a euphemism for "God."

[8] See Matt 21:26: "But if we say, 'From men,' *we fear the multitude*, for all count John as a prophet." The people sided with both John and Jesus. Herod Antipas had recently been defeated by the Nabateans, and it was said that this was divine recompense for his killing of John (Josephus, *Ant.* XVIII: 119).

[9] See Lindsey, *Jesus*, 147–48.

[10] The question about fasting relates not to accepted fast days, but to the special fasts of the Pharisees and John the Baptist.

[11] The Greek υἱοὺς τοῦ νυμφῶνος ("children of the bride chamber") translates the Hebrew בני החופה; see Matt 9:15.

bridegroom will be **taken**[12] away from them, and then they will fast in those days. **36** And he also spoke a parable to them: No one puts a piece of a new garment on an old. Otherwise, then, the new makes a tear, and the piece that was taken out of the new does not match with the old. **37** And no one puts **new wine**[13] into old wineskins, lest the new wine burst the wineskins, and spill out, and the wineskins be destroyed. **38** But new wine must be put into new wineskins; and both are preserved. **39** And no one having drunk old wine desires new; for he says: **The old is better**.[14]

Like Children in the Marketplace

Luke 7:31–35 (Matthew 21:28–32) most likely belong here, as these verses also relate to John the Baptist. (Jesus is saying that the inconsistency of the arguments of his opponents is an indication of their foolishness.)

---

[12] The Greek ἀπαρθῇ ("taken") translates the Hebrew לוקח, which is a euphemism for death; see Isa 53:8: "By oppression and judgment he was **taken away**" (מֵעֹצֶר וּמִמִּשְׁפָּט לֻקָּח). Jesus' mission of "renewal" is therefore linked with his death.

[13] "New wine" (Gr. οἶνον νέον) was unfermented "grape juice" or "sweet wine" (γλεῦκος) as in Acts 2:13 (Heb. תירוש). See Ben Sira 9:10: "A new friend is like *new wine*; when it has aged, you can drink it with pleasure."

[14] Jesus may be seen as wanting to revitalize, not radically redefine Judaism. Note *m. Avot* 4:20: "He who learns from the young, to what is he compared? To one who eats unripe grapes, and drinks wine from his vat; And he who learns from the old, to what is he compared? To one who eats ripe grapes, and drinks *old wine*. Rabbi said: don't look at the container but at that which is in it: there is a new container full of *old wine*, and an old [container] in which there is not even new [wine]." הַלּוֹמֵד מִן הַקְּטַנִּים לְמַה הוּא דוֹמֶה, לְאֹכֵל עֲנָבִים קֵהוֹת וְשׁוֹתֶה יַיִן מִגִּתּוֹ. וְהַלּוֹמֵד מִן הַזְּקֵנִים לְמַה הוּא דוֹמֶה, לְאֹכֵל עֲנָבִים בְּשֵׁלוֹת וְשׁוֹתֶה יַיִן יָשָׁן. רַבִּי אוֹמֵר, אַל תִּסְתַּכֵּל בַּקַּנְקַן, אֶלָּא בְמַה שֶׁיֶּשׁ בּוֹ. יֵשׁ קַנְקַן חָדָשׁ מָלֵא יָשָׁן, וְיָשָׁן שֶׁאֲפִלּוּ חָדָשׁ אֵין בּוֹ); *b. Sof.* 15:7: "The world cannot exist without water, it cannot exist without *wine*, and it cannot exist without spiced-wine; but a rich man enjoys all three of them. So, too, it is impossible for the world to exist without Scripture" אי אפשר לעולם בלא מים ואי אפשר לעולם בלא יין ואי אפשר; *Sifre Deut.* 48:6: לעולם בלא קונדיטון ואיש עשיר מתכלכל בשלושתן כך אי אפשר לעולם בלא מקרא "And just as with *wine*, you taste the flavor of *wine* from the beginning, but the more it *ages* in the bottle, the more its flavor is enhanced, so, words of Torah—the older they grow in the body, the more their 'flavor' is enhanced" (ומה יין, אתה טועם טעם יין מתחילתו, כל זמן שהוא **מתיישן** בקנקן סופו להשביח—אף דברי תורה, כל זמן שהם מתיישנים בגוף סופם להשביח).

Luke 7:31 And the Lord said: **To what then shall I liken**[15] the men of this generation? and to what are they like? **32** They are like to children sitting in the marketplace, and calling one to another, and saying: We have **piped** to you, and you have not **danced**; we have **sung a dirge**, and you have not **wept**.[16] **33** For John the Baptist came neither eating bread nor drinking wine; and you say: **He has a demon.**[17] **34** The **Son of Man**[18] has come eating and drinking; and you say: Behold a gluttonous man, and a drunkard, a friend of tax collectors and sinners! **35** But **wisdom**[19] is justified by all of her children.

The "incident" of Jesus being questioned by the "temple committee" is theoretically followed by a teaching (about children in the marketplace) and two parables. One features a son who opposes his father's directive but later repents; the other features a son who acts foolishly with his inheritance but "comes to himself." The "Parable of the Two Sons" is transposed from Matthew's Gospel (21:28–32) and is echoed by the "Parable of the Lost Son," transposed from Luke 15 (11–32).[20]

---

[15] This is similar to the Hebrew expression: ?למה הדבר דומה ("To what is this comparable?"). This exact language frequently appears in rabbinic literature (including the Mishnah and Gemara). It serves as an introduction to an example or parable.

[16] Note the Hebraic parallelism: "piped"/"danced"; "sung a dirge"/"wept."

[17] See Mark 3:22, where the original story likely did not include the charge of demon possession. This represents a "pickup" from the charge against John the Baptist.

[18] The Aramaic בר אנוש ("son of man") links to Dan 7:13; authority being the theme.

[19] The Greek σοφία is the equivalent of the Hebrew חכמה, which can denote shrewdness, craftiness, or in some cases (unlike Greek) stupidity, in the sense that one who says something "smart" may in reality have said something "stupid." To be truly "bright," an argument must be consistent. Jesus is saying that since his opponents' arguments are so inconsistent, they are an indication of "stupidity"/capriciousness.

[20] See Lindsey, *Jesus*, 148–49.

Parable 1: The Two Sons

Matthew 21:28 But what do you think? A certain man had two sons;[21], and he came to the first, and said: Son, go work today in my vineyard. 29 He answered and said: I will not: but afterward he repented, and went. 30 And he came to the second, and said likewise. And he answered and said: I go, sir: but he did not go. 31 Which of the two did the will of his father? They said to him: The first. Jesus said to them: Truly, I say to you, that the tax collectors and the harlots enter the kingdom of God before you. 32 For John came to you in the way of righteousness,[22] and you did not believe him: but the tax collectors and the harlots believed him: and you, when you saw it, did not repent afterward and believe him.

Parable 2: The Lost Son (ANT)

The emphasis here should be placed on the compassionate father rather than the repentant son.[23] A Hasidic parable references a king who exiled a son who had gone astray. The King later sent messengers asking the son to return. The son replied that he could not, whereupon the king then sent another message: "Return as far as you can, and I will come the rest of the way to meet you."

---

[21] See *Ex. R.* 27: "A king had a field and decided to turn it over to a tenant farmer. He called to the first and said: 'Will you take this field?' He said to him, 'I don't have the strength ...' So it was with the second, the third, and the fourth. He called to the fifth and said, 'Will you take this field?' He said 'Yes!' ... When the tenant farmer entered the field he left it unworked. With whom should the king be angry?"

[22] The Dead Sea sect believed that the "good principle" walks in the way of good; the "evil principle" walks in the way of evil, i.e. "double predestination" (see Rom 9:22–23). John the Baptist believed in "two ways" between which one must choose. Jesus alludes to this motif. Note the word "righteousness" (Heb. צדקה). For John this meant "redemption."

[23] For a detailed discussion of the parable, see Young, *The Parables,* 130–57.

Luke 15:11 And he said: **A certain man had two sons;**[24] **12** And the younger of them said to his father, **Father, give me the portion of property that falls to me.**[25] And he divided the property between them. **13** And not many days afterward the younger son gathered it all together, and went away into a **distant country;**[26] and there wasted his estate with riotous living. **14** And when he had spent all, there arose a severe famine in that land; and he began to be in need. **15** And he went and joined himself to a citizen of that country; and he sent him into his fields to feed the pigs. **16** And he was longing to fill his belly with the husks that the pigs were eating; but no one gave to him. **17** And when **he came to himself,**[27] he said: How many hired servants of my father's have abundant bread, and I am perishing with hunger! **18** I will rise and go to my father, and say to him: **Father, I have sinned against heaven,**[28] **and before you,**[29] **19** And am **no longer worthy to be**

---

[24] Note *b. San.* 99a (edited out): "A King who had *two sons*, one who went the proper way, the other who went out to evil culture ..." (Geniza frag.). Perhaps Luke is the source, or perhaps some other source lady beneath both. Note the rabbinic parable, *Midrash Devarim Rabbah*, ed. S. Liebermann, trans. Brad Young, *The Parables*, 152: "To what may Israel be compared? To the son of a man who said to his father, 'I intend to depart into a far country by way of the sea.' The father warned ... 'Even if the ship is wrecked, you lose everything in it and all of your personal belongings are swept away ... Do not be ashamed to return to me ...'"

[25] The Mishnah allows a father to divide the inheritance while yet alive. The son acquires the right of possession, but not disposal. The father retained usufruct rights, allowing him use of his property. This is why (in the parable) the father still gave orders to the servants. When the estate was sold (likely at an exceptional price) the buyer had to wait for the father's death before taking possession.

[26] Better: "a country across the sea" (in Hebrew: מדינת הים).

[27] "Coming to himself" (εἰς ἑαυτὸν δὲ ἐλθὼν εἶπε) makes no sense. The Greek may be seen as translating the Hebrew חזר בו, from *Deut. R.* 2:24 (on Deut 4:24): "... and he said to him: Return (repent), my son" (וְאָמַר לוֹ חֲזֹר בְּךָ בְּנִי). Note *Lam. R.* 1:7 §34: "When a son [abroad] goes barefoot, he remembers the comfort of his father's house" (כַּד וְחוּפָה בְרָא מִדְּכַר שַׁלְוָתָא דְּבֵיתֵיה דַּאֲבוּי). See Young, *The Parables*, 156.

[28] I.e. "against God."

[29] Pharisaism did accept repentance; note *Cant. R.* 5:3: "The Holy One, blessed be He, said to Israel: My children, make for Me an opening of repentance no bigger than the point of a needle, and I will widen it for you into openings through which wagons and carriages can pass" (אָמַר הַקָּדוֹשׁ בָּרוּךְ הוּא לְיִשְׂרָאֵל, בָּנַי, פִּתְחוּ לִי פֶּתַח אֶחָד שֶׁל תְּשׁוּבָה כְּחֻדָּהּ שֶׁל מַחַט, וַאֲנִי פּוֹתֵחַ לָכֶם פְּתָחִים שֶׁיִּהְיוּ עֲגָלוֹת וּקְרוֹנִיּוֹת נִכְנָסוֹת בּוֹ); see also *Pes. K.* 24:12.

called your son.[30] Make me like one of your hired servants. **20** And he rose, and came to his father. But when he was still a long way off, his father saw him, and had compassion, and ran, and fell on his neck, and kissed him. **21** And the son said to him: Father, I have sinned against heaven, and in your sight, and am no more worthy to be called your son. **22** But the father said to his servants, Bring forth the best robe, and **put**[31] it on him; and put a ring on his hand, and sandals on his feet; **23** And bring here the fattened calf, and kill it; and let us eat, and be merry. **24** For this son of mine was dead, and is alive again; he was lost, and is found. And they began to be merry. **25** Now his elder son was in the field; and as he came and drew near to the house, he heard music and dancing. **26** And he called one of the servants, and asked what these things meant. **27** And he said to him: Your brother has come; and your father has killed the fattened calf, because he has received him safe and sound. **28** And he was angry, and would not go in. Therefore his father came out, and begged him. **29** And he, answering, said to his father: **Behold,**[32] so many years I have served you, and never disobeyed a commandment of yours; and **yet you never gave me a young goat, that I might make merry**

---

[30] Note *b. Qid* 36a: "'You are the *sons* to the Lord your God,' indicates that when you act like *sons* and cleave to the Holy One, Blessed be He, you are called *sons*, but when you do not act like *sons* you are not called *sons*. This is the statement of Rabbi Yehuda. And Rabbi Meir says: Either way you are still called *sons*" (בנים אתם לה' אלהיכם‎ בזמן שאתם נוהגים מנהג בנים אתם קרוים בנים אין אתם נוהגים מנהג בנים אין אתם קרוים בנים דברי ר' יהודה רבי מאיר אומר בין כך ובין כך אתם קרוים בנים‎). Note also *Deut. R.* 2:24: "To what is the matter like? It is like the son of a king who took to evil ways. The king sent a teacher to him who appealed to him, saying, '*Repent, my son*.' But the son sent him back to his father [saying], '*How can I have the effrontery to return*? I am ashamed to come before you.' Thereupon his father sent back word: 'My son, is a son ever ashamed to return to his father? And *is it not to your father that you will be returning*?' Thus the Holy One Blessed Be He sent Jeremiah to Israel" (לְמָה הַדָּבָר דּוֹמֶה, לְבֶן מֶלֶךְ שֶׁיָּצָא לְתַרְבּוּת רָעָה, וְהָיָה הַמֶּלֶךְ מְשַׁלֵּחַ פַּדְגוֹגוֹ אַחֲרָיו, וְאָמַר לוֹ חֲזֹר בְּךְ בְּנִי, וְהָיָה הַבֵּן מְשַׁלְּחוֹ וְאָמַר לְאָבִיו בְּאֵלוּ הַפָּנִים אֲנִי חוֹזֵר בִּי וַאֲנִי מִתְבַּיֵּשׁ לְפָנֶיךָ. וְהָיָה אָבִיו מְשַׁלְּחוֹ וְאוֹמֵר לוֹ בְּנִי, יֵשׁ בֵּן מִתְבַּיֵּשׁ לַחֲזֹר אֵצֶל אָבִיו, וְאִם אַתָּה חוֹזֵר, לֹא אֵצֶל אָבִיךְ אַתָּה חוֹזֵר, כָּךְ הַקָּדוֹשׁ בָּרוּךְ הוּא מְשַׁלֵּחַ יְרְמְיָה לְיִשְׂרָאֵל‎).

[31] The Greek imperative ἐνδύσατε ("wear"/"put on") renders the Hebrew imperative שים‎/"put."

[32] The Greek ἰδοὺ is used in imitation of the Hebrew הִנֵּה‎.

with my friends.[33] **30** But as soon as this son of yours has come, who has devoured your living with prostitutes, you have killed for him the fattened calf. **31** And he said to him: Son, you are always with me, and all that I have is yours. **32** It is fitting for us to make merry, and be glad, for this brother of yours was dead, and is alive again; and was **lost,**[34] and is found.

Scene 3:
Is It Lawful to Pay Taxes to Caesar? (RCT)

When Jesus is asked about paying taxes to Caesar, it is noteworthy that he will not even touch a coin bearing a pagan image. Some argue that the passage is a later addition, to mask any insurrectionist attitudes on the part of Jesus and his followers. Another view is that pious Jews were well aware that since everything belongs to God, nothing belongs to Caesar; therefore the tax need not be paid, depending on one's interpretation.

Luke 20:20 And they watched him, and sent forth spies, themselves pretending to be righteous, that they might catch him in his words, in order to deliver him to the power and authority of the governor. **21** And they asked him, saying: Teacher, we know that you speak and teach rightly, not accepting the person of any, but teaching the way of God truly. **22** Is it lawful for us to give **tribute**[35] to Caesar, or not? **23** But he perceived their craftiness, and said to them: Why do you tempt me? **24** Show me a denarius. Whose image and inscription does it have? They answered and

---

[33] Note *m. Avot* 1:3: "Do not be like servants who serve the master in the expectation of receiving a reward, but be like servants who serve the master without the expectation of receiving a reward, and let the fear of Heaven be upon you" (אַל תִּהְיוּ כַעֲבָדִים הַמְשַׁמְּשִׁין אֶת הָרַב עַל מְנָת לְקַבֵּל פְּרָס, אֶלָּא הֱווּ כַעֲבָדִים הַמְשַׁמְּשִׁין אֶת הָרַב שֶׁלֹּא עַל מְנָת לְקַבֵּל פְּרָס, וִיהִי מוֹרָא שָׁמַיִם עֲלֵיכֶם).

[34] The elder son is also "lost" because he still views the father as his "employer" who demands obedience rather than a parent to be loved.

[35] This "poll tax" had to be paid in Roman coinage, bearing an idolatrous figure of Caesar. It was applied in Judea (under direct Roman rule) but not in Galilee, which was ruled by Herod Antipas. Judah the Galilean had fought against this tax (Josephus, *Ant.* XVIII.1.1).

said: Caesar's. **25** And he said to them: **Therefore, give back to Caesar the things that are Caesar's, and to God the things that are God's.**[36] **26** And they were not able to catch him in his words before the people; and they marveled at his answer, and held their peace.

Scene 4:
The Sadducees: What About the Resurrection?

When the Sadducees query Jesus regarding resurrection, his response is congruent with Talmudic teaching: "In the world to come, there is no eating and drinking, or procreation and childbearing."

Luke 20:27 Then he was approached by some of the Sadducees, who deny that there is any resurrection; and they questioned him, **28** Saying: Teacher, Moses wrote to us, If anyone's brother dies, having a wife, and he dies without children, his brother should take his wife, and raise up seed to his brother. **29** There were therefore seven brothers; and the first took a wife, and died without children. **30** And the second took her as his wife, and he died childless. **31** And the third took her; and likewise the seven also; and they

---

[36] Possibly a later emendation, Jesus appears to commend paying taxes to Caesar while ascribing divinity to God. However, like the Zealots, Jesus would not handle a pagan coin. See Josephus, *Ant.* XVIII, 23, referencing the Zealot saying, "We have no ruler but God!" Jesus could also be interpreted as saying that since Tiberius claimed divinity (the inscription reading "son of the divine Augustus"), nothing belonged to him. Note *b. Pes.* 104a: "Who is this person called the son of sacred ones? Rabbi Menaḥem bar Simai. And why did they call him the son of sacred ones? Because **he would not look at the forms on coins**" (מַאן נִיהוּ "בְּנָן שֶׁל קְדוֹשִׁים"? רַבִּי מְנַחֵם בַּר סִימָאי. וְאַמַּאי קָרוּ לֵיהּ "בְּנָן שֶׁל קְדוֹשִׁים"? **דְּלָא אִסְתַּכַּל בְּצוּרְתָא דְזוּזָא**). Note also *b. B.K.* 113b: "The law of the kingdom is the law" (דִּינָא דְמַלְכוּתָא דִּינָא); *b. A.Z.* 6b; *Lev. R.* 34:3 (referencing Hillel in a pagan bath house): "Just like regarding the statues of kings, that are set up in the theaters and the circuses, the one who is appointed over them bathes them and scrubs them, and they give him sustenance, and furthermore, he attains status with the leaders of the kingdom; I, who was created **in the [Divine] Image and Form**, as it is written, 'For in the Image of G-d He made Man (Genesis 9:6),' even more so!" (מָה אִם אִיקוֹנִין שֶׁל מְלָכִים שֶׁמַּעֲמִידִים אוֹתָן בְּבָתֵּי טַרְטִיאוֹת וּבְבָתֵּי קַרְקְסִיאוֹת, מִי שֶׁנִּתְמַנֶּה עֲלֵיהֶם הוּא מוֹרְקָן וְשׁוֹטְפָן וְהֵן מַעֲלִין לוֹ מְזוֹנוֹת, וְלֹא עוֹד אֶלָּא שֶׁהוּא מִתְגַּדֵּל עִם גְּדוֹלֵי מַלְכוּת, אֲנִי שֶׁנִּבְרֵאתִי **בְּצֶלֶם וּבִדְמוּת**, דִּכְתִיב: כִּי בְּצֶלֶם אֱלֹהִים עָשָׂה אֶת הָאָדָם, עַל אַחַת כַּמָּה וְכַמָּה).

left no children, and died. **32** Finally, **the woman also died.**[37] **33** Therefore, in the resurrection whose wife does she become? For seven had her as a wife. **34** And Jesus answering said to them: The sons of this age marry, and are given in marriage. **35** But those who are considered worthy to obtain that age, and the resurrection from the dead, **neither marry, nor are given in marriage.**[38] **36** Neither can they die anymore: for they are **like the angels;**[39] and are the sons of God, being the sons of the resurrection. **37** That the dead are raised, however, even Moses showed at the bush, when he called the Lord the God of Abraham, and the God of Isaac, and the God of Jacob. **38** For he is not the God of the dead, but of the living; for all live to him. **39** Then some of the scribes, answering, said: Teacher, you have well spoken. **40** And after that they dared not ask him anything at all.

---

[37] In Tannaitic times, a woman who had been married several times was not allowed to remarry. Note *b. Yeb.* 64b: "If a man divorced his wife after ten years without children, she is permitted to marry a second man, who may remain married to her for ten years. A second husband, yes, but a third one, no ... Abaye relied on this report and went and married Ḥuma, the daughter of Isi, son of Rav Yitzḥak, son of Rav Yehuda. Ḥuma had previously married Raḥava of Pumbedita, and he died, and then she married Rav Yitzḥak, son of Rabba bar bar Ḥana, and he died; and he, Abaye, married her nevertheless, without concern that she had been established to be a woman whose husbands die; and he died" (סמך עלה אבי ואזל נסבה ... שני אין שלישי לא :שני אין שלישי וכו'. לחומה ברתא דאיסי בריה דרב יצחק בריה דרב יהודה דנסבה רחבא דפומבדיתא ושכיב רב יצחק בריה דרבה בר בר חנה ושכיב ונסבה הוא ושכיב). See Matt 22:23–32. Note the story of the seven brothers who were martyred, along with their mother, during the Antiochan persecution (2 Mac 7:1–41). The story concludes: "And finally *after her sons, the mother died*."

[38] Note *b. Ber.* 17a: "The World-to-Come is not like this world. In the World-to-Come *there is no eating, no drinking, no procreation*, no business negotiations, no jealousy, no hatred, and no competition. Rather, the righteous sit with their crowns upon their heads, enjoying the splendor of the Divine Presence" (הָעוֹלָם הַבָּא. לֹא כָעוֹלָם הַזֶּה הָעוֹלָם הַבָּא **אֵין בּוֹ לֹא אֲכִילָה וְלֹא שְׁתִיָּה וְלֹא פְּרִיָּה וּרְבִיָּה** וְלֹא מַשָּׂא וּמַתָּן וְלֹא קִנְאָה וְלֹא שִׂנְאָה וְלֹא תַּחֲרוּת, אֶלָּא צַדִּיקִים יוֹשְׁבִין וְעַטְרוֹתֵיהֶם בְּרָאשֵׁיהֶם וְנֶהֱנִים מִזִּיו הַשְּׁכִינָה). Note also *b. San.* 90b: "From where is resurrection of the dead derived from the Torah? As it is stated with regard to the Patriarchs: 'I have also established My covenant with them to give to them the land of Canaan' (Exodus 6:4). The phrase: To give to you the land of Canaan, is not stated; rather, 'To give to them.' From here is it derived that the resurrection of the dead is from the Torah" (מניין לתחיית המתים מן התורה שנאמר את הקימותי את בריתי אתם לתת להם את ארץ כנען. לכם לא נאמר אלא להם מכאן לתחיית המתים מן התור).

[39] Note En 104:6: "You shall become companions of the hosts of heaven."

Jesus: How Can David Call His Descendant Lord?

Psalm 110 is prominently quoted by Jesus, who, like many early Israelite Sages, understood the psalm messianically. Did Jesus, as a historical personage in the context of Second Temple Judaism, evince a conviction, consistent with early mystical concepts, of the Messiah as a pre-existent being, who was David's Lord and who would become incarnate as his son? Did he go as far as to equate himself with such a personage?

Luke 20:41 And he said to them: How do they say that the messiah is David's son? **42** For David himself says in the book of Psalms: The Lord said to my Lord, Sit at **my right hand,**[40] **43** Until I make your enemies your footstool. **44** David therefore calls him Lord; how is he then his son?

Jesus issues another condemnation, not of the Pharisees (as in Matthew 23:14) but of the scribes:

Luke 20:45 Then in the hearing of all the people he said to his disciples: **46** Beware of the **scribes,**[41] who desire to walk in long robes, and love greetings in the markets, and the first seats in the synagogues, and the first places at feasts; **47** Who **devour**[42] widows' houses, and for a show make long prayers. These will receive greater condemnation.

---

[40] See Luke 22:69; Ps 110:1: "The LORD said to my lord: 'Sit *at* **My right** hand,** until I make your enemies your footstool'" (נְאֻם יְהוָה לַאדֹנִי שֵׁב **לִימִינִי** עַד-אָשִׁית אֹיְבֶיךָ, הֲדֹם לְרַגְלֶיךָ). In *Avot d'Rabbi Natan* (34:6) it is said that David's "Lord" is the Messiah of Israel, with reference Zechariah's vision of the four craftsmen: "From this verse we know that the *messianic king* is even more beloved than a rightful priest" (הֲרֵי יוֹדֵעַ שֶׁמֶּלֶךְ **הַמָּשִׁיחַ** חָבִיב יוֹתֵר מִכֹּהֵן צֶדֶק).

[41] The condemnation is not of the Pharisees (as in Matthew 23:14), but of the scribes.

[42] This likely refers to creditors who would come to take the sons as bondmen. See 2 Ki 4:1; Prov 30:14.

Scene 5:
The Poor Widow's Offering

The account of the widow's offering is paralleled by rabbinic teaching, that God prefers "...one handful of a free-will offering of the poor to the heap of incense which is offered by the high priest" (Koh. R. 4:6).

Luke 21:1 And he looked up, and saw the rich men casting their gifts into the **treasury.**[43] **2** And he saw also a certain **poor widow**[44] casting in two lepta. **3** And he said: Truly I say to you, that this poor widow has cast in more than all of these: **4** For all these have out of their abundance cast in to the offerings of God. But she out of her poverty has cast in **all the livelihood that she had.**[45]

R. Lindsey suggested that three prophecies may be identified in Luke 21, culled by the editor of RCT from three separate occasions.[46] They may be reconstructed as follows:

---

[43] Probably one of the thirteen receptacles in the form of trumpets in the temple, used for charity.

[44] A reconstruction of the narrative involves an incident (the poor widow's offering; Luke 21:1–4), a prophecy (Luke 21:5–7) and a teaching (the destruction of Jerusalem; Luke 21:20–24, Luke 21:29–33), followed by two parables: the barren fig tree (Luke 13:6–9) and the wicked vinedressers/only son (Luke 20:9–18/Matt 21:33–44).

[45] Note *m. Men.* 13:11: "One who brings a substantial offering and one who brings a meager offering have equal merit, provided that he directs his heart toward Heaven" (אֶחָד הַמַּרְבֶּה וְאֶחָד הַמַּמְעִיט, וּבִלְבַד שֶׁיְּכַוֵּן אָדָם אֶת דַּעְתּוֹ לַשָּׁמָיִם). Note also *Lev. R.* 3:5: "There is a story of a woman who brought a handful of meal as an offering. A priest despised it and said, 'See what they offer!' What is in it that one could eat, what is in it that can be sacrificed?' It was shown to him in a dream 'Do not despise her; it is as if she has **sacrificed herself** (נפשה) as the sacrifice.' If in regard to one who does not **sacrifice himself**, the text uses the term **soul** (נפש), how much more one who **sacrifices himself**!"
מַעֲשֶׂה בְּאִשָּׁה אַחַת שֶׁהֵבִיאָה קֹמֶץ שֶׁל סֹלֶת, וְהָיָה כֹּהֵן מְבַזֶּה עָלֶיהָ, וְאָמַר, רְאוּ מָה הֵן מַקְרִיבוֹת, מַה בָּזֶה לֶאֱכֹל,) מַה בָּזֶה לְהַקְרִיב, נִרְאָה לַכֹּהֵן בַּחֲלוֹם אַל תְּבַזֶּה עָלֶיהָ, כְּאִלּוּ **נַפְשָׁהּ הִקְרִיבָה.** וַהֲרֵי דְּבָרִים קַל וָחֹמֶר, וּמַה אִם מִי **שֶׁאֵינוֹ מַקְרִיב נֶפֶשׁ** כְּתִיב בּוֹ **נֶפֶשׁ**, מִי שֶׁהוּא **מַקְרִיב נֶפֶשׁ**); *Koh. R.* 4:6: "For God said: I prefer one handful of a free-will offering of the poor to the heap of incense which is offered by the high priest" וְאַף הַקָּדוֹשׁ בָּרוּךְ הוּא אָמַר חָבִיב עָלַי קֻמְצוֹ שֶׁל עָנִי מִנְחַת נְדָבָה, מִמְּלֹא חָפְנָיִם שֶׁל כֹּהֵן (גָּדוֹל קְטֹרֶת הַסַּמִּים).

[46] See Lindsey, *Jesus,* 154–55.

1. *The destruction of the temple (occurring after the incident on the Temple Mount regarding the poor widow's offering) 21:5–7; 20–24; 29–32*
2. *The coming of the Son of Man; 21:8–11; 25–28; 34–36*
3. *Coming persecution; 21:12–19*

The second two prophesies are theorized to be post-resurrection sayings and have been moved to follow Luke 24:50/Acts 1:3.

Scene 6:
Prophecy #1: The Destruction of the Temple

Jesus' prophecy of the coming destruction of Jerusalem and the temple in 70 C.E. is often thought to represent a later addition to the text. However, given the revolutionary fervor already present in the land during his lifetime, some (David Flusser included) have argued that such a prediction is entirely within the realm of possibility.

Luke 21:5 And as some spoke about the temple, how it was adorned with goodly stones and gifts, he said: **6** As for these things which you behold, the days will come, in the which **there will not be left one stone upon another, that will not be thrown down.**[47] **7** And they asked him, saying: Teacher, **when will these things be?**[48] and what will be the sign when these things are about to come to pass?

---

[47] Note *b. Sanh.* 96b: "This blood is the blood of a priest and a prophet who prophesied for the Jewish people with regard to **the destruction of Jerusalem** and whom they killed" (האי כהן ונביא הוא דאינבי להו לישראל **בחורבנא דירושלם** וקטלוהו). Note also *Test. Levi* 10: "He shall not bear with Jerusalem because of your wickedness; but the veil of the temple shall be rent, so as not to cover your shame"; *Apoc. Bar.* 1:4: "Behold I bring evil upon this city, and upon its inhabitants, and it shall be removed from before Me for a time, and I will scatter this people among the Gentiles …"

[48] The Greek πότε ταῦτα ἔσται ("when will be these things?") parrots a semitic construction; e.g. Dan 8:13: "How long shall be the vision?" (עַד-מָתַי הֶחָזוֹן).

The Destruction of Jerusalem

Luke 21:20 And when you shall see Jerusalem encircled by armies, then know that its desolation is near. **21 Then let those who are in Judea flee to the mountains;**[49] and let those who are in the midst of it depart; and do not let not those who are in the countries enter into it. **22** For these are the days of vengeance, that all things which have been written may be fulfilled. **23** But **woe**[50] to those who are with child, and to those nursing in those days! For there will be great distress in the land, and wrath upon this people. **24** And they will fall by the edge of the sword, and will be led away captive into all nations: and Jerusalem will be trodden down by the Gentiles until the times of the Gentiles are fulfilled.

The Fig Tree

Luke 21:29–33 should possibly be added here. The example of the fig tree is read by the writer of Luke as referring to the parousia, which he falsely equates with the kingdom of God (which should always be understood as present tense). The reference is instead to the prophecy of Jerusalem's destruction at the hands of the Romans (70 CE).

Parable 1: The Fig Tree

Luke 21:29 And he spoke to them **a parable:**[51] Behold the fig tree, and all the trees; **30** When they have already sprouted, you see and know for yourselves that **summer**[52] is already near at hand.

---

[49] Note the debatable tradition related by Eusebius (*EH* III:5) and Epiphanius (*de Mens. et Pond.*, 15) regarding the flight of the Judeo-Christian community to Pella during the Great Revolt (66–70 CE); see also Rev 12:14.

[50] The Greek Οὐαί is used in the Septuagint chiefly for הוֹי and אוֹי.

[51] This should be understood as the beginning of a longer parable, the barren fig tree, continued in Luke 13:6–9 and complemented by a second parable, the wicked vinedressers/only son (Luke 20:9–1).

[52] A play on the words appears in the Hebrew for "summer" (קיץ) and "end" (קץ). The fig tree puts forth its leaves long before the vines.

31 So likewise you, when you **see these things**[53] come to pass, know that **the kingdom of God is near at hand.**[54] **32 Truly I say to you,**[55] **This generation shall not pass away, until all is fulfilled.**[56] **33** Heaven and earth will pass away, but my words will not pass away.

Parable 1 (continued): The Barren Fig Tree (ANT)

Luke 13:6–9 theoretically belongs here, completing the fig tree parable. Fig trees (which were sometimes planted in vineyards) were taken to represent the leaders of Israel, standing in dignity above the vineyard. Jesus seems to be offering one more chance for the leaders of the nation to reform themselves before the coming judgment.[57]

Luke 13:6 [He spoke also this parable:][58] A certain man had a **fig tree**[59] planted in his vineyard; and he came and sought fruit on it, and found none. **7** Then he said to the dresser of his vineyard:

---

[53] See Luke 9:27, where the writer/redactor picked up the idea of "seeing" because of the way the editor revised Luke 21:31.

[54] The "kingdom of God" in this verse appears to be a later addition (and secondary usage), wrongly viewing it as eschatological. By "the kingdom of God is near," the editor meant the coming of the Son of Man while the immediate context was the destruction of Jerusalem.

[55] "Amen"/"assuredly" (אמן) added after a strong statement. Jer 28:6 - כֵּן, **אָמֵן** יַעֲשֶׂה יְהוָה יָקֵם יְהוָה, אֶת-דְּבָרֶיךָ אֲשֶׁר נִבֵּאתָ ("Amen! The Lord do so; the Lord perform your words which you have prophesied…"). See Luke 4:24; Matt 5:18.

[56] The Lucan redactor understands "this generation …" as referring to the *parousia* (which he wrongly equates with the kingdom of God), when the verse is actually about the destruction of Jerusalem.

[57] See Lindsey, *Jesus*, 156.

[58] Perhaps an editorial gloss, placing the barren fig tree parable in a different context (Luke 13).

[59] Occasionally, fig trees were planted in vineyards, here perhaps representing the leaders of Israel, standing above in dignity. The imagery suggests one more chance for the leadership to reform itself. Note *Story of Ahikar* 35 (Syriac): "My son, you have been to me like that palm tree that stood by a river and cast all its fruit into the river; and when its Lord came and cut it down, it said to him: 'Let me alone this year, and I will bring forth carobs.' And its Lord said to it: 'You have not been industrious with what is yours; how will you be industrious with what is not yours?'" (Charles, *Apocrypha and Pseudepigrapha*, 2: 775).

Behold,[60] throughout these three years I have come seeking fruit on this fig tree, and have found none. Cut it down; why should it even use up the ground? **8** And he answering said to him: Lord, leave it alone this year also, until I dig around it, and put in manure. **9** And if it should bear fruit in time, so be it. And if not, then after that you will cut it down.

Parable 2: The Wicked Vinedressers/"Only Son" (RCT)

The parable of the "Wicked Vinedressers" would be better titled the "Parable of the Only Son." This may be the most messianic text in the Gospels, often missed if the focus is on the vineyard instead of the son. Jesus' real opponents are the leaders of the temple, who collaborated with Rome.[61] In Luke, the parable is intended as a condemnation of the scribes and priests (together with the elders), whereas in Mark the priests, scribes, and elders are equally challenged. Matthew substitutes "Pharisees" for "scribes." We see (theorizing Lucan priority) the progressive identification of the Pharisees as Jesus' adversaries. Wrongly used to support replacement theology, the tenants to whom the vineyard is leased are often taken to represent the Jewish people. Instead, they should be understood as corrupt temple leadership.

---

[60] The Greek ἰδοὺ is used in imitation of the Hebrew הִנֵּה.
[61] See Flusser, *Judaism,* 558.

Luke 20:9 *Then began he to speak to the people this* **parable:**[62] *A certain man planted a* **vineyard,**[63] *and rented it out to* **farmers (vinedressers),**[64] *and went abroad for a long time.* **10** *And at the season he sent a servant to the farmers, that they should give him from the fruit of the vineyard. But the farmers beat him, and sent*

---

[62] This parable is found after the question of authority in all three synoptics; therefore, it must have been told on the Temple Mount. Only Matthew places this parable between "Authority" and the "Husbandmen." It is cast as an affront to the *Pharisees* and priests in Matthew (reflecting anti-Jewish sentiment). In Mark 11:27, the priests, scribes, and *elders* are challenged. The leaders of the temple, who collaborated with Rome, are the real opponents. The Greek text suffers from severe redaction, and it is doubtful whether the original language can be recovered. Matthew's two groups of servants may be an editorial gloss (Luke and Mark have three individual servants). Originally, there were likely three sendings of individual servants, climaxed with the son (see *Thomas Logion* 65, where there are only two). Also, in Luke, the slaves are not killed.

[63] The background is "Song of the Vineyard," Isa 5:1–7. The parable reflects an *early* setting (before the Roman destruction) when vineyards were profitable and often run by tenant farmers. Herod established new forms of tenant farming, confiscating farms from many Jewish enemies (Josephus, *Ant.* 5:5). These were owned by absentee landlords. The proud descendants of the Hasmoneans would have been enraged seeing their vineyards stolen by Herod and given to his friends, and even more-so when a foreigner came to collect the tax. The quotation is from Isa 5:2: "*And he dug it*/and cleared it of stones, and planted it with the choicest vine (וַיְעַזְּקֵהוּ וַיְסַקְּלֵהוּ, וַיִּטָּעֵהוּ שֹׂרֵק)/"He *built a watchtower* in the midst of it, and *hewed out a wine vat in it*" (וַיִּבֶן מִגְדָּל בְּתוֹכוֹ,)/"and he looked for it to yield grapes, but it yielded wild grapes" (וְגַם-יֶקֶב חָצֵב בּוֹ וַיְקַו לַעֲשׂוֹת עֲנָבִים, וַיַּעַשׂ בְּאֻשִׁים). This verse was likely added by Mark (12:1) and picked up by Matthew since Luke obviously refers to this scripture. Mark (as a "targumist") "explains" Luke, interpreting **יעזקהו** ("and he dug it") as "putting a wall around it."

[64] Greek γεωργοῖς translates the Hebrew אריסים ("tenant farmers"/ "sharecroppers"). The parable has been wrongly used to support replacement theology (i.e. that the tenants are the Jewish people). The "tenants" actually represent the corrupt temple leadership. See Mark 11:27; Matt 21:23. Note *Sifre Deut.* 312: "An analogy: A king had a field **and gave it to tenant-farmers**, who began to steal from it—upon which he gave it to their sons—who began to be worse than the first. When *a son* was born to him, he said to them: Get out of what is mine. You cannot remain there. Give me my portion so that I can recognize it" (משל למלך שהיה לו שדה **ונתנה לעריסין**, התחילו העריסין נוטלים וגונבים אותה. נטלה מהם ונתנה לבניהם, התחילו להיות רעים יותר מן הראשונים. נולד לו **בן**, אמר להם צאו מתוך שלי, אי אפשר שתהיו בתוכה, תנו לי חלקי שאהיה מכירו); *Ex. R.* 27: "An analogy to a king had a field and decided **to turn it over to tenant farmers**. He called to the first and said, 'Will you take this field?' He said to him, 'I don't have the strength....' So it was with the second, third, and fourth. He called to the fifth and said, 'Will you take this field?' He said, 'Yes.' ... When the tenant farmer entered the field, he left it unwalled. With whom should the king be angry?" (מָשָׁל לְמֶלֶךְ שֶׁהָיָה לוֹ שָׂדֶה וְהָיָה מְבַקֵּשׁ **לְמָסְרָה לַאֲרִיסִים.** קָרָא לָרִאשׁוֹן וְאָמַר לוֹ, תְּקַבֵּל אַתָּה אֶת הַשָּׂדֶה הַזּוֹ, אָמַר לוֹ אֵין בִּי כֹּחַ ... וְכֵן לַשֵּׁנִי וְלַשְּׁלִישִׁי וְלָרְבִיעִי וְלֹא קִבְּלוּהָ מִמֶּנּוּ. וְקָרָא לַחֲמִישִׁי וְאָמַר לוֹ תְּקַבֵּל אַתָּה הַשָּׂדֶה הַזּוֹ, אָמַר לוֹ הֵן ... מִשֶּׁנִּכְנַס לְתוֹכָהּ הוֹבִירָהּ, עַל מִי הַמֶּלֶךְ מַקְפִּיד). See also *Seder Eli. Rab.* 28: "A king who went to a far country, and decided to send **his son** to an evil guardian ..." (למלך ב"ו שצריך לצאת למדינת הים ובקש למסור את **בנו** ביד אפוטרופוס רשע). Subsequently, the king's city is destroyed and the son is killed.

him away empty-handed. 11 And he proceeded to send another servant; and they beat him also, and dishonored him shamefully, and sent him away empty-handed. 12 And he proceeded to send a third; and they wounded him also, and cast him out. **13 Then the owner of the vineyard said: What shall I do? I will send my beloved/only son. Perhaps they will respect him when they see him.**[65] *14 But when the farmers saw him, they reasoned among themselves, saying:* **This is the heir. Come, let us kill him, so that the inheritance may be ours.**[66] *15 So they cast him out of the vineyard, and killed him.* **What therefore will the owner of the vineyard do to them?**[67] *16 He will come and destroy these farmers, and will give the vineyard to others. And when they heard this, they said:* **May it never be.**[68] *17 And he looked at them, and said:* **What then is this that is written,**[69] *The stone*[70] *which the builders*

---

[65] The Greek ἀγαπητόν ("beloved") translates the Hebrew יחיד ("only"). This is unusual in light of very large Middle Eastern families. Hypothetical Hebrew reconstruction (Brad Young): ויאמר בעל הכרם. מה אעשה? אשלח לכם את בני את יחידי ואתו יכבדו.

[66] It is likely that the householder is a proselyte since, when a proselyte died intestate, his property became ownerless and went to the first claimant; see *b. Kid.* 17b: "By Torah law and by rabbinic law a gentile does not inherit property from his father who is a convert, nor does a convert inherit property from his father who is a convert" (עובד כוכבים את הגר וגר את הגר אינו לא מדברי תורה ולא מדברי סופרים). Here, the tenant had the first chance to claim by possession. Hypothetical Hebrew reconstruction (Brad Young): הנה היורש. נהרוג אותו ולנו תהיה הירושה.

[67] Editorially, Luke and Mark simply say, "What will the owner of the vineyard do to them?" Matthew makes an eschatological point. In reality, the parable is a prophetic warning to the temple leadership; recall Josephus, *War* 6:300: Four years before the revolt, Jesus son of Ananias cried in the streets "against Jerusalem and the Sanctuary."

[68] It is the friends of Jesus on the Temple Mount who say "May it never be" (Μὴ γένοιτο/Heb. חלילה) when the son in the story is killed. This is similar to the Pharisees, who warn Jesus (Luke 13:31) that Herod Antipas wants to kill him.

[69] "That is written" (γεγραμμένον) is not as good as Matt 21:42: "read in the Scriptures (γραφαῖς)." Hypothetical Hebrew reconstruction: אמר להם ישוע הלא קראתם הכתובים ...

[70] The words "son"/"stone"/"builders" (בן/אבן/בונים) are a play on words in Hebrew. The "stone" is the son of David. The words "has become head of the corner" refer to David since he became the "head of kings," as referenced in *Midrash Ha-Gadol* Deut 1:11. *Midrash Ha–Gadol* (*Midrash Tannaim*) relates Psalm 118 to David, who was despised in the eyes of his father. It explains (along with Dead Sea Psalm 151) that he was destined to rise to power. Note *Esther R.* 7:10 (Billerbeck): "If a *stone* falls on a pot, woe to the pot; it a pot falls on a *stone*, woe to the pot. In either case, woe to the pot!" (נָפְלָה כִּיפָה עַל קִידְרָא, וַוי לְקִידְרָא. נָפְלָה קִידְרָא עַל כִּיפָה, וַוי לְקִידְרָא). The author wrote in Greek, but appears to have been thinking (with regard to the "stone") in Hebrew. Jesus uses this verse (see also Matt 21:42) to reference himself as a stone to trip over. See Dan 2:34–35; 44–45.

*rejected has become the **head of the corner?**71 18 Whoever shall fall upon that stone shall be broken; **but on whomever it shall fall, it will grind him to powder.**72 19 And the scribes and the chief priests sought to lay hands on him in that same hour. And **they feared the people;**73 for they perceived that he had spoken this parable against them.*

Luke 21:20–24; 25–28, 34–36 are theorized to follow Luke 24:50/ Acts 1:3.

Scene 7:
Retiring to the Mount of Olives

Luke 21:37 And during the day he was teaching in the temple; and **at night he went out, and lodged on the mount that is called the Mount of Olives.**74 **38** And all the people came to him early in the morning in the temple, to hear him.

Luke 22 begins by noting that it is the chief priests and scribes, the "Temple Committee" (not the Pharisees) who seek Jesus' execution.

-----

71 See Ps 118:22: "The *stone* which the builders rejected is become the *chief cornerstone*" (אֶבֶן, מָאֲסוּ הַבּוֹנִים הָיְתָה, לְרֹאשׁ פִּנָּה). This is linked in the Dead Sea Scrolls to Isa 28:16: "Behold, I lay in Zion for a foundation *a stone, a tried stone, a costly cornerstone* of sure foundation" (הִנְנִי יִסַּד בְּצִיּוֹן אָבֶן: אֶבֶן בֹּחַן פִּנַּת יְקָרַת. מוּסָד מוּסָד). Note 1QS 8:7–10: "They will be '*the tested wall, the precious cornerstone*' (Isaiah 28:16) whose foundations shall neither be shaken nor swayed, a fortress, a Holy of Holies for Aaron, all of them knowing the Covenant of Justice and thereby offering a sweet savor. They shall be a blameless and true house in Israel, upholding the covenant of eternal statutes. They shall be an acceptable sacrifice, *atoning for the land* and ringing in the verdict against evil, so that perversity ceases to exist" (היאה **חומת הבחן פנת יקר** בל יזדעזעו יסודותיהו ובל יחישו" ממקומם מעון קודש קודשים לאהרון בדעת כולם לברית משפט ולקריב ריח ניחוח ובית תמים ואמת בישראל להקם ברית לחוקות עולם. והיו לרצון **לכפר בעד הארץ** ולחרוץ משפט רשעה בתמים דרך ואין עולה).

72 The point is that whatever happens, the stone (Jesus) will remain.

73 This indicates that the crowd is sympathetic to Jesus.

74 This may have been because the city was crowded for Passover.

Scene 8:
The Plot to Kill Jesus

Shimon Gibson has argued that Jesus likely did not have revolutionary intent, being interested in establishing an alternative movement of ritual immersion involving special purification and healing techniques. It was Jesus' actions at the temple which likely offended the Sadducee-oriented chief priests and scribes, who subsequently sought his execution for sedition.[75]

Luke 22:1 Now the feast of unleavened bread drew near, which is called the Passover. **2** And the **chief priests and scribes**[76] sought how they might kill him; for they feared the people. **3** Then **Satan**[77] entered into Judas who was called Iscariot, being of the number of the twelve. **4** And he went his way, and spoke with the chief priests and captains, how he might betray him to them. **5** And they were glad, and agreed to give him money. **6** And he promised, and sought opportunity to betray him to them, apart from the multitude.

Scene 9:
Jesus and Disciples Prepare the Passover

Jesus instructs his disciples to prepare the Passover meal, but there is no indication that it is ever consumed. James Tabor has theorized that Jesus was most likely crucified on a Thursday when the Passover lamb was slaughtered.[78] A possible Qumranic allusion in the Gospels' Passover narrative is the unexpected presence of a man (rather than a woman) carrying a pitcher of water. Perhaps such details indicate a sectarian "overlay" to a

---

[75] It is the chief priests and scribes, the "Temple Committee" (not the Pharisees) who seek Jesus' execution.

[76] Shimon Gibson, *The Final Days of Jesus: The Archaeological Evidence* (New York: HarperCollins, 2010), 205.

[77] See Luke 4:3 n.

[78] See James Tabor, *The Jesus Dynasty*, 199–202.

more traditionally "Jewish" narrative. Moreover, Jesus' final repast may have been transformed from a traditional Jewish meal into, not just a Passover meal, but a Qumran-inspired "Messianic Banquet," influenced by a secondary Pauline wave of Judeo-Christianity.

Luke 22:7 Then came the day of Unleavened Bread, **when the Passover lamb must be sacrificed.**[79] **8** And he sent Peter and John, saying: **Go and prepare us the Passover, that we may eat.**[80] **9** And they said to him: Where do you wish that we prepare it? **10** And he said to them: **Behold,**[81] when you have entered into the city, **a man will meet you, carrying a pitcher of water.**[82] Follow him into the house into which he enters. **11** And you shall say to the master of the house: The Teacher says to you, Where is the guest room, **where I may eat the Passover**[83] with my disciples? **12** And he will show you a large furnished **upper**

---

[79] James Tabor argues that since Jesus was crucified on the day "when the Passover lamb is sacrificed," it would have been on a Thursday (assuming that Passover fell on Friday, essentially creating two back-to-back Sabbaths). This is also congruent with a Talmudic passage which relates (*b. San.* 43a): "*On Passover Eve* they hung the corpse of Jesus the Nazarene. And a crier went out before him for forty days, publicly proclaiming: Jesus the Nazarene is going out to be stoned because he practiced sorcery, incited people, and led the Jewish people astray. Anyone who knows of a reason to acquit him should come forward and teach it on his behalf. And the court did not find a reason to acquit him, and so they stoned him and hung his corpse *on Passover eve*" (בערב הפסח תלאוהו לישו והכרוז יוצא לפניו מ' יום ישו יוצא ליסקל על שכישף והסית והדיח את ישראל כל מי שיודע לו זכות יבא וילמד עליו ולא מצאו לו זכות ותלאוהו **בערב הפסח**).

[80] However, we are never told that they actually prepare it or that it is ever consumed. Passover arguably fell on a Friday that particular year, thus creating (in essence) two back-to-back Sabbaths.

[81] The Greek ἰδοὺ is used in imitation of the Hebrew הִנֵּה.

[82] It would have been rare to see a man (rather than a woman) carrying water. This may possibly have been an Essene since they supposedly had a colony on Mt. Zion. According to the Essene calendar, Passover always fell on Wednesday. In that case, what may have been observed as Passover by Jesus and his disciples (if they followed the sectarian calendar) was not Passover for the rest of the population of Jerusalem. This "solution," however, would place the Last Supper/Seder on a Tuesday night, in conflict with the rest of the Gospel chronology and effectively turning Jesus into a quasi-Essene. It has also been argued that Passover in the Qumran calendar (if it were intercalated) would have fallen *after* Passover, as in the lunar Jewish calendar.

[83] John's Gospel (13:13) simply relates that the Last Supper occurred "before the festival of the Passover." The meal is never identified as a Passover Seder, and the Passover itself is said to have commenced a few hours after Jesus' death.

room.[84] There make it ready. **13** And they went, and found it as he had said to them. And they made ready the Passover.

Scene 10:
The Last Supper

The so-called "Messianic Rule" of the Dead Sea Scrolls describes an eschatological "banquet," involving bread and wine (in that order), blessed by a priestly/messianic figure (1QSa 2:17–21). This is the order depicted by Paul (1 Cor 11:23–25), as well as by the Gospels of Mark (14:22–25) and Matthew (26:26–29), in which Jesus refers to the "blood of the covenant" or, according to other ancient texts, "new covenant" (as in Qumranic parlance). By contrast, Luke has Jesus take the cup first, as common in Jewish ritual, followed by a second cup, which becomes, theologically, "the new covenant in my blood."[85] The problematic reference to the drinking of blood (an atrocious concept in Jewish thought and dietary customs) might represent a later redaction of the Lucan account.

Luke 22:14 And when the hour had come, he **reclined,**[86] and the twelve apostles with him. **15** And he said to them: With desire I have desired to eat this Passover with you before I suffer. **16** For I say to you, I will not any more eat of it, **[until it is fulfilled in the**

---

[84] Some have linked the "beloved disciple" of John's Gospel (not the fisherman from Galilee but a different "John") with the Essene sect (since he had been a disciple of John the Baptist, who also may have had links with the sect), suggesting that he came from a Jerusalem priestly family and that the Last Supper may have taken place at a priestly villa in Jerusalem's Upper City. See Acts 1:13.

[85] See Flusser, *Judaism*, 203.

[86] In the Greco-Roman world, only free men were allowed to recline at table, hence its significance at the "Festival of Freedom."

kingdom of God.][87] **17** And **he took the cup, and gave thanks,**[88] and said: Take this, and divide it among yourselves. **18** For I say to you, **I will not drink of the fruit of the vine**[89] until the kingdom of God comes. **19** And he took bread, and gave thanks, and broke it, and gave to them, saying: **This is my body**[90] [which is given for you: this do in remembrance of me. **20** Likewise also the cup after supper, saying: This cup is the new covenant in my blood, which is shed for you.][91] **21** But, **behold,**[92] the hand of him who betrays me is with me on the table. **22** For truly the **Son of Man**[93] **goes,**[94] as it was determined; but **woe**[95] to that man by whom he is betrayed! **23** And they began to question among themselves, who among them it might be who would do this thing.

---

[87] This statement is arguably a secondary usage. It does not appear in Matthew or Mark. Later manuscripts render the text as "eat it *again*," most likely to make it appear as if the Last Supper were in fact a Seder.

[88] Note *m. Pes.* 10:7: "They poured for the leader of the seder the third *cup of wine, and he recites the blessing* over his food, [Grace After Meals]. Next, they pour him *the fourth cup. He completes hallel over it*" (מָזְגוּ לוֹ **כּוֹס שְׁלִישִׁי, מְבָרֵךְ** עַל מְזוֹנוֹ. **רְבִיעִי, גּוֹמֵר עָלָיו אֶת הַהַלֵּל**). This is the last cup at the Seder. See also *m. Ber.* 6:1: "Over wine one recites: Who creates fruit of the vine" (שֶׁעַל הַיַּיִן אוֹמֵר בּוֹרֵא פְּרִי הַגָּפֶן). Note *Didache* 9:11: "We thank You, O our Father, for the *Holy Vine of David*," conveying a messianic message in the cup. The *Didache*, as in rabbinic tradition, begins with the cup, followed by the bread.

[89] Consider the "wine of paradise" (*b. Sanh.* 99a): "What is that which no eye has seen? R' Yehoshua ben Levi said: This is *wine* preserved in its grapes since the six days of Creation. Reish Lakish says: This is *Eden*" (מאי עין לא ראתה אמר רבי יהושע בן לוי זה **יין** המשומר בענביו מששת ימי בראשית ר"ל אמר זה **עדן**).

[90] Here ends the Lucan text, according to the Latin Codex Bezae. Theoretically, the "original" account begins and ends with the cup. In fact, the cup came first, as in normative Jewish practice (rather than the Dead Sea sectarian custom of bread first). See 1QSa 2:17–21: "When they gather at the *communal table*, having set out bread and wine so the communal table is set for eating and the wine poured for drinking, none may reach for the first portion of the *bread or the wine* before the Priest. For he shall bless the first portion of the *bread and the wine, reaching for the bread first*. Afterward the *Messiah of Israel shall reach for the bread...*" (ואם **לשולחן יחד** יועדו או לשתות התירוש וערוך השולחן היחד ומסוך התירוש לשתות אל ישלח איש את ידו ברשית **הלחם והתירוש** לפני הכוהן. כיא הוא מברך את **רשית הלחם והתירוש ושלח ידו בלחם לפנים**. ואחר **ישלח משיח ישראל ידיו בלחם**). Notably, Jesus never uses the word "covenant," which is a later interpolation.

[91] This language is picked up from 1 Cor 11:24–25. See Flusser, *Judaism*, 202–6.

[92] The Greek ἰδοὺ is used in imitation of the Hebrew הִנֵּה.

[93] The Aramaic בר אנוש ("son of man") links to Dan 7:13; authority being the theme.

[94] The Greek πορεύεται ("goes") renders the Hebrew הוֹלֵךְ, a Hebraism referring to his death.

[95] The Greek Οὐαί is used in the Septuagint chiefly for הוֹי and אוֹי.

The Disciples Argue About Greatness

The discussion/quarrel about who among the disciples should be the greatest may involve the question of who would take the leadership of the movement after Jesus' departure.

Luke 22:24 And there was also a dispute among them, which of them should be thought to be the greatest. **25** And he said to them: The kings of the Gentiles rule over them; and those who exercise authority upon them are called benefactors. **26** But you shall not be so; but he who is greatest among you, let him be as the younger; and **he who is the leader, as he who serves**.[96] **27** For who is greater, the one who reclines, or **the one who serves**[97]? Is not the one reclining? But I am among you as he who serves. **28** You are those who have remained with me in my trials. **29** And I appoint to you a kingdom, as my Father has appointed to me; **30** so that you may eat and drink at my table in my kingdom, and sit on **thrones**[98] **judging**[99] the twelve tribes of Israel.

---

[96] The leader will be the one who works the hardest in caring for others; e.g. at a communal meal the host does the serving.

[97] It was the obligation of disciples to serve sages. Note *ARN* 12: "Anyone who debases himself for the sake of the words of Torah, in the end they will elevate him" (כל המשפיל עצמו על דברי תורה סוף שמגביהין אותו). Note also *b. Hag.* 15b: "If the rabbi is similar to an angel of the Lord of hosts, perfect in his ways, they should seek Torah from his mouth" (אם דומה הרב למלאך ה׳ צבאות יבקשו תורה מפיהו). Note R. Yohanan (*b. Ber.* 7b): "The **service of Torah** is greater than its study" (גדולה שמושה של תורה יותר מלמודה); Avot 6:6: "Greater is learning Torah than the priesthood and than royalty, for royalty is acquired by thirty stages ... **by attending to the sages**" (גדולה תורה יותר מן הכהנה ומן המלכות, שהמלכות נקנית בשלשים מעלות ... **בשמוש חכמים**); *b. Taan.* 10b: "A person should not say: I am only a student, and consequently I am unworthy to be considered an individual. Rather, all Torah scholars are individuals. Who is an individual and who is a student? An individual is anyone who is learned in Torah and **worthy to be appointed leader and teacher over the community**" (תנו רבנן אל יאמר אדם תלמיד אני איני ראוי להיות יחיד אלא כל תלמידי חכמים יחידים [איזהו יחיד ואיזהו תלמיד יחיד כל **שראוי למנותו פרנס על הצבור**]).

[98] A reference to Ps 122:5: "For there were set **thrones** for judgment, the **thrones** of the house of David" (כי שמה, ישבו כסאות למשפט: כסאות לבית דוד). The tribes of Israel are depicted as coming to Jerusalem and to the messiah in order to be "judged," i.e. "delivered." Here, the disciples sit judging the twelve tribes, i.e. continuing to lead the people in the kingdom of God/heaven movement.

[99] I.e. "saving"/"delivering."

Jesus Predicts Peter's Denial

Contrary to much contemporary thought, that Jesus' "Last Supper" amounted to a traditional Passover seder, it might be better understood as a prophetic vehicle to showcase the immanent betrayal by Judas.

Luke 22:31 And the Lord said: Simon, Simon, **behold,**[100] **Satan**[101] has desired to have you, that he may sift you as wheat. **32** But I have prayed for you, that your faith may not fail; and when **you have turned back,**[102] strengthen your brothers. **33** And he said to him: Lord, I am ready to go with you, both to prison, and to death. **34** And he said: I tell you, Peter, the **rooster will not crow**[103] this day, until you deny three times that you know me.

Supplies for the Road

Jesus' directive to sell one's cloak and buy a sword is taken by some to be a veiled reference to a more militant messianic leader, at the very least sympathetic to the Zealot cause.[104]

---

[100] The Greek ἰδού is used in imitation of the Hebrew הִנֵּה.

[101] See Luke 4:3 n.

[102] The Greek ἐπιστρέψας ("you have turned back") mimics the Hebrew concept of "repentance" as "turning around" (שׁב).

[103] An early tradition declares that while the Temple stood, there were no roosters in Jerusalem; see *m. B.K.* 7:7: "One may not raise **chickens/roosters** in Jerusalem, due to the sacrificial meat" (אֵין מְגַדְּלִין **תַּרְנְגוֹלִים** בִּירוּשָׁלַיִם, מִפְּנֵי הַקֳּדָשִׁים). The cock's crow indicating the break of day is common in rabbinic literature, e.g. *m. Yom.* 1:8: "Every day the priests would remove the ashes from the altar at the crow of the *rooster*" (בְּכָל יוֹם תּוֹרְמִין אֶת הַמִּזְבֵּחַ בִּקְרִיאַת הַגֶּבֶר); *m. Tam.* 1:2: "And at what time does the appointed priest arrive? The times of his arrival are not all the same. There are times that he comes at the call of the *rooster*" (וְכִי בְאֵיזוֹ שָׁעָה הַמְמֻנֶּה בָא. לֹא כָל הָעִתִּים שָׁוֹות. פְּעָמִים שֶׁהוּא בָא מִקְּרִיאַת הַגֶּבֶר).

[104] Zev Garber notes (*Judaism and Jesus*, 64): "The *ipsissima verba* of Jesus, recorded in Matt 10:34, namely, 'I have not come to bring peace but a sword,' supports the militancy in the Jesus party mentioned in the Gethsemane tradition: Luke 22:35–38 portrays Jesus asking his disciples if they are armed and they reply that they are doubly armed."

Luke 22:35 And he said to them: When I sent you without purse, and bag, and sandals, did you lack anything? And they said: Nothing. **36** Then said he to them: But now, the one who has a purse, let him take it, and likewise his bag; and **the one who has no sword, let him sell his cloak, and buy one. 37 For I say to you, that what has been written must yet be accomplished in me: And he was reckoned among the transgressors.**[105] For the things concerning me have an end. **38** And they said, Lord, **behold,**[106] here are two swords. And he said to them: **It is enough.**[107]

Scene 11:
The Prayer in Gethsemane

Many have noted the similarity between Jesus' prayer in Gethsemane and the Lord's Prayer (Luke 11:1–3; Matt 6:9b–13), suggesting that Gethsemane was assimilated into the Lord's Prayer, foreshadowing the passion.[108]

Luke 22:39 And he came out, and went, according to his custom, to the Mount of Olives; and his disciples also followed him. **40** And when he was at the place, he said to them: Pray that you do not enter into temptation. **41** And he withdrew from them about a stone's throw, and knelt down, and prayed, **42** Saying: Father, if you are willing, remove this cup from me. Nevertheless, not my will, but yours, be done. **43** And there appeared to him an angel from heaven, strengthening him. **44** And being in an agony he prayed more earnestly; and his sweat was as if it were great drops of blood falling down to the ground. **45** And when he rose up from

---

[105] Quoting Isa 53:12: "He bared his soul unto death, *and was numbered with the transgressors*" (הֶעֱרָה לַמָּוֶת נַפְשׁוֹ, **וְאֶת-פֹּשְׁעִים נִמְנָה**). Since he is to be counted among evildoers, it is only appropriate that there should be a sword or two. The statement is sometimes taken as sympathetic to the Zealot cause.

[106] The Greek ἰδού is used in imitation of the Hebrew הִנֵּה.

[107] See Neumann, "Thy Will Be Done: Jesus's Passion in the Lord's Prayer," *JBL* 138, 1 (2019): 161–82.

[108] The Greek ἰδού is used in imitation of the Hebrew הִנֵּה.

prayer, he came to his disciples, and he found them **sleeping for sorrow,**[109] **46** And said to them: Why are you sleeping? Rise and pray, that you might not enter into temptation.

Scene 12:
Betrayal and Arrest in Gethsemane

When Jesus is arrested in Gethsemane, we see at least one of the disciples resorting to violence, cutting off the ear of the high priest's servant. Zev Garber and others have suggested ties to the Zealots among the disciples and even Jesus himself.[110]

Luke 22:47 And while he was still speaking, **behold,**[111] a multitude, and he who was called Judas, one of the twelve, went before them, and drew near to Jesus **to kiss him.**[112] **48** But Jesus said to him: Judas, do you betray the **Son of Man**[113] with a kiss? **49** When those who were around him saw what would follow, they said to him: Lord, shall we strike with the sword? **50** And **one of them struck the servant of the high priest, and cut off his right ear.**[114] **51** And Jesus answered and said: No more of this. And he touched his ear, and healed him. **52** Then Jesus said to the chief priests, and **captains of the temple,**[115] and the elders, who had come to him: Have you come out, as against a thief, with swords

---

[109] It could be that in the hypothetical Hebrew *grundschrift*, the Hebrew word "weariness" (יגיעה) was misread as "sorrow" (יגוח), and rendered in Greek as λύπης. The phrase might instead be read: "sleeping *from weariness.*"

[110] See Zev Garber, "A Partisan's Imagination," in Garber and Hanson, *Judaism and Jesus* (Newcastle Upon Tyne: Cambridge Publishing, 2020), 60–67.

[111] The Greek ἰδοὺ is used in imitation of the Hebrew הִנֵּה.

[112] The kiss here is a type of salutation. A disciple was not permitted to greet his master first since this would imply equality. Therefore, Judas' kiss could be taken as an affront.

[113] The Aramaic בר אנוש ("son of man") links to Dan 7:13; authority being the theme.

[114] This unnamed disciple may, by resorting to the sword, may be identifying himself as a member of the Sicarii. Some speculate that this could this be Peter.

[115] I.e. the temple guard. See John 18:3. The author of John likely used a Jewish Christian source with Jewish nationalist tendencies (emphasizing Jesus' messiahship). He was more anti-Roman than the other Gospel writers. The synoptics suggest that Jesus is taken prisoner by the temple guard, but John 18:12 introduces Roman soldiers.

and clubs? **53** When I was **daily**[116] **with you in the temple,**[117] you did not stretch forth your hands against me; but this is your hour, and the power of darkness.

Scene 13:
Peter Denies Jesus and Weeps Bitterly

Many unanswered questions are raised by the following sequence of events, as it is difficult to explain why, given that Jesus' behavior was thought to be seditious, he was taken directly to the high priest, rather than to the prison at the Praetorium.

Luke 22:54 Then they took him, and led him away, and brought him into the high priest's house. And Peter followed from a distance. **55** And when they had kindled a fire in the midst of the courtyard, and had sat down together, Peter sat down among them. **56** But a certain servant girl saw him as he sat by the fire, and earnestly looked upon him, and said: This man was also with him. **57** But he denied it, saying: Woman, I do not know him. **58** And after a little while another saw him, and said, You are also of them. And Peter said: Man, I am not. **59** And after about one hour, another confidently affirmed it, saying: Of a truth this one was also with him; for **he is a Galilean.**[118] **60** And Peter said: Man, I do not know what you are saying. And immediately, as he yet spoke, the rooster crowed. **61** And the Lord turned, and looked upon Peter. And Peter remembered the word of the Lord, how he had said to

---

[116] The verse may also be read "*By day* I sat in the temple," implying audacity in seizing him by night. Jesus objects, not that he is arrested, but that it happens by night (and with swords), when a rebel leader might be seized, taking him to be a member of Josephus' "Fourth Philosophy," i.e. the Zealots.

[117] Sitting in the court of the temple was forbidden except for kings of the house of David. By sitting, Jesus may have been indicating that he is the messianic king. He wryly comments that he should have been arrested then; see *y. Pes.* 5:7 (32d); *Yom.* 3 (40b); *Sot.* 7:7 (22a).

[118] Galileans were noted for a slurring of the gutturals and were looked down upon by Judeans.

him: Before the rooster crows, you will deny me three times. **62** And Peter went out, and wept bitterly.

Scene 14:
Jesus Mocked and Beaten

Luke 22:63 And the men who held Jesus mocked him, and struck him. **64** And when they had blindfolded him, they struck him on the face, and questioned him, saying: **Prophesy,**[119] who is it that struck you? **65** And they said many other blasphemous things against him.

Scene 15:
Jesus Faces the Temple Committee

When Jesus faces the elders, the chief priests, and scribes, it is again clear that his adversaries are not the Pharisees but the Sadducee-oriented "Temple Committee." It is suggested that this was not the Sanhedrin but merely the place where the Sanhedrin met (the Chamber of Hewn Stone). No such interrogation would have taken place after the onset of Passover, which could indicate that Jesus was crucified on Thursday and that this interrogation occurred on Wednesday night. Jewish law, propounded by the Pharisees, strictly forbade handing a Jew over to a foreign authority. Jesus' declaration that the Son of Man will sit on the right hand of the power of God is laden with messianic references, linking back to Psalm 2:7 and Psalm 110:3–4. This is not, however, a true trial, and the charge of blasphemy, present in Mark and Matthew, is notably absent. Arguably, Luke is less inflammatory than the other two synoptic Gospels, which could have significant implications in understanding the genesis of the charge of "deicide."

---

[119] The Sadducees, who denied the existence of angels, mocked those who possessed the "spirit of prophecy." The guards would have been playing a brutal, traditional game.

Luke 22:66 And as soon as it was day, **the elders of the people and the chief priests and the scribes**[120] came together, and led him into their council, saying: **67** Are you the messiah? Tell us. And he said to them: If I tell you, you will not believe; **68** And **if I also ask you, you will not answer me,**[121] nor let me go. **69** Hereafter the **Son of Man**[122] will sit **on the right hand of the power**[123] of God. **70** Then they all said: Are you then the **Son of God?**[124] And he said to them: **You say that I am.**[125] **71** And they

---

[120] I.e. the temple committee (not the Pharisees; see Luke 20:1). See Matt 26:57; Mark 15:1. Matthew (as opposed to Mark) omits "Sanhedrin." If the Sanhedrin had met, where are the Pharisees? (Compare John 18:3: "officials from the chief priests and the Pharisees"). The chief priests delivered Jesus to the Romans because of his intervention in the temple market and his prophesies of destruction. The chief priests also opposed the disciples; see Acts 4:1, 5–6; 5:17, 24. Here, the priests incited the crowd (see Mark 15:11). Note *m. San.* 4:1: "In cases of capital law, the court judges during the daytime, and concludes in the daytime" (דִּינֵי נְפָשׁוֹת דָּנִין בַּיּוֹם וְגוֹמְרִין בַּיּוֹם). It could be that the "Sanhedrin" here is merely the place where the Sanhedrin met, i.e. the Chamber of Hewn Stone, as in Acts 4:15; 5:27, 34; 6:12, 15. See Mark 14:55; Matt 26:59. It is only assumed that Luke was referring to the Great Sanhedrin. Handing a Jew over to a foreign authority (thereby "separating from the community") was considered a sin that could not be forgiven; see *Seder Olam Rabbah*, 3:2: "Those who *separated from the ways of the community*, like the *Sadducees*, and the betrayers and the hypocrites and the heretics, and those who 'spread their terror in the land of the living,' and those who denied the resurrection, and those who say Torah is not from heaven, and those who scoff at the words of the Sages—*Gehinnom is locked before them* and they are judged there forever" מִי שֶׁפֵּירְשׁוּ מִדַּרְכֵי צִבּוּר כְּגוֹן הַצְּדוֹקִין וְהַמְּסוֹרוֹת וְהַחֲנִיפִין וְהָאֶפִּיקוֹרוֹסִין וְשִׁנְּתְנוּ חֲתִיתָם בְּאֶרֶץ הַחַיִּים) וְשֶׁכְּפְרוּ בִּתְחִיַּת הַמֵּתִים וְהָאוֹמְרִים אֵין תּוֹרָה מִן הַשָּׁמַיִם וְהַמַּלְעִיגִין עַל דִּבְרֵי חֲכָמִים גֵּיהִנָּם נִנְעֶלֶת בִּפְנֵיהֶם וְנִידוֹנִין בְּתוֹכָהּ לְעוֹלְמֵי עוֹלָמִים).

[121] Jesus will not use the word "Messiah/anointed one" (משיח). The priests use it in order to prompt from him a candid answer. In rabbinic debate, the one questioned can ask a question in return, but they will not answer.

[122] See Dan 7:13: "There came with the clouds of heaven one like a *son of man*" (וַאֲרוּ עִם עֲנָנֵי שְׁמַיָּא כְּבַר אֱנָשׁ).

[123] The Greek τῆς δυνάμεως ("the power") translates the Hebrew הגבורה, and is a euphemism for God; see Prov 8:14: "power is mine" (אֲנִי בִינָה לִי גְבוּרָה). See also Ps 110:1: "The LORD said to my lord: 'Sit at My right hand'" (נְאֻם יְהוָה לַאדֹנִי שֵׁב לִימִינִי).

[124] The priests respond with reference to Ps 2:7: "The LORD said to me: 'You are **My son**, this day I have begotten you'" (יְהוָה, אָמַר אֵלַי בְּנִי אַתָּה אֲנִי, הַיּוֹם יְלִדְתִּיךָ). An early tradition read it *y'laditikha* ("I have revealed you", as a midwife "reveals" a baby), as opposed to the Masoretic reading, *y'lid'tikha*, ("begotten/sired you"). Note Ps 110:3–4: "You have the dew **of Your youth [I have birthed/revealed you]**. The Lord has sworn and will not relent, 'You *are* a priest forever According to the order of Melchizedek.'" טַל (יַלְדֻתֶיךָ נִשְׁבַּע יְהוָה וְלֹא יִנָּחֵם אַתָּה כֹהֵן לְעוֹלָם עַל-דִּבְרָתִי מַלְכִּי-צֶדֶק).

[125] This could mean, "What you have said is correct."

said: **What need do we have of any further witness?**[126] For we ourselves have heard it from his own mouth.

Scene 16:
Jesus Handed Over to Pontius Pilate

Pontius Pilate appears in Luke's account as inwardly conflicted, torn between cruelty and cowardice since he feared the people. This is reflected in an earlier event at Caesarea when he threatened to behead a protesting mob but ultimately lost courage and gave in to their demands. In this case, he knows that Jesus poses no serious threat of insurrection, and he attempts to avoid the issue by sending him to Herod.

Luke 23:1 And the whole multitude of them arose, and led him to **Pilate.**[127] **2** And they began to accuse him, saying: We found this fellow misleading the nation, and forbidding to give tribute to Caesar, saying that he himself is the messiah, a King. **3** And Pilate asked him, saying: Are you the **King of the Jews?**[128] And he answered him and said: **You say so.**[129] **4** Then Pilate said to the

---

[126] The charge of "blasphemy" is absent, as opposed to Mark 14:64 and Matt 26:66. This was not a true "trial," but an "interrogation."

[127] According to D. Flusser (*Judaism*, 593–603), Pilate evinced a mixture of cruelty and cowardice, having surrendered to the crowd in Caesarea, demanding the removal of Roman standards from Jerusalem. See Josephus, *War* 2.169–72: "These came zealously to Pilate to Cesarea, and besought him to carry those ensigns out of Jerusalem, and to preserve them their ancient laws inviolable; but upon Pilate's denial of their request, they fell down prostrate upon the ground, and continued immovable in that posture for five days and as many nights... Pilate was greatly surprised at their prodigious superstition, and gave order that the ensigns should be presently carried out of Jerusalem"; *Ant.* 18.55–59: "...when the Jews petitioned him again, he gave a signal to the soldiers to encompass them routed, and threatened that their punishment should be no less than immediate death, unless they would leave off disturbing him, and go their ways home. But they threw themselves upon the ground, and laid their necks bare, and said they would take their death very willingly, rather than the wisdom of their laws should be transgressed; upon which Pilate was deeply affected with their firm resolution to keep their laws inviolable, and presently commanded the images to be carried back from Jerusalem to Caesarea."

[128] Jews would never have used the Greek term "King of the Jews" (Βασιλεὺς τῶν Ἰουδαίων). A Jew would refer to himself as an "Israelite" or a "son of Israel."

[129] This could mean, "What you have said is correct"; see Luke 22:70.

chief priests and to the crowds: I find no guilt in this man. **5** And they kept insisting, saying: He stirs up the people, teaching **throughout all of Judea,**[130] beginning from Galilee to this place.

Scene 17:
Jesus Faces Herod

Luke 23:6 When Pilate heard this, he asked whether the man were a Galilean. **7** And as soon as he knew that he belonged to Herod's jurisdiction, he **sent him to Herod, who himself also was at Jerusalem at that time.**[131] **8** And when Herod saw Jesus, he was exceedingly glad; for he had been wishing to see him for a long time, because he had heard many things of him, and he was hoping to see some miracle done by him. **9** Then he questioned with him with many words; but he answered him nothing. **10** And the chief priests and scribes stood and vehemently accused him. **11** And Herod with his troops set him at nought, and mocked him, and arrayed him in splendid apparel, and sent him again to Pilate. **12** And the same day Pilate and Herod became friends; for before they were at enmity between themselves.

Scene 18:
Taking the Place of Barabbas

Pilate ultimately gives in to a Sadducee-dominated crowd. Pilate would have preferred to execute Barabbas, who possibly belonged to Josephus' "Fourth Philosophy," i.e. the Zealots. Notably, Luke does not contain the "blood curse" that Matthew records as being uttered by the crowd: "Let His blood be on us and on our children" (Matt 27:25).

---

[130] A possible reference to an earlier Judean sojourn.

[131] As argued by J. Tabor, no such interrogation would have taken place after the onset of Passover, which means that Jesus may have been crucified on Thursday, and that Herod's interrogation may have occurred on Wednesday night.

Luke 23:13 And Pilate, when he had called together the chief priests and the rulers and the people, **14** Said to them: You have brought this man to me, as one who misleads the people; and, **behold,**[132] I, having examined him before you, and have found no guilt in this man regarding the things of which you accuse him. **15** No, not even Herod: for he sent him back to us; and, **behold,**[133] nothing worthy of death is done by him. **16** I will therefore chastise him, and release him. **17** For of necessity he must release one to them at the feast. **18** And they cried out all at once, saying: Away with this man, and release to us **Barabbas;**[134] **19** Who, for a certain insurrection made in the city, and for murder, was cast into prison. **20** Pilate therefore, willing to release Jesus, spoke again to them. **21** But they cried out, saying: **Crucify him, crucify him.**[135] **22** And he said to them a third time: Why, what evil has he done? I have found no cause of death in him. I will therefore chastise him,

---

[132] The Greek ἰδοὺ is used in imitation of the Hebrew הִנֵּה.

[133] The Greek ἰδοὺ is used in imitation of the Hebrew הִנֵּה.

[134] The Greek Βαραββᾶν transliterates the Aramaic בר אבא ("Son of the Father"). Note *b. Ber.* 18b: "[Shmuel] went after his father to the cemetery and said to the dead: I want Abba. The dead said to him: There are many Abbas here. He told them: I want **Abba bar Abba**. They said to him: There are also many people named Abba **bar Abba** here" (אָזַל אַבַּתְרֵיהּ לַחֲצַר מָוֶת. אֲמַר לְהוּ: בָּעֵינָא אַבָּא! אֲמַרוּ לֵיהּ: אַבָּא טוּבָא אִיכָּא הָכָא. אֲמַר לְהוּ: בָּעֵינָא **אַבָּא בַּר אַבָּא**. אֲמַרוּ לֵיהּ: **אַבָּא בַּר אַבָּא** נָמֵי טוּבָא אִיכָּא הָכָא). The use of this name may represent a play on Jesus' relationship with God, as an ancient Hasid. In the *Gospel According to the Hebrews*, Barabbas is presented as a "son of their *teacher*" ("father" understood as "teacher"). Origen said that in an old manuscript, he is called "Jesus Barabbas," in which case Pilate's question would have been "Which Jesus?" Solomon Zeitlin, *Who Crucified Jesus?* (New York: Harper Collins, 1947), 167, among others, suggested that Barabbas was a member of the "Fourth Philosophy."

[135] Scholars are divided over whether the Jews had the right to inflict capital punishment. John 18:31 says: "It is not lawful for us to put anyone to death." However, some maintain that in exceptional cases the Jews did inflict capital punishment. Note Dead Sea Scrolls 11Q19 64:7–12: "If a man is a traitor against his people and gives them up to a foreign nation, so doing evil to his people, you are *to hang him on a tree until dead*. On the testimony of two or three witnesses he will be put to death, and they themselves *shall hang him on the tree*. If a man is convicted of a capital crime and flees to the nations, cursing his people and the children of Israel, *you are to hang him, also, upon a tree until dead. But you must not let their bodies remain on the tree overnight; you shall most certainly bury them that very day*. Indeed, anyone hung on a tree is accursed of God and men ..." (יהיה איש רכיל בעמו ומשלים את עמו לגוי נכר ועושה רעה בעמו) **ותליתמה אותו על העץ וימת**. על פי שנים עדים ועל פי שלושה עדים יומת והמה **יתלו אותו העץ**. כי יהיה באיש חטא משפט מות ויברח אל תוך הגואים ויקלל את עמו ואת בני ישראל **ותליתמה גם אותו על העץ** (**וימות. ולוא תלין נבלתמה על העץ כי קבור תקוברמה ביום ההוא**. כי מקוללי אלוהים.

and let him go. **23** But they were urgent with loud voices, asking that he might be crucified. And the voices of them and of the chief priests prevailed. **24** And Pilate gave sentence that it should be done as they demanded. **25** And he released to them the one who was cast into prison for **insurrection**[136] and murder, for whom they asked. But he delivered Jesus to their will.

Scene 19:
Jesus Led Away; Utters Lament

Instead of the "blood curse," a great multitude, including women, lament Jesus' fate. Jesus' own lamentation recalls the words of grief uttered over the destruction of the Second Temple. "Blessed is he who was not born, Or he, who having been born, has died ... And, you women, pray not that you may bear ..." (2 Bar. 10:6–16).

Luke 23:26 And as they led him away, they laid hold upon one **Simon, a Cyrenian,**[137] coming out of the country, and on him they laid the cross, that he might carry it behind Jesus. **27** And there followed him a **great multitude**[138] of people, and of women, who also mourned and **lamented**[139] him. **28** But Jesus turning to them said: Daughters of Jerusalem, do not weep for me, but weep for yourselves, and for your children. **[29** For, **behold,**[140] the days are coming, in the which they will say, **Blessed are the barren, and**

---

[136] It has been argued that Pilate was prepared to release Jesus not because he respected him, but because Barabbas was quite possibly a leader of the Zealots.

[137] The Romans often demanded the compulsory services of pilgrims on holidays, a humiliation for Jews. See Mark 15:21; Matt 27:32.

[138] References to the sympathetic multitude, and Jesus' words to the women who lamented him are missing in Mark and Matthew, indicating an early tendency to paint the Jews as complicit in Jesus' execution. The Lucan account is superior in that it reflects genuine sympathy for Jesus among the common people.

[139] The Greek ἐθρήνουν ("lamenting") translates the Hebrew מקוננות, reflecting the authentic Jewish practice of singing laments.

[140] The Greek ἰδοὺ is used in imitation of the Hebrew הִנֵּה.

the wombs that never bore,[141] and the breasts that never nursed.][142] **30** Then they will begin to say to the mountains, Fall on us; and to the hills, Cover us. **31** For **if they do these things in a green tree, what shall be done in the dry?**[143]

It is possible that Jesus' famous lament over Jerusalem, elsewhere depicted as occurring on the Mount of Olives (Matt 23:37–39; Luke 19:41–44), more appropriately belongs at this juncture.[144] Generally considered to be a later interpolation, it can be argued that a "prophecy" of the city's destruction would not have been beyond the realm of possibility given the geopolitical realities.

---

[141] The blessing of Luke 1:42 is reversed. Note the lamentation composed over the destruction of the temple (2 Bar 10:6–16): "Blessed is he who was not born, Or he, who having been born, has died. But as for us who live, woe unto us, Because we see the afflictions of Zion …   And, ye women, pray not that ye may bear … Or why, again, should mankind have sons?"

[142] This statement possibly belongs after Luke 8:21, followed by the declaration of the woman in the crowd: "Blessed is the womb that bore you …"

[143] A rabbinic *a fortiori* ("light and heavy"/קַל וָחוֹמֶר) statement. Note Ezek 21:3: "Behold, I will kindle a fire in you, and it shall devour every *green tree* in you, and every dry tree, it shall not be quenched, even a flaming flame; and all faces from the south to the north shall be seared thereby" (הִנְנִי מַצִּית-בָּךְ אֵשׁ וְאָכְלָה בָךְ כָל-**עֵץ-לַח** וְכָל-עֵץ יָבֵשׁ לֹא-תִכְבֶּה, לַהֶבֶת שַׁלְהֶבֶת, וְנִצְרְבוּ-בָהּ כָּל-פָּנִים, מִנֶּגֶב צָפוֹנָה). "Green tree" was used as a pseudonym for the Messiah; i.e., what will happen when the Messiah is taken from you? See Bivin and Blizzard, 120–23.

[144] See Lindsey, *Jesus*, 170.

Jesus Laments over Jerusalem

Matt 23:37 Jerusalem, Jerusalem,[145] who kills the prophets, and stones[146] those who are sent to you. How often I would have gathered your children together, even as a hen gathers her chicks under her wings,[147] and you were not willing! 38 Behold,[148] your house[149] is left to you desolate.[150] 39 For I say to you, You will not see me again, until you say, Blessed is he who comes in the name of the Lord.

Jesus Weeps over Jerusalem (RCT)

Luke 19:41 [And when he had come near, he beheld the city, and wept over it, **42** Saying:][151] If you had known, even you, at least in

---

[145] This connects Jesus to the prophetic strand. Yohanan b. Zakkai was said to have prophesied the Temple's destruction. Note *b. Gittin* 56a-b: [Yoḥanan ben Zakkai] "said to him: As for what you said about yourself: I am not a king, in truth, you are a king [if not now, then in the future]. As if you are not a king, Jerusalem will not be handed over into your hand, as it is written: 'And the *Lebanon shall fall by a mighty one*' (Isaiah 10:34). And "mighty one" means only a king, as it is written: 'And their mighty one shall be of themselves' (Jeremiah 30:21) [indicating that 'mighty one' parallels 'ruler.'] *And "Lebanon" means only the Temple*" (דקאמרת לאו מלכא אנא איברא מלכא את דאי לאו מלכא את) לא מימסרא ירושלים בידך דכתיב (ישעיהו י, לד) **והלבנון באדיר יפול** ואין אדיר אלא מלך דכתיב (ירמיהו (ל, כא) והיה אדירו ממנו וגו' **ואין לבנון אלא ביהמ"ק**.

[146] A few decades earlier, the ancient Hasid, Honi ha-Me'agel, was stoned; see Josephus, *Ant.* 14.2.1: "Now there was one named Onias, a righteous man and beloved of God ... the wicked Jews that stood about him, as soon as he had made this prayer, *stoned him to death.*"

[147] Note *Lev. R.* 25: "*The hen, when her chicks are young, gathers them together and places them under her wings* and warms them and digs up the earth before them. But when they grow bigger, if one of them wants to come near to her as she pecks him on the head and says to him, 'Dig in your own dirt!'" (הָדָא תַּרְנְגוֹלְתָּא כַד אֶפְרוֹחֶיהָ דַּקִיקִין הִיא מְכַנְּשָׁא לְהוֹן וְיָהֲבַת לְהוֹן תְּחוֹת אֲגַפַּיָּא וּמְשַׁחֲנָה לְהוֹן וּמְעַדַּרְנָה קֳדָמֵיהוֹן, וְכַד אִינּוּן רַבְיָה חַד מִנְהוֹן בָּעֵי לְמִקְרַב לְוָתֵיהּ וְהִיא נָקְרָה לֵיהּ בְּגוֹ רֵישֵׁיהּ, וַאֲמְרַת לֵיהּ זִיל עֲדוֹר בְּקוּקַלְתָּךְ). *Lev. R.* 2 speaks of how proselytes are brought "beneath the wings of the *Shekhinah.*" "When a proselyte who comes to convert, extend one's hand to bring him **beneath the wings of the Shekhinah**" (גֵּר שֶׁבָּא לְהִתְגַּיֵּיר פּוֹשְׁטִין לוֹ יַד לְהַכְנִיסוֹ **תַּחַת כַּנְפֵי הַשְּׁכִינָה**).

[148] The Greek ἰδοὺ is used in imitation of the Hebrew הִנֵּה.

[149] The Hebrew for "house" (בית) is a euphemism for the temple.

[150] Note *b. Shab.* 119b: "Any city in which there are no schoolchildren studying Torah, they destroy it. Ravina said: They leave it *desolate.*" כָּל עִיר שֶׁאֵין בָּהּ תִּינוֹקוֹת שֶׁל בֵּית (רַבָּן מַחֲרִיבִין אוֹתָהּ, רָבִינָא אָמַר: **מַחֲרִימִין** אוֹתָהּ).

[151] Possibly an editorial gloss, used to place this passage earlier in the narrative.

this day, the things which belong to **peace;**[152] but now they are **hidden from you eyes.**[153] **43** For the days will come upon you, in which your enemies will cast a barricade around you, and surround you, and hem you in on every side, **44** And will level you to the ground, and your children within you; and they will not leave in you **one stone upon another;**[154] because you did not know the time of your **visitation.**[155]

Jesus' words from the cross, "Father, forgive them, for they do not know what they do," were likely on behalf of the Romans, since rank-and-file Jews were on his side. As already stated (23:27), there were "multitudes," including women, who mourned and lamented his execution. The rulers who scorned him were undoubtedly Sadducee-oriented.

Scene 20:
Two Criminals and Words from the Cross

Luke 23:32 And there were also two other, criminals, led with him to be put to death. **33** And when they had come to the place, which

---

[152] A word play on "Jerusalem (ירושלים)," which means "city of peace." Note *Gen. R. 56*: "*I call it Yerushalayim [Jerusalem]*, as they called it together: *Yireh Shalem*. Jerusalem. Rabbi Berechiah said in Rabbi Helbo's name: While it was *Shalem*, the Holy One of Blessing made for himself a *sukkah* [booth] and prayed in it, since it says 'In *Shalem* is set His tabernacle, and His dwelling-place in Tzion' (Psalms 76:3). And what did He say? 'May it happen that I see the building of My house.' Another interpretation: It [this verse] teaches that the Holy One of Blessing showed him the Temple *destroyed and built, destroyed and built* [a second time], since it says: 'the name of that place *Ad-nai Yireh*' (Ad-nai sees)" (רַבִּי. יְרוּשָׁלַיִם. יְרָאֶה שָׁלֵם, שְׁנֵיהֶם כְּמוֹ שֶׁקְּרָאוּ **הֲרֵינִי קוֹרֵא אוֹתוֹ יְרוּשָׁלַיִם** בְּרָכְיָה בְּשֵׁם רַבִּי חֶלְבּוֹ אָמַר עַד שֶׁהוּא שָׁלֵם עָשָׂה לוֹ הַקָּדוֹשׁ בָּרוּךְ הוּא סֻכָּה וְהָיָה מִתְפַּלֵּל בְּתוֹכָהּ, שֶׁנֶּאֱמַר (תהלים עו, ג): וַיְהִי בְשָׁלֵם סֻכּוֹ וּמְעוֹנָתוֹ בְצִיּוֹן, וּמַה הָיָה אוֹמֵר יְהִי רָצוֹן שֶׁאֶרְאֶה בְּבִנְיַן בֵּיתִי. דָּבָר אַחֵר, מְלַמֵּד שֶׁהֶרְאָה לוֹ הַקָּדוֹשׁ בָּרוּךְ הוּא בֵּית הַמִּקְדָּשׁ **חָרֵב וּבָנוּי חָרֵב וּבָנוּי**, שֶׁנֶּאֱמַר: שֵׁם הַמָּקוֹם הַהוּא ה' יְרָאֶה).

[153] The Hebrew "Hidden from your eyes" (נסתר מעניך) suggests: "You have no answers."

[154] Note *b. Yom.* 9a: "'But the years of the wicked will be shortened;' that is a reference to the *Second Temple*" ("יּשְׁנוֹת רְשָׁעִים תִּקְצֹרְנָה" זֶה **מִקְדָּשׁ שֵׁנִי**); *b. Shab.* 119b: "*Jerusalem was destroyed* only because there were no more trustworthy people there …" (לֹא **חָרְבָה יְרוּשָׁלַיִם** אֶלָּא בִּשְׁבִיל שֶׁפָּסְקוּ מִמֶּנָּה אַנְשֵׁי אֱמָנָה).

[155] See Luke 1:68.

is called **Calvary,**[156] there they **crucified**[157] him, and the criminals, one on the right, and the other on the left. **34** Then Jesus said: **Father,**[158] **forgive them; for they do not know what they do.**[159] And they divided his garments, and cast lots. **35** And the people stood **beholding.**[160] And **the rulers also with them derided him,**[161] saying: He saved others; let him save himself, if he is the messiah, the chosen of God. **36** And the soldiers also mocked him, approaching him, and offering him sour wine, **37** And saying: If you are the king of the Jews, save yourself. **38** And an inscription was also written over him in Greek, and Latin, and Hebrew letters: This Is The **King Of The Jews.**[162] **39** And one of the criminals who was hanged railed at him, saying, **If you are Christ, save yourself and us.**[163] **40** But the other answering rebuked him, saying: Do you not even fear God, since you are under the same condemnation? **41** And we indeed justly; for we are receiving the due reward of our deeds. But this man has done nothing wrong. **42** And he said to Jesus: Lord, **remember**[164] me when you come

---

[156] The Greek κρανίον ("skull") translates the Hebrew גולולת; in Latin *Calvaria*.

[157] Note *Targ. Ruth* 1:17: "Naomi said, 'We have four death penalties for the guilty: stoning with stones, burning with fire, execution by the sword, and hanging on a tree (צליבת קיסא).'"

[158] See Luke 2:49. Jesus addresses God as would a Hasid (אבי).

[159] Omitted in Mark. Jesus may have been praying for the Roman soldiers since the Jewish multitude was sympathetic to him.

[160] The Greek θεωρῶν ("beholding") translates the Hebrew רואה—a sympathetic word.

[161] See Ps 22:8: "All those who see me laugh me to scorn; they shoot out the lip, they shake the head" (כָּל-רֹאַי יַלְעִגוּ לִי; יַפְטִירוּ בְשָׂפָה, יָנִיעוּ רֹאשׁ).

[162] See Luke 23:3; Jews would never have used the Greek term "King of the Jews" (Βασιλεὺς τῶν Ἰουδαίων). A Jew would refer to himself as an "Israelite" or a "son of Israel."

[163] Zealots (presumably pro-Barabbas) had little sympathy for a crucified messiah; see Matt 27:38–44; Mark 15:27–32.

[164] The Greek μνήσθητί μου ("remember me") translates the Hebrew זכרני. The Hebrew verb also indicates "favor." Note Gen 40:14: "... *and make mention of me* to Pharaoh" (וְהִזְכַּרְתַּנִי אֶל-פַּרְעֹה); Jud 16:29: "And Samson called unto the LORD, and said: 'O Lord GOD, *remember me*'" (וַיִּקְרָא שִׁמְשׁוֹן אֶל-יְהוָה, וַיֹּאמַר: אֲדֹנָי יֱהוִה זָכְרֵנִי). The verb can also convey a messianic motif.

into your kingdom. **43** And Jesus said to him: **Truly I say to you,**[165] Today you will be with me in paradise.

Scene 21:
Jesus Dies on the Cross

David Flusser noted the tradition in ancient Judaism of martyrs having died on behalf of the Jewish people, as a propitiation for their transgressions:

> *Since the age of the Hasmoneans, Jews had believed that the saints who died to sanctify the name of God atoned for the sins of Israel. The story of the mother and her seven sons in the Second Book of Maccabees acquires a greater significance in the Fourth Book of Maccabees, where their death is seen as an atoning sacrifice. In another Jewish source, Midrash Sifre, the idea is expressed that the killing of the Children of Israel by the Gentiles atones for the former's sins (Sifre to Deut 32:43).[166] It is reasonable to assume that during the Roman period this idea was applied not only to Jesus, but also to all those who were executed by the authorities. Even Jews who did not accept Christianity evidently believed that Jesus, like the other martyrs of the Roman authorities, had atoned for the sins of Israel.[167]*

Luke 23:44 And it was about the sixth hour, and there was a darkness over all the earth until the ninth hour. **45** And **the sun**

---

[165] "Amen"/"assuredly" (אמן) added after a strong statement. Jer 28:6 - כֵּן ,אָמֵן יַעֲשֶׂה יְהוָה יָקֵם יְהוָה אֶת-דְּבָרֶיךָ אֲשֶׁר נִבֵּאתָ ("Amen! The Lord do so; the Lord perform your words which you have prophesied …"). See Luke 4:24; Matt 5:18.

[166] "Whence is it derived that the killing of Israel by the nations atones for them (Israel) in the world to come? From (Psalm 79:1) 'A psalm of Asaf: O G-d, nations have entered Your inheritance… (3) They have shed their blood like water…'" (מנין אתה אומר שהריגתן של ישראל ביד אומות העולם כפרה היא להם לעולם הבא? שנא' [תהלים עט] מזמור לאסף אלהים באו גוים בנחלתך... שפכו דמם כמים).

[167] Flusser, *Jewish Sources*, 59.

was darkened,[168] and the **veil of the temple was torn in the middle.**[169] **46** And when Jesus had cried with a loud voice, he said: **Father, into your hands I commit my spirit.**[170] And having said thus, he breathed his last. **47** Now when the centurion **saw**[171] what had taken place, he glorified God, saying, Certainly this was a **righteous man.**[172] **48 And all the people who came together to**

---

[168] See Joel 2:10: "Before them the earth quakes, the heavens tremble; *the sun and the moon are become black*, and the stars withdraw their shining" (לְפָנָיו רָגְזָה אֶרֶץ, רָעֲשׁוּ שָׁמָיִם; שֶׁמֶשׁ וְיָרֵחַ קָדָרוּ, וְכוֹכָבִים אָסְפוּ נָגְהָם).

[169] This may also represent a prophetic precursor of the coming destruction. There are two curtains, an inner and an outer; here the outer is meant, being visible to the populace. Note *b. Yom.* 39b: "Forty years prior to the destruction of the Second Temple, the lot for God did not arise in the High Priest's right hand at all. So too, the strip of crimson [that was tied to the head of the goat that was sent to Azazel] did not turn white, and the westernmost lamp of the candelabrum did not burn continually. And the doors of the Sanctuary opened by themselves as a sign that they would soon be opened by enemies, until Rabban Yoḥanan ben Zakkai scolded them. He said to the Sanctuary: Sanctuary, Sanctuary, why do you frighten yourself with these signs? I know about you that you will ultimately be destroyed, and Zechariah, son of Ido, has already prophesied concerning you: "Open your doors, O Lebanon, that the fire may devour your cedars" (Zechariah 11:1) [Lebanon being an appellation for the Temple]" אַרְבָּעִים שָׁנָה קוֹדֶם חוּרְבַּן הַבַּית לֹא הָיָה גּוֹרָל עוֹלָה בְּיָמִין, וְלֹא הָיָה לָשׁוֹן שֶׁל זְהוֹרִית מַלְבִּין, וְלֹא הָיָה נֵר מַעֲרָבִי דּוֹלֵק וְהָיוּ דַּלְתוֹת הַהֵיכָל נִפְתָּחוֹת מֵאֲלֵיהֶן, עַד שֶׁגָּעַר בָּהֶן רַבָּן יוֹחָנָן בֶּן זַכַּאי. אָמַר לוֹ: הֵיכָל הֵיכָל! מִפְּנֵי מָה אַתָּה מַבְעִית עַצְמְךָ? יוֹדֵעַ אֲנִי בְּךָ שֶׁסּוֹפְךָ עָתִיד לֵיחָרֵב, וּכְבָר נִתְנַבֵּא עָלֶיךָ זְכַרְיָה בֶּן עִדּוֹא: "פְּתַח לְבָנוֹן דְּלָתֶיךָ וְתֹאכַל אֵשׁ בַּאֲרָזֶיךָ" y. *Yom.* 6, 43c (61); *b.Git.* 56b: "What did Titus do when he conquered the Temple? He took a prostitute with his hand, and entered the Holy of Holies with her. He then spread out a Torah scroll underneath him and committed a sin, i.e., engaged in sexual intercourse, on it. Afterward he took a sword and cut into the curtain separating between the Sanctuary and the Holy of Holies. And a miracle was performed and blood spurted forth" (מה עשה תפש זונה בידו ונכנס לבית קדשי הקדשים והציע ספר תורה ועבר עליה עבירה ונטל סייף וגידר את הפרוכת ונעשה נס והיה דם מבצבץ ויוצא); *b. M.Q.* 26a: "And upon seeing the cities of Judea that were destroyed or the destroyed Temple or Jerusalem in ruins. He first *rends* his garments for the Temple and then extends the rent for Jerusalem" (וְעַל עָרֵי יְהוּדָה וְעַל הַמִּקְדָּשׁ וְעַל יְרוּשָׁלַיִם וְקוֹרֵעַ עַל מִקְדָּשׁ וּמוֹסִיף עַל יְרוּשָׁלַיִם). See also 2 Kgs 2:12, relating that when Elisha witnessed Elijah's ascent, he rent his clothes. Earthquakes and splitting rocks were signs of judgment; see Jud 5:4; 2 Sam 22:8; 1 Kgs 19:11; Ps 68:9. Note Josephus, *War* VI.5.3–4: "There was a star, resembling a sword, which stood over the city; and a comet, that continued a whole year … Moreover the eastern gate of the inner [court of the] temple, which was of brass, and vastly heavy, and had been with difficulty shut by twenty men, and rested upon a basis armed with iron, and had bolts fastened very deep into the firm floor; which was there made of one entire stone: was seen to be opened of its own accord, about the sixth hour of the night …"

[170] See Ps 31:5: "Into your hand I commit my spirit" (בְּיָדְךָ, אַפְקִיד רוּחִי). Mark 15:34 (and Matthew 27:46) replaces this with Ps 22:2 "My God, my God, why have you forsaken me?" (אֵלִי אֵלִי, לָמָה עֲזַבְתָּנִי), though employing the Aramaic *targum* "למה שבחתני."

[171] See v. 35. The Hebrew verb "saw" (ראה) is a sympathetic word.

[172] As opposed to "son of God" in Mark 15:39 (and Matthew 27:54), arguably influenced by later theology.

that spectacle, seeing the things which took place, beat their breasts,[173] and returned home. **49** And all his acquaintances, and the women who followed him from Galilee, stood afar off, beholding these things.[174]

Scene 22:
Jesus Buried in Joseph's Tomb

At Jesus' burial, we are introduced to Joseph of Arimathea, who may well have been present at a council meeting at the High Priest's home on the evening before the crucifixion. At that time he may have been designated to ensure that Jesus received a proper burial. It is possible that when Jesus' body disappeared, Joseph was held responsible by the Romans, hence his disappearance from the narrative.[175]

Luke 23:50 And, **behold,**[176] there was a man named **Joseph, a council member;** and he was a good man, and righteous. **51** He

---

[173] This indicates Jewish sympathy for Jesus, which is not in Mark or Matthew.

[174] Rabbinic sources recount strange occurrences at the death of notable rabbis. Note *b. MQ* 25b: "When Rabbi Abbahu passed away, the pillars of Caesarea, his city, ran with water [as if they were shedding tears over him]. When Rabbi Yosei passed away, the gutters of Tzippori, his city, flowed with blood. When Rabbi Ya'akov passed away, the stars were visible during the day. When Rabbi Asi passed away, all the trees were uprooted in a storm. When Rabbi Ḥiyya passed away, fiery stones fell from the sky. For Rabbi Menaḥem, son of Rabbi Yosei, the faces of the statues became smooth as if they had been smoothed with a plasterer's trowel [*meḥlatzaya*]. When Rabbi Tanḥum bar Ḥiyya passed away, every statue [*andartaya*] of the king were mutilated. When Rabbi Elyashiv passed away, seventy tunnels of thieves were dug in Neharde'a. When Rav Hamnuna passed away, hail stones fell from the sky. When Rabba and Rav Yosef passed away, the tops of the bridges of the Euphrates collapsed and touched each other. When Abaye and Rava passed away, the tops of the bridges of the Tigris collapsed and touched each other. When Rabbi Mesharshiyya passed away, the palm trees became laden with thorns [*shitzei*]" (כִּי נָח נַפְשֵׁיה דְּרַבִּי אָבָהוּ אַחִיתוּ עַמּוּדֵי דְקַסְרִי מַיָא דְּרַבִּי יוֹסֵי שָׁפְעוּ מַרְזְבֵי דְצִיפּוֹרִי דְּמָא דְרַבִּי יַעֲקֹב אִתְחֲמִיאוּ כּוֹכְבֵי בִּימָמָא דְּרַבִּי אַסִי אִיעֲקַרוּ כָּל אִילָנַיָא דְרַבִּי חִיָּא נְחִיתוּ כֵּיפֵי דְנוּרָא מֵרְקִיעָא דְרַבִּי דְרַבִּי תַּנְחוּם בַּר חִיָּא אִיתְקְצַצוּ כֹּל אַנְדַּרְטַיָא דְּרַבִּי אֶלְיָשִׁיב(מְנַחֵם בְּרַבִּי יוֹסֵי אִישְׁתַּעוּ צַלְמָנַיָא וַהֲווֹ (לְמַחְלָצַיָיא) אִיחֲתָרוּ שִׁבְעִין מַחְתַּרְתָּא בִּנְהַרְדְּעָא דְרַב הַמְנוּנָא נְחִיתוּ כֵּיפֵי דְבַרְדָּא דְרַבָּה דְרַבָּה מֵרְקִיעָא וְרַב יוֹסֵף נָח נַפְשֵׁיה כֵּיפֵי נָשׁוּק דִּיקְלֵי שִׁיצֵי מְשַׁרְשָׁיָא טְעוּן דְּרַבִּי (אֲהֲדָדֵי דְּאַבַּיֵי וְרָבָא נְשׁוּק כֵּיפֵי דְּדִגְלַת אֲהֲדָדֵי כִּי נָח נַפְשֵׁיה). Note also *y. A.Z.* 3, 42c (1). See Mark 15:38; Matt 27:51–53.

[175] See Shimon Gibson, *The Final Days of Jesus: The Archaeological Evidence* (New York: HarperCollins, 2010), 127–47.

[176] The Greek ἰδού is used in imitation of the Hebrew הִנֵּה.

had not consented to the counsel and deed of them. He was from **Arimathaea,**[177] a city of the Jews, and he was also waiting for the kingdom of God. **52** This man went to Pilate, and begged for the body of Jesus. **53** And he took it down, and wrapped it in **linen,**[178] and laid it in a **tomb**[179] that was hewn in stone, in which no one had yet been laid. **54** And **that day was the preparation,**[180] and the Sabbath was just beginning. **55** And the women also, who came with him from Galilee, followed after, and saw the tomb, and how his body was laid. **56** And they returned, and prepared spices and ointments; and **rested on the Sabbath day**[181] according to the commandment.

---

[177] Probably Haramataim, ten miles east of Lod.

[178] The Patriarch Gamliel II decreed that all Jews, regardless of their station in life, were to be buried in linen shrouds; see *b. MQ* 27b: "At first taking the dead out for burial was more difficult for the relatives than the actual death [because it was customary to bury the dead in expensive shrouds, which the poor could not afford. The problem grew] to the point that relatives would sometimes abandon the corpse and run away. This lasted until Rabban Gamliel came and acted with frivolity by leaving instructions that he be taken out for burial in *linen* garments. And the people adopted this practice after him and had themselves taken out for burial in *linen* garments" (בְּרִאשׁוֹנָה הָיְתָה הוֹצָאַת הַמֵּת קָשָׁה לְקְרוֹבָיו יוֹתֵר מִמִּיתָתוֹ עַד שֶׁהָיוּ קְרוֹבָיו מַנִּיחִין אוֹתוֹ וּבוֹרְחִין עַד שֶׁבָּא רַבָּן גַּמְלִיאֵל וְנָהַג קַלּוּת רֹאשׁ בְּעַצְמוֹ וְיָצָא בִּכְלֵי **פִשְׁתָּן** וְנָהֲגוּ הָעָם אַחֲרָיו לָצֵאת בִּכְלֵי **פִשְׁתָּן**).

[179] Tombs had to be located at least fifty cubits from a city; see *m. B.B.* 2:9: "One must distance animal carcasses, and graves, and a tannery, a place where hides are processed, *fifty cubits from the city*" (מַרְחִיקִין אֶת הַנְּבֵלוֹת וְאֶת הַקְּבָרוֹת וְאֶת הַבֻּרְסָקִי **מִן הָעִיר חֲמִשִּׁים אַמָּה**). Rolling stones are described in *m. Ohal* 2:4: "The *covering stone* and the buttressing stone [of a grave] defile by contact and overshadowing but not by carriage" (הַגּוֹלֵל וְהַדּוֹפֵק מְטַמְּאִין בְּמַגָּע וּבְאֹהֶל, וְאֵינָן מְטַמְּאִין בְּמַשָּׂא); *b. Ket.* 4b; *San.* 47b: "[Mourning does not take effect] until the covering of the grave is sealed" (עַד שֶׁיִּסָּתֵם הַגּוֹלֵל). The dead had to be buried on the day of death, and the body was not to be left uncovered; note *Sifre Deut.* 221: "Whence is it derived that if one allows his dead one [i.e., one that he must bury] to remain overnight, he transgresses a negative commandment? From (ibid.) 'You shall not leave his body overnight on *eitz* [wood]'..." (מנין למלין את מתו, שעובר בלא תעשה? תלמוד לומר לֹא תָלִין נִבְלָתוֹ עַל הָעֵץ); *b. San.* 47a. Note also Josephus, *War* IV.5.2: "The Jews used to take so much care of the burial of men, that they took down those that were condemned and crucified, and buried them before the going down of the sun."

[180] I.e. the day before the feast, specifically, between the hours of 3:00 p.m. and 6:00 p.m.; see Josephus, *Ant.* XVI.6.2: "The Jews have liberty to make use of their own customs ... that they be not obliged to go before any judge on the Sabbath day, nor on *the day of the preparation* to it, after the ninth hour."

[181] J. Tabor (*The Jesus Dynasty*, 199) has argued that Passover fell on a Friday that year, thus creating (in essence) two back-to-back Sabbaths. The Gospels suggest that the body of the crucified Jesus had to be taken down from the cross and interred prior to the Sabbath; yet if Jesus had been crucified on Friday (the first day of Passover), it would already have been a high holy day, and the rush to burial would have been moot.

Resurrection and
Post-Resurrection

T he Gospel narrative of the resurrection finds a parallel in certain tales in the Hebrew Bible, in which people are said to have risen from the dead. These include the son of a widow in Zarephath (1 Kgs 17:17–24), a Shunammite woman's son (2 Kgs 4:18–37), and an Israelite man thrown into Elisha's tomb (2 Kgs 13:20–21). Rabbinic literature also considers the doctrine of resurrection to be fundamental to Judaism. The account of the resurrection of Jesus is understandably the culmination of the entire narrative of his life and mission, becoming the focal point of what would evolve as the Christian faith. His multiple appearances to his disciples in a resurrected body are emphasized, making it clear that his resurrection was not in a gnostic "phantom body," but physical and corporeal. This is why the text takes pains to point out that the resurrected Jesus breaks bread with the disciples and eats fish before them.

Importantly, many of Jesus' prior sayings relating to "end time" themes and the *parousia* are not consistent with the thrust of his present-tense kingdom of God/heaven message. Far from being the eschatological prophet of Albert Schweitzer's imagination, the proto-rabbinic Jesus was arguably concerned with the day-to-day struggles (and illnesses) of the inhabitants of the cities and towns he frequented. The assorted sayings relating to the end of the age and the coming of the Son of Man are currently found in various locations across the Gospel narratives. However, an attractive hypothesis is that in the hypothetical Hebrew *grundscrhift* they were uttered after the account of his physical resurrection. Both the end of Luke and the beginning of Acts recount that Jesus was seen alive on many occasions and for an extended period and that he taught them many things. It is reasonable to assume that among them were the eschatological messages subsequently scattered among the texts of both ANT and RCT, and ultimately scattered across the traditional Lucan narrative. These "resurrection sayings" are repositioned to this location, and though it is beyond the current work to reconstruct the exact order in which they might originally have appeared in the theorized Gospel undertext, they are presented here following Acts 1:8 and the ascension accounts of Luke 24:51–53 and Acts 1:9–11.

Scene 1:
Returning to the Tomb (RCT)

Some have speculated that the body of Jesus was stolen by his disciples, and others suggest that it was left to decay on the cross. However, the concern here is the immediate Jewish cultural, religious and textual context of the Gospel. Taking into account Matthew's narrative, some speculate that when the empty tomb is said to be discovered "very early in the morning," the theorized Hebraic subtext would have referred to the end of the Sabbath (motzei Shabbat/שבת מוצאי) and the beginning of the first day, that is, Saturday night. Since there was insufficient time to complete the anointing of the body prior to the onset of the Sabbath, the women would have hurried to return to the tomb in the darkness immediately following the Sabbath. According to Jewish tradition, the relatives and friends of a deceased person gather together for a period of seven days, to mourn and comfort one another. The Lucan narrative relates that the disciples had gathered together in Jerusalem, presumably for this purpose, when the women told them of the empty tomb.

Luke 24:1 Now **on the first day of the week, very early in the morning,**[1] **they came to the tomb,**[2] bringing the spices they had prepared. **2** And they found the stone rolled away from the tomb. **3** And they entered in, and did not find the body of the Lord Jesus. **4 And it came to pass,**[3] as they were perplexed about this, **behold,**[4] two men stood by them in shining garments. **5** And as they were afraid, and bowed down their faces to the earth, they said to them: Why do you seek the living among the dead? **6** He is not here, but has risen. Remember how he spoke to you when he was still in Galilee, **7** Saying: The **Son of Man**[5] must be delivered into the hands of sinful men, and be crucified, and the third day rise again. **8** And they remembered his words, **9** And **returned from the tomb, and told all these things to the eleven, and to all the rest.**[6] **10** It was Mary Magdalene and Joanna, and Mary the mother of James, and other women who were with them, who told these things to the apostles. **11** And their words seemed to them as folly, and they did not believe them. **12** Then Peter arose, and ran to the tomb; and stooping down, he saw the linen strips only, and departed, wondering in himself at that which had come to pass.

Scene 2:
The Road to Emmaus

The scene on the road to Emmaus is consistent with the doctrine of the Pharisees, who, unlike the Greco-Romans, strongly proclaimed the concept of the resurrection of the dead. For the Pharisees, a

---

[1] Note Matt 28:1: "toward the dawn of the first day of the week." The Greek (τῇ ἐπιφωσκούσῃ εἰς μίαν σαββάτων) is equivalent to the Hebrew "light to one of Sabbath" (אור לאחד בשבת), i.e. at the beginning of the succeeding Sabbath. It has been suggested that these events occurred not on Sunday morning, but on Saturday night, immediately following the Sabbath.

[2] Note *m. Sem.* 8:1: "We go out to the cemetery and examine the dead within three days ..." (יוצאין לבית הקברות ופוקדין על המתים עד ג׳ ימים).

[3] The Greek καὶ ἐγένετο translates the Hebrew וַיְהִי; see Luke 1:23.

[4] The Greek ἰδοὺ is used in imitation of the Hebrew הִנֵּה.

[5] The Aramaic בר אנוש ("son of man") links to Dan 7:13; authority being the theme.

[6] The disciples were gathered when Mary returned (in the fashion of mourning/ *shivah*).

central tenet was a belief in the literal resurrection of the physical body, which would be rejoined with the spirit of an individual. The appearances of the resurrected Jesus hint at this worldview, embracing a future restoration of the divine plan for the world. At such a time of redemption, the physical and ethereal realms would be realigned.[7]

Luke 24:13 And, **behold,**[8] two of them went that same day to a village called **Emmaus,**[9] which was distant from Jerusalem sixty stadia. **14** And they talked with each other of all these things that had happened. **15 And it came to pass,**[10] that, while they talked together and reasoned, Jesus himself drew near, and went with them. **16** But their eyes were held, that they should not know him. **17** And he said to them: What manner of words are these that you exchange with one another, as you walk, and are sad? **18** And the one of them, whose name was **Cleopas,**[11] answering, said to him: Are you only a stranger in Jerusalem, and have not known the things that have come to pass there in these days? **19** And he said to them: What things? And they said to him: Concerning Jesus of Nazareth, who was a mighty **prophet**[12] in deed and word before God and all the people; **20** And how the **chief priests and our rulers**[13] delivered him to be condemned to death, and crucified him. **21** But we trusted that it had been he who should have

---

[7] See Brad Young, *Paul, The Jewish Theologian: A Pharisee Among Christians, Jews, and Gentiles* (Grand Rapids: Baker Academic, 1997), 123.

[8] The Greek ἰδού is used in imitation of the Hebrew הִנֵּה.

[9] The location of Emmaus is uncertain, but the word may derive from the Hebrew חמה or חמת, referring to a hot spring.

[10] The Greek καὶ ἐγένετο translates the Hebrew וַיְהִי; see Luke 1:23.

[11] J. Tabor has theorized that a certain "Alphaeus" (the equivalent of "Clophas") possibly took the place of Joseph (Mary's husband) after he died. See Luke 6:15. While it is tempting to identify the Cleopas mentioned here with Clophas/Alphaeus, Tabor notes that they do not appear to be the same person and that their names in Greek are different. See Tabor, *The Jesus Dynasty*, 332 n.11.

[12] The term "prophet" could be used messianically, echoing Deut 18:15: "A **prophet** will the LORD your God raise up to you, from your midst, of your brethren, like me; to him you shall listen" (נָבִיא מִקִּרְבְּךָ מֵאַחֶיךָ כָּמֹנִי, יָקִים לְךָ יְהוָה אֱלֹהֶיךָ: אֵלָיו, תִּשְׁמָעוּן). See Luke 4:24; 7:16, 13:33.

[13] "Our rulers" is vague, but "chief priests" suggests the culpability of the Sadducees and their allies.

redeemed[14] Israel; and beside all this, today is the **third day**[15] since these things were done. **22** However, certain women also of our company astonished us, having been early at the tomb; **23** And when they did not find his body, they came, saying that they had also seen a vision of angels, who said that he was alive. **24** And certain of them who were with us went to the tomb, and found it just as the women had said; but they did not see him. **25** Then he said to them: O fools, and slow of heart to believe all that the prophets have spoken. **26** Was it not necessary for the messiah **to have suffered these things,**[16] and to enter into his glory? **27** And beginning from Moses and all the prophets, he expounded to them in all the scriptures the things concerning himself.

Scene 3:
The Disciples' Eyes Opened

As noted, the narrative strains to point out that Jesus' resurrection is physical, not mystical or purely spiritual, as in gnostic thought. The breaking of bread serves to emphasize the physicality of the shared experience.

Luke 24:28 And they drew near to the village, where they were going; and he appeared as though he would have gone further. **29** But they constrained him, saying: Abide with us: for it is toward evening, and the day has declined now. And he went in to abide

---

[14] See Luke 1:52, 68; note Dead Sea Scrolls 1QM 14:4–15: "Blessed is the God of Israel, who guards lovingkindness for His covenant and the appointed times of *salvation* (*yeshuah*) for the *people He redeems*. He has called those who stumble unto wondrous accomplishments ..." (... **ישועה לעם** ברוך אל ישראל השומר חסד לבריתו ותעודות **פדותו**. ויקרא כושלים לגבורות פלא).

[15] See Luke 9:22. Prophecy of rising again possibly added by later redactor. However, consider the "Gabriel Revelation": "In three days, live, I, Gabriel, command you" (לשלושת ימים חיה אני גבריאל גוזר עליך). A slain messianic leader would be resurrected within three days, and rise to heaven in a chariot.

[16] Rabbinic literature references the "pangs of the Messiah"; *b. Shab.* 118a: "Anyone who fulfills the obligation to eat three meals on Shabbat is rescued from three punishments: From the *pangs of the Messiah*, and from the judgment of Gehenna, and from the war of Gog and Magog" (כָּל הַמְקַיֵּים שָׁלֹשׁ סְעוּדוֹת בְּשַׁבָּת נִיצוֹל מִשָּׁלֹשׁ פּוּרְעָנִיּוֹת: מֵחֶבְלוֹ **שֶׁל מָשִׁיחַ**, וּמִדִּינָהּ שֶׁל גֵּיהִנָּם); see Luke 21:25.

with them. **30 And it came to pass,**[17] as he reclined with them, **he took bread, and blessed it, and broke it,**[18] and gave it to them. **31** And their eyes were opened, and they knew him; and he vanished out of their sight. **32** And they said one to another: Did not our hearts burn within us, while he talked with us on the road, and while he opened to us the scriptures? **33** And they rose up the same hour, and returned to Jerusalem, and found the eleven gathered together, and those who were with them, **34** Saying: The Lord has risen indeed, and has appeared to Simon. **35** And they told of the things that were done on the road, and how he was known to them in the breaking of bread.

Scene 4:
Jesus Appears to His Disciples

When the resurrected Jesus is depicted as eating broiled fish in front of his disciples, the text is emphasizing the Jewish insistence on bodily resurrection, as distinct from gnostic and Greek ideas of disembodied spirits.

Luke 24:36 And as they spoke of these things, Jesus himself stood in the midst of them, and said to them: Peace to you. **37** But they were terrified and frightened, and thought to themselves that they had seen a spirit. **38** And he said to them: Why are you troubled? And why do doubts arise in your hearts? **39** See, my hands and my feet, that it is I myself. **Touch me, and see; for a spirit does not have flesh and bones,**[19] as you see I have. **40** And when he had said this, he showed them his hands and his feet. **41** And while they still did not believe, for joy, and amazement, he said to them:

---

[17] The Greek καὶ ἐγένετο translates the Hebrew וַיְהִי; see Luke 1:23.

[18] The text strains to point out that Jesus had not resurrection in a mystical, spiritual or "phantom" body, but, consistent with Jewish thought, in physical form, here seen breaking and distributing bread. The Hebrew blessing for bread later became standardized: בָּרוּךְ אַתָּה יְהֹוָה אֱלֹהֵינוּ מֶלֶךְ הָעוֹלָם הַמּוֹצִיא לֶחֶם מִן הָאָרֶץ.

[19] This description counters gnostic ideas regarding resurrection, emphasizing (in Jewish fashion) the physicality of the resurrected body.

Have you here anything to eat? **42** And they gave him **a piece of a broiled fish.**[20] **43** And he took it, and ate it before them.

The Scriptures Opened

In resurrected form, Jesus is said to interpret many passages in the Hebrew Scriptures messianically, referring to himself. He emphasizes the idea of rising from the dead after three days, which may already have been a theme in Jewish messianism during the Second Temple period (as in the so-called Gabriel Revelation).

Luke 24:44 And he said to them: These are the words which I spoke to you, while I was yet with you, that all things must be fulfilled, which were written **in the law of Moses, and in the Prophets, and in the Psalms,**[21] concerning me. **45** Then he opened their mind, that they might understand the Scriptures, **46** And said to them: Thus it is written, and that the messiah was to suffer, and **to rise from the dead the third day;**[22] **47** And that repentance and forgiveness of sins should be proclaimed in his name among **all nations,**[23] beginning at Jerusalem. **48** And you are witnesses of these things. **49** And, **behold,**[24] I send the promise of my Father upon you; but remain in the city of Jerusalem, until you are clothed with **power**[25] from on high.

---

[20] This emphasizes the Jewish concept of bodily resurrection, as distinct from gnostic and Greek ideas of disembodied spirits.

[21] There is indication here that the tripartite division of the Hebrew Scriptures was already recognized in the first century, CE.

[22] See Luke 9:22. The prophecy of rising again possibly added by later redactor. However, consider the "Gabriel Revelation"; Luke 24:21 n.

[23] Only in resurrection does Jesus mention "all nations," appearing to contradict his statement the he was sent only to the "lost sheep of the house of Israel" (Matt 15:24) and his directive that the disciples should not to go into the "way of the gentiles" (Matt 10:5). This may reflect later editorializing.

[24] The Greek ἰδοὺ is used in imitation of the Hebrew הִנֵּה.

[25] Note Dead Sea Scrolls 1QHa 12:33–34: "… to perfect a way for humankind so that they may know all His works by His mighty ***power*** and the abundance of His mercies upon all the sons of His will" (להתם דרך לבני אדם למען ידעו כול מעשיו ב**כוח** גבורתו ורוב רחמיו על כול בני רצונו).

The Holy Spirit Promised (ANT)

Acts 1:3–8 (presumably also of Lucan authorship) is repositioned here, as it transitions from narrative to verbal instructions. A reconstruction of the hypothetical Hebrew grundschrift is not possible, and a good deal of editorializing is likely in evidence, as Jesus' message shifts from the land of Israel to the "end of the earth." However, the presumed post-resurrection sayings of Jesus are relevant in this section of the Lucan account.

Acts 1:3 ... he showed himself alive after his passion by many infallible proofs, being seen of them forty days, and speaking of the things pertaining to the kingdom of God. **4** And, being assembled together with them, commanded them that they should not depart from Jerusalem, but wait for the promise of the Father, which, he said, you have heard from me. **5** For John truly baptized with water; but you shall be baptized with the **Holy Spirit**[26] not many days from now. **6** When they therefore had come together, they asked him, saying: Lord, will you at this time **restore again the kingdom**[27] to Israel? **7** And he said to them: It is not for you to know the times or the seasons, which the Father has put in his own authority. **8** But you shall receive **power,**[28] after the **Holy Spirit**[29] has come upon you: and you shall be witnesses to me both in

---

[26] See Luke 1:15. Note Jub. 1:23: "And I shall create for them a *holy spirit*, and I shall purify them." Note also Dead Sea Scrolls 1QS4:21: "... cleansing from every wicked deed by a *holy spirit*" (ולטהרו ברוח קודש מכול עלילות רשעה). The term is falls out of use in the rabbinic period, though the concept is carried on in the idea of the *shekhinah*, referring to the divine presence, or "dwelling."

[27] "Restore again the kingdom" carries an eschatological tone, inconsistent with the present tense understanding of the kingdom of heaven referenced in rabbinic literature.

[28] Note Dead Sea Scrolls 1QHa 12:33–34: "... to perfect a way for humankind so that they may know all His works by His mighty *power* and the abundance of His mercies upon all the sons of His will" (להתם דרך לבני אדם למען ידעו כול מעשיו בכוח גבורתו ורוב רחמיו על כול בני רצונו).

[29] See v. 5.

Jerusalem, and in all Judea, and in Samaria, and **to the end of the earth**.[30]

Scene 5:
Blessings and Teachings (RCT)

Luke 24:50 And he led them out as far as Bethany, and he lifted up his hands, and blessed them.

An Eschatological "Beatitude"

Immediately before the ascent of Jesus into heaven, various eschatological prophecies from elsewhere in the Lucan account (wrongly transposed by the final redactor) should arguably be inserted. These deal with situations (persecution and the parousia) faced by the disciples/followers of Jesus in the years to come. The exact order of these sayings cannot be determined, as it was disrupted when the "sayings" of Jesus were collected in the anthological text referred to as ANT. However, since Jesus was said to have remained with them and taught them for forty days following his resurrection, such teachings may have been included in that part of the hypothetical Hebrew grundschrift.

Luke 6:22 Blessed are you, when men hate you, and when they separate you from their company, and reproach you, and **cast out your name as evil**,[31] for the **Son of Man's**[32] sake. **23** Rejoice in

---

[30] See Luke 24:47. Only in resurrection does Jesus mention "the end of the earth," appearing to contradict his statement the he was sent only to the "lost sheep of the house of Israel" (Matt 15:24) and his directive that the disciples should not to go into the "way of the gentiles" (Matt 10:5). This may reflect later editorializing.

[31] Note the equivalent Hebrew expression: להוציא שם רע ("to bring out an evil name"). The rabbinic term לשון הרע (*lashon hara*) was used to describe derogatory speech about a person. See Bivin and Blizzard, 156–57.

[32] The Aramaic בר אנוש ("son of man") links to Dan 7:13; authority being the theme.

that day, and leap for joy: for, **behold,**[33] your reward is great in heaven; for in the like manner their fathers did to the prophets.

Matthew 5:11–12 is added here, as a post-resurrection saying paralleling Luke 6:22–23. Jesus would not likely have been speaking of future persecutions as part of his "present tense" kingdom of God/heaven message, but this theme does befit his resurrection appearances.[34]

Matthew 5:11 Blessed are you, when men revile you, and **persecute you,**[35] and say all manner of evil against you falsely, for my sake. **12** Rejoice, and be exceedingly glad, for great is your reward in heaven; for so they persecuted the prophets who were before you.

The Fear of God (ANT)

The following reference to "those who kill the body" is relevant at this point, continuing the warning of coming persecution.

Luke 12:4 And I say to you **my friends,**[36] Do not be afraid of those who kill the body, and after that have no more that they can do.[37] **5** But I will show you whom you should fear. Fear the one, who after he has killed has power to cast into hell. Yes, I say to

---

[33] The Greek ἰδού is used in imitation of the Hebrew הִנֵּה.

[34] See Lindsey, *Jesus*, 184.

[35] This ninth Beatitude in Matthew's narrative was originally unrelated to the eighth. It was added to the others because the editor assumed that the eighth dealt with eschatological persecution: "Blessed are those who are persecuted for righteousness' sake, for theirs is the kingdom of heaven" (Matt 5:10). If, however, "kingdom of heaven" is understood as a present tense experience, there is no eschatological context to the saying.

[36] "My friends" (חברי) may involve a play on words with *Haverim* (חברים), as members of a Pharisaic *havurah* were called. This term may be behind John 15:13–15. See Luke 14:12.

[37] Better than Matt 10:28. Note 4 Macc 13:14: "Let us not fear him who thinks he kills. Great is … the danger laid up in eternal tribulation for those who transgress the commandment of God."

you, fear him. **6** Are not five **sparrows**[38] sold for two assarion, and not one of them is forgotten before God? **7** But even **the hairs of your head are all numbered.**[39] Do not fear not therefore; you are of more value than many sparrows.

Confess the Son of Man Before Men

The message here is that one may criticize the Son of Man with impunity, but one may not deny the working of the Holy Spirit in his divine call. Jesus appears not to have been interested in a "cult of personality" surrounding himself. This is a better rendering than its parallel in Mark 3:28, which deletes the notion of forgiveness for those who speak against "the Son of Man," making the message more general: "...all sins will be forgiven the sons of men, and whatever blasphemies with which they shall blaspheme." Mark may therefore represent a later recension of Jesus' words.

Luke 12:8 Also I say to you, Whoever will confess me before men, him also will the **Son of Man**[40] confess before the angels of God. **[9** But **he who denies me before men will be denied before the angels of God.]**[41] **10** And whoever will speak a word against the **Son of Man,** it will be forgiven him. But the one who has **blasphemed against the Holy Spirit will not be forgiven.**[42] **11** And **when they bring you to the synagogues, and to the**

---

[38] Note *m. Hul.* 12:5. The sparrow is the cheapest life in the market but is not outside of God's care. Shimon b. Yochai declared: "No bird perishes without God; how much less man" (*y. Shev.* 9.1.38d 22). See Matt 10:26.

[39] Note *b. B.B.* 16a: "I have created many **hairs** [*nimin*] on a person, and for **each hair** I created its own follicle" (הַרְבֵּה **נִימִין** בָּרָאתִי בְּאָדָם וְכָל **נִימָא וְנִימָא** בָּרָאתִי לָהּ גּוּמָא), בִּפְנֵי עַצְמָהּ.).

[40] Aramaic בר אנוש ("son of man") links to Dan 7:13; authority being the theme.

[41] Doublet; this is likely the original context of Luke 9:26.

[42] The parallel in Mark 3:28, appears to be an exaggerated expansion of this verse. Note *ARN* 39: "Five kinds of people *cannot be forgiven* ... Anyone whose sin publicly *desecrates God's name*" (חמשה **אין להם סליחה** ... וכל שיש בידו **חלול השם**); *m. Avot* 4:5: "whoever *profanes the name of heaven* in secret, he shall be punished in the open. Unwittingly or wittingly, it is all one in profaning the name" (כָּל **הַמְחַלֵּל שֵׁם שָׁמַיִם** בַּסֵּתֶר,, נִפְרָעִין מִמֶּנּוּ בְּגָלוּי. אֶחָד שׁוֹגֵג וְאֶחָד מֵזִיד בְּחִלּוּל הַשֵּׁם).

rulers and the authorities,[43] take no thought how or what you should answer, or what you should say; **12** For the **Holy Spirit**[44] will teach you in the same hour what you ought to say.

Tasteless Salt Is Worthless

Jesus raises a purely rhetorical question. Salt cannot become unsavory; therefore, the disciples will always preserve the world from judgment.

Luke 14:34 Salt is good;[45] but if the **salt has lost its flavor, with what will it be seasoned?**[46] **35** It is neither fit for the soil, nor for manure; but they cast it out. The one having ears to hear, let him hear.[47]

Matthew 5:13–16 is added here, as a post-resurrection teaching, paralleling Luke 14:34–35.[48]

Matthew 5:13 You are the **salt of the earth: but if the salt has lost his savor, with what shall it be salted?** It is henceforth good for nothing, but to be cast out, and to be trodden under foot of men.

---

[43] Likely a later interpolation, reflecting subsequent strife with traditional Jews.

[44] See Luke 1:15. Note Dead Sea Scrolls 1QS4:21: "… cleansing from every wicked deed by a **holy spirit**" (ולטהרו ברוח קודש מכול עלילות רשעה).

[45] Note Lev 2:13: "And every meal-offering of yours you will season with **salt**; neither shall you allow the **salt** of the covenant of your God to be lacking from your meal-offering; with all your offerings you shall offer **salt**" (וְכָל-קָרְבַּן מִנְחָתְךָ, **בַּמֶּלַח** תִּמְלָח, וְלֹא תַשְׁבִּית **מֶלַח** בְּרִית אֱלֹהֶיךָ, מֵעַל מִנְחָתֶךָ; עַל כָּל-קָרְבָּנְךָ, תַּקְרִיב **מֶלַח**).

[46] Salt is seen as delaying decay and judgment; note *m. Sof.* 15:8: "The world cannot exist without *salt*" (וא"א לעולם בלא **מלח**); *b. Bekh.* 8b: "When *salt* is spoiling, with what does one *salt* it to preserve it? Rabbi Yehoshua said to them: With the placenta of a mule. They said to him: But is there a placenta of a mule? Rabbi Yehoshua said to them: And does *salt* spoil?" (**מילחא** כי סריא במאי **מלחי** לה אמר להו בסילתא דכודניתא ומי איכא סילתא דכודנתא **ומילחא** מי סרי). See Mark 9:50.

[47] Theorized as "post-resurrection" sayings since it describes attributes relating to a time of future persecution.

[48] See Lindsey, *Jesus*, 183–84.

14 You are the light of the world. A **city [fire]**[49] that is set on a hill cannot be hid. **15** Neither do men light a **lamp,**[50] and put it under a basket, but on a lamp stand; and it gives light to all who are in the house. **16** Let your light so shine before men, that they may see your **good works,**[51] and glorify your Father in heaven.

The Sign of the Son of Man (ANT)

R. Lindsey theorized that Luke 17:22–27 belongs before Prophecy #2 in Luke 21 (21:8–11; 25–28; 34–36), conforming to the template of an incident (Jesus' address on the Mount of Olives before his ascension), followed by a teaching and two parables.[52]

---

[49] The hypothetical original Hebrew "torch/flame" (נור) may have been rendered "city" (עיר). The word "city" disrupts the "light" imagery. See *m. R.H.* 2:4: "And from which mountains would they light the torches? They would transmit the message from the Mount of Olives in Jerusalem to Sartava, and from Sartava to Gerofina, and from Gerofina to Ḥavran, and from Ḥavran to Beit Baltin. And from Beit Baltin they would not move. Rather [the one who was appointed for this task] would wave the torch back and forth and up and down, until he would see the entire Diaspora before him alight like one large bonfire" (וּמְנַיִן הָיוּ מַשִּׂיאִין מַשּׂוּאוֹת, מֵהַר הַמִּשְׁחָה לְסַרְטְבָא, וּמִסַּרְטְבָא לִגְרוֹפִינָא, וּמִגְּרוֹפִינָא לְחַוְרָן, וּמֵחַוְרָן לְבֵית בַּלְתִּין, וּמִבֵּית בַּלְתִּין לֹא זָזוּ מִשָּׁם, אֶלָּא מוֹלִיךְ וּמֵבִיא וּמַעֲלָה וּמוֹרִיד עַד שֶׁהָיָה רוֹאֶה כָל הַגּוֹלָה לְפָנָיו כְּמְדוּרַת הָאֵשׁ).

[50] Note *Sifre Num.* 93: "What was Moses like at that time? Like a **lamp placed upon a menorah**, from which many lamps are lighted without the first losing any of its light. So, the wisdom of Moses was in no way diminished thereby" (למה משה דומה באותה שעה?—**לנר שמונח על גבי מנורה**, ודלקו ממנו נרות הרבה ולא חסר אורו כלום; כך לא היתה חכמתו של משה חסרה כלום). The Torah ("wisdom of Moses") is here equated with light. Note *Mid. Tehillim,* 113: "If a man has a dwelling, where does he set a lamp? … In the middle of the dining room." See Luke 11:33; 8:16; Mark 4:21; John 8:12.

[51] Jesus, like the early *hasidim,* stressed good deeds more than knowledge. Note *m. Avot* 1:17: "Study is not the most important thing, but actions" (וְלֹא הַמִּדְרָשׁ הוּא הָעִקָּר, אֶלָּא הַמַּעֲשֶׂה); *m. Avot* 3:12: "Rabbi Hanina ben Dosa said: anyone whose fear of sin precedes his wisdom, his wisdom is enduring, but anyone whose wisdom precedes his fear of sin, his wisdom is not enduring. He [also] used to say: anyone whose deeds exceed his wisdom, his wisdom is enduring, but anyone whose wisdom exceeds his deeds, his wisdom is not enduring" (רַבִּי חֲנִינָא בֶן דּוֹסָא אוֹמֵר, כָּל שֶׁיִּרְאַת חֶטְאוֹ קוֹדֶמֶת לְחָכְמָתוֹ, חָכְמָתוֹ מִתְקַיֶּמֶת. וְכָל שֶׁחָכְמָתוֹ קוֹדֶמֶת לְיִרְאַת חֶטְאוֹ, אֵין חָכְמָתוֹ מִתְקַיֶּמֶת. הוּא הָיָה אוֹמֵר, כָּל שֶׁמַּעֲשָׂיו מְרֻבִּין מֵחָכְמָתוֹ, חָכְמָתוֹ מִתְקַיֶּמֶת. וְכָל שֶׁחָכְמָתוֹ מְרֻבָּה מִמַּעֲשָׂיו, אֵין חָכְמָתוֹ מִתְקַיֶּמֶת); *Test. Naph.* 8:4: "God shall be glorified among the Gentiles through you, but through him who does not do what is good ... he is dishonored"; *Deut. R.* 3: "When the Israelites do God's will, he Name is exalted in the world. When they do not ... his Name is profaned." In a parable, Shimon b. Shetah buys a donkey from an Ishmaelite, but returns a precious stone hanging from its neck. The Ishmaelite says, "Blessed be the God of Shimon b. Shetah!"

[52] See Lindsey, *Jesus,* 188.

Luke 17:22 Then he said to the disciples: The days will come, when you will desire to see one of the days of the **Son of Man,**[53] and you will not see it. **23** And they will say to you: **behold,** here; or, **behold,**[54] there. Do not go after them, or follow them. **24** For as the **lightning,**[55] that flashes from **one end of the heavens, shines to the other**[56] end of the heavens; so also will the **Son of Man**[57] be in his day. [**25 But first must he suffer many things, and be rejected of this generation.**][58]

Parable 1: As in the Days of Noah

In a theoretical Hebraic story unit, a teaching would be followed by two parables. Parable # 1 relates to Noah.

Luke 17:26 And as it was in the days of Noah, so will it be also in the days of the **Son of Man.**[59] **27** They ate, they drank, they married wives, they were given in marriage, until the day that Noah entered into the ark, and the flood came, and destroyed them all.

---

[53] Aramaic בר אנוש ("son of man") links to Dan 7:13; authority being the theme.

[54] The Greek ἰδού is used in imitation of the Hebrew הִנֵּה.

[55] The messiah is often described as coming on a cloud with lightning. Note *Apoc. Bar.* 72:1–2: "Hear now also regarding the bright *lightning* which is to come at the consummation after these black (waters): this is the word. After the signs have come, of which you were told before, when the nations become turbulent, and the time of My Messiah is come …"

[56] "From one end … to the other" is an explanation for a gentile audience (vs. "from the east and west" in Matt 8:11).

[57] The Aramaic בר אנוש ("son of man") links to Dan 7:13; authority being the theme.

[58] v. 25 is likely an editorial gloss (by the redactor of ANT) to place this group of post-resurrection sayings in an earlier context.

[59] Aramaic בר אנוש ("son of man") links to Dan 7:13; authority being the theme.

Parable 2: As in the Days of Lot

Parable # 2 relates to Lot leaving Sodom.

Luke 17:28 Likewise also as it was in the days of Lot; they ate, they drank, they bought, they sold, they planted, they built; **29** But the same day that Lot went out of Sodom it rained fire and brimstone from heaven, and destroyed them all. **30** Even so will it be in the day when the **Son of Man**[60] is revealed.

The Coming of the Son of Man

Compare and contrast the directives that a person on the roof should not come down and that one in the field should not return with Luke 21:21, where Jesus declares: "Let those who are in Judea flee to the mountains."

Luke 17:31 In that day, the one who will be upon the housetop, and his goods in the house, let him not come down to take them away. And the one who is in the field, let him likewise not return. **32** Remember Lot's wife. **33 Whoever may seek to save his life will lose it; and whoever will lose his life will preserve it.**[61] **34** I tell you, in that night there will be **two in one bed; the one will be**

---

[60] Aramaic בר אנוש ("son of man") links to Dan 7:13; authority being the theme.

[61] See Luke 9:24—a "doublet." This is likely the original context of the saying, which suits a time of persecution alluded to in the "post-resurrection" sayings. Note *b. Tam.* 32a (attributed to Alexander of Macedon): "He said to them: What must a man do and thereby ensure that he will live? They said to him: Such a man must figuratively *kill himself* [by living moderately]. Alexander further inquired: What must a man do and ensure that he will die? They said to him: Such a man must *keep himself alive* [i.e., lead an extravagant and indulgent life]" (אמר להן מה יעביד איניש ויחיה אמרו ליה **ימית עצמו** מה יעביד **אינייש וימות יחיה את עצמו**).

taken,[62] and the other will be left.[63] 35 Two women will be grinding together; the one will be taken,[64] and the other left. 36 Two will be in the field; the one will be taken, and the other left.[65] 37 And they answered and said to him: Where, Lord? And he said to them: Where the **body[66]** is, there will the vultures be gathered together.[67]

Prophecy #2: The Signs of the Times and the End of the Age (RCT)

The second of three prophetic themes ultimately redacted into Luke 21 (the coming of the Son of Man; 21:8–11; 25–28) has been moved to this location. The general teaching of Jesus should be considered as "present tense." Consequently, eschatological statements regarding the end of the age should most likely also be seen as post-resurrection sayings.[68]

---

[62] The Greek παραλημφθήσεται ("will be taken") translates the Hebrew יכרת ("will be cut off").

[63] See Ps 37:9: "For evildoers **shall be cut off**; but those that wait for the LORD, they shall **inherit the land**" (כִּי-מְרֵעִים יִכָּרֵתוּן וְקֹוֵי יְהוָה הֵמָּה יִירְשׁוּ-אָרֶץ); see also vv. 11, 20, 22, 28, 34. Jesus refers to this psalm when he speaks of one being "taken" and one remaining. The wicked are taken out, not the righteous, who will "inherit the earth." The Qumranic *Pesher* on this verse declares that the "earth" is the "earth" of eschatology, involving the physical retaking of the temple. Note 4Q171 f1_2ii:5–8: "'But those who trust in the Lord are the ones who will **inherit the earth'** (Psalm 37:9b). This refers to the company of his chosen, those who do his will. 'Very soon there will be no wicked man; look where he was, he's not there' (Psalm 37:10). This refers to all of the wicked at the end of the forty years. When they are completed, **there will no longer be any wicked person on the earth**" (וקואי יהוה המה **ירשו ארץ**. פשרו המה עדת בחירו עושי רצונו. ועוד מעט ואין רשע ואתבוננה על מקומו ואיננו. פשרו על כול הרשעה לסוף ארבעים השנה אשר יתמו **ולוא ימצא בארץ כול איש רשע**). For Jesus the process is arguably spiritual. See Matt 24:40–41.

[64] παραλημφθήσεται = יכרת ("will be cut off").

[65] Matt 24:40–41 reads better: "Then shall two be in the field; one shall be taken, and the other left. Two women shall be grinding at the mill; one shall be taken, and the other left." The context involves the Roman practice of impressing people into compulsory government service (*angaria*).

[66] Whereas Luke reads σῶμα ("body"), Matt (24:28) reads πτῶμα ("carcass") since vultures eat carrion.

[67] See Job 39:30: "Her young ones also suck up blood; and where the *slain* are, there is she" (וְאֶפְרֹחָו יְעַלְעוּ-דָם; וּבַאֲשֶׁר חֲלָלִים שָׁם הוּא). In this context the text suggests that when Jesus appears, the believers will be in his presence. This section is hypothetically followed by Luke 21:8–11; 21:25–28.

[68] See Lindsey, *Jesus*, 155.

Luke 21:8 And he said: Take heed that you are not deceived; for **many will come in my name, saying, I am the one;**[69] and the time is drawing near. Do not go after them. **9** But when you hear of wars and commotions, do not be terrified. For these things must first come to pass; but the end is not yet. **10** Then he said to them: **Nation will rise against nation,**[70] and kingdom against kingdom. **11** And great earthquakes will be in various places, and famines, and pestilences; and there will be fearful sights and **great signs**[71] from heaven.

---

[69] Josephus speaks of many false prophets at the time of the siege of Jerusalem, who tried to delude the people; *War* VI. 5.2. Note also *Apoc. Bar.* 48:34: "And there shall be many rumors and tidings not a few, And the doing of phantasms shall be manifest, And promises not a few be recounted, Some of the idle …" See Mark 13:8; 2 Thes 2:3–4; Rev 13:8. From such references it is clear that the idea of an "Antichrist" is both Jewish, and proto-Christian. Note *Ascension of Isa.* 4:2–16, where the Antichrist is Belial incarnated, perpetrating matricide, like Nero.

[70] See Dan 7:27; note Qumran fragment 4Q ps Dan. A (4Q246 f1i:5–f1ii:6): *"Amid great signs, tribulation is coming upon the land* … After much killing and slaughter, a prince of nations will arise … the king of Assyria and Egypt … he will be ruler over the land … will be subject to him and all will obey him. Also his son will be called The Great, and be designated by his name. He will be called the *Son of God*, they will call him the *son of the Most High*. But like the meteors that you saw in your vision, so will be their kingdom. They will reign only a few years over the land, while *people tramples people and nation tramples nation*. Until the people of God arise; then all will have rest from warfare. *Their kingdom will be an eternal kingdom*, and all their paths will be righteous. They will judge the land justly, and all nations will make peace. Warfare will cease from the land" (מלך … במדינתא רב ונחשירין … **ארעא על תתא עקה רברבין**). אתור ומצרין … רב להוה על ארעא … יעבדון וכלא ישמשון … רבא יתקרא ובשמה יתכנה. **אל די ברה** יתאמר **ובר עליון** יקרונה. כזיקיא די חזותא כן מלכותהן תהוה. שנין ימלכון על ארעא וכלא **ידשון עם לעם ידוש ומדינה למדינה.** עד יקום עם אל וכלא ינוח מן חרב. **מלכותה מלכות עלם** וכל ארחתה בקשוט. ידין (ארעא בקשט וכלא יעבד שלם. חרב מן ארעא יסף). Note *Gen. R.* 42:4: "When you see *kingdoms fighting against one another* look and expect the foot of the Messiah" (מַלְכֻיּוֹת רָאִיתָ אִם מְשִׁיחַ שֶׁל לְרַגְלוֹ צַפֵּה בָּאֵלוּ אֵלוּ מִתְגָּרוֹת); Jub. 23:13: "For calamity follows calamity, and wound on wound, and *tribulation on tribulation*, and evil tidings on evil tidings, and illness on illness, and all evil judgments such as these, one with another, illness and overthrow, and snow and frost and ice, and fever, and chills, and torpor, and famine, and death, and sword, and captivity, and all kinds of calamities and pains" (על פגע הוה על הוה כי) פגע **צרה על צרה** רעה על רעה מחלה על מחלה וכל שפטים רעים כאלה יחד יבואו: מדוה וכאב בטן וברד (וקרח ושלג וכפור ומכאובים וקפאון ומות וחרב ושבי וכל עונש וצוקה).

[71] See Josephus, *War* VI 288–310.

The Coming of the Son of Man

Luke 21:25–28 is presumed to belong here, continuing the theme of coming "signs."[72]

Luke 21:25 And there will be **signs in the sun, and in the moon, and in the stars;**[73] and upon the earth **distress of nations,**[74] with perplexity; the sea and the waves roaring; **26** Men's **hearts failing them for fear,**[75] and expectation of that which is coming on the

---

[72] See Lindsey, *Jesus*, 155.

[73] Note *b. Sanh.* 91b: "It is written (Isa 24:23): 'Then **the moon shall be confounded and the sun ashamed**, when the Lord of hosts will reign.' And it is written (Isa 30:26): 'And the light of the moon shall be as the light of the sun, and the light of the sun shall be sevenfold, as the light of seven days.' This is not difficult. The verse here, is written with regard to **the days of the Messiah**; the verse there is written with regard to **the World-to-Come**" (כתיב **וחפרה הלבנה ובושה החמה** כי מלך ה' צבאות וכתיב והיה אור הלבנה כאור). Note also **ב**"**לעוה** כאן **המשיח** **לימות** כאן קשיא לא הימים שבעת כאור שבעתים יהיה החמה ואור (החמה). En 80:4–6: "And the **moon** shall alter her order, And not appear at her time. And in those days the **sun** shall be seen and he shall journey in the evening on the extremity of the great chariot in the west, And shall shine more brightly than accords with the order of light. And many chiefs of the **stars** shall transgress the order (prescribed). And these shall alter their orbits and tasks, And not appear at the seasons prescribed to them …"; 4 Esd 5:4: "… the **sun** shall suddenly shine again in the night, and the **moon** thrice in the day."

[74] Rabbinic literature references the "pangs of the Messiah"; *b. Shab.* 118a: "Anyone who fulfills the obligation to eat three meals on Shabbat is rescued from three punishments: From the **pangs of the Messiah**, and from the judgment of Gehenna, and from the war of Gog and Magog" (מַחְבְּלוֹ מִשָּׁלֹשׁ פּוּרְעָנִיּוֹת: נִיצּוֹל בְּשַׁבָּת סְעוּדוֹת שָׁלֹשׁ הַמְקַיֵּים כָּל גֵּיהִנָּם שֶׁל וּמִדִּינָהּ **מָשִׁיחַ** שֶׁל); *Pes.* 118a: "… the exodus from Egypt, the splitting of the Red Sea, the giving of the Torah, the resurrection of the dead, and the pangs of the Messiah" (**מָשִׁיחַ** שֶׁל **וְחֶבְלוֹ** הַמֵּתִים, וּתְחִיַּית תּוֹרָה, וּמַתַּן סוּף, יַם קְרִיעַת מִצְרַיִם, יְצִיאַת); *m. Sot.* 9:15: "**In the times of the approach of the Messiah**, impudence will increase and high costs will pile up. Although the vine shall bring forth its fruit, wine will nevertheless be expensive. And the monarchy shall turn to heresy, and there will be no one to give reproof about this. The meeting place of the Sages will become a place of promiscuity, and the Galilee shall be destroyed, and the Gavlan will be desolate, and the men of the border shall go round from city to city to seek charity, but they will find no mercy. And the wisdom of scribes will putrefy, and people who fear sin will be held in disgust, and the truth will be absent" (תּוֹכֵחָה, וְאֵין לְמִינוּת, תֵּהָפֵךְ וְהַמַּלְכוּת בְּיֹקֶר, וְהַיַּין פְּרִיָהּ תִּתֵּן הַגֶּפֶן יַאֲמִיר, וְיֹקֶר יִסְגֵּא, חֲצָפָּא **מְשִׁיחָא** בְּעִקְבוֹת סוֹפְרִים וְחָכְמַת יֵחוֹנֵנּוּ, וְלֹא לָעִיר מֵעִיר יְסוֹבְבוּ הַגְּבוּל וְאַנְשֵׁי יִשֹּׁם, וְהַגָּבְלָן יֶחֱרַב, וְהַגָּלִיל לְזָנוּת, יִהְיֶה וַעַד בֵּית נֶעְדֶּרֶת תְּהֵא וְהָאֱמֶת יִמָּאֵסוּ, חֵטְא וְיִרְאֵי תִּסְרַח,). See Luke 24:26, above.

[75] 4 Ezra 5:1: "Behold, the days come when the inhabitants of the earth shall be seized with **great panic** and the way of truth shall be hidden, and the land of faith be barren. And iniquity shall be increased above that which you yourself now see or that you have heard of long ago."

earth. For the **powers of the heavens**[76] will be shaken. **27** And then they will see the **Son of Man**[77] **coming in a cloud**[78] with power and great glory. **28** And when these things begin to come to pass, then look up, and lift up your heads; for your redemption draws near.

The Importance of Watching

Luke 21:34–36 presumably belong here, as these verses deal with eschatological themes and the coming of the Son of Man.[79] They frame a teaching, followed by two parables, echoing themes of watching and waiting.

Luke 21:34 And take heed to yourselves, lest at any time your hearts become burdened with dissipation, and drunkenness, and the cares of this life, so **that day might come upon you unawares.**[80] **35** For as a snare it will come upon all of them who dwell on the face of the whole earth. **36** Watch therefore, and pray always, that you may have the strength to escape all these things that are about to come to pass, and to stand before the **Son of Man.**

Parable 1: The Faithful Servant and the Evil Servant

Luke 12:35 Let your waist be girded about, and your lamps burning; **36** and you yourselves like to men waiting for their

---

[76] The Greek δυνάμεις τῶν οὐρανῶν translates the Hebrew צבא השמים/"armies of heaven."

[77] The Aramaic בר אנוש ("son of man") links to Dan 7:13; authority being the theme.

[78] See *b. Sanh.* 98a: "If the Jewish people merit redemption, the Messiah will come *with the clouds of heaven*. If they do not merit redemption, the Messiah will come lowly and riding upon a donkey" (זכו **עם ענני שמיא** לא זכו עני רוכב על חמור); 4 Esd 13:3: "And I beheld, and, lo, that man waxed strong with the thousands of heaven ..."

[79] See Lindsey, *Jesus*, 155.

[80] There is a tradition that Elijah or the Messiah will come on the fourteenth of Nisan, but not on a Sabbath or holiday; see *y. Pes.* 3.6, 30b (39); *b. Pes.* 13a: "The Jewish people have already been assured that *Elijah will come neither on a Friday nor on the eve of a Festival*, due to the exertion involved preparing for the upcoming holy day" (כְּבָר מוּבְטָח לָהֶן לְיִשְׂרָאֵל שֶׁאֵין אֵלִיָּהוּ בָּא לֹא בְּעַרְבֵי שַׁבָּתוֹת וְלֹא בְּעַרְבֵי יָמִים טוֹבִים, מִפְּנֵי הַטּוֹרַח).

master, when he returns from the wedding; that when he comes and knocks, they may open to him immediately. **37 Blessed are those servants, whom the master, when he comes, shall find watching. Truly**[81] I say to you, that he will gird himself, and make them recline, and will come forth and serve them. **38** And if he comes in the second watch, or in the third watch, and finds them so, blessed are those servants. **39** And know this, that if the master of the house had known what hour the thief would come, he would have watched, and not have allowed his house to be invaded. **40** Be you therefore ready also; **for the Son of Man comes at an hour you do not expect.**[82]   **41** Then Peter said to him: Lord, do you speak this parable to us, or also to all? **42** And the Lord said: Who then is that faithful and wise manager, whom his master will make ruler over his household, to give them their portion of food in due season? **43** Blessed is that servant, whom his master, when he comes, shall find him so doing. **44** Of a truth I say to you, that he will set him over all his possessions. **45** But if that servant says in his heart: My master delays his coming; and begins to beat the men-servants and maid-servants, and to eat and drink, and to become drunk; **46** The master of that servant will come in a day he does to expect, and at an hour when he is not aware, and will cut him in two, and will appoint his portion with the unbelievers. **47** And that servant, who knew his master's will, and did not prepare himself, nor did according to his will, shall be beaten with many lashes. **48** But **the one who did not know,**[83] and did commit things worthy of lashes, will be beaten with few. For to whomever much is given, much shall be required: and to whom much has been committed, the more they will ask of him.

---

81 See Luke 4:24. The word "Amen" (Ἀμὴν = אמן) would conclude a statement, not begin it. Jesus patterns his use of "Amen" after Jer 28:5–7.

82 Note *b. San.* 97a: "There are three matters that come only by means of diversion of attention, and these are they: The Messiah, a lost item, and a scorpion" ('ג באין בהיסח הדעת אלו הן משיח מציאה ועקרב).

83 Note *y. Sot.* 15.10 p. 320: "It is better to sin unknowingly than to sin willfully."

Parable 2: The Wise and Foolish Virgins

The parable of the waiting virgins has been imported from Matthew's Gospel and matches the parable of the faithful and evil servants waiting for the return of their master. This preserves the template of an incident, a teaching, and two parables.[84]

Matthew 25:1 Then shall the kingdom of heaven be likened to ten virgins, who took their lamps, and went forth to meet the bridegroom. **2** And five of them were wise, and five were foolish. **3** Those who were foolish took their lamps, and took no oil with them: **4** But the wise took oil in their vessels with their lamps. **5** While the bridegroom delayed, they all slumbered and slept. **6** And at midnight there was a cry, **Behold, the bridegroom**[85] comes; go out to meet him. **7** Then all those virgins arose, and trimmed their lamps. **8** And the foolish said to the wise, Give us of your oil; for our lamps have gone out. **9** But the wise answered, saying: Not so; lest there not be enough for us and you: but go rather to those who sell, and buy for yourselves. **10** And as they went to buy, the bridegroom came; and those who were ready went in with him to the marriage: and the door was shut. **11** Afterward, the other virgins also came, saying: Lord, Lord, open to us. **12** But he answered and said: **Truly, I say to you,**[86] I do not know you. **13** Watch therefore, for you know neither the day nor the hour in which the **Son of Man**[87] comes.

---

[84] See Lindsey, *Jesus*, 193.

[85] Note *PRE* 41: "And Moses went forth and came to the camp of the Israelites, and he aroused the Israelites from their sleep, saying to them: Arise ye from your sleep, for behold, your God desires to give the Torah to you. Already ***the bridegroom*** wishes to lead the bride and to enter the bridal chamber" (ויצא משה ובא למחנה ישראל והיה מעורר ישראל משינתם ואמ' להם עימדו משינתכם שהרי אלהיכם מבקש ליתן לכם את התורה, כבר **החתן** מבקש להביא את הכלה להכניס לחופה).

[86] "Amen"/"assuredly" (אמן) added after a strong statement. Jer 28:6 - כֵּן ,אָמֵן, יַעֲשֶׂה יְהוָה יָקֶם יְהוָה אֶת-דְּבָרֶיךָ אֲשֶׁר נִבֵּאתָ ("Amen! The Lord do so; the Lord perform your words which you have prophesied …"). See Luke 4:24; Matt 5:18.

[87] The Aramaic בר אנוש ("son of man") links to Dan 7:13, authority being the theme. The Greek υἱὸν τοῦ ἀνθρώπου is awkward.

Prophecy #3: Expect Persecution (RCT)

The last of three prophetic themes ultimately redacted into Luke 21 (the coming persecution; 21:12–19) has been moved to this location.[88]

Luke 21:12 But before all these things, they will lay their hands on you, and persecute you, **delivering you up to the synagogues,**[89] and into prisons, being brought before kings and rulers for my name's sake. **13** And it will result to you for a testimony. **14** Settle therefore in your hearts, not to premeditate what you will answer: **15** For I will give you a mouth and wisdom, which all your adversaries will not be able to resist, nor be able to reply. **16** And you will be betrayed both by parents, and brothers, and relatives, and friends; and some of you they will put to death. **17** And you will be hated by all men for my name's sake. **18** But not a hair of your head will perish. **19** By your patient endurance you will gain your souls.

Scene 6:
Jesus Ascends

The final verses of Luke, recounting that the disciples returned to Jerusalem and the temple, connect the narrative to the book of Acts (1:12). Luke-Acts (or at least the first half of Acts) should therefore be viewed as a single narrative.

Luke 24:51 And it came to pass,[90] while he blessed them, that he was separated from them, and carried up into heaven. **52** And **they**

---

[88] See Lindsey, *Jesus*, 177.

[89] This likely reflects a later time of animosity between early Christianity and rabbinic Judaism. It may represent a subsequent editorial gloss.

[90] The Greek καὶ ἐγένετο translates the Hebrew וַיְהִי; see Luke 1:23.

worshipped him,[91] and **returned to Jerusalem**[92] with great joy; **53** And were continually in the temple, praising and blessing God. Amen.

Jesus Ascends to Heaven

Acts 1:9 And when he had spoken these things, while they beheld, he was taken up; and a cloud received him out of their sight. **10** And while they looked steadfastly toward heaven as he went up, **behold,**[93] two men stood by them in white apparel; **11** Who also said: You men of Galilee, why do you stand gazing up into heaven? This same Jesus, who has been taken up from you into heaven, shall also come in like manner as you have seen him go into heaven.

Afterword

The reconstruction of the book of Luke presented here is hardly intended as a fully authoritative work on the subject. It is designed to stimulate further thought and serious research on approaches that have long been ignored by the bulk of New Testament scholarship. Not only does this modest volume serve as a resource for those investigating parallels with rabbinic literature and Second Temple Judaism, but it provides ample evidence of Lucan priority and Mark having expanded on individual verses found in Luke. The idea that the synoptic Gospels ultimately rest, not merely on oral traditions, but a Hebraic undertext/*grundschrift* should no longer be dismissed out of hand and is worthy of due consideration.

Moreover, the reordering of the text, while purely hypothetical, represents a potentially important contribution to understanding the chronological sequence of Jesus' words and

---

[91] This is the only reference in Luke that the disciples actually worshipped Jesus. Perhaps a later addition.

[92] Connect to Acts 1:12.

[93] The Greek ἰδοὺ is used in imitation of the Hebrew הִנֵּה.

deeds. The result places Jesus (*Yeshua m'Nazeret*) within the context of the Second Jewish Commonwealth, arguably as never before. We see Jesus, not as an opponent of Jewish/rabbinic tradition, not as a radical revisionist about Jewish law or religious precepts, but as a fervent pietist, thoroughly in line with early, pre-rabbinic approaches to faith, practice, and spirituality. This is not a Jesus outside of Judaism or in conflict with Judaism; this is Jesus *within* Judaism. Hopefully, we have at least made a beginning of the formidable task of illuminating the Sage of Galilee.

Bibliography

Barag, Dan and Flusser, David. "The Ossuary of Yehohanah Granddaughter of the High Priest Theophilus," *Israel Exploration Journal* 36, no. 1–2 (1986): 39–44.

Bivin, David and Blizzard, Roy. *Understanding the Difficult Words of Jesus*. Arcadia, CA: Makor Foundation, 1983.

Bivin, David and Tilton, Joshua. "Widow's Son in Nain," *Jerusalem Perspective*, May 19, 2022: https://www.jerusalemperspective.com/13167/.

Buth, Randall. "Hebrew Poetic Tenses and the Magnificat," *Journal for the Study of the New Testament*, 21 (1984): 67–83.

Buth, Randall and Notley, R. Steven, eds. *The Language Environment of First Century Judaea*. Leiden: Brill, 2014.

Charles, Robert Henry, ed. *The Apocrypha and Pseudepigrapha of the Old Testament*, I. London: Oxford University Press, 1913.

Charlesworth, James H., ed. *Jesus and the Dead Sea Scrolls*. New York: Doubleday, 1992.

———. *The Old Testament Pseudepigrapha*, vols. 1–2. Garden City, NY: Doubleday, 1983–1985.

Crossan, John Dominic. *The Historical Jesus: The Life of a Mediterranean Jewish Peasant*. T. & T. Clark, 1993.

———. *Jesus: A Revolutionary Biography*. HarperOne, 2009.

Daube, David. *The New Testament and Rabbinic Judaism*. London: Althlone Press, 1956.

Davies, W. D. *The Setting for the Sermon on the Mount*. London: Cambridge University Press, 1977.

Edersheim, Alfred. *The Life and Times of Jesus the Messiah*, vols. 1–2. London: Longmans, Green & Co., 1912.

Farmer, William. R. *The Synoptic Problem*. New York: Macmillan, 1964.

Fitzmeyer, James A. T*he Gospel According to Luke: Introduction, Translation and Notes*, vols. 1–2. Garden City, NY: Doubleday, 1981–1985.

Flusser, David. *Jewish Sources in Early Christianity*. New York: Adama Books, 1987.

———. "Jesus and Judaism." In *Eusebius, Christianity and Judaism,* 80–109. H. W. Attridge and G. Hata, eds. Detroit: Wayne State University Press, 1992.

———. *Judaism and the Origins of Christianity.* Jerusalem: Magnes Press, 1988.

———. 1982 ,ספרית הפועלים :ישראל *.יהדות ומקורות הנצרות*

Gabriel, Richard A. *Gods of Our Fathers: The Memory of Egypt in Judaism and Christianity.* Westport, CT: Greenwood Press, 2002.

Garber, Zev and Hanson, Kenneth. *Judaism and Jesus*. Newcastle Upon Tyne: Cambridge Scholars, 2020.

Gibson, Shimon, *The Cave of John the Baptist: The First Archaeological Evidence of the Truth of the Gospel Story.* London: Century, 2004.

———. *The Final Days of Jesus: The Archaeological Evidence.* New York: HarperCollins, 2010.

Grinz, Jehoshua. "Hebrew as the Spoken and Written Language of the Second Temple." *JBL* 79 (1960): 32ff.

Haupt, Paul. "Magnificat and Benedictus." *American Journal of Philology* 40 1 (1919): 64–75.

Hogeterp, Albert L. A. and Denaux, Adelbert. *Semitisms in Luke's Greek: A Descriptive Analysis of Lexical and Syntactical Domains of Semitic Language Influence in Luke's Gospel.* Tübingen: Mohr Siebeck, 2018.

Jastrow, Marcus. *A Dictionary of the Targumim, the Talmud Babli and Yerushalmi, and the Midrashic Literature*, vols. 1–2. New York: Pardes, 1950.

Jeremias, Joachim. *Jerusalem in the Time of Jesus: An Investigation in Economic and Social Conditions during the New Testament Period*. Philadelphia: Fortress Press, 1989.

Klausner, Joseph. *Jesus of Nazareth*. New York: Menorah, 1979.

Knohl, Israel. *Messiahs and Resurrection in 'The Gabriel Revelation.'* London: Continuum, 2009.

———. *The Parables of Jesus*. New York: C. Scribner's Sons, 1963.

Lapide, Pinchas. "The Missing Hebrew Gospel." *Christian News From Israel*, XXIV (1974): 167–70.

Levine, Amy-Jill and Marc Zvi Brettler, eds. *The Jewish Annotated New Testament: New Revised Standard Version Bible Translation*. New York: Oxford University Press, 2011.

Lightfoot, John. *A Commentary of the New Testament from the Talmud and Hebraica*, vol. 3, Luke - John. Peabody, MA: Codex Hendrickson, 1989.

Lindsey, Robert. *A Hebrew Translation of the Gospel of Mark*. Jerusalem: Dugith Publishers, 1973.

———. "A Modified Two-Document Theory of the Synoptic Dependence and Interdependence." *Novum Testamentum* 6 (1963): 239–63.

———. ed. *Greek Concordance to the Synoptic Gospels*, vols. 1–3. Jerusalem: Dugith Publishers, 1985–1989.

———. *Jesus Rabbi & Lord: the Hebrew Story of Jesus Behind our Gospel*. Oak Creek, WI: Cornerstone, 1989.

Marshall, I. Howard. *Commentary on Luke: A Commentary on the Greek Text*. Grand Rapids: Eerdmans, 1978.

Meier, John P. *A Marginal Jew: Rethinking the Historical Jesus, Vol. 5*. New Haven, CT: Yale University Press, 2009.

Milik, J. T. *The Books of Enoch*. Oxford: Clarendon Press, 1976.

Montefiore, C. G. *Rabbinic Literature and Gospel Teachings.* New York: KTAV, 1970.

Neumann, James N. "Thy Will Be Done: Jesus's Passion in the Lord's Prayer." *JBL* 138, 1 (2019): 161–82.

Neusner, Jacob, *The Study of Ancient Judaism*, vols. 1–2. New York: KTAV, 1981.

Notley, R. S. "The Kingdom of Heaven Forcefully Advances." In *The Interpretation of Scripture in Early Judaism and Christianity: Studies in Language and Tradition,* 279–311. C. A. Evans, ed. Sheffield: Sheffield Academic Press, 2000.

Notley, R. S., M. Turnage and B. Becker, eds. *Jesus' Last Week: Jerusalem Studies in the Synoptic Gospels,* vol. 1. Leiden: Brill, 2006.

Notley, Steven and Safrai, Zeev. *Parables of the Sages: Jewish Wisdom from Jesus to Rav Ashi.* Jerusalem: Carta, 2013.

Safrai, Chana and Safrai, Zeev. "Rabbinic Holy Men." In *Saints and Role Models in Judaism and Christianity,* 59–78. Edited by Marcel J. H. M. Poorthuis and Joshua J. Schwarts. Leiden: Brill, 2004.

Safrai, Shmuel, Menahem Stern, David Flusser, and W. C. van Unnik, eds. *The Jewish People in the First Century*, vols. 1–4. Amsterdam: Van Gorcum, 1974–1987.

Safrai, Shmuel. "Ḥasidim and Men of Deeds." *Zion* 50 (1985): 133–54 (Heb.).

———. "Jesus as a Hasid." *Proceedings of the Tenth World Congress of Jewish Studies.* Jerusalem: World Congress of Jewish Studies, 1990.

———. "Literary Languages in the Time of Jesus." *Jerusalem Perspective* 31 (March–April 1991): 3–8.

———. "Mishnat Ḥasidim in the Literature of the Tannaim." In *In Times of Temple and Mishnah: Studies in Jewish History* (Heb.), 2:501–17. Jerusalem: Magnes, 1996.

———. "The Pharisees and the Ḥasidim (Heb.)." *Sidic* 10 (1977): 12–16.

————. "The Teaching of Pietists in Mishnaic Literature." *JJS* 16 (1965): 27–31.

_____. "Which is the Straight Way that a Man Should Choose for Himself? (*M Ab 2.1*)." In *Judaism in the Second Temple Period* 2, 232–47. Grand Rapids: Eerdmans, 2009.

Safrai, Shmuel and Menahem Stern, eds. *The Jewish People in the First Century*, vols. 1–2. Amsterdam: Brill, 1976.

Sanders, E. P. *Jesus and Judaism.* London: SCM Press, 1985.

Schonfield, Hugh H. *The Original New Testament.* San Francisco: Harper & Row, 1985.

Schürer, Emil. *History of the Jewish People in the Age of Jesus (175 B.C.–A.D. 135),* vols. 1–4, G. Vermes and F. Millar, eds. Edinburgh: T & T Clark, 1973–1987.

Schweitzer, Albert. *In Quest of the Historical Jesus: A Critical Study of Its Progress from Reimarus to Wrede.* New York: Macmillan, 1968.

Spolsky, Bernard. *The Languages of the Jews: A Sociolinguistic History.* New York: Cambridge University Press, 2014.

————. "Triglossia and Literacy in Jewish Palestine of the First Century." *International Journal of the Sociology of Language* 42 (1985): 95–110.

Stern, Menahem, *Greek and Latin Authors on Jews and Judaism*, vols. 1–3. Jerusalem: Israel Academy of Sciences and Humanities, 1974–1984.

Tabor, James. *The Jesus Dynasty: The Hidden History of Jesus, His Royal Family, and the Birth of Christianity.* New York: Simon & Schuster, 2006.

————. *Paul and Jesus: How the Apostle Transformed Christianity.* New York: Simon & Schuster, 2012.

Thackeray, H. J., ed. and trans. *Josephus; With an English Translation* (in nine volumes). Oxford: Harvard University Press, 1978.

Urbach, Ephraim E. *The Sages*, vols. 1–2. Jerusalem, Magnes Press, 1979.

Vermes, Geza. "Ḥanina ben Dosa." *JJS* 23 (1972): 28–50.

————. *Jesus and the World of Judaism.* Philadelphia: Fortress, 1983.

————. *Jesus the Jew.* London: William Collins Sons, 1973.

Wilcox, Max. "Semitisms in the New Testament." *ANRW* II.25.1 (1984): 978–1029.

Wise, M. O., Abegg, M. G. Jr, and Cook, E. M. *Dead Sea Scrolls: A New Translation.* San Francisco: Harper Collins, 1996.

Yadin, Yigael. *Masada: Herod's Fortress and the Zealots' Last Stand.* New York: Random House, 1997.

————. *The Scroll of the War of the Sons of Light against the Sons of Darkness.* Oxford: Oxford University Press, 1962.

————. *The Temple Scroll: The Hidden Law of the Dead Sea Sect.* New York: Random House, 1985.

Young, Brad. *Jesus and His Jewish Parables: Rediscovering the Roots of Jesus' Teaching.* New York: Paulist Press, 1989.

————. *Jesus the Jewish Theologian.* Grand Rapids: Baker Academic, 1993.

————. *The Parables: Jewish Tradition and Christian Interpretation.* Grand Rapids: Baker Academic, 1998.

————. *Paul the Jewish Theologian: A Pharisee Among Christians, Jews, and Gentiles.* Grand Rapids: Baker Academic, 1997.

Zeitlin, Solomon. *Who Crucified Jesus?* New York: Harper Collins, 1947.

Index

A

Abraham, 18, 23, 25, 35, 37, 40–41, 43, 64, 66, 89–90, 117, 126, 148, 162, 180
Adultery, 60, 75–77, 133, 143, 154, 168
Aesop (fable), 111
Anna (the Prophetess), 31
Annas, 35–36, 100, 167, 171
Arrest (of Jesus), 143, 171, 197
Atonement, 19, 90

B

Baptism, 34, 36, 38, 111, 145, 172
Barabbas, 141, 202–204, 208
Beatitudes, 57–59
Beelzebub, 3, 69–70
Bethlehem, 22, 26, 28, 66
Birth (of Jesus), 1, 15–16, 18, 20–21, 23, 26–27, 32, 49, 55, 170
Burial (of Jesus), 211–212

C

Caesar, 26, 35–36, 178–179, 201
Caesarea, 201, 211
Caiaphas, 35–36, 100, 171
Capernaum, 35, 45, 93–94, 97, 108–109, 132

Centurion, 8, 108–109, 210
Chorazin, 132
Circle-Drawer, 69.
    See also: Honi HaMe'aggel
Crucifixion, 8, 126–127, 170, 211

D

David, 1–2, 4, 10, 16, 20–22, 25–28, 40–41, 48–50, 66–67, 73, 96, 125, 142, 160, 162, 166, 171, 181, 183, 188, 193–194, 198, 209
Day of Atonement, 19
Death, 2, 5, 26, 30, 43, 53, 59, 69, 74, 89, 122, 125–126, 142, 159, 162, 173, 176, 191, 193, 195–196, 201, 203, 206–209, 211–212, 216, 229, 234
Disciples (calling of), 47, 49–50, 54, 58, 65–68, 72, 82–83, 86, 93, 99–102, 104–105, 108–110, 112, 114, 117, 122, 124, 128–131, 134–135, 139, 144, 151–152, 155, 158, 165–166, 172, 181, 190–191, 194–197, 200, 213–215, 217–219, 221, 224, 226, 234–235
Dragnet Parable, 143, 146

E

Elect, 25, 27, 108
Elijah, 18, 35, 98, 120, 122–125,
    127, 144, 150, 210, 231
Emmaus, 215–216
Enoch, 41–42, 59, 78, 96, 144,
    148
Eschatology, 158, 228
Essenes, 36–37, 48, 130–131, 134
Evil, 36, 39, 42–43, 46, 63, 65,
    68, 70–71, 75, 78, 80, 89–90,
    96, 100, 104, 106, 110, 112,
    116–118, 138–139, 175–177,
    183, 187, 189, 203, 221–222,
    229, 231, 233.
    See also: Faithful
Exorcism, 45–46, 119

F

Faithful, 58, 106, 150, 152, 231–
    233.
    See also: Evil
Family (of Jesus), 9, 21, 24, 31,
    49, 62, 100, 132, 161, 171, 188,
    192
Fear (of God), 18, 20, 23–27, 43,
    50, 54, 73, 100, 107, 111, 120–
    121, 137–139, 150, 172, 178,
    208, 222–223, 225, 230
Feet, 26, 38, 76–77, 85–86, 91–
    92, 118–120, 131, 144, 157,
    177, 218
Fig Tree Parable, 170, 182, 184–
    186
Fool, 76, 85–89, 134, 136, 217.
    See also: Wise
Forgiveness, 25, 53, 79, 219, 223

G

Galilee, 9, 11, 13, 20, 26, 31, 34,
    36, 44–45, 47–50, 52, 93, 95,
    97, 99, 101, 103, 105, 107, 109,
    111, 113, 115, 117–119, 121,
    123, 125, 127, 129, 131, 133,
    135, 137, 139–142, 156–157,
    161, 163, 178, 192, 202, 211–
    212, 215, 230, 235–236
Genealogy (of Jesus), 13, 34, 40
Gentile, 30, 97–98, 132, 159,
    183–184, 188, 194, 209, 216,
    219, 221, 225–226
Gethsemane, 171, 195–197
Good Samaritan Parable, 72, 80
Great Supper Parable, 162–163

H

Hanina ben Dosa, 119, 225
Hasidim, 31–32, 40, 53, 63, 121,
    134, 139, 225
Herod, 17, 26, 35–39, 112, 122–
    123, 148, 172, 178, 187–188,
    201–203
Herod Antipas, 37–39, 172, 178,
    188
Herodias, 38–39, 123
Hillel, 40, 48, 55, 57, 60, 71, 77,
    80, 102, 129, 136, 143, 153–
    154, 163, 179
Holy Spirit, 16, 18, 21–22, 25,
    30, 38, 42, 134–135, 220, 223–
    224
Honi HaMe'aggel, 69, 107.
    See also: Circle-Drawer
House on the Rock Parable, 112,
    115
Hypocrisy, 37, 137–139

I

Illness, 53–54, 213, 229
Isaac, 22, 41, 64, 128, 148, 180

J

Jacob, 21, 37, 41, 59, 135, 148, 180
James, 14, 19, 21, 57, 78, 100–101, 121, 126, 144, 190–191, 215
Jeremiah, 98, 159, 177, 206
Jerusalem, 1, 4–6, 9, 11, 13, 16–17, 20, 22, 29–33, 43, 49–52, 56, 66, 68–69, 71, 78, 81–82, 85, 90–91, 93, 101, 126–127, 130, 140–145, 147–151, 153, 155, 157, 159, 161, 163, 165–170, 182–185, 188, 191–192, 194–195, 201–202, 204–207, 210, 214, 216, 218–221, 225, 229, 234
Job, 75, 87, 228
John the Baptist, 15–16, 22–23, 30–31, 34–36, 38–39, 70, 79, 91, 104, 110–111, 124, 131, 153, 155, 172–175, 192
Joseph of Arimathea, 211
Josephus, 18, 32–33, 38, 44, 50, 93, 96–97, 109, 118–119, 130–131, 141, 150, 172, 178–179, 187–188, 198, 201–202, 206, 210, 212, 229
Judas, 101, 190, 195, 197

K

King of the Jews, 201, 208
Kingdom of God, 7, 35, 46–48, 57–58, 61–63, 65, 69–70, 97, 99, 105, 110–112, 114, 117–118, 123, 126, 128, 130–133, 135, 138, 142, 144–145, 148, 150, 153, 157–159, 175, 184–185, 193–194, 212–213, 220, 222
Kingdom of Heaven, 48, 57–58, 60, 75, 99, 104, 135, 145–146, 148, 153, 162, 220, 222, 233

L

Last Supper, 27, 56, 170, 191–193, 195
Law, 9, 29–31, 33, 36, 39, 46, 49, 52, 54, 60, 66, 68, 70, 72, 74, 80–81, 84, 93, 98–100, 108–109, 123, 135–136, 142, 145, 153, 158, 161–163, 168, 179, 188, 199–201, 219, 236
Lazarus, 85, 88–90.
    See also: Rich Man Parable
Leaven, 62–63, 138–139
Lillies, 87–88
Lost Coin Parable, 82–84
Lost Sheep Parable, 82–84, 219, 221
Lost Son Parable, 170, 174–175
Lot, 17–18, 24, 60, 208, 210, 227

M

Maccabees (Book of), 23, 209
Mary, 20–23, 27–28, 30, 85–86,
    100, 112, 215–216
Mary Magdalene, 215
Messiah, 22, 27–28, 30, 33–35,
    38, 42, 44, 47, 55, 91, 96, 111,
    122–127, 145, 155, 162, 165,
    181, 193–194, 200–201, 205,
    208, 217, 219, 226, 229–232
Messianic Banquet, 55, 57, 105,
    171, 191
Minas Parable, 149–151.
    See also: Talents Parable
Moses, 24–25, 29, 35, 38, 43, 48,
    51, 74, 84–85, 90, 116, 122,
    126–128, 165–166, 168, 179–
    180, 217, 219, 225, 233
Mount of Olives, 165–166, 168,
    189, 196, 205, 225
Mustard Seed Parable, 62–63,
    155–156

N

Nazareth, 2, 20, 26, 31, 33, 35,
    45, 93–94, 97–98, 160, 216
Noah, 226

O

Offense, 111, 154–155

P

Parable, 5–6, 12, 49, 55, 61–63,
    72, 80–85, 87–88, 103, 106–
    108, 112, 114–115, 135, 142–
    143, 145–147, 149–151, 160,
    162–163, 170, 173–176, 182,
    184–189, 225–227, 231–233
Passover, 32, 49, 56–57, 67, 90,
    93, 126–127, 143, 170, 189–
    192, 195, 199, 202, 212
Persistent Friend Parable, 106–
    107
Persistent Widow Parable, 106–
    107, 160
Peter, 44, 46, 61, 93, 99–101,
    121–124, 126–127, 155, 167,
    191, 195, 197–199, 215, 232
Pharisee, 9, 33, 52–55, 59–60,
    67–70, 75, 80–83, 85, 90–91,
    111, 136–139, 143–144, 148,
    153, 157, 162–163, 166–168,
    170–172, 181, 186–190, 199–
    200, 215–216.
    See also: Tax Collector;
    Scribes
Pilgrimage, 32, 49
Pontius Pilate, 35–36, 201
Proselytes, 37, 63, 149, 206

R

Ravens, 85–86, 88
Reincarnation, 123
Repentance, 36–38, 61, 83–85,
    176, 195, 219
Resurrection, 5, 13, 57, 125, 138,
    142, 158–159, 168, 179–180,
    183, 200, 213–231, 233, 235
Rich Fool Parable, 85–88

Rich Man Parable, 61, 85, 88–90,
  151, 173, 182.
  See also: Lazarus
Righteousness, 25–26, 71, 73, 75,
  89, 100, 123, 127, 175, 222
Roman, 4, 8, 26, 34, 43–44, 48,
  101, 108–109, 140, 149, 167,
  178, 187, 192, 197, 201, 208–
  209, 228

S

Sabbath, 45–46, 54–55, 59, 65–
  69, 89, 94, 191, 212, 214–215,
  231
Sadducees, 81, 85, 137, 153, 168,
  179, 199–200, 216
Samaritans, 81, 144, 156
Sanhedrin, 76, 171, 199–200
Satan, 3, 42–43, 66, 70–71, 89,
  133, 155
Scribes, 53, 68–70, 75, 82–83,
  125, 137–138, 167–171, 180–
  181, 186–187, 189–190, 199,
  202, 230.
  See also: Pharisee
Shammai, 77, 136, 153–154
Shimon ben Shetakh, 69
Simeon, 29–31, 41, 103
Son of God, 8, 21, 24, 42–44, 47,
  119, 200, 210, 229
Son of Man, 53, 67, 97, 108, 125,
  127, 129, 144, 158–159, 162,
  174, 183, 185, 193, 197, 199–
  200, 213, 215, 221, 223, 225–
  228, 230–233
Sons of Light, 152
Sower Parable, 112, 114

T

Talents Parable, 149, 151.
  See also: Minas Parable
Tares, 3, 143, 145, 147
Tax Collector, 37, 82–83, 89,
  111, 142–143, 161–164, 174–
  175.
  See also: Pharisee
Temple, 3, 13, 16–17, 19–20, 29–
  34, 36, 38–39, 44, 48–49, 51,
  66–67, 69, 82–83, 96–97, 109–
  110, 113, 123, 134, 138, 142–
  143, 149, 154, 162, 166–175,
  177, 179, 181–183, 185–191,
  193, 195, 197–201, 203–207,
  209–211, 219, 228, 234–235
Temple Committee, 170–172,
  174, 189–190, 199–200
Testament of Solomon, 97
Tiberius, 35–36, 179
Tomb, 13, 118–119, 137, 170–
  171, 173, 175, 177, 179, 181,
  183, 185, 187, 189, 191, 193,
  195, 197, 199, 201, 203, 205,
  207, 209, 211–215, 217
Transfiguration, 56, 126
Trial (of Jesus), 8, 35, 43, 143,
  171, 194, 199, 201
Triumphal Entry, 143, 161, 165,
  170
Two Sons Parable, 170, 174–176
Two Ways, 36, 74, 175

U

Unjust Steward Parable, 149, 151

V

Vinedressers, 170, 182, 184, 186–187.
   See also: Wicked
Virgins, 233

W

Washing of Feet, 91
Wedding Feast Parable, 55
Wheat and Tares Parable, 147
Wicked, 18, 21–23, 25, 30, 38, 42, 73, 78, 89, 133–134, 137, 146–147, 151, 170, 182, 184, 186, 206–207, 220, 224, 228.
   See also: Vinedressers
Wise, 4, 64, 85, 134, 137, 232–233.
   See also: Fool
Woes, 58–59

Y

Yohanan ben Zakkai, 115, 161

Z

Zacchaeus, 142, 161
Zealots, 48, 140–141, 144, 179, 197–198, 202, 204, 208
Zechariah, 17–19, 21–22, 24–25, 36, 39, 137, 165, 181, 210

GCRR PRESS

INTERNATIONAL DISTRIBUTION

39,000 online and in-store outlets like Amazon, Walmart, Target, and Barnes & Noble

EXPANDED ADVERTISING

Developed with search optimization technology, we offer an expanded Advertising package that involves delivery of your book to one of the industry's largest book distributors, as well as circulating information about the book to 7,000 top U.S. booksellers and librarians, as well as to over 27,000 international and domestic customers with more than 150,000 monthly views and 70,000 registered users.

HIGHER AUTHOR ROYALTIES!

Lightning Source UK Ltd.
Milton Keynes UK
UKHW021523100223
416696UK00001B/45